Geographical Targeting
for Poverty Alleviation

WORLD BANK
REGIONAL AND
SECTORAL STUDIES

Geographical Targeting for Poverty Alleviation

Methodology and Applications

EDITED BY

DAVID BIGMAN AND

HIPPOLYTE FOFACK

THE WORLD BANK
WASHINGTON, D.C.

Library of Congress Cataloging-in-Publication Data

Geographical targeting for poverty alleviation : methodology and applications / edited by David Bigman, Hippolyte Fofack.
    p. cm. -- (World bank regional and sectoral studies)
    ISBN 0-8213-4625-3
    1. Poverty--Developing countries--Data processing. 2. Poverty--Developing countries--Mathematical models. 3. Geographic information systems--Developing countries. I. Bigman, David. II. Fofack, Hippolyte, 1963- III. Series.

HV29.5.D5 G46 2000
362.5'8'091724--dc21   00-036817

Contents

v

Tables

Acknowledgments

IN RECENT YEARS, the potential applications of spatial analysis were broadened significantly with the advances in geographical information systems (GIS) methods and the accumulation of a large volume of increasingly more reliable data that also contain spatial references. The interest in these applications for the design of development strategies in general and of poverty alleviation programs in particular was reflected in the large and lively participation in the Conference on Geographical Targeting for Poverty Alleviation organized by the Poverty Reduction and Social Development Division of the Africa Region of the World Bank in the fall of 1997.

This conference led to a fruitful collaboration between the editors of this volume and a large number of researchers in the World Bank, in other multinational organizations, and in various research institutes in industrial and developing countries. Many researchers sent us their work for consideration and made it possible for us to select for this volume chapters that address most effectively the issues raised by the choice of spatial characteristics as criteria for targeting the allocation of public resources and the methods that can be used for geographical targeting. We wish to thank all these researchers for their interest in our work and to express our sincere appreciation to the contributors to this volume. We are also grateful to the three anonymous reviewers whose valuable comments on an earlier draft of the manuscript led to considerable improvements in some of the chapters.

We are particularly indebted to Jack W. van Holst Pellekaan, formerly Lead Specialist Poverty in the Africa Region of the World Bank, for his invaluable guidance at the beginning of this project and for his continuous support, which was essential in bringing this project to completion. Several other colleagues have helped us in the preparation of this volume, and we would like to extend our sincere gratitude to all of them, particularly to Ye Xiao and Francoise Genouille for their assistance during the organization of the conference. The completion of this project also profited from the working environment provided by the Poverty Reduction Group within the Africa Region of the World Bank under the leadership of Roger Sullivan, Sector Manager. We are also grateful to the Government of Norway for providing financing to support this project through the Norwegian Trust Fund, managed by Antoine Simonpietri, and to the Government of the Netherlands, particularly Ms. Margreet Moolhuijzen, for financing the overall costs of printing this volume through the Dutch Trust Fund, managed by Lionel Demery. Product development, design, editing, production, and dissemination were directed and managed by the World Bank's Office of the Publisher.

Foreword

RISING POVERTY AND DECLINING public resources present a major challenge for the majority of developing countries. In Sub-Saharan Africa (SSA), the problem is especially acute. After nearly two decades of low rates of economic growth that, in many countries, fell well below the rates of population growth, the size of the poor population in the subcontinent increased substantially, and at the end of the 1990s nearly two-fifths of the population in this region live in poverty. However, countries in SSA were not equally affected by these trends. A number of countries adopted sound macroeconomic policies that yielded encouraging results. In these countries, economic growth rates gradually accelerated, and poverty was reduced. These countries, which represent a growing number in Sub-Saharan Africa, suggest that persistent efforts to improve economic policies can lead to significant poverty reduction.

The task of renewing economic growth must also include concerted efforts to stabilize the government budget with the goal of breaking the vicious circle of rising public deficits, ensuing runaway inflation, and rising poverty. Successful implementation of these stabilization programs, however, requires considerable sacrifices and painful tradeoffs in the short run. For poverty reduction programs to be successful, it is necessary to explore creative solutions that will allow the governments of these countries to target their limited resources to the most needy, and to use these resources in the most effective way. Programs that cover a country's entire population, such as general food subsidies that were common in the 1960s and 1970s, were of limited effectiveness in reaching the poor, led to bloated public deficits and debts, and are no longer sustainable.

During the past decade, the need for effective targeted programs that provide significant support to the poor within the tightening budget constraints has become more apparent than ever. The design of efficient programs that are tailored to the specific conditions and needs of each country presents a challenge that government agencies and international development institutions must confront. This book is intended to contribute to this challenge by addressing the complex factors that need to be taken into account in the design of successful poverty alleviation programs. The book presents alternative methods of geographical targeting aimed at improving the living standards of the poor, and carefully evaluates their effect on social welfare and their implications for public resource allocation.

The book demonstrates that the use of geographical information systems (GISs) makes possible a detailed mapping of the incidence of poverty in the country that can be used, in turn, for more precise targeting. The incorporation of data from a wide variety of sources by means of GISs also reveals the multidimensional aspects of poverty and enables a more accurate identification of factors relevant for the design of effective poverty alleviation programs within the tight budget constraints. Finally, the book also shows that GIS methods can be more broadly applied in support of targeting service delivery and access to the poor, for instance by optimizing the planning and location of health and education centers in poor and under-served areas.

We welcome this contribution to our work. We are confident that our staff in the Africa Region and other groups in the World Bank, in other development institutions, and in developing countries themselves will benefit from the methods presented in this book. Use of these methods will improve the effectiveness of targeted programs in reaching the poor and will help to achieve the greatest poverty reduction impact within today's stringent limits on public resources.

CALLISTO MADAVO
VICE PRESIDENT
AFRICA REGION
THE WORLD BANK

JEAN-LOUIS SARBIB
VICE PRESIDENT
AFRICA REGION
THE WORLD BANK

Preface

THIS BOOK GREW OUT OF TWO PROJECTS undertaken by the Poverty Reduction and Social Development Group of the World Bank's Africa Region: The first was a study on targeting public projects and allocating resources for health, education, and development across rural communities in Burkina Faso. The second was a conference on "Geographical Targeting for Poverty Alleviation" that was organized by the Division in the fall of 1997 in order to explore the potential contribution of GIS applications to improving the distribution of public resources across a country's geographical areas and securing more effective targeting on the poor. These two projects were by no means the World Bank's first endeavors to draw attention to the significance of the spatial dimension in project design and the implementation of antipoverty policies and programs. Nevertheless, for all too many projects and programs, a careful design of the general structure of the project and a meticulous evaluation of its total costs and benefits are still followed by much less scrupulous attention when it comes to the decision on *where*—that is, *in which specific village or urban community*—to implement the project. In rural areas in particular, this is often the most important decision that determines the benefits to the local population from the project.

The widening availability and growing use of spatial data, organized in a computer system as a geographical information system (GIS), significantly advance the possibilities of analyzing the spatial impact of projects and programs and of achieving more effective targeting. Nevertheless, the actual use of GISs, both in development organizations and in developing countries themselves, is still limited. The discrepancy between the extensive possibilities that this tool opens up and the very slow pace at which it is applied by economists and social scientists working in development, was the main motivation for the initiative of bringing together the papers presented at the conference, as well as several other papers that were submitted for consideration at a later stage, in this volume.

The book has three objectives. First, it introduces the basic concepts of GISs to readers who are not yet familiar with this tool, and demonstrate the forms of organizing geographic and nongeographic data in this system for potential users. Second, the book presents different methods for using the data from a Household Income and Expenditure Survey together with other surveys and the population census in order to provide estimates for the standard of living and the poverty incidence in different geographical areas of a country. The ultimate objective of these estimates is to establish guidelines for targeting poverty alleviation projects and programs. Third, the book illustrates different applications of GISs for identifying the target population of a program, determining the spatial "sphere of influence" of a project, or deciding on the location of public facilities. These illustrations are for a variety of projects or programs in health, nutrition, and education. The focus in this book is primarily on the methodology, and, in principle, the same method that is being presented in one of the chapters for calculating the sphere of influence of a disease, for example, can later be used to calculate the sphere of influence of a hospital.

Although the potential contribution of a thorough analysis of the spatial effects of projects or policies to improve their effectiveness is obvious, the obstacles to a more extensive use of spatial analysis in general and of GISs in particular in most developing countries are still enormous. They include the difficulties in collecting and properly organizing all the data required for the analysis and the resources needed for acquiring the know-how and the hardware in order to use this system. It is clear that no single project, large as it may be, will be able to justify these expenses by itself. It is also clear, however, that, with only minor modifications, this system can serve *all* projects over an extended period of time. To secure the availability of all the data and the resources necessary for this system, all projects will have to combine their efforts and share these expenses. This, in turn, will require considerable cooperation between the different units that work on development project in the country and a long-term perspective.

ALAN HAROLD GELB
CHIEF ECONOMIST AND SECTOR DIRECTOR
ECONOMIC MANAGEMENT AND SOCIAL POLICY
AFRICA REGION, THE WORLD BANK

Introduction and Overview

David Bigman and Hippolyte Fofack

LARGE INEQUALITIES IN THE STANDARD OF LIVING between geographic areas and "pockets of poverty" are common in all countries, rich and poor. The northern region of Nigeria; the Indian states of Bihar, Orissa, and West Bengal; the "inland" provinces in China; the southern regions in Italy; and the Deep South of the United States are just a few examples of geographic areas in which the incidence of poverty is much higher than in the other parts of these countries. The main reasons for such marked inequalities are the unequal distribution of natural resources (including water), differences in agro-climatic conditions, and differences in geographic conditions (primarily the distance to the centers of commerce, to the main transport routes, and to seaports.). Another factor that leads to income disparities between regions, districts, and communities is geographic bias in infrastructure policy decisions, reflected in the poor quality of such local infrastructure as access roads and the availability of public services.

Studies on income inequality and poverty generally use an individualistic, human-capital model that seeks to explain differences in income and consumption by individual and household characteristics. Spatial (that is, geographic) variables are added in some studies to explain these differences, but usually in an ad hoc way.[1] The formal argument of the individualistic model is straightforward: In a country where internal migration is free and the economy is in equilibrium, the standard of living must be fully determined by characteristics of individuals and households other than geography. If spatial characteristics did have an effect on the well-being of individuals and households, so the argument goes, then they would tend to move to better locations.[2]

Nevertheless, large differences in the incidence of poverty between different geographic areas do exist. Their magnitude is often far too large to be explained by differences in individual or household characteristics alone. One reason for the persistence of these differences is that internal migration is not really free—in some countries because of deliberate government policies, and in all countries because of economic, demographic, and cultural obstacles. Migration between rural areas, for example, is often constrained by the lack of available land for cultivation, and rural-to-urban migration leaves behind the very young and the very old. Moreover, migration is costly and risky, and frequently individuals do not have the necessary information to make such a decision. Even migration from rural to urban areas, while common, is often a gradual process, beginning with the move of a single household member to an urban center to look for work; it may take a long time for other members of the household to follow. And there are further barriers to migration that help account for large inter-regional income disparities. Particular aspects of poverty, such as large households, poor health conditions, low levels of human capital, and, in some countries, the "feminization of poverty," reduce the capacity of the poor to migrate. Wealthier individuals in poor regions are less restricted in their decisions to migrate, and when they leave, the standard of living in these areas declines still further.[3] In addition, geographic areas with a low standard of living often have a much lower quality of public services, particularly education and health, which impedes their residents' accumulation of human capital, and therefore their earning capacity and prospects for migration. Binswanger and others (1993) evaluated the significance of rural infrastructure for local investments and growth. Foster and Rosenzweig (1995) emphasized the varying conditions in different rural communities, and the resultant impact on the diffusion of new farm technologies; the low level of human capital in the poor communities demonstrably slows down the adoption of new technologies by the local farmers and reduces earning capacity. All these factors increase the likelihood that households in poor regions will retain individual and community characteristics that doom them and their offspring to continued poverty.

The *spatial* dimension of the economic activities, decisions, and characteristics of individuals, despite its importance, has long been given only little attention in economic theory. Until the mid-1990s, the early writings on spatial economics of Harris (1954) and Myrdal (1957) had only a handful of followers. In a series of lectures published as *Development, Geography, and Economic Theory* (1995), Paul Krugman asked why spatial issues remained a blind spot for the economic profession, observing that "economic geography—the location of activity in space—is a subject of obvious practical importance and presumably considerable intellectual interest. Yet it is almost completely absent from the standard corpus of economic theory."[4] In recent years, though, a growing body of economic research seeks to explain the mechanisms and rules by which economic forces operate in geography, thus putting spatial considerations into the mainstream of economic theory. One aspect of this research analyzes the factors that determine the location of and the spatial interactions between industrial and market centers (see, for example, Krugman 1993, Ades and Glaser 1995, and Fujita and Mori 1996). Another branch of this research analyzes the geographic characteristics of cities, regions, or countries, the impact of these characteristics on the pace of economic development, and their implications for inequality among regions and among nations (Fujita and Mori 1996; Krugman 1991, Krugman and Venables 1995).

These studies represent what has become known as the "new economic geography," and they give center stage to the evaluation of the effects of *distance* on the economic growth of and income disparities between nations and regions. They emphasize the important, sometimes critical role that distance—to and from sources of raw materials, main transport routes, seaports, and large population centers—plays in determining the division of production between industrial and primary-producing regions, and in augmenting the divergence of incomes between North and South. In these studies, the comparative advantage of regions and nations has been determined not only by their factor endowments, but also by their geographic attributes. Warner and Sachs (1997) argue that because Africa is more land-locked and has fewer navigable rivers than almost any other area in the world (except for Central Asia), distance is the main factor inhibiting its economic growth. Although technological progress has gradually reduced the importance of distance and has provided cheaper, alternative means of transportation— thereby changing the comparative advantage and disadvantage of geographic areas—this change has been slow, with a noticeable impact only in the last 150 years. Until that progress arrived (and in many developing countries it has yet to come), the geography of a nation and a region determined not only their historical and political lot, but also their economic fate.

Climate, distance, and *access* are the primary components of economic geography, and their respective importance varies when explaining the large differences in the pace of development between regions, and even between communities. In most countries, *climate* is the primary factor determining the prospects of development of the agricultural sector, and with it, the rate of growth of the entire economy. In industrial countries, this factor gradually became less significant, but in the majority of developing countries, where agriculture remains the dominant sector, climate continues to be the most significant factor that determines the country or region's level of development. With the spread of industry and commerce, *distance*—to the sources of raw materials and energy on the one hand, and to the main population centers on the other—became more important to growth. Equally important are the ease of *access* to the ports and to the main centers, and the availability of passable and safe roads.

At the local level of the village and the urban community, the relevant *distances* are to the nearest town, to the main transport route, and to public services. *Access* to the community year round and the absence of natural or man-made obstacles to access are equally important for development. In many developing countries, and particularly in Sub-Saharan Africa, villages located more than 5 kilometers from the main transport routes are likely to have significantly lower standards of living than closer villages, and villages without a passable access road during the rainy season are noticeably poorer than villages with year-round access.

The incorporation of these geographic factors can significantly enrich economic analysis and policy decisions. By identifying the spatial and environmental factors that affect the standard of living in a community, it is possible to formulate the policies that are necessary in order to raise living standards. The information on distance and access needed for this analysis is difficult to obtain, and in many developing countries, the process of generating and collecting this information is still at an early stage. In recent years, however, these geographic indicators have received much greater attention and their importance for the design of public policies has been widely recognized. This process took a large leap forward with the development of new and sophisticated methods for incorporating spatial data by organizing them as a geographic information system (GIS), suitable for computer analysis, and by a surge of technological innovations, particularly satellite imagery, which advanced the ability to collect spatial and climatic data. In a GIS, the database contains information not only on the value of social, economic, climatic, or environmental observations, but also on their location and spatial arrangement. This allows the presentation of data in the form of maps and overlaying interfaces for cross-comparisons, and the performance of spatial analysis assessing the relationships between these data according to their geographic location.[5] In many countries, and at all levels of development, these systems have become the single most important analytical tool for the analysis of a wide range of geographic and socioeconomic data and for the design of policy measures that account for *space*.

The great interest in this subject was evident from the high attendance and the lively participation generated by a conference on "Geographical Targeting for Poverty Reduction," organized by the Institutional and Social Policy Division of the World Bank's Africa Region in the Fall of 1997.[6] The conference highlighted the potential of GIS applications to improve project and program design and to provide guidelines for effective targeting of aid to selected geographic areas, with the goal of cost-effective reductions in poverty. In view of the mounting constraints on resources available for development projects, and the growing pressures to achieve *better results on the ground*, GIS applications gain increasing significance. However, currently available books on GIS methodology and its applications are not tailored to the needs and professional background of economists and social scientists working on development issues. By bringing together the papers presented at the World Bank's 1997 conference, this volume aims to provide an introduction to the basic concepts of GISs and a sample of their different applications to spatial analysis. This introductory chapter also provides a brief overview of the economic motivation for targeting public projects in general, and of the pros and cons of geographic targeting in particular.

Economic Criteria for Targeting

Targeting poverty alleviation programs to a subgroup of the population has an intuitive appeal for policymakers and economists, but also considerable perils. The principle that guides policymakers in planning programs of this type is how to use the available resources in order to provide the greatest possible amount of assistance to those who need it most. The intuitive method of targeting subgroups identifies poor individuals and directs all benefits only to them, but this practice is marred with problems and difficulties. First, the costs of identifying poor individuals can be very significant, and requires information that is not available in most developing countries. Second, even in industrial countries where this information can be obtained, it is impossible to ascertain if targeted programs will indeed reach all the poor, and only the poor. The costs of obtaining this information can be very high, higher than the costs of implementing the first best solution of reducing leakage to individuals who are not poor. Third, benefits to the poor provide incentives to non-poor households to change their behavior in order to qualify for the program, thus raising the costs of the program and reducing the impact of social welfare. Fourth, targeted programs tend to stigmatize the poor, both in their own eyes and in the eyes of their fellow citizens, potentially leading to reactions that can frustrate efforts to break the cycle of poverty and thus undermining the goal of the program. The negative effects of targeted programs are exacerbated when information necessary for identifying the poor cannot be obtained, causing governments to resort to second-best solutions of identifying the poor by means of indirect criteria. These difficulties have led some economists to conclude that targeted programs should be discarded altogether in favor of programs with universal coverage.

Nevertheless, the constraints on public resources available for social welfare programs make targeting the only viable alternative for practically all developing countries. In these countries, growing budget constraints prevent governments from providing universal coverage programs such as general food subsidies that were highly popular in earlier years. Difficulties in gathering information and the weak administrative capacity of the government also dictate the form of intervention.[7] There are two general alternatives for managing social welfare. The first is the use of indirect criteria to determine eligibility, such as the household size, the number of children in the household, the size of the household's landholdings or other assets, or the place of residence. The second is the use of self-targeting programs, such as food-for-work, subsidies for commodities that are consumed primarily by the poor, or targeting research and extension services on the agricultural products of the poor

Targeted programs that use indirect criteria are bound to involve considerable leakage of benefits to the non-poor, while excluding many of the poor not found eligible under the program's criteria, and the savings compared to nontargeted programs may therefore be quite low. For example, in family assistance programs implemented in a number of Latin American countries, eligibility was determined by the number of children in the household; the costs of these programs were pushed to intolerably high levels by slack entitlement conditions and large leakage of benefits, and they had, in addition, negative effects on the fertility rates of the poor. In Tanzania, difficulties in establishing clear eligibility criteria for the distribution of food aid forced the government to delegate the distribution operation to specialized local NGOs and village committees that drove up the costs. In Sri Lanka, nearly half the population has access to food stamps while less than 30 percent are eligible under the program's criteria (Subbarao and others 1997).

The effectiveness of targeted programs for poverty reduction thus depends on the availability of an efficient and inexpensive mechanism for identifying the poor, on the cost reduction achieved by the exclusion of non-poor households from the program, and on the organizational capacity of the government to administer the program. Despite the leakage in targeted programs that use indirect indicators as eligibility criteria, the savings compared with universal coverage programs make targeting the choice by default in view of the mounting budget constraints. Grosh (1994) also noted the *political feasibility* of a program as one of the central factors that determine its effectiveness, since the main obstacles to targeted programs have often been political. Unfortunately, targeted programs tend to isolate and stigmatize the target population, thus reducing the political support for the programs, while universal coverage may provide the political leverage to mobilize the support of the population not covered by the program, particularly middle-income consumers. Anand and Kanbur (1990) reported that, after the introduction of a targeted food stamp program in Sri Lanka, the real value of the food stamps was allowed to fall quite sharply during periods of high inflation as the interest of the middle class shifted to other issues and public support for the program declined. In some countries, particularly in Sub-Saharan Africa, targeted programs may also exacerbate ethnic tensions if the target group is perceived to be predominantly of a specific ethnic origin.

Income-based programs and means testing are common in industrial and middle-income developing countries; these programs are highly cost effective, and rank high in terms of the principal performance measures— that is, leakage and coverage (see further discussion below). Nevertheless, these programs are often more divisive than universal coverage, and raise political problems due to the stigma attached to beneficiaries (see Rainwater 1982; Besley and Coate 1992; and Smolensky and others 1995). Besley and Kanbur (1993) point out that stigmatizing beneficiaries of income-based programs can reduce the ability of welfare recipients to acquire skills and grow out of poverty. The stigma is particularly divisive when the costs of the program are being borne by a relatively small portion of the general population. Moffitt (1983) describes the stigma in terms of the "disutility arising from participation in the welfare program;" and Besley and Coate (1992) emphasize the "psychic costs of being on welfare." Smolensky and others (1995) distinguish between *external* and *internal* stigma; that is, the stigma created because the welfare program lowers the self-esteem of the recipients, and the stigma imposed by the society at large. Often, however, the most significant reason for political tensions and opposition to targeted programs is the leakage of benefits to ineligible households, and the perception that they are perceived to take a free ride on the back of the taxpayers. Improved targeting can therefore go a long way toward reducing such tensions. Rainwater (1982) pointed out, however, that more accurate targeting may also have the opposite effect of further stigmatizing the poor by identifying them more accurately (p. 46). This will be the case particularly if more stringent eligibility conditions require the recipient to submit very personal information (for example, the name of the father of a child born out of wedlock).

The next section of this chapter ("An Overview of Alternative Targeting Methods") provides an overview of the main targeted programs implemented in developing countries, and examines the pros and cons of geographic targeting in comparison to other methods of targeting. Several examples that illustrate advantages of and problems with targeted programs are discussed. While the subject of the overview is poverty alleviation programs, similar principles apply also to other targeted programs in which poverty alleviation is only one of several objectives. Other programs might include education for girls or children of a specific age group (irrespective of their parent's income), health programs for women of childbearing age or for households with a large number of children, nutrition programs for mothers and young children, and so forth. As background to this overview, the remainder of this section summarizes the main measures that are commonly used for evaluating the performance of targeted poverty alleviation programs. These measures include the following:

- Type I errors—the error of inclusion, which denotes the number of non-poor individuals who are *included* in the program due to inaccurate specification of the criteria for entitlement and their proportion in the total number of the benefit recipients (also referred to as "vertical inefficiency").
- Type II errors—the error of exclusion, which denotes the number of poor individuals who are *excluded* from the program due to inaccurate specification of the criteria for entitlement and their proportion in the country's total number of poor (also referred to as "horizontal inefficiency").
- The budgetary costs of the program—including the costs of collecting the data necessary for the design of the criteria of entitlement, as well as the program's administrative costs.
- The effects of the program on the behavior of households and the implications for the households' welfare and the government budget.
- The effects of the program on poverty reduction.

The performance of the program, as indicated by these measures, depends on the *criteria* that are used to determine eligibility, and the *instruments* that are used to transfer benefits to the target population.

Among the above criteria, the errors of inclusion and exclusion generally receive the greatest attention due to their intuitive appeal and their direct budgetary implications. Ravallion and Chao (1989) suggest a quantifiable performance measure for targeted programs which takes into account both of these errors: the gains from targeting are defined as the amount by which the budget for a nontargeted program would have to be increased in order to achieve the same reduction in poverty, as measured by the poverty gap ratio. They termed this measure the "equivalent gain from targeting." Clearly, the larger the type I error, the higher the costs of the targeted program, and the smaller the equivalent gain. Likewise, the larger the type II error, the smaller the cost increase with a nontargeted program that provides the same reduction in poverty, and the smaller the equivalent gain.

A complete specification of these performance measures must also include the choice of a measure for the *reduction* in poverty, and therefore a proper measure of poverty. The Headcount measure of poverty is not a proper measure for this purpose: if poverty is measured by the Headcount measure, then a program of income transfers would achieve the greatest reduction in poverty if targeted to the persons (or regions) who are the *least* poor, leaving the poorest people uncovered. The Headcount measure is also not the proper measure for comparing programs: Datt and Ravallion (1993) evaluated the reduction of regional disparities through income transfers (while leaving *intra*-regional inequalities unchanged), and concluded that this program would yield only a marginal reduction in the Headcount measure of poverty. The methods of Datt and Ravallion fail, however, to measure the reduction in the *poverty gap* of the remaining poor population.[8] If poverty in the target region(s) is well below the poverty line, the income transfer program may fail to lift the extreme poor out of poverty, whereas a nontargeted program will also reach the least poor, and by lifting them out of poverty, may generate an even larger reduction in the Headcount measure.

When measuring poverty by the poverty gap ratio, the gains from geographic targeting can be calculated as follows: Let S_i be the share of the *i*th region's population in the country's total population, and let H_i be the Headcount measure of poverty in that region. Consider a targeted program that transfers income to the persons residing in that region. To simplify the illustration, assume that the income transfer does not change the number of poor in the region and, to simplify the notations, let this transfer be of 1 rupee per person. This transfer will raise the income of the poor population residing in this region—and thus reduce their income gap below the poverty line—by a total of $(S_i \cdot H_i \cdot N)$, where N is the total number of persons in the entire economy. The budgetary costs of the program will be $(S_i \cdot N)$. Consider now the nontargeted program, and let w be the amount transferred to *all* persons in the country under the latter program. If the number of poor does not change (much) with this transfer, then the poor's poverty gap is reduced with the nontargeted program by a total of $(\omega \cdot N \cdot H)$, and the budgetary costs of this program are $(N \cdot \omega)$. By equating the reduction in the poverty gap under the targeted program with the reduction in the gap under the nontargeted program, we can calculate the transfer ω that equates these two reductions, given by equation 1:

$$\omega = \frac{S_i \cdot H_i}{H}. \tag{1}$$

Inserting this value into the formula for calculating the budgetary costs with the nontargeted program, and comparing these costs with the costs of the targeted program, determines the equivalent gain (EG), given by equation 2:

$$EG = \frac{H_i}{H}. \tag{2}$$

The target region is typically the one in which the incidence of poverty is higher than average, and the *EG* ratio is therefore larger than 1.

Another performance criterion for evaluating a targeted program is the reduction in the poverty gap that can be achieved with a targeted program compared with the reduction in the gap that can be achieved with a nontargeted one, when the *costs* of the two programs are the same. By comparing the costs of a targeted program that transfers 1 rupee to each person in the target area with the costs of a universal coverage program that transfers e rupees to each person in the country at large, we can conclude that the transfer in this case would be $\varepsilon = S_i$; the expression of *EG* in equation 2 then measures the ratio of the reduction in poverty with a targeted program relative to the reduction in poverty with a universal coverage program. In India, the percentage of the rural population in poverty was, in 1983, 43.9 percent, while that percentage in the state of Bihar was 60.8 percent (Datt and Ravallion 1993). With the same budgetary costs, a program targeted on the state of Bihar can therefore bring about a 50 percent larger reduction in the poverty gap compared with a universal coverage program.

Equation 2 can also have a different interpretation. To see this, define the benefits from the targeted program as the *average* reduction in the poverty gap of the poor. Obviously, the larger the number of poor persons that are *excluded* from the program, the smaller the average reduction in the poverty gap of the poor and the smaller the benefits. When the total number of poor persons remains unchanged, the benefits per person would be equal to the share of the poor population covered by the program, given by: $[(S_i \cdot H_i)/H]$, and the budgetary costs per person would be equal to S_i. The benefit/cost ratio would therefore be given by the ratio (H_i/H), which is also equal to the value of the *EG* in equation 2.

An alternative performance measure compares the costs and effectiveness of a targeted program with the costs and effectiveness of *another* targeted program. Here we consider two alternatives to a given targeted program: one is a program targeted on *all other* regions of the country; the other is a program targeted on another *subgroup* of regions in which targeting may be more effective. We can term these measures the "opportunity costs of targeting" (OC). The opportunity cost of targeting region R_j is the value of the foregone alternative action of targeting any other region R_i with $i + j$.

Using the same notation and the same procedure as above, the first alternative is determined by equating the reduction in poverty in the two programs, and comparing the respective costs of achieving that reduction with the targeted program and the program targeted on all other regions. After some algebra, that cost ratio is given by equation 3:

$$OC = \frac{(1 - S_i) \cdot H_i}{H - H_i S_i} = \frac{H_i}{HC_i} \tag{3}$$

where HC_i is the share of the poor individuals in the population of all other regions that are not covered by the target program under consideration. We provide two equations of opportunity costs of targeting and this expression can also be written as equation 4:

$$OC = EG \cdot \frac{1 - S_i}{\left[1 - (S_i H_i / H)\right]} . \tag{4}$$

The expression $(1 - S_i)$ measures the share of the general population that is not covered by the program; the expression $1 - (S_i H_i / H)$ measures the share of the poor population that is not covered by the program (the error of exclusion). It is easy to verify that

$$OC > EG \Leftrightarrow H_i > H \Leftrightarrow EG > 1.$$

The measure OC can also be defined as the reduction in poverty that could have been achieved with the same budget, had the program been targeted on the *other* regions. The second measure of the opportunity costs compares the respective reductions in poverty of two programs with the same budget: the program under consideration, and a program targeting another subgroup of regions. These two performance measures can be applied in order to determine the subgroup of regions in which targeting will be most effective.

To illustrate this application, we use the data calculated by Datt and Ravallion (1993) on poverty in the 20 states of India in 1983. Table 1 presents these data and the states are ranked according to the value of the corresponding Headcount measure. The large differences between states in the extent of poverty are highlighted, ranging from a Headcount ratio of over 60 percent in Bihar to less than 20 percent in Punjab, Jamu, and Kashmir. Notice that although this rank is highly correlated with the rank established by the poverty gap measure, there are noticeable differences between the two ranks. Moreover, in some states (such as Madhya Pradesh and Assam), the values of the Headcount measure are nearly identical, whereas the values of the poverty gap measures are significantly different.

Table 2 presents the result of a comparative analysis in which three alternative targeting programs are considered: In the first program, the only target is the state of Bihar. In the second program, the targets are the five poorest states (according to the Headcount measure). In the third program, the targets are the ten poorest states, in all of which the Headcount measure is over 40 percent. The table highlights the difference between the two performance measures EG and OC: When the program is expanded to include rural areas in more states, the EG is reduced monotonically (as an effect of the rise in the budgetary costs) at higher a rate than the rise in the benefits from the program. The reason for the monotonic decline of the EG in table 1 is the way in which the states were selected in this illustration: the program is expanded from Bihar to the five poorest states, and then to the ten poorest states, thus adding at each step the poorest among the remaining states. With this expansion, the *average* Headcount measure in the states included in the programs declines monotonically, and with it, the ratio

Table 1 Population Shares and Poverty Measures in India, 1983

State	Population share (percent)	Headcount measure measure	Share in poor population (percent)	Poverty gap (percent)
Bihar	10.4	60.8	14.3	18.52
Orissa	3.9	55.2	4.9	16.71
West Bengal	8.1	54.4	10.0	18.02
Tamil Nadu	7.1	51.6	8.3	16.41
Maharashtra	9.3	46.5	9.9	13.62
Karnataka	5.5	45.1	5.7	13.57
Gujarat	5.1	43.0	5.0	9.81
Madhya Pradesh	7.8	41.8	7.4	10.88
Assam	3.0	41.6	2.8	8.32
Uttar Pradesh	16.5	41.5	15.6	10.88
Kerala	3.7	38.8	3.3	9.96
Meghalaya	0.2	38.4	0.2	11.87
Tripura	0.3	35.0	0.2	7.76
Rajastan	5.1	33.6	3.9	12.29
Manipur	0.2	30.9	0.2	5.94
Andhra Pradesh	7.9	30.3	5.5	7.27
Himachal Pradesh	0.6	28.9	0.4	5.62
Haryana	1.9	21.7	1.0	4.33
Jammu and Kashmir	0.9	19.6	0.4	3.14
Punjab	2.5	19.4	1.1	3.94
All	100.0	43.9	100.0	12.29

Source: Datt and Ravallion (1993).

(H_i/H) also declines. The EG measure of 1.39 for Bihar, for example, indicates that the targeted program is 39 percent more effective than the nontargeted one. With the expansion of the program from Bihar to the five poorest states, the share of the poor that are covered by the program rises from

Table 2 Performance Measures for Regional Targeting in India

Target states	Population share (percent)	Headcount P_0	Share of poor in target states (percent)	EG	OC_1	Type I error (%)	Type II error (%)
Bihar	10.4	60.8	14.3	1.38	1.45	4.1	37.6
5 Poorest	38.7	53.7	47.4	1.22	1.43	17.9	23.0
10 Poorest	76.5	48.1	83.8	1.10	1.59	36.8	7.1

Source: Authors' calculations.

16.3 percent to 48.2 percent—a rise of nearly 200 percent, whereas the budgetary costs rise, with the rise in the population covered by the program, by 222 percent. The decline in the EG measure thus reflects the more rapid rise in the average budgetary costs per poor person covered by the program, thereby reducing the program's benefit to cost ratio. The decline in the proportion of poor persons that are *not* covered by the program (the type II error of exclusion) is reflected by the rise in the OC measure. OC rises from 1.46 to 1.53 with the expansion of the program from the state of Bihar to the five poorest states as the type II error declines by 38 percent; the proportion of the *general* population not covered by the program declines only 30 percent. These two changes counter the decline in EG, as shown in the expression of OC in equation 4, leaving EG nearly unchanged.

Table 3 presents a comparison of targeted programs in urban and rural areas. The value of the EG for a program targeted on rural areas shows a modest gain of 3 percent compared with a universal coverage program, primarily because the population in rural areas constitutes more than three-quarters of the country's general population. The value of OC shows, however, that a program targeted on the rural areas in India will be 13 percent more effective than a program targeted on urban areas because, with the same budget, the reduction in the poverty gap with the former program will be 13 percent larger than the reduction with the latter.

Finally, table 4 evaluates the desirability of a program targeted on the four southern states—Karnataka, Kerala, Tamil Nadu, and Andra Pradesh—evaluated against two alternatives: one is a universal coverage program and the other is targeting on the country's three poorest states. Compared to a universal coverage program, the EG measure is equal to 0.91, indicating that this targeted program is less effective than a universal coverage program, since, with the same overall budget, the latter could achieve a further reduction in the poverty gap of 9 percent. In the comparison of the reference program with an alternative program targeted on the three poorest states, the OC_2 measure indicates that, with the same budget, the reduction in poverty with the program targeted on the four southern states is 30 percent lower than the reduction in poverty with the alternative

Table 3 Performance Measures for Rural and Urban Targeting in India

Target	Population share (percent)	Headcount P_0	Share of poor in target area (percent)	EG	OC_1	Type I error (percent)	Type II error (percent)
Rural	76.7	45.0	78.7	1.03	1.13	42.2	9.34
Urban	23.3	40.0	21.3	0.91	0.89	13.4	34.57

Source: Authors' calculations.

Table 4 Performance Measures for Targeted Programs in India

Target states	Population share (percent)	Headcount P_0	Share of poor in target states (percent)	EG	OC_1 (%)	OC_2 (%)
South	24.3	41.0	22.8	0.94	0.92	0.72
three poorest	22.3	57.2	29.2	1.31	1.44	...

Source: Authors' calculations.

program. Comparison with the second alternative program has the advantage of offering a criterion whose objectivity is less likely to be disputed for comparing and selecting states for targeting.

These criteria offer a systematic method of selecting target areas for the program that maximizes reduction in poverty for given budgetary costs: starting with a low (but essentially arbitrary) budget for the targeted program, select the state (or states) in which the incidence of poverty is highest and in which costs will not exceed budget. In figure 1 below this initial budget is expressed as four percent of the national income. At each subsequent step, increase the budget incrementally and add the state(s) in which poverty is the highest, so that the expanded program meets the (expanded) budget constraints. For example, with a budget equal to 8 percent of the national income, the target state will be West Bengal; an increase of the budget to 9.5 percent of the national income will change the target states to Orissa and Karanataka; and a further increase in the budget to 10.5 percent of the national income will change the target state to Bihar. Figure 1 shows the percentage of the poor covered by an optimal selection of the target states for each level of the program's budget.

An Overview of Alternative Targeting Methods

Targeted programs for poverty alleviation vary widely between countries, and most countries implement several programs with the general goal of poverty alleviation. The main differences between programs stem from their secondary objectives, specific target groups, criteria of eligibility, and the instruments used to administer benefits to the poor. The variety of targeted programs also reflects differences between countries' administrative capacities, political conditions, the availability of relevant information, and budget constraints. (For a survey of targeting methods with applications for developing countries see Glewwe 1992, Grosh 1994, and Kanbur and others 1994). The methods of targeting, such as the criteria of eligibility, fall into the following main categories: targeting by household income; targeting by other indicators of households; targeting by commodities; and geographic targeting. This section provides an overview of the main targeting methods

Figure 1 Targeting Performance under Optimal Selection of States

Percentage of the Poor Covered by the Targeted Program

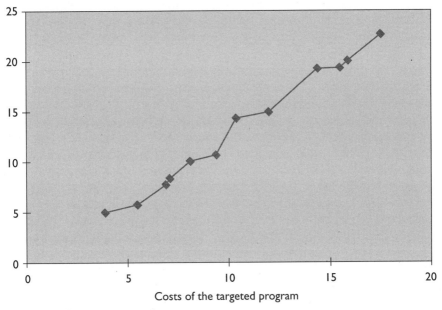

Source: Authors' calculations.

and their merits. This background is necessary for evaluating the merits of geographic targeting, since these other forms of targeting are the alternatives against which geographic targeting should be evaluated.

Targeting by Household Income (Means Testing)

Income-based targeting is the most obvious method, because poverty is generally defined in terms of household income. Once the minimum income necessary for subsistence—the *poverty line*—is established, the target group can be determined as the group of households whose incomes fall below the poverty line. The use of means testing to differentiate between the poor and the non poor requires, however, very detailed data on households, which are available in few developing countries. The leakage due to the error of inclusion (type I) with means testing reflects not only errors in the estimation of the households' income, but also the incentives that the program's benefits may give households to misrepresent their true income, or even to reduce their work effort and labor supply to qualify for the program. In industrial countries, where these programs are common, individual income

reports to the tax authorities are the main source of information on households' income. However, many of the poor—and even nonpoor, for that
matter—do not work in positions that oblige them to file income tax statements, and separate statements that go through extensive verification by
local social workers must be submitted to the social welfare administration
to qualify for aid. Despite this comprehensive data, the error of exclusion
(type II) can be quite substantial, overlooking many of the homeless that are
among the poorest of the poor. In developing countries, comprehensive
data and the means of verification are not available, making programs
based on means testing infeasible.

In principle, income support programs based on means testing need not
be based on equal transfers to all poor households; transfers can vary
according to the household's income or other characteristics of the household's members. Transfers based on the households' income amount to a
negative income tax scheme, discussed extensively in the economic literature (see De Donder and Hendriks 1998, and Kanbur and others 1994).
Under one scheme transfers are proportional to the gap between the household income y and the poverty line z. The tax rate can then be calculated as
$T(z, y) = c(\frac{1}{\delta} y - z)$, where $c > 0$ and $0 < \delta \le 1$; the transfers are positive for
households with income below the poverty line, and equal to zero when
$y = z\delta$. The transfers per poor household fall, however, as a household's
income rises to the poverty line, implying that the marginal tax rate is positive. In addition, means testing need not be limited to income transfers; it
can determine eligibility for a wide range of other programs, such as food
stamps, subsidized health services, subsidized housing, and so forth.

Targeting by Household Indicators

The informational and administrative difficulties of means-testing programs and their high costs forced many countries, including some industrial countries, to take a different route. Instead of (or in addition to) means
testing to determine eligibility, they selected one or more key indicators
which are easily observable and monitorable and highly correlated with
household income. Such programs require much lower administrative costs
to determine eligibility, and information on the key indicators is more widely available. The motivation in the economic literature for the use of indicators is provided by a large number of models that use regression analysis to
correlate a household's (log) level of consumption or income with a variety
of household characteristics. A number of characteristics are highly correlated with a household's earning capacity and human capital. They include
the number of children, (or the number of children under five), the age distribution of household members, programs for pregnant or lactating

women, woman-headed households, school-age girls, the amount of the land owned, and the neighborhood or the region in which the household resides. The latter two characteristics are used for geographic targeting. The degree of correlation between these characteristics and household income varies, however, from country to country.

The theoretical analysis of targeting by a set of social indicators was first advanced by Akerlof (1978), and further developed by Kanbur (1987), Ravallion (1987), and Glewwe (1990, 1992), among others. Akerlof compared a welfare system in which transfers are based on a set of household characteristics with a system in which transfers have the form of a negative income tax and are based on means testing. In the former system, age, employment status, female headed households, the number of children, and so forth were used to determine eligibility. While this system is more likely to create dependency and stigma, it does not create the disincentives to work associated with the negative income tax system, and is therefore likely to be cheaper to operate. Akerlof noted that, while determining eligibility by household characteristics uses information that is much easier and less costly to obtain and monitor, this method of targeting could have a negative impact on households' behavior, decisionmaking, and self image.

Kanbur (1987) emphasized the savings in administrative costs that can be achieved with the use of indicators based on household characteristics. He developed a framework for determining the optimal set of non-income information for targeting the poor by dividing the population into several mutually exclusive groups that differ from each other in their labor supply decisions and household characteristics. The model compares the marginal cost of researching additional indicators for each population subgroup to the marginal gain due to reduction in leakage, which lowers program costs. The optimal set of indicators includes all indicators for which marginal gain exceeds marginal cost. A targeted program based on indicators was used in a food subsidies program in Columbia (World Bank 1986a). The indicators were the number of children under five years old, and whether the household included a pregnant or lactating woman. The use of these two transparent and easily monitored indicators was sufficient to significantly reduce the number of beneficiaries in the program, as well as its administrative costs. Ravallion (1987) evaluated a targeting scheme using indicators based on land ownership. A clear advantage of this indicator is its transparency, and the study showed that substantial cost reductions can be achieved by using land ownership as the main eligibility indicator. Glewwe (1992) used the household survey in Côte d'Ivoire to determine a *set* of indicators that identify with the greatest efficiency the non-poor households in urban areas. They include households that live in an apartment; households that have flush toilets; and households that have drinking water from indoor plumbing.

Glewwe found that the use of multiple criteria to determine eligibility offered an effective way to reduce the error of inclusion (type I), the error of exclusion (type II), and budgetary costs.

The use of indicators often broadens the objective of the program. For example, antipoverty programs targeted on households having more than a certain number of children combine the objectives of poverty alleviation—because the majority of the households with many children are poor—and education promotion. The result of broadened objectives, however, may be substantially different from the a priori expectations. In the Indian state of Tamil Nadu, the eligibility criterion was the weight of the child. Preschool children were admitted to the program when their weight fell below the standard for their age. In some cases mothers seem to have used the supplements as an excuse to feed their children less at home (World Bank 1986b). The same indicators can also be used in a number of different programs. For example, a program targeted on households with many children can employ several alternative instruments to distribute benefits, including income transfers, food stamps, transfers in kind, an education allowance, subsidized medical treatment for the children or all household members, and so forth.

Although the effectiveness of these indicators varies widely between countries, the following general conclusions emerge from the experience of many developing countries:

- The use of land ownership as an indicator can be attractive in certain rural areas because it is often highly correlated with a household's income and is easily observable. In some countries this indicator may introduce a large bias because it does not account for the income of family members that work in the city; nor does it account for the cattle owned by the household. Type I and type II errors associated with this indicator may vary even between regions, depending on their agro-climatic conditions and on the crops they grow. There may also be a difference between villages, depending on their proximity to the urban center or to the main road.

- Benefits to the elderly in the form of income support or free or highly subsidized health services are common in many countries, including most industrial countries These programs are often controversial, however, because they include many non-poor individuals. Proposals to reduce program costs by excluding high-income elderly individuals or taxing old age benefits are charged however, with political tensions—despite the fact that budget constraints forced open debate on these proposals even in the more affluent countries. In some cases, old age benefits provide an incentive to withhold notice of the death of the entitled person, thus raising costs.

- The number of children in the household is a good indicator of low income in many more developed countries, where the average number of children per household is relatively low. Many of these large families migrated from developing countries, therefore giving this criterion a powerful stigma that may create strong pressures to reduce benefits. Furthermore, in most developing countries, a household's number of children may not be a good poverty indicator for three reasons. First, many families have a large number of children and the error of inclusion can be quite large. Second, high child mortality, which primarily afflicts the poor, leaves many poor families with a relatively small number of children, thus excluding them from the program. Third, this entitlement criterion may provide incentives to households, primarily the poor ones, to have more children in order to qualify for aid.
- School meal programs are very popular in many Latin American countries. They have a direct impact on a child's nutrition and an indirect, positive impact on school attendance and learning. In some countries (Costa Rica, for example), these programs cover the entire population, while in other countries (Chile, for example), they cover only schools in poor neighborhoods. However, these programs do not reach children not attending school, the vast majority of whom are poor.

Targeting on Commodities

The rationale for targeting by commodities is based on the differences observed in the consumption basket of poor and non-poor households, and the objective is to reduce the costs of those commodities that are heavily consumed by the poor, thus increasing their purchasing power and consumption of staple foods. Subsidies also induce non-poor households to change their consumption habits and purchase more of the subsidized goods, thus raising the program's costs. The choice of commodities is therefore critical in reducing the error of inclusion and its budgetary costs: the higher the price elasticity and the higher the income elasticity of demand for these commodities, the larger will be the government expenses. *Inferior* goods—those with a negative income elasticity—are a particularly attractive choice for these programs, since the subsidies for these goods will be progressive. These subsidies may fail, however, to reach those consumers, primarily in rural areas, who have limited access to the (primarily urban) markets where inferior commodities are sold. This is perhaps the main reason why a program of general food subsidies tends to benefit urban more than the rural areas and the non-poor more than the poor. The urban bias of these programs reflects not only their stated objectives, but also the political pressures that motivate the government to implement such programs. This bias is further exacerbated when the government implements price controls or imposes producer taxes to prevent the price of these goods from rising or to cover program expenses. Price controls amount to net income transfers from the rural to the urban population even without a subsidy program, and their net effect is therefore an exacerbation of poverty. Nevertheless, pressure from the politically influential urban population and the relative simplicity of administering such programs motivates governments in many developing countries to resort to commodity targeting in times of high inflation.

To improve targeting, subsidized items are sometimes sold in commercial outlets located in poor neighborhoods. However, with the rise in the difference between the subsidized price and the free market price, consumers from other neighborhoods are increasingly attracted to these outlets. General food subsidies or subsidies for selected staple foods have been used in many developing countries over the years. These interventions are particularly common in years when drought or an increase in the world price of food grains inflates food prices. In many countries, particularly in Sub-Saharan Africa, food subsidy programs have been implemented primarily in urban markets to which the rural population has only limited access.

Self-Targeting

In self-targeting programs, the participants receive money income or payment in kind for their work, and the wage rate, set slightly below the market rate for unskilled labor, is the main regulatory mechanism that ensures the poor are the main beneficiaries. By relying on self-regulatory mechanisms to select the beneficiaries, these programs can overcome the information limitations that plague and reduce costs (Besley and Kanbur 1993). The work requirements and the low wage rate are used to discourage non-poor workers from participating in the program, thus screening the eligible households. Another argument in favor of a lower wage rate for participants is the lower opportunity cost of poor individuals' working time relative to others. The lower wage rate can therefore keep the program sufficiently attractive to the poor while deterring the non-poor. The assumption that the opportunity cost of non-poor individuals' working time is significantly higher may not be applicable, however, to many developing countries where unemployment is high. In rural areas, cash payments under these programs are often higher than the income generated from agricultural work and may provide an incentive for the non-poor to leave their lands uncultivated in favor of the public work program. Moreover, the government in many countries sets the minimum wage for unskilled labor, and it may be difficult for the government to set a lower wage in the public work program than the minimum wage. For all these reasons, the wage rates in the public work programs often fail as a self-regulating mechanism to target the program on the poor.

A workfare scheme was extensively used in the Indian famine relief program (Drèze 1990). Empirical evidence on the impact of this scheme in alleviating poverty was provided by Ravallion (1991), who found that participants generally came from households with income in the lowest quintile of the income distribution. The public work program in India continued to be very widespread, and in the mid-1990s employment under this program reached billions of workdays. The overall cost-effectiveness of the program cannot be measured, however, by the reduction in poverty alone, since the program also affects the supply of labor and the market wage rate. In some countries, the scale of public works operations can exceed 10 percent of the labor force (such as Chile in the mid-1980s), and it is bound to have an effect on the market wage rate and possibly on market prices. In addition, the costs of creating jobs under these programs are often much larger than the direct wage costs. In a sample of developing countries in Asia and SSA, the ratio of the wage costs to total costs in public work programs varied between 0.5 to 0.2 (Subbarao and others 1997).

Another argument in favor of self-targeted programs is their long-term benefits such as on-the-job training and the acquisition of skills, although the extent of this training depends on the nature of the job and the opportunity for program participants to make use of these skills in the private sector. Food-for-work programs are also an effective response to severe droughts and floods.

Geographic Targeting

Another method of targeting on the basis of household indicators is geographic targeting, based on the household's place of residence. Geographic targeting can be used at different levels, ranging from the region, to the district, to the village and the urban neighborhood, and it can apply a wide variety of instruments to transfer benefits to the residents of target areas. The motivation for targeting poverty alleviation programs on the basis of a household's location is the large variation in the standard of living between different geographic areas, and the concentration of poverty in particular areas. The western (inland) areas of China, parts of northeastern India, northwestern rural areas in Bangladesh, northern Nigeria, the rural savannah in Ghana, and the northeast region of Brazil are just a few examples of "pockets of poverty." Geographic conditions, particularly the distance from seaports and urban centers, had a significant impact on a region's pace of development in all countries until this century, and geography still has a strong impact on living standards of an area's residents in most developing countries. Isolation from urban centers and seaports slows growth, and also inhibits trade, the growth of specialized industries, and the use imported inputs. Isolation also creates obstacles to the diffusion of farm technologies (Foster and Rosenzweig 1995), as well as wider access to and use of credit.

In many developing countries, particularly in SSA, the quality of the roads—primarily all-weather roads—is an equally important factor determining an area's development and capacity to trade. As a result, there are differences in the standard of living between villages even within the same agro-climatic regions, depending upon their road infrastructure. In the urban areas, large disparities between neighborhoods are common; the shantytowns of Johannesburg, the *favelas* of Rio de Janeiro, and the slums of New York exist side by side with affluent neighborhoods. These neighborhoods are differentiated by housing prices and quality, physical infrastructure, the socioeconomic characteristics of the population, and the quality of health and education services, including public schools and health clinics. The low housing costs in poor neighborhoods attract migrants from rural areas while detracting the households that manage to increase their incomes, thus exacerbating income disparities between neighborhoods and deepening pockets of poverty.

Large disparities in the standard of living between geographic areas and their consequences for the design and implementation of poverty reduction programs have been widely discussed (see Besley and Kanbur, 1993, for a review). The potential benefits from geographical targeting for poverty alleviation, relative to other methods of targeting, were estimated in several empirical studies (see Bigman 1987, Ravallion 1993, Datt and Ravallion 1993, Ravallion and Wodon 1997, and Baker and Grosh 1994). The main question examined in these studies is whether geographic targeting can offer a cost-effective alternative to other targeting methods that use proxy indicators as substitutes for means testing. The absence of accurate and reliable income data in most developing countries, and their limited resources for effective universal programs, make targeting programs by means of indirect indicators the only viable alternative; among these programs, geographical targeting is in many cases the most cost-effective option.

Ravallion and Wodon (1997) examined the significance of two sets of indicators in determining households' level of well-being: one based on household characteristics, and the other based on a household's place of residence. Their empirical study with household data from Bangladesh shows that the geographic profile was a more significant indicator of poverty than other household characteristics. Their results for Bangladesh indicated, however, that the gains from geographical targeting at the regional level were quite small. In a similar study with data from Indonesia, Ravallion (1993, p. 464) concluded that the gains to the poor from geographical targeting at the level of regions could be quite small, even with large regional disparities in poverty. These studies were conducted at the regional level, however, where geographic indicators may not satisfactorily identify the poor, because a region's population is typically heterogeneous and includes many non-poor households. Considerably less leakage to the non-poor is likely in smaller geographic areas, because the socioeconomic characteristics of smaller communities, particularly in rural areas, are typically more homogeneous and the population is affected by the same agro-climatic and geographic conditions. Targeting large administrative regions may therefore result in a sizeable error of inclusion (type I) due to differences in living standards within regions, and a substantial reduction of leakage can be achieved by targeting interventions on smaller geographic areas (Grosh 1994). Data requirements may, however, be the major constraint on the design of targeting programs at the district or village level. This book presents several methodologies for applying the sophisticated tools of spatial analysis that have become available in recent years with the development of geographical information systems. The book also combines a variety of surveys with the Household Income and Expenditure Survey and the population census in order to effectively target smaller geographic areas.

Baker and Grosh (1994) evaluated the impact on poverty reduction of geographic targeting, at different levels of geographic aggregation, with household survey data from Venezuela, Mexico, and Jamaica. Their results indicate that geographic targeting can be a useful mechanism for transferring resources to the poor, and the reduction in poverty is larger than the reduction with an equally costly universal distribution program. These results were consistent both for a program of general food subsidies, and a food stamp program that used means testing as a self-selection process. Baker and Grosh also demonstrated that the level of geographic aggregation has a noticeable impact on the targeting outcome, and improved efficiency and greater reduction in poverty can be achieved by targeting on smaller geographic areas.

For many developing countries, geographic targeting offers significant advantages over other methods of targeting. First, it provides a clear criterion for identifying the target population and avoids the informational constraints that impede most other targeted programs. Second, it is relatively easy to monitor and administer and its implementation can be greatly assisted by local administrative institutions and nongovernmental organizations (NGOs). Third, geographic targeting has relatively little influence on household behavior since it is difficult and costly to change the place of residence. Fourth, it is possible to combine the location criterion with other criteria based on individual or household characteristics for determining eligibility and thereby improve targeting. Examples of these combinations include programs for school-age children in rural areas, food rations for pregnant and lactating women in certain regions or states, public work programs that are restricted to the poorer districts, and so forth. Fifth, the instruments of geographically targeted programs can include not only direct income transfers to the target population, but also a variety of other measures aimed at increasing the income of the population. Development measures include precipitating growth through investments in infrastructure, provision of public services, and provision of financial services. Measures to develop the target areas can be particularly important at the local level of the village or urban neighborhood, where the physical infrastructure is often a critical constraint. Geographic targeting can thus provide guidelines for both the allocation of benefits under a country's welfare program, and the allocation of resources under the country's development program.

Geographical Information Systems and Their Applications

In statistical and econometric analyses the use of spatial data has often been limited by the lack of an easy and effective way to explicitly incorporate spatial characteristics. This problem has been largely solved during the past decade by significant advancements in the technology of geographical information systems. Nevertheless, the use of a GIS in the social sciences has progressed very slowly, and the application of spatial data analysis in econometric studies is still quite limited. As result, the primary uses of a GIS are still in the display, organization, and simple manipulation of spatial data.

The common definition of a GIS is a computer-based system used to capture, store, edit, display, and plot geographically referenced data. Mapping by means of a computer replaces the traditional cartography process and can greatly reduce production time and costs. An important source of data for mapping is satellite remote sensing, which is used, for example, to identify and map natural resources. The sheer volume of data made available by remote sensing technology makes it necessary to use a computer for storage and display. In addition, a GIS is an instrument not only for mapping, but also for the analysis of geographic data.

In a GIS, the database contains information on both the value of individual observations and on their location and spatial arrangement. This information, known as data *typology*, goes beyond mere description of the location and geometry of observations; it also includes information on how observed areas are bounded, how they are connected, which areas are neighboring, and so forth. The spatial information for each observation thus has three dimensions: *nodes*, *lines*, and *areas* (also termed as *points*, *arcs*, and *polygons*). Each *node* is uniquely numbered and its location is determined by its geographic coordinates. *Lines* are also uniquely numbered and are described by pairs of geographic coordinates depicting their shape, where each two pair describes the linear segment of a line. The *area* is identified by its boundaries, in turn defined by the *lines* forming the boundaries. The analysis of these data proceeds in the following stages:

- Sample selection and the choice of the proper scale.
- Data manipulation, namely the partitioning, aggregation, overlay, and interpolation procedures needed to convert the data in the sample into

meaningful maps. The techniques used for these presentations are the main commercial applications of a GIS.

- Data extrapolation, namely first-round analysis of the data aimed at exploring the basic patterns and relations without resorting to more complex models.
- Data confirmation, namely evaluating spatial models and processes using the common statistical and econometric techniques for testing hypotheses, simulations, and predictions (Anselin 1988).

To highlight the main features of spatial data and the complications in their analysis, an analogy with time-series data and analysis can be instructive. In time-series analysis, the discount factor expresses the fact that variables in the near past or the near future have a greater impact than more distant variables. The same applies to spatial data: The relations between variables are determined not only by their attributes, but also by their proximity, and closer variables tend to have a greater impact.[9] In addition, distance itself is an important explanatory variable.

In a time-series analysis, the *time distance* is measured linearly and at equal intervals; in spatial analysis, the *spatial distance* may be different for different variables. For some variables, this is simply the geometric distance along a straight line on a map; for others, it is the distance along the available *access roads*, taking into account in some cases the quality of the road; for still other variables, the distance is measured by actual *travel time*, which may depend on the mode of transportation; for another group of variables, the area's topology plays a significant role. Spatial analysis therefore requires a very detailed data set to take into account all these dimensions of distance, and only the organization of these data as a GIS and the use of computers make the complete analysis possible. Even though a GIS is now more widely available, model-driven analysis of spatial data is still quite limited, and most applications of these data in regression analysis are very similar to the application of time-series data in that they exploit only a fraction of the information on the observations contained in a GIS. Below is a more detailed description of the different applications of a GIS in spatial analysis.[10]

Data Integration

The predominant use of a GIS is for data management and retrieval, and rapid update of large amounts of geographically referenced information. In research, a GIS is also used for integrating heterogeneous, geographically referenced data sets and to provide a common reference framework for the analysis of spatial data in different subjects and over different time periods. The spatial coordinates of the data make it possible, for example, to combine socioeconomic information on village populations from household and community surveys with information on the surrounding farming systems from an agriculture survey, and with information on climate and soil conditions in these areas from an agro-climatic study. By combining these data sets, a GIS allows the comprehensive analysis of social and economic phenomena that would not be possible otherwise.

A GIS allows many forms of data integration. One layer of data (for example, districts) can be presented on top of another (such as climate zones), not only for visual display, but also to combine the two sets of data and generate a new data set in which each point (or line or polygon) has attributes from both data sets. The points in the integrated data set can then be used in the analysis of social, economic, and spatial relationships, either via cross tabulation or by means of formal statistical and econometric methods. For example, information on the distance from a village to the urban center can be combined with area-based soil data in order to assess the agricultural potential of rural communities; and road network information can be combined with information on population density to generate indicators of transportation density for each district. Standard computations with data from a GIS include computation of straight-line and network distances, the area that lies within a specified threshold distance from selected features or places, and so forth. Applications for these functions include the determination of the nearest hospital for each of a number of settlements, or the identification of all villages located within a certain distance from public schools.

Data Visualization

The widespread applications of a GIS are due largely to the visualization capabilities of these systems. Maps have long been used for exploring patterns over space and developing hypotheses for subsequent formal testing. A GIS makes it possible to map large amounts of spatially referenced data almost instantaneously with various symbols and colors, and thus allow the identification of spatial patterns of the data as well as the *spatial outliers*, particularly the areas for which the observations have unusual values. Without this visualization of the data, the spatial outliers may not be obvious when the data are tabulated; nor will they necessarily reveal themselves in a statistical analysis. The following example is indicative. A direct statistical test of the relations between adult literacy rates and child malnutrition in a country may fail to reveal any pattern or significant relationship. When the data are drawn on a map, however, it can be seen that in one of the regions where literacy rates are relatively high, child malnutrition is also quite high due to specific environmental conditions. In all other regions, however, there is a clearly unfavorable relationship between adult literacy rates and child malnutrition. The identification of spatial outliers may provide insights not only into the relationships between economic, social, and spatial variables, but also into the quality of the data by identifying apparent errors.

An initial exploration of the relationships between spatial variables by means of visualization has long been used in the natural sciences, but has so far been comparatively neglected in the social sciences. In policy-oriented analysis, maps can play an important role by presenting complex relationships in a way that is easy to interpret, and by identifying the spatially relevant policy alternatives. The targets of policy actions are often specified in terms of target *areas,* and the application of a GIS can help identify the relevant policy options and the areas in which they are most effective. Maps are also an effective means of communicating the results of the analysis, and synthesize complex ideas into a generally comprehensible form.

Data Analysis

Certain to become the most significant applications of a GIS are the statistical and econometric analyses made possible, and the option to test rather complex hypotheses about the relationships among geographically referenced observations. These analyses can also evaluate the impact of distance, proximity, adjacency, or contiguity on certain behavioral patterns, and can be used to answer research questions concerning the spatial association among observations. For example, the analyst can evaluate the impact of the travel time to a health care center on child morbidity, in addition to the impact of a population's socioeconomic characteristics and the quality of services in a health care center. Another example is analysis of the impact of relevant geographic attributes—often summarized by means of a *distance* or *contiguity matrix*—on the spatial diffusion of health innovations, or of diseases.

A GIS analysis requires considerable care, however. In some cases, the strong association between variables revealed in an econometric analysis, or the explanatory power of some variables, may simply be due to their geographic proximity rather than to any inherent attribute or causal relationships.[11] The formal analysis may fail to show the distinct impact of distance if spatial dimensions are not taken separately and explicitly into account. Indeed, the distribution of social or economic observations over space is often as important as their distribution over time. A GIS makes it possible to analyze the spatial characteristics of variables in all statistical or econometric modeling, and to demonstrate the impact of distance as distinct from the impact of other attributes of these variables.

In other cases, spatial association may shed light on the process that generated the observed structure and the causal relations between variables. For example, similar rates of adoption of a new agricultural technology in neighboring villages may well be the result of personal communication driven by the villages' proximity. The distance directly influences processes that are driven by interaction and exchange, such as the distribution of information or the spread of diseases. This is one reason why neighboring villages tend to have very similar standards of living. The concentration of the poor in "pockets of poverty" is likely to be influenced by the agro-climatic conditions, the distance to the urban center, the quality of the access roads, and the area's poor resource endowment. Jalan and Ravallion (1997) also highlighted the "spatial poverty traps" in which the underlying agro-climatic and spatial conditions impoverish the local population. At the same time, the low standard of living increases the spread of infectious diseases and slows down private sector initiatives, helping to keep the local population in dire poverty.

Spatial dependence and spatially autocorrelated data require proper statistical and econometric tools for geographically referenced data. A GIS can be very useful for testing spatial autocorrelation, either by means of suitable statistical methods or by mapping and direct observation. In addition, the data integration capabilities of a GIS allow fast and efficient retrieval of neighborhood and proximity relationships among the observations. This will allow the analyst to account for, specify, or disregard the spatial dependence between variables, according to the specific objectives of the analysis.

A GIS can be a powerful tool for mapping the geographic distribution of poverty and analysis of the factors that create pockets of poverty. The data most commonly used for estimating poverty come from the Household Income and Expenditure Survey. The sample in this survey is typically very small and the analysis must rely on additional sources of relevant data. In most developing countries, the principal sources of information on all households are the population and housing censuses. A census is typically conducted only once a decade; the census questionnaire is very concise and contains only limited information on the standard of living. Even so, census data remain one of the most important sources of information on demographic and social conditions in a country. In Chapter 3 of this volume, Hentschel and others make effective use of census data in combination with the data of the Household Income and Expenditure Survey to assess the geographic distribution of poverty at subregional levels in Ecuador.

Surveys provide more detailed data, but they cover only a randomly selected sample of households. Two examples of comprehensive household survey programs in developing countries are the World Bank's Living Standards Measurement Survey (LSMS) and the U.S. Agency for International Development (USAID)–funded Demographic and Health Survey (DHS). The LSMS concentrates on household income and consumption, while the DHS focuses on measuring health indicators, including anthropometric measures that indicate the adequacy of food consumption and health care. Because the sample size in these two surveys, as well as in all other surveys, is relatively small, it is not possible to generate statistically reliable information for geographic areas smaller than a region, and the data cannot be used to map poverty in smaller areas. With the aid of a GIS, it is possible to aggregate the survey data for geographic areas, such as agro-climatic zones, that are different from the administrative regions in which the sample of households was selected. For example, per capita expenditure indicators can be aggregated for agro-climatic zones, and health indicators can be aggregated for areas classified according to their access to health services. Additional information from other surveys or from the population census organized as a GIS can then be used to determine for each survey cluster, for example, the distance to the market town or the quality of the access road. In Chapter 4, Bigman and others apply data from the population census, and from the Household Income and Expenditure Survey, and from a wide variety of surveys to determine the geographic distribution of poverty at the village level in Burkina Faso.

Auxiliary data was extensively used for estimating the geographic distribution of food insecurity and vulnerability in two recent initiatives: the USAID's Famine Early Warning System (FEWS), and the Food Insecurity and Vulnerability Mapping System (FIVIMS) of the Food and Agricultural Organization (FAO). These two systems generated comprehensive spatial indicators that are related to the population's level of well-being. A GIS database can also be used to generate indicators of accessibility, using high-resolution census data, information on transport networks, and the location of villages, towns, and service centers. This database can be used, for instance, to identify communities and estimate the proportion of the population that live an unacceptable distance from a school or health clinic. Measures of accessibility, which are generated rather easily with a GIS, can be a powerful tool for identifying vulnerability and for targeting public expenditures.

Survey of the Chapters in the Book

The book is divided into three parts. The chapters in the first part provide an overview of a GIS and its potential applications in project design and project evaluation. Chapter 1 compares the methods of analyzing spatial data as currently practiced in economic and social studies with the methods that become available when the data are organized as a GIS. Typically, geographic considerations are incorporated into economic studies by means of dummy variables that represent the effects of a country's main regions on the dependent variable. This method places severe restrictions on the analysis, and therefore on the conclusions that can be drawn. First, it restricts the number of regions (= dummy variables) that can be included, thereby restricting the analysis itself to a high level of aggregation across geographic areas. Second, it does not permit a straightforward incorporation of data from other studies. Third, this method of analyzing the impact of spatial attributes may identify the target regions, but not the reasons that make these regions eligible for targeting, which may in turn lead to misguided policies. Chapter 1 also demonstrates how the analysis can be conducted after the data have been organized in a GIS, and how additional data from other sources can be incorporated. It also demonstrates how survey data can be extrapolated from an analysis of a sample of communities to all communities in the region or the country to allow improved inference in welfare.

Chapter 2 illustrates an application of spatial and georeferenced economic and social data in project evaluation. Instead of using the data to determine where future projects or facilities should be located, the chapter describes the use of the data for evaluating the impact of projects and programs that were implemented in the past. This method, developed by the USAID, shifted the focus of impact evaluation from the level of the individual project to the level of the entire program in a country, and later from the country program level to the level of the entire West Africa region. This evolution, made possible by a GIS, created in turn a growing demand for geographic analysis of existing data and for more advanced analytical methods. The impact evaluation is focused on a statistical inference aimed at estimating the impact of a sample of projects for which suitable data on the local population are available. Rather than focusing on mean values of variables describing principal attributes of the various geographic areas in which assistance was provided, impact analysis focuses on the characteristics of the *population groups* that were the beneficiaries of assistance and on the impact of assistance on these groups. The impact evaluation is key to increasing the use of performance budgeting, which aims at targeting expenditures based on results.

Alternative Methods of Geographical Targeting

The chapters in the second part of the book describe different methods of using spatial data for geographical targeting. Chapter 3 develops a method for poverty mapping to guide geographical targeting and allocation of resources on public projects. This method combines the household survey data on income and consumption, which are available for only a sample of communities and households, with the census data, which are available for all communities and households, to determine estimates of per capita consumption for all households included in the census. Chapter 3 shows that poverty measures calculated with these consumption estimates, using census data, closely match the measures calculated from the original household survey data. While the consumption estimates are unbiased, their standard errors remain quite large, and can provide only a first draft of a detailed poverty map.

Chapter 4 presents a different method of bringing together and analyzing data from different sources to map poverty. In order to conduct the analysis, the data from all sources were georeferenced and brought together at the village level on the basis of the names of the villages and the geographic coordinates that identified their location. Agro-climatic and environmental data were integrated into the analysis at the provincial or regional levels. Organization of the data as a GIS also made it possible to incorporate data on the distance from village to village, from villages to towns, and from villages to public facilities such as schools and health clinics. Some of the data sources were available for all the villages in the country; others, including household expenditures and health data, were available only for a sample of households and villages. Econometric estimations were made in the sample of villages in which the household survey was conducted to identify community variables that best explain, for each village, the average level of well being and the prevalence of poverty. These variables were then used to estimate the level of well-being of *all* the villages in the country. From this estimate, all the villages in the country were divided into four categories of well being, ranging from the very poor to the least poor. These estimates thus identified not only villages that should be the target of anti-poverty programs, but also villages that should be the target of cost-recovery programs.

Chapter 5 considers another method of utilizing the data collected in the household surveys to obtaining criteria for geographic targeting. The method is based on the use of a light monitoring survey, in which households are only asked about a small sample of their expenditure items and household effects, rather than the full Living Standards Measurement Survey (LSMS) or Integrated Surveys (IS), which are more comprehensive and typically cover several dozens of household expenditure items. The use of the light monitoring survey may, however, lead to significant errors in resource allocation. An evaluation of the costs and leakage that can result from these errors shows that they can be significant enough to far outweigh the savings made by using the light monitoring instruments instead of the full household survey. The chapter then presents a methodology for estimating total household expenditure consisting of light monitoring surveys and integrated surveys, and demonstrates the reduction in mistargeting and leakage of benefits to non-eligible households that can be achieved. The regional poverty predictors derived by this methodology are shown to provide an effective instrument for targeting poverty alleviation programs.

Chapter 6 takes the analysis of geographic targeting of public projects in health, education, and rural development one step further: once the regions that should be the target of the public expenditures have been identified, it still must be decided where in these regions the public health or education facility should be located. Distances from the various villages within each target region to public facilities are among the most important parameters determining the benefits that individuals in that region can obtain. Nevertheless, project design is all too often predominantly concerned with direct costs, even though ease and speed of access for the population is sometimes key in facilitating use of the services. Chapter 6 outlines the method of designing accessibility indicators for communities through a GIS and develops criteria based on these indicators, incorporating considerations of *equity* and *fairness* to determine the socially desirable location of public facilities. After reviewing the criteria for accessibility that have been suggested in the geographic literature, the chapter presents an alternative set of criteria for determining the location of public facilities in the form of economic indices of inequality and poverty. The application of these criteria is illustrated in an analysis of family planning service centers in Madagascar

Applications of a GIS for Geographic Targeting

The use of geographical information systems grew rapidly in the 1980s, and it has become the central tool in the work of geographers and regional planners. The core of a GIS is a database comprising geographic, economic, demographic, social, and other information organized into digital form, which allows easy addition of any new geo-referenced data. This system makes it possible to produce both statistical tables for an analysis of attributes of the data, as well as maps that display cartographic information together with their associated characteristics.

Economists and sociologists have yet to make full use of the potential of a GIS in their work. In particular, the application of a GIS for evaluating the spatial impact of government policies and for targeting public projects and programs in health, education, and rural development is still quite limited, even though these applications offer clear benefits in streamlining government expenditures on social programs and making them more effective. In part, lack of familiarity with a GIS explains their limited use; another reason is the lack of information required for the creation of the database and the methodological problems arising from the use of social and economic data. These problems are due to incomplete georeferencing and extensive use of data covering only a sample of communities and households. Nevertheless, the growing need to improve the cost-effectiveness of social programs and development projects requires first and foremost more precise targeting and better evaluation of results across different regions and communities; and for this purpose, the use of a GIS is particularly advantageous. Organization of data in a computer system makes the scope of applications of a GIS analysis very broad, going far beyond the mere presentation of geographic data. The following is a partial list of possible applications of a GIS analysis:

- Calculating distance (taking, whenever necessary, transport routes into account) from the community to the main city, to the nearest health-care facility, and so forth.

- Verification of spatial data that already exist in some data sets, particularly data obtained in surveys (for instance, the distance to the nearest town).
- Determining and displaying the "area of influence" of a project or facility like a school or hospital, based on specific criteria such as the maximum distance from the facility. This area of influence depends on the location of the facility, its capacity, the means of transportation, and the attributes of the population (density, income, and so forth) in that area.
- Calculating the "area of influence" of a disease (or a drought) based on the characteristics of the population, the geographic and climatic conditions in that area, and the attributes of the disease.
- Estimating the values of variables that depend on geographic factors, and that can therefore be extrapolated from their values in the surrounding communities where the data were collected using statistical or econometric analysis.
- Assessing the impact of an existing or new facility or project on the surroundings.
- Extending the spatial analysis when the value of the dependent variable is a function not only of the characteristics of the population in that community, but also of its distance from the sphere of influence of the neighboring communities.

The third part of this book presents different applications of a GIS for the geographical targeting of a variety of projects and programs. The chapters in this part were selected in order to illustrate not only different applications, but also different methods of using spatial data in analysis, and different forms of presenting the results. Clearly, the most advanced applications are the ones in public health and the environment. More so than projects in education and rural development, these projects rely on data that cover the entire population of a region or a country, and the application of a GIS for these projects is relatively straightforward. The analytical methods developed for these projects, together with the methods presented in the second part of this book for analyzing survey data, can provide guidance for similar applications in other projects.

Chapter 7 demonstrates the use of the large amount of agro-climatic data collected in the past decade in most Sub-Saharan African countries for determining indicators of vulnerability to food insecurity and evaluating the consequences of food insecurity in different geographic regions. The chapter illustrates how the agro-climatic data and data on the attributes of the population collected in a number of different studies can be brought together and used to analyze the spatial dimension of the vulnerability to food insecurity in the countries of West Africa. The indicators of food insecurity are then used to show the variations in vulnerability across population groups and geographic regions and to evaluate the implications for regional development planning activities. The analysis is based on the data collected within the framework of USAID's Famine Early Warning System project and the West Africa Spatial Analysis Prototype (WASAP), including the geo-referenced Demographic and Health Survey data.

Chapter 8 illustrates another application of a GIS to determine target areas for the treatment of one of the most common and damaging diseases in West Africa and Central America: onchocerciasis, or river blindness. Since treatment is ultimately delivered at the community level, target areas must also be determined for communities. This method was developed and applied in Guatemala, which embarked a decade ago on a strategy of community therapy and onchocerciasis control. The principal source of data was a complete set of 1:50,000 maps, in which all the communities in the affected area were identified. These data were combined with the comprehensive epidemiological data set of the Ministry of Health, and analyzed in order to calculate community endemicity and identify three categories of communities according to the prevalence of the disease. The data were then used to determine the "disease endemic areas" by calculating the area in which the black fly that spreads the disease is likely to stay, and thereby identify communities that are not yet affected but at high risk. The division of all communities according to these categories determined the road map for the fight against the disease, and the specific measures to be taken in each category to contain the disease.

Chapter 9 illustrates the application of a GIS in public health planning. Specifically, the chapter demonstrates how a GIS can be combined with a satellite-based surveying system known as a global positioning system (GPS) in differentiated mode (DGPS) to achieve greater accuracy of geographical targeting. The methodology is described in this chapter and is applied to identify the geographic parameters of one of the most prevalent diseases in developing countries—malaria. This disease, transmitted by mosquitoes, is the cause of high rates of child mortality in tropical regions of Africa and Latin America. Malaria can be effectively controlled, however, if mosquito-infested areas are targeted, and special measures taken to protect households located in these areas. For decisionmakers, the issue is how to optimally select communities that should be targeted. The chapter reports on the experience of combining a GIS and DGPS to select target communities in Kenya. The process of selecting these communities involves the following steps. First, a database is created with information on household identifiers for all villages and communities in the wider target area. Second, location information is linked to parasitology and entomology databases through common identifiers. Third, DGPS is used to compute the shortest distance between location points in the community database and location points of mosquito sites in the parasitology and entomology database. These distances are the basis for estimating the household rate of exposure to the disease and for allocating resources for preventive care. The study shows that DGPS greatly reduces the errors in these positional measurements. The method has potential for planning public expenditure allocations in many other applications. It can be used, for example, to calculate the shortest distance between communities and health care facilities or schools, in order to determine the location of additional facilities; it can also be used to calculate the shortest distance between communities and urban centers or main roads in order to plan road infrastructure. The method can also include income or consumption data of households in these communities in order to introduce poverty-alleviation considerations into this planning process.

Chapter 10 describes the application of a GIS for the effective management of animal health in a developing country where low productivity of the livestock and diseases are endemic. In countries that have health information on livestock, it is typically passive in the sense that it includes information collected during the routine operation of veterinary services. While such systems can be improved, the chapter presents the case for a more strategic approach in which information on animal health is collected by using active surveillance techniques. On-site surveillance cannot cover all animals, however, and must be based on a sample (or samples) of locations and animals. The most critical element in active surveillance is therefore the selection of the sample and the data collection techniques. The chapter shows that if data is organized as a GIS, analysis can be made simpler, more robust, and generate more reliable, useful results at lower cost. A system is described that has been established in three northern provinces of Thailand and in the Lao People's Democratic Republic. Using a GIS for mapping background data such as spatial distribution of the various animal populations, the administrative organization of veterinary services delivery, and other relevant data, the chapter applies a modified version of Random Geographic Coordinate Sampling as the core element of the active surveillance strategy. This system produced much more data at lower costs than existing surveillance techniques.

Chapter 11 examines the application of geographic, demographic, and social data for determining the placement of branches and introducing location criteria into the decisions of micro-credit institutions and NGOs providing credit to the poor in Bangladesh. Targeted interventions are disaggregated to the level of administrative units (*thana*), and the study uses secondary-level data to identify the determinants of branch locations. These determinants may include the incidence of poverty, the demand for credit, the expected costs, and an index of riskiness for the geographic areas under consideration. The study shows, however, that in practice the main factor determining branch location was not the extent of poverty in administrative areas, but the state of local infrastructure—particularly in transportation and communication. Because of the dependence of NGOs on the location of branches of the major commercial banks where their funds are deposited, the concentration of NGOs and micro-credit institutions providing credits for poverty alleviation is quite low in poor areas, while their concentration in the better-off areas of Bangladesh is much higher. The authors demonstrate, however, that much greater outreach and improved targeting of the micro-credit institutions could be achieved if the operating NGO were to broaden their functions to include a network of branch offices that perform all functions of money transfers.

The different methods of combining survey data with a wide variety of data on agro-climatic, spatial, health, education, and demographic conditions presented in this book, and the demonstrations on how the extended data sets can be utilized to determine target areas and effective policy instruments, are aimed at motivating and inspiring economists and other social scientists to make more extensive use of social and economic data in regional planning, and to incorporate spatial analysis in their work. By including a wide range of methods and applications, the book allows potential GIS users to tailor methods of analysis and presentation of the results to their specific needs and preferences, and according to data availability. The broad range of applications and analytical methods highlights the potential role of a GIS as an essential tool in the analysis of social programs, development projects, and economic policies. A GIS requires a large volume of data that characterize not only the population affected by these programs, projects, and policies, but also the geographic conditions in the regions and communities in which they live. The analysis, and, equally important, an effective presentation of the results, requires sophisticated methods of organizing, analyzing, and displaying the data. For these tasks, a GIS is a valuable tool with great and largely unexploited potential to help those working on development issues to come up with innovative and efficient solutions for the formidable challenges presented by their work.

Notes

David Bigman was at the World Bank while this work was done and is currently at the International Service for National Agricultural Research (ISNAR). Hippolyte Fofack is at the World Bank.

1. See, for example, Jalan and Ravallion 1995.
2. See, for example, Ravallion and Wodon 1997.
3. This, however, should be captured by the individual rather than the spatial characteristics that explain inter-regional inequalities.
4. Krugman illustrated this neglect by noting that the very thorough economic

principles textbook of Joseph Stiglitz, *Economics*, more than 1,100 pages long, does not contain a single reference to the words "location" or "spatial economics."

5. The section below titled "Geographical Information Systems and Their Applications" provides further details on the main applications of GIS. Chapter 1 provides a more rigorous and detailed discussion on GIS and its applications.

6. The Institutional and Social Policy Division has become the Poverty Reduction and Social Development Group.

7. Sri Lanka is a typical example: In the late 1970s, the costs of a universal ration program reached 5 percent of GDP; these high costs drove the government into a food stamp program that cut costs to 1.3 of GDP (Subbarao and others 1996).

8. See also Ravallion (1993)

9. This is sometimes referred to as Tobler's First Law of Geography (Tobler 1970).

10. For further details see Chapter 1 in this volume.

11. Spatial dependence may also be the result of omitted variables.

References

Ades, A., and E. Glaser. 1995. "Trade and Circuses: Explaining Urban Giants." *Quarterly Journal of Economics* 110: 195–227.

Akerlof, G. A. 1978. "The Economics of 'Tagging' as Applied to the Optimal Income Tax, Welfare Programs, and Manpower Planning." *American Economic Review* 68: 8–19.

Anselin, L. 1988. *Spatial Econometrics. Methods and Models.* Dordrecht, The Netherlands: Kluwer.

Anand, Sudhir, and Ravi Kanbur. 1990. "Public Policy and Basic Needs Provision: Intervention and Achievement in Sri Lanka." In Jean Drèze and Amartya Sen, eds., *The Political Economy of Hunger.* Vol. 3, *Endemic Hunger.* Oxford: Clarendon Press.

Baker, J., and M. Grosh. 1994. "Measuring the Effects of Geographical Targeting on Poverty Reduction." *LSMS Working Paper* 99. Washington D.C.: The World Bank.

Besley, T., and S. Coate. 1992. "Understanding Welfare Stigma: Taxpayer Resentment and Statistical Discrimination." *Journal of Public Economics* 40: 165–183.

Besley, T., and R. Kanbur. 1993. "The Principles of Targeting." In Michael Lipton and Jacques Van Der Gaag, eds., *Including the Poor.* Washington D.C.: The World Bank.

Bigman, David. 1987. "Targeted Subsidy Programs under Instability: A Simulation and Illustration for Pakistan." *Journal of Policy Modeling* 9: 483–501.

Binswanger, Hans, S.R. Khandker, and M. Rosenzweig. 1993. "How Infrastructure and Financial Institutions Affect Agricultural Output and Investment in India." *Journal of Development Economics* 41: 337–66.

Datt, G., and M. Ravallion. 1993. "Regional Disparities, Targeting, and Poverty in India." In Michael Lipton and Jacques Van Der Gaag, eds., *Including the Poor.*

Washington D.C.: The World Bank.

De Donder, P., and J. Hindriks. 1998. "The Political Economy of Targeting." *Public Choice* 95: 177–200.

Drèze, Jean. 1990. "Famine Prevention in India." In Jean Drèze and Amartya K. Sen, eds., *The Political Economy of Hunger.* Vol. 2, *Famine Prevention.* Oxford: Clarendon Press.

Foster, A. D., and M. Rosenzweig. 1995. "Learning by Doing and Learning from Others: Human Capital and Technical Change in Agriculture." *Journal of Political Economy* 103: 1176–1209.

Fujita, M., and T. Mori. 1996. "Structural Stability and Evolution of Urban Systems." *Regional Science and Urban Economics.* [WHERE IS REST OF CITATION?]

Glewwe, P. 1990. "Efficient Allocation of Transfers to the Poor: The Problems of Unobserved Household Incomes." LSMS Working Paper 70. Washington D.C.: The World Bank.

Glewwe, Paul. 1992. "Targeting Assistance to the Poor: Efficient Allocation of Transfers when Household Income is Not Observed." *Journal of Development Economics* 38: 297–321.

Grosh, Margaret. 1994. *Administering Targeted Social Programs in Latin America: From Platitudes to Practice.* Washington D.C.: The World Bank.

Harris, C. D. 1954. "The Market as a Factor in the Localization of Production." *Annals of the Association of American Geographers* 44: 315–48.

Jalan, J., and M. Ravallion. 1995. "Are there Dynamic Gains from a Poor Area Development Program?" Paper presented at the Winter Econometric Society Meeting, San Francisco.

Jalan, J., and M. Ravallion. 1997. "Spatial Poverty Traps?" Working Paper, Development Research Group. Washington D.C.: The World Bank.

Kanbur, R. 1987. "Transfers, Targeting and Poverty." *Economic Policy* 4: 141–47.

Kanbur, R., M. Keen, and M. Tuomala. 1994. "Labor Supply and Targeting in Poverty Alleviation Programs." *The World Bank Economic Review* 8: 191–211.

Krugman, P. 1991. "Increasing Returns and Economic Geography." *Journal of Political Economy* 99: 183–199.

———. 1995. *Development, Geography, and Economic Theory.* Cambridge, Massachusetts: MIT Press.

———. 1993. "On the Number and Location of Cities." *European Economic Review* 37: 293–298.

Krugman, P., and A. Venables. 1995. "Globalization and Inequality of Nations." *Quarterly Journal of Economics* 110: 857–80.

Moffit, R. 1983. "An Economic Model of Welfare Stigma." *American Economic Review* 73: 1023–35.

Myrdal, G. 1957. *Economic Theory and Under-developed Region.* London: Duckworth.

Nichols, A., and R. Zeckhauser. 1982. "Targeting Transfers through Restrictions on Recipients." *American Economic Review* 72: 372–377.

Rainwater, L. 1982. "Stigma in Income-Tested Programs." In I. Garfinkel, ed., *Income Tested Transfer Programs: The Case For and Against.* New York: Academic Press.

Ravallion, M. 1987. "Land-Contingent Poverty Alleviation Schemes." *World Development* 17: 1223–33.

———. 1991. "Reaching the Rural Poor through Public Employment: Arguments, Evidence and Lessons from South Asia." *World Bank Research Observer* 6: 153–175.

Ravallion, M. 1993. "Poverty Alleviation through Regional Targeting: A Case Study for Indonesia." In Karla Hoff, Avi Braverman, and Joseph E. Stiglitz, eds., *The Economics of Rural Organization.* Oxford: Oxford University Press.

Ravallion, M., and K. Chao. 1989. "Targeted Policies for Poverty Alleviation under Imperfect Information: Algorithms and Applications." *Journal of Policy Modeling* 11: 213–24.

Ravallion, M., and Q. Wodon. 1997. "Poor Areas or Only Poor People?" LSMS Working Paper 1798. Washington D.C.: The World Bank.

Smolensky, E., S. Reilly, and E. Evenhouse. 1995. "Should Public Assistance be Targeted?" *Journal of Post Keynesian Economics* 18: 3–28.

Subbarao, Kalanidhi, Aniruddha Bonnerjee, Jeanine Braithwaite, Soniya Car Valho, Kene Ezemenari, Carol Graham, and Alan Thompson. 1997. "Safety Net Programs and Poverty Reduction." Lesson from Cross-Country Experience. Washington, D.C.: The World Bank.

Tobler, W. R. 1970. "A Computer Movie Simulation of Urban Growth." *Economic Geography* 46: 234–240.

Warner, A., and J. Sachs. 1997. "Sources of Slow Growth in African Economies." *Journal of African Economies (U.K)* 6: 335–76.

World Bank. 1986a. *World Bank Studies.* Washington, D.C.

———. 1986b. *Poverty and Hunger: Issues and Options for Food Security in Developing Countries.* Washington, D.C.

Part One

Geographical Targeting and GIS:
An Overview

1

Geographical Targeting:
A Review of Different
Methods and Approaches

David Bigman and Uwe Deichmann

WHILE ECONOMISTS AND OTHER SOCIAL SCIENTISTS have used spatial data only sporadically, physical planners, geographers, and natural resource scientists have routinely relied on these data as the basis of their work for many years (Scholten and Stillwell 1990). Growing concerns with location, spatial interaction, and, consequently, the uses of spatial data have also led to a rapidly growing use of geographical information systems for the collection, processing, archiving, and distribution of georeferenced data. In addition, GISs have been instrumental in social and economic studies that apply spatial statistics or spatial econometrics to determine the location of projects, the target areas of programs, or the regional impact of policies.

However, the development and implementation of an automated georeferenced database has not been easy, even in industrialized countries. In most developing countries, this is a daunting task that presents many obstacles, ranging from the lack of precise georeferencing to the lack of resources for transforming the data collected into a computer-readable format. In most European and North American countries, the analysis of population census statistics had already provided an incentive to establish an automated geographic database by the late 1960s and early 1970s. In developing countries, the application of GISs in the population census started only in the 1990s, primarily in Latin America, while in Africa, Zambia was the first country to use automated mapping in its 1992 census.

Slow progress in the development of an automated georeferenced database in developing countries also restricted application of spatial analysis in economic and social studies, and prevented physical planners from utilizing social and economic data. However, for several reasons, spatial analysis in general and the use of a GIS in particular can offer significant advantages to developing countries, particularly in Sub-Saharan Africa. First, in many developing countries, there are large differences in economic conditions and the standard of living between regions, and even between communities within the same region. In many countries, poverty has a clear geographic dimension, since the poor are often concentrated in pockets of poverty. Therefore, the design of poverty alleviation policies must also have a significant spatial component. Second, in many developing countries, there are differences in the ethnic composition of the populations in different regions. This makes the regional distribution of government expenditures a sensitive political issue requiring clear and objective criteria based on reliable data and impartial spatial analysis. Third, a GIS can be a very powerful tool for presenting the data, the results, and the implications of spatial analysis, thus assisting in building a wide consensus for the resulting policy recommendations. Fourth, the lack of proper infrastructure in rural areas makes the location of projects or public facilities a highly significant decision that determines the benefits of a project or facility for the population in that area.

One of the bigger methodological barriers to a wider use of GISs in social and economic research is the fact that these studies often rely on survey data collected in a sample of areas and a sample of households in each area. The methods currently used in many of these studies to analyze the spatial impact on households' decisions can considerably restrict the scope of the analysis. However, the application of GIS in this analysis can significantly broaden the scope of spatial analysis and allow far more comprehensive results and policy recommendations. The objective of this chapter is to provide a general overview of the basic concepts of GIS and illustrate its applications in social and economic studies. The first section discusses the current methods of evaluating the spatial impact in social and economic studies and presents an alternative method using a GIS to incorporate data from a variety of studies into spatial evaluation. The second section focuses on the three areas in which the tools of spatial analysis can benefit the decision-making process most: data integration, data visualization, and data analysis. Special attention is given in this review to the methods of incorporating survey data into the database and in the spatial analysis.

The Use of Spatial Data in Economic and Social Studies

Economic and social studies that evaluate the impact of spatial factors often encounter severe restrictions due to the use of survey data. Typically, a study of household or individual behavior that also examines regional factors focuses on an econometric analysis of a reduced form equation of the following general structure:

$$Y_i = \sum_q \alpha_q x_{iq} + \beta_1 D_1 + \ldots + \beta_m D_m \qquad (1.1)$$

where Y_i is the income of the ith individual (or household), $(x_{i1}, \ldots, k_{iq})$ is a vector of the relevant personal characteristics, and $(D_1, \ldots, D_m)$ is a set of dummy variables which identify the m regions from which household data were collected. This reduced-form equation, in which the location impact is presented by means of a dummy variable, is bound to restrict the analysis and interpretation of the results for several reasons. First, it imposes restrictions on the number of location dummy variables, which in turn limits the number of regions that can be considered. This confines the spatial analysis to large regions and therefore does not allow an assessment of the impact of local factors which are manifested at the level of the community, such as the distance to an urban center or to the source of drinking water. Second, the analysis at the level of large administrative areas may obscure, rather than highlight, the impact of location factors, since these areas are generally arbitrary units. Third, under this structure of the equation, the analysis is restricted to an evaluation of whether or not a person's place of residence (or work) has a significant impact on the decisions that are expressed by the dependent variable. It does not allow an evaluation of the specific characteristics of the place of residence that affect these decisions, thereby limiting the policy implications that can be drawn from the results.[1] For example, if the objective of the study is to determine criteria for targeting public projects, an analysis of the location impact by means of dummy variables can identify the areas that should be selected for targeting, but cannot determine the characteristics that qualify these areas for targeting. However, knowledge of these characteristics can be pivotal in determining the type of projects that should be implemented in order to achieve the best results. Some of these projects—such as improving the access road to the community—can change the impact of the location factor and thereby the households' decisions.

The organization of data as a geographical information system can provide the necessary vehicle for conducting a comprehensive analysis of the spatial characteristics that affect the households' decisions. It also allows the incorporation of survey data—and the social and economic information contained in these surveys—in physical and environmental planning. A detailed overview of GIS issues and an illustration of its possible applications will follow this section's more general discussion of the merits of geographic targeting of projects and programs. The focus of this discussion will be on poverty alleviation programs.

The Motivation for Targeting Poverty Alleviation Programs

In most welfare programs, the optimum solution, from a theoretical point of view, is to identify the target population and design the most effective program for this group. In the majority of cases, however, it is not possible to identify the target population since this requires information that is not observable and thus difficult to verify. In poverty alleviation programs, for example, the target population is the group of households with incomes below a certain minimum level necessary to provide basic needs. Household income is often difficult to observe, however, and efforts to assess its value and thus identify the target group may involve prohibitive costs. These costs consist not only of direct administrative expenses for collecting the necessary information on income, but also of indirect costs due to incentives that the program may give individuals either to modify their behavior or to falsify information on their income in order to qualify for the program's benefits. Poverty alleviation programs such as income transfers or food subsidies to the poor, for example, may provide incentives to work less, cut earnings, or underreport income in order to qualify. Even in countries that have an accurate income reporting system, frequent means testing is necessary to verify that only households that meet the criteria remain on the eligibility lists.

The difficulties and expenses involved in identifying eligible households leave two options: either to implement universal programs that cover the entire population, or to use observable indicators that are highly correlated with the relevant unobserved variables, such as income, in order to determine eligibility. Universal programs are too expensive for most developing countries, and even many industrial countries find the rising welfare costs daunting. The only viable option, therefore, is to use some form of targeting. This, however, requires a careful choice of the targeting criteria, the observable indicators that will determine eligibility, and the programs that best fit the specific conditions in the country. The following summary of experience with a food coupon program in Brazil illustrates the difficulties involved in these choices:

> Food coupons were distributed through government-run supermarkets. Initially, income testing was used to determine who could participate. Income reporting was arbitrary, however, could not be checked, and the program incurred substantial administrative costs. On the basis of this experience, the program was modified by targeting only on low-income neighborhoods. That change proved to be very effective. Leakage of benefits to people not in need was much reduced, and the program proved to be much less expensive than administering the cumbersome coupon program. (World Bank 1986, p. 35)

As a background for the discussion on geographic targeting, a brief outline of the other options available to developing countries is useful.[2] These options fall into three categories: self-targeted programs, programs targeted on the basis of household characteristics—such as female-headed households—and programs targeted on the households' place of residence. Among these options, self-targeting seems to be the most attractive. The experience with self-targeting programs such as food for work was often mixed, however. A number of studies in African countries indicated that the poorest of the poor often could not benefit from these programs because of various restrictions that the poor have (single mothers of small children were not able to work far from their home, poor health of the head of the household, and so forth). Another form of self-targeting is the careful selection of benefits from the programs. A typical example is a food distribution program that focuses on food items that are the main staples of the poor.

The other two categories of targeted programs are based on a classification of the population into two groups: those that are eligible for the program and those that are not. This division is made on the basis of certain criteria that are specified in terms of clearly observed indicators, such as families with a large number of children, households that reside in low quality or crowded dwellings, female headed households, or households that reside in certain geographic areas. A combination of targeting criteria has also been used. In Colombia, for example, areas of poverty were first identified as part of the national development plan. Targeted food subsidies were then provided to households in national development plan areas with children under five years old or with a pregnant or lactating woman. This reduced the number of possible beneficiaries and thus lowered administrative and fiscal costs (World Bank 1986).

The Costs and Effectiveness of Targeted Programs

The effectiveness of a targeted program depends on the share of the target population—that is, the percentage of the total poor population—that is actually covered by the program. This, in turn, depends on the accuracy with which the observable indicators predict the unobserved variables that are the basis for determining eligibility. In the case of poverty alleviation programs, the desired indicators are those that are highly correlated with income. The effectiveness of the set of indicators $(\gamma_1, ..., \gamma_m)$ depends on the probability expressed in equation 1.2:

$$\text{Prob}(y_i < z \mid \gamma_{ik} > \gamma_k^* \text{ for } k = 1, ..., K): \text{ for all households} \qquad (1.2)$$

where γ_{ik} is the household's level of the kth indicator (for example, the number of children) and γ_k^* is the critical value of the indicator that determines eligibility, y_i is the (unobservable) income of the ith household, and z is the poverty-line income, below which the household is considered poor and therefore eligible for the program. Studies that seek to identify the most suitable set of indicators can use the data of a Household Income and

Expenditure Survey to estimate the correlation between the indicators and household income for those households that were included in the survey—and for which there is complete information on both income and the indicators. The reduced form equation in this analysis is similar to equation 1.1 and can be written as equation 1.3:

$$P_i = \sum_q \alpha_q x_{iq} + \beta_1 \mu_1 + \ldots + \beta_m \mu_m \qquad (1.3)$$

where P_i is either the level of consumption expenditures or a dummy variable which indicates whether the household is considered to be poor or not. In this analysis, we can distinguish between two types of indicators: $(x_{i1}, \ldots, x_{iq})$ are household or personal indicators, and $(\mu_1, \ldots, \mu_m)$ are "dummies" that identify the place of residence. When the dependent variable P_i is itself a dummy variable, the econometric analysis is transformed into a logit analysis, and the equation then estimates the probability of a person being poor, assuming that his personal indicators are within a given range and his place of residence is in a given area.

The overall costs of the program have the following three components: (1) the direct (administrative) costs of obtaining the information on these indicators; (2) the indirect costs due to incentives that eligibility for the program may provide; and (3) the costs of providing the benefits to the population covered by the program.

To illustrate the method of accounting for the effectiveness of the program and its costs, consider an income transfer program aimed at reducing poverty:[3] If incomes were observed, the problem of designing an effective program could be stated as equation 1.4:

$$\min P(y+t;z) \quad \text{subject to:} \ \sum_{i \in F} t_i \leq T \qquad (1.4)$$

where $t = (t_i)$ is the vector of transfers which are positive for the individuals included in the group Φ which is covered by the program, and zero for the others, y is the vector of incomes, $P(y; z)$ is the poverty index, and T is the total amount of financial resources available for the program. The solution to this problem depends on the functional form of the poverty index, on the poverty line, and on the resources available. That solution can be denoted as $t^* = t(y, z, T)$. When incomes are not observable, a decision has to be made on the set of observable indicators, denoted by the vector $\gamma = (\gamma_1, \ldots, \gamma_k)$, which will be selected to estimate income. The group that will be covered by the program and the income transfers will then be determined on the basis of the observable indicators, and the problem then becomes the minimization of *expected* poverty, given the joint probability distribution of y and γ as shown in equation 1.5:

$$\min E[P(y+t(\gamma);z)] \quad \text{subject to:} \ \sum_{i \in F} t_i(\gamma) + C(\gamma) \leq T \qquad (1.5)$$

where $\sum_{i \in \Phi} t_i(\gamma)$ are the transfer payments to all the households covered by the program and $C(\gamma)$ are the costs of collecting information on the indicators $\gamma = (\gamma_1, \ldots, \gamma_K)$ in *all the households in the population*. For a given set of indicators, the decision whether or not to add another indicator thus depends on the cost of collecting the information on this indicator, on the effect that the addition of this indicator will have on the selection of the target group, and on the reduction in expected poverty that can be achieved by adding this indicator. Let $(\gamma_1, \ldots, \gamma_K)$ be a given set of indicators. The decision whether or not to add another indicator, γ_{K+1}, depends on the expected increase in effectiveness, that is, the expected reduction in poverty:

$$\min \ E[P(y + t(\gamma'); z)] - \min \ E[P(y + t(\gamma); z)] \leq 0 \tag{1.6}$$

where $\gamma' = (\gamma_1, \ldots, \gamma_K, \gamma_{K+1})$; and it also depends on the net change in costs.

The change in costs has three components. The first is the additional costs for collecting the information on the indicator γ_{K+1}, given by equation 1.7:

$$\Delta C(\gamma_{K+1}) = C(\gamma') - C(\gamma) > 0 \tag{1.7}$$

The second component is the change in costs of providing benefits to the population covered by the program—equal to the change in transfer payments due to the change in the group covered under the new set of indicators (which determine also new criteria of eligibility). The third component is the change in indirect costs due to the incentives that the addition of this indicator may give individuals to change their behavior or falsify the reported information in order to qualify for the program. To simplify the presentation, this third cost component will not be considered in these accounts. The change in direct costs is given by equation 1.8:

$$\sum_{i \in \Phi'} \tau_i(\gamma') - \sum_{i \in \Phi} \tau_i(\gamma) \leq 0 \tag{1.8}$$

where Φ' is the group entitled for benefits under the indicators γ'. The additional indicator can reduce the direct costs of the transfer payments by reducing the number of non-poor households included in the group Φ— which was selected with the indicators γ. The additional indicator can also enhance the effectiveness of the program by increasing the number of poor that are included in the new target group Φ'. These changes in costs and effectiveness are discussed further below.

Equations 1.6, 1.7, and 1.8 provide the criteria for selecting the best indicators from the list of all possible indicators. In an analysis of household data in Côte d'Ivoire, Paul Glewwe (1992) examined a list of indicators that included the following:

- What is the region of residence?

- Does the dwelling have stone walls?
- Does the household have flush toilet?
- Is the household's drinking water from indoor faucet?
- What is the ethnic group of the head of the household?
- What is the level of education of the head of the household?
- Does the household own a bike?
- Does the household own a refrigerator?

The econometric analysis determines the most effective subset of indicators—the indicators that minimize the expected poverty. This, however, is only one part of the analysis; in the second part, the costs of obtaining the information on these indicators must be evaluated. Even a superficial appraisal of the costs and the efforts that may be necessary to obtain information on the above list of indicators from all households in the population illustrates the potential difficulties. Information on the quality of the dwelling is sometimes included in the population census, but in most developing countries, a census is conducted only once every 5 to 10 years. If households will also be asked about the level of education of the head of the household, his or her ethnic group, or even ownership of certain household effects, they may have incentives to falsify their replies if they suspect that this information will determine their eligibility for the program.

Indicators of Geographic Attributes

Among the various indicators, the easiest to determine for all households and one that is difficult to falsify is the place of residence. Although geographically targeted welfare programs may give incentives to households to change their place of residence, the costs involved in this change are likely to reduce that incentive and thus also the indirect costs of the program. The information on the place of residence need not be limited, however, to a binary (zero/one) variable which indicates whether or not the household resides in a certain area. It can also include much more detailed information on the *attributes* of that area: Is the household's place of residence rural or urban? What are the agro-climatic conditions in that area? How far is this place from the urban center? How far is it from an intercity highway? What is the quality of the access road to this place? How far is it from public facilities such as schools or health clinics? All this information can be very important in determining the standard of living of the households residing in that area. A household study in Java, for example, found that distance from the urban center was one of the most important factors affecting the incomes of the local population. In villages situated more than 6 kilometers from the regional center, the average per capita income was at least 20 percent lower and the incidence of poverty more than 70 percent higher than in the closer villages (Mason, 1996). In other words, what determines the stan-

dard of living and the incidence of poverty in an area is not its specific iden-
tity—which the dummy variable establishes—but its attributes. Populations
in two communities that have similar geographic attributes are likely to
have a similar standard of living and incidence of poverty.

The problem from an operational point of view is that Household
Surveys typically contain only very limited information on a community's
geographic attributes.[4] To determine which attributes of a household's place
of residence affect its decisions and behavior, most of these data must be collected from other sources. These sources may include the agricultural surveys, health and demographic surveys, the population census, and various
geographic and climatic surveys. The data can be strictly geographic—location, altitude, administrative boundaries, roads, and so forth—but they can
also include georeferenced social and economic data, such as the population's size in the area, their age and ethnic distribution, the main crops
grown in the area, other sources of income, the availability of public facilities such as schools or hospitals, and so forth. In order to prepare these data
for econometric analysis, it is necessary to merge the data at the level of the
geographic unit under consideration—the region, district, or village. This
can be done by the name of the area and the geographic coordinates (for villages), or the geographic boundaries (for the district or the region). This part
of the work is where a GIS can be most instrumental.

With this information, both the exact geographic reference of all the
supplementary data and the place of residence of each of the households in
the Household Survey can be established. In the next step, attributes of the
area are incorporated into the econometric analysis, and the corresponding
coefficients that determine their impact on the household's income can be
estimated. In the econometric analysis, the estimation equation is transformed from that shown in 1.1 or 1.3 to an equation of the following form:

$$P_i = \Sigma_q \alpha_q x_{iq} + \Sigma_d \beta_d \mu_{di} \qquad (1.9)$$

where $(\mu_{1i}, \ldots, \mu_{Di})$ are now the D *attributes* of the place in which the ith
household resides—rather than zero/one variables that establish the identi-
ty of that place. This analysis of the Household Survey data will provide
estimates and the significance value of the coefficients $(\beta_1, \ldots, \beta_D)$ which
measure the contribution of the geographic attributes, thus identifying the
subset of attributes with the most significant impact on the standard of living of the populations in these places. These attributes can serve as the indicators that identify all areas in the country that will be covered by the geographically targeted program.

Several comments on this part of the work should be noted:

1. If the econometric analysis is using only the Household Survey data—
   as in equation 1.1—it is bound to be restricted to an analysis of the

impact of large areas such as an entire region, since the size of the sample in each region must be sufficiently large and representative. At the regional level, geographic attributes are likely to include primarily agro-climatic indicators that affect the standard of living of the population; they cannot include, however, more local indicators such as the distance to the urban center or to a public facility.

2. If the place of residence is defined in terms of relatively large areas, it is less likely to be correlated with income; the larger the area, the more heterogeneous its population is likely to be, and the larger, therefore, the relative number of non-poor households residing in the target areas. At the village level, the population is generally much more homogeneous in terms of standard of living, because all households are equally influenced by its geographic attributes.

3. A GIS makes it possible to determine the place of residence of households as well as the geographic reference of most geographic attributes at the level of the community—that is, the village in rural areas, and the neighborhood in urban areas. This allows the entire econometric analysis of the effects of geographic attributes to be conducted at the level of the community, thereby making it possible to determine criteria for targeting on individual communities.

4. This method of using the Household Survey data together with other georeferenced data to estimate the impact of geographic attributes can be applied with any other survey, thus allowing physical planners to make more extensive use of survey data in their analysis.

Criteria for Selecting the Target Areas

Once estimates of the standard of living and the incidence of poverty in all of a country's "areas"—the regions, districts, or communities—have been determined on the basis of the indicators, target areas can be selected. This selection requires, however, specific criteria of cost-effectiveness. Kanbur (1987) suggested a measure of "poverty alleviation efficiency" (PAE) as a criterion for evaluating the cost-effectiveness of a transfer payment program that compares the increase in incomes of the poor as an effect of transfers with the program's total costs. When income transfers to all eligible persons are equal, program effectiveness is determined by the *number* of poor persons covered, and the measure of effectiveness is their share in the total *poor* population. When the costs accounted for in this evaluation are only the direct costs of the transfer payments themselves, then, in a universal program, the PAE ratio of a transfer payment of US$1 is simply the Headcount ratio, H. For a regional program that covers only one region, say area j, the PAE ratio is the Headcount ratio in that area, H_j. A first-order indicator of the efficiency of a program targeted on that area is the ratio H_j/H: if that ratio is larger than 1, then the PAE of the targeted program is larger than that of the universal program.

This criterion suggests the following process of selecting the areas for targeting a transfer program under a fixed resource constraint. First, select the area that has the highest Headcount ratio and subtract from the budget the costs of implementing the program in that area. Second, select the area that has the highest Headcount ratio among the remaining regions and subtract from the total budget the costs of implementing the program in the *two* areas. Proceed in this way until the total budget is exhausted. When the transfer payment is equal to US$1 per eligible person, the costs per region are simply the size of the population in area j—that is, N_j—and the cost constraint is given by $\sum_{j \in \Theta} w_j H_j \leq \{T/N\}$, where Θ is the set of all areas that are covered by the program, T is the program's budget, N is the size of the total population, and $w_j = N_j/N$ is the share of the population in the jth area in the country's total population. This process determines the most cost-effective targeting program under the PAE criterion when the values of all the variables that are necessary for the calculation are known with certainty. The cost-effectiveness ratio—or the PAE ratio—of this program is given by:

$$\left\{ \sum_{j \in \Theta} w_j H_j \right\} / \left\{ \sum_{j \in \Theta} w_j \right\} \qquad (1.10)$$

If the values of the variables that are needed for this calculation—primarily the areas' Headcount ratios—are not known and must be estimated by means of certain indicators, the cost-effectiveness criterion would be the expected value of the PAE.

The measure of effectiveness under this criterion can also be expressed in terms of the effect of the program on the poor that reside in the *other* areas and are therefore *not* eligible for any transfer payments. The share of this group in the total poor population is given by

$$\sum_{j \notin \Theta} w_j \left\{ H_j / H \right\} \qquad (1.11)$$

where the summation is over the set of the areas that are *not* targeted under the program. This sum is known as the Type II error of targeting, namely the probability that a poor person who qualifies, in principle, for the transfer payment will not be covered by the program. The PAE measure of effectiveness thus seeks to minimize the Type II error, which measures the program *ineffectiveness*.

The measure of costs which complements this measure of ineffectiveness is known as the Type I error of targeting, defined as the probability that a non-poor person will receive the transfer payment under the targeted program. This probability is given by

(1.12) $$\left\{ \Sigma_{j\in\theta}\, w_j \left(1 - H_j\right) \right\} / \left\{ \Sigma_{j\in\theta}\, w_j \right\}.$$

The Type I error can be regarded as a measure of the *cost-ineffectiveness* of the program and is equal to 1 minus the PAE ratio. The process of selecting the target areas with this criterion involves eliminating from the program areas that have the highest cost-ineffectiveness. At each step in this process, the area that will be eliminated is the one in which the ratio $(1-H_j)$ is the highest among the remaining areas. This process clarifies that areas selected under the PAE criterion—and which therefore minimize the type II error— will also be the ones that minimize the type I error.

To provide numerical estimates of the cost-effectiveness of the program, we can use once again the Household Survey. Divide the sample of households in the survey into two groups: those residing in areas that are covered by the program, and those residing in areas that were not selected for targeting. For these two groups, we can estimate, on the basis of their income (or expenditure) data in the survey, the size of the total population, and the percentage of *poor* households that are included in each. On the basis of the parameters of the program—the size of the income transfers or other criteria of eligibility (age, employment status, and so forth)—we can calculate the costs of the program according to the income transfers and the relative size of the poor population that is covered.

Application of GIS in Spatial Analysis

This section surveys the role that a GIS can play in economic and social analysis in general, and in studies aimed at establishing criteria for geographic targeting of economic development projects and programs in particular. The focus of this overview is on three areas: data integration, data visualization, and data analysis.

Data Integration

The predominant use of a GIS remains in inventory-type applications, where large amounts of geographically referenced information need to be retrieved and updated quickly. Such applications, which stress database management functions, are common in the utilities sectors and in facility management. For research and policy analysis, the more important aspect of geographic data storage and management is a GIS's ability to integrate heterogeneous data sets (Shepherd 1991). By providing a common reference framework for information drawn from a range of subject areas, GISs allow the user to perform comprehensive, multidisciplinary analyses. Spatial data integration by means of GIS functions can thus help to overcome the difficulties of analyzing socioeconomic and biophysical data within a common reference framework. A GIS can also be used to reconcile data sets collected at different time periods for incompatible area units. This problem is commonly encountered in the analysis of census data where reporting zone boundaries were modified between enumerations.

Data integration is achieved by using space as an indexing system (Goodchild 1987): a common geographic reference system allows us to represent all features in a database at their true spatial location. This vertically integrated information can be overlaid and combined to create new information. For example, village or community information from the community survey can be combined with information on the surrounding farming systems from the agriculture survey. District-level economic indicators from the Income and Expenditure Survey can be integrated with data on climate or soil quality from an agro-climatic study. These GIS functions thus make it possible to combine data sets that would otherwise be difficult or impossible to analyze jointly. This enables the analyst to tackle a wider range of questions and also increases the returns on investment in building spatial databases, since many more users can benefit from them. Many countries, for example, are now building a national spatial data infrastructure consisting of basic *framework data* such as roads, hydrology, settlements, and various types of political and administrative boundaries.

The chapters in this book present alternative methods of integrating spatial data in economic and social studies. In Chapter 3, Hentschel and others examine the integration of the census data and the data of the Household Income and Expenditure Survey at the regional and sub-regional levels. In Chapter 6, Bigman and others integrate village-level data collected in a survey with information on agro-climatic conditions and distance to services. In Chapter 7, McGuire combines health, economic, and environmental information that had been compiled by various studies to analyze food security issues in West Africa.

Geographical information systems provide many data integration functions. For instance, a polygon overlay is a function that, in some ways, defines the essence of a GIS. Polygon overlay goes beyond drawing one data layer (for example, districts) on top of another (such as climate zones) for visual display. Rather, the two sets of area features are intersected and logically combined. The output is a new data set that contains all areas of intersection, and each new polygon has the attributes from both input data sets—such as district-level census information and climatic characteristics. Variables from the resulting integrated data set can be cross-tabulated to analyze, for example, whether the agricultural endowment of a region has an influence on indicators of well-being that are available from a census. Relationships that are summarized in the cross-tabulations can subsequently be analyzed more formally using statistical methods. Similar techniques exist for point or line features. Village location information, for example, can be combined with area-based soil data to assess the agricultural suitability around each community. Road network information can be used to generate a simple indicator of transportation density for each district.

Other data integration functions may result in complete new data layers. For instance, by using a set of station recordings of rainfall or temperature, interpolation functions allow the estimation of a complete surface of those values that can later be combined with other information. Such techniques are common in natural sciences applications but, for reasons outlined below, have not found widespread use in socioeconomic analysis. Location and distance are at the core of a GIS. Standard functions include computation of straight-line and network distances, as well as so-called *buffer operations* that define a region around selected features that lie within a specified threshold distance. Example applications for these functions are finding the nearest hospital for each of a number of settlements, or identifying all villages within a certain distance in a behavioral study of neighborhood influence. This discussion of basic GIS functions is by no means exhaustive. Standard GIS textbooks contain extensive discussions of GIS data integration functions (for example, Jones 1997 and DeMers 1996).

Data Visualization

The exploratory paradigm in statistics relies heavily on the graphing and charting of data. New techniques implemented in standard statistical packages use innovative displays to allow searching for patterns in multivariate data sets (Cleveland and McGill 1988). This supports a mode of analysis that relies on intuition as much as statistical theory. Similarly, the widespread acceptance of GISs owes much to the visualization capabilities of these systems, which are rooted in the cartographic tradition. Maps have been used for a long time as aids in exploring patterns and to develop hypotheses that can then be tested more formally. The most famous example is John Snow's London cholera map, which led to the discovery of the relationship of the disease with contaminated drinking water (Snow 1855).

A GIS adds a dynamic component to the traditional cartographic approach. Large amounts of spatially referenced data can be mapped almost instantaneously with symbols and colors. This supports, for example, the identification of observations with values that are unusual in relation to their surroundings (see, for example, Haining 1990). Such spatial outliers, which may have been generated by substantive underlying factors, might not be obvious from looking at a data table or chart alone. The scatter plot in figure 1.1, for example, does not show any unusual values. A map of the two variables, however, shows that one district has unusually high rates of literacy and income compared to the surrounding districts. This

Figure 1.1 Spatial Outliers

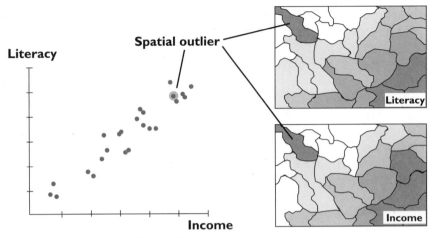

Source: Illustrative data generated by the authors.

information may provide an insight into the conditions that caused this particular region to be different from its neighbors. It is possible, for instance, that the higher literacy rates are due to much better economic conditions in that district, which make better education possible. An actual example is the unusually low birthrates in the southern Indian state of Kerala, which are mainly due to the traditionally high status of women in the local society and consequently their higher level of education (Repetto 1994). Spatial outliers or groups of observations for which certain characteristics have unusual values may also lead to significant insights about the data generation mechanism. Where no substantive meaning can be attributed to an unusual pattern, visualization may simply help to identify errors in the data.

Developments in dynamic graphics in statistics have also quickly found their equivalent in geographic applications (Anselin 1998 provides an overview). In many commercial statistical software packages, different representations of the same data set, for example scatter plots and histograms, are dynamically linked. If a subset of the data is selected in one representation, such as a bar in a histogram, the corresponding observations in all other representations are highlighted as well. Some mapping packages support the use of maps as an added representation of the data (for example, Haslett and others 1991). If an analyst selects on the map a set of districts or villages that appear to show an interesting pattern, these observations are automatically indicated on the statistical charts as well. This feature provides significant support in exploring multivariate relationships in a comprehensive data set. The exploratory paradigm has been adopted more quickly in data-rich natural sciences applications, but has been comparatively neglected in the social sciences. Economic analysis tends to be hypothesis driven rather than data oriented. However, with the emergence of more comprehensive socioeconomic data sets and the move toward multidisciplinary research, as supported by the data integration capabilities of GISs, the highly visually oriented methods in exploratory statistics and mapping are also likely to find wider application in the social sciences.

Moving from research applications to more policy-oriented analysis, maps also have an important role in focusing debate in situations where the decisionmaking process involves a number of participants. By presenting complex relationships in a way that can be easily interpreted by anyone, maps can focus public debate concerning policy alternatives and thus help to reach consensus decisions in politically sensitive situations. In targeting or other allocation applications, models can be linked directly with a GIS. As discussions proceed, comments and objections can be translated into changed model parameters, new results can be generated quickly, and the resulting maps can immediately influence the ongoing debate.

Finally, besides supporting exploratory analysis and participatory decisionmaking, maps have an important role in communicating results of analysis. Presentation quality maps, as shown in several chapters of this book, are powerful tools in supporting tabular and text output. Maps help put things in context and allow us to synthesize complex ideas into a generally comprehensible form.

Data Analysis

Although at present most GIS applications tend to be limited to inventory-type applications or simple mapping, these systems also support more formal analysis, such as hypothesis testing that follows hypothesis generation. Recent developments in GISs have thus led to a revival of the spatial analysis tradition in geography. Central to this tradition is *spatial structure*: the arrangement of observations in geographic space and how the relationships among geographically referenced observations influence the results of statistical analysis (Anselin and Getis 1992). Spatial analysis considers geographic referencing not only in terms of absolute location, but also in terms of relative position. Concepts such as distance, proximity, adjacency, or contiguity of observations are implicitly stored within a spatial database and can be called upon to answer research questions that might concern the spatial association among observations. Advanced data structures, for instance, store information on which districts border another district. Other information, such as which villages are located within a half-day's travel from a village, can be generated quickly using standard GIS functions. The influence of geography on the spatial diffusion of innovations, or of diseases, can thus be tested by evaluating adoption rates or disease incidence among people who live in close proximity, or who are neighbors. In a formal analysis, this information is summarized by means of a *distance* or *contiguity matrix*. These matrices indicate in each cell the distance between observations i and j, or simply whether i and j are neighbors.

Geographic structure and association relates to what Tobler (1970, p.235) called the *first law of geography*: "everything is related to everything else, but near things are more related than more distant things." This is variously called spatial dependence, spatial autocorrelation, or spatial association, and implies that similar values tend to be clustered, which has obvious implications for hypothesis testing.[5] Sometimes, geographic proximity explains the association between variables in an econometric analysis, and the explanatory power of other variables (behavioral or policy related) may be insignificant once the spatial relationships are taken into account. Therefore, spatial data sets usually cannot be regarded as independent samples. This loss of sample information results in reduced efficiency of statistical inference. In analogy to time-series analysis, the geographic dependence structure of the data needs to be taken into account in statistical or econometric modeling.

In addition to this concept of spatial dependence as a "nuisance"—something that yields statistical estimation problems rather than substantive insights—there is a second, more substantive implication: spatial association may shed light on the process that generated the observed dependence structure. For example, if neighboring communities or villages show similar values for important variables, this might be the result of a diffusion pattern driven by personal communication, copycatting, spatial spillovers, or a bandwagon effect (see, for example, Case 1991 and 1992). In addition to *spatial diffusion*, where an attribute of a population is distributed and adopted by a fixed population, Haining (1990) identifies three other types of spatial processes: *spatial dispersal* or spread, where the population itself, rather than an attribute, disperses; *exchange and transfer*, where, for example, goods or services are exchanged and these functional linkages generate a convergence of income or other traits (see, for example, Lewis and Thorbecke 1992); and *spatial interaction*, where events at one location influence events at another, as in interregional price transmittal (see, for example, Alderman 1993). In addition, a spatially dependent variable might be the result of the distribution of an underlying variable that had not been considered in the analysis.

Spatial processes occur within a specific *context*, and spatial autocorrelation may thus be a problem not only in the dependent variable, but also in any number of explanatory variables. A concentration of poor persons may therefore be caused by poorly developed labor markets, limited resource endowments, or restricted access to social services within a region—this is what Jalan and Ravallion (1997) termed "spatial poverty traps" (see also Ravallion 1996 and 1998). Clearly, spatial autocorrelation, whether as a result of a spatial process or limited geographic capital, is an essential condition for geographic targeting to be meaningful. Poor people tend to live together where land and housing costs are low. Infectious disease incidence tends to be clustered. People tend to adopt beneficial programs such as rural credit if their neighbors do so as well. And low educational attainment tends to be concentrated where school infrastructure is inadequate.

Spatial dependence has several practical implications for the analysis of geographically referenced data. The first is that standard statistical tools are only of limited use in the analysis of spatial data. Just as the specific issues in the analysis of temporally autocorrelated data have given rise to a set of specific tools, spatial econometrics and spatial statistics provide a range of methods and models that allow the incorporation of spatial dependence in formal estimation (see Anselin 1988, Griffith 1988, Cressie 1991, as well as Anselin and Bera 1998, for a more recent survey). The data integration and visualization capabilities of a GIS clearly support this mode of analysis. GISs are useful for the identification of potential spatial autocorrelation through mapping and data query. Furthermore, the data integration capabilities of these systems allow for the fast and efficient retrieval of the neighborhood and proximity relationships among the observations—a requirement for more formal testing for the presence of spatial dependence and for spatial econometric modeling.

Spatial dependence also has consequences for sample design. If the objective of a study is to establish valid econometric relationships using standard estimation techniques—in impact analysis, for example—then a sampling distance beyond the range of spatial dependence should be chosen. If, however, we are interested in exploiting the structure of a spatial process for prediction—for targeting applications, for example—we might design a sample in which neighbors are deliberately included and the neighborhood structure is considered in the estimation. In a spatial context, prediction usually refers to the estimation of values for a variable at locations that were not sampled, using information available for a set of sample sites. For example, a complete surface of rainfall values can be interpolated using information from a set of climate stations. Here, spatial dependence is a necessary condition for the interpolation to be valid, since the rainfall at any given location is estimated as a distance-weighted function of the rainfall at the closest climate stations. Choosing the appropriate parameters for the interpolation is equivalent to specifying the structure of spatial dependence. By contrast, prediction—say of average income for all villages in a region based on a survey sample of villages—cannot be done on the basis of distance alone, but must consider many other characteristics that are available for the sample villages as well as for all communities (see Hentschel and others in Chapter 3).

Geographic Data Issues

Most socioeconomic data have a spatial component. Typically, such data are collected for micro-units such as individuals, households, or settlements, or they are aggregated by community, village, district, province, or nation-state. Most often, the geographic reference is simply an address or a consistent code for each observation that indicates its administrative unit. In a GIS, reference units are explicitly represented as discrete geometric features with a known position on the earth's surface. In practice, these will either be points that specify the location of a farm or household, or boundaries that delineate districts or other administrative or natural units. The areas delineated by boundaries are usually called *polygons* in GIS terminology. Points are often also used to summarize the location of villages in applications at smaller cartographic scales—that is, those that cover a large area. An example in this volume is the village level data set for Burkina Faso in Chapter 4.

Censuses

Two types of data sources dominate in socioeconomic analysis: censuses and surveys. Population and housing censuses provide basic demographic and social data, although in some countries, civil registration systems make censuses increasingly unnecessary. Exhaustive data collection is expensive and time consuming.[6] Therefore, censuses are at best carried out at ten-year intervals, and the scope of the census questionnaire is usually kept to a small number of variables that are useful for the largest number of government and private census data users (see United Nations 1998). National statistical organizations collect census data for individuals and households. For privacy reasons, they usually release information only at aggregate levels, such as census blocks or enumeration areas, which may have a population size of a few hundred people.[7] Unfortunately, many countries in the past have only released information at even more aggregate levels such as districts or provinces, and access to more detailed information is frequently difficult or impossible.

Given that a census is usually the only source of local area data that are not sampled or estimated, this lack of access to disaggregated data is unfortunate. Much energy, time, and resources must be spent by researchers to reverse the aggregation and to obtain small-area data that were collected at this level of detail in the first place. More powerful computers, better software allowing flexible cross-tabulations, and the growing demand for local-area data in public and commercial applications may encourage more statistical offices to release data at the highest level of resolution that does not compromise legitimate privacy concerns. In the meantime, however, an array of shortcut methods needs to be used to disaggregate census data to a level that is useful for analysis or targeting.

Aggregate data hide possibly large internal heterogeneity. In the spatial domain, this causes problems if the units of analysis are not designed by meaningful aggregation procedures—those that minimize intraregional variance while maximizing interregional variance. Since socioeconomic data are usually aggregated for more or less arbitrary administrative or political units, we cannot expect that the internal distribution of each region is homogeneous. The same underlying distribution of a variable such as income may therefore give rise to different aggregate patterns.

Consider the two aggregations in figure 1.2, which are derived from the same underlying distribution (also shown in the illustration). The actual distribution of the variable, which could be income or rainfall, is referenced for a regular array of grid cells (a so-called *raster* GIS data set). The distribution displays a high degree of spatial autocorrelation since neighboring grid cells tend to have similar values. Table 1.1 shows summary statistics for the three spatial representations of the same data. Clearly, the first aggregation reflects the actual distribution much better than the second aggregation in which the spatial variability is strongly underestimated. This problem is

Figure 1.2 Illustration of Aggregation Problems

Actual distribution

800
1100
1400
1700
2000
2300

Aggregation 1

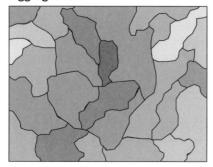

Aggregation 2

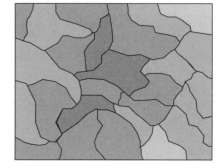

Source: Illustrative data generated by the authors.

Table 1.1 Summary Statistics of the Three Different Realizations in Figure 1.2

	Actual distribution	*Aggregation 1*	*Aggregation 2*
Minimum	514	896	1367
Maximum	2690	2338	2053
Mean	1686	1644	1689
Standard Deviation	352	351	221

Source: Authors' computation.

known as the *modifiable areal unit problem* (MAUP) and has been recognized in many fields that deal with geographically aggregated information (see Haining 1990 and Jelinski and Wu 1996). It implies that virtually any number of possible correlation or autocorrelation structures can be derived from the same underlying distribution.

The MAUP is related to the problem of *aggregation bias*, which is the loss of information as individual units are aggregated. This, in turn, is associated to the so-called *ecological fallacy problem* (Robinson 1950): relationships observed at an aggregate level do not necessarily hold at the individual level. In fact, as King (1997) points out in the context of voting behavior, the true individual-level relationships can even be the reverse of the relationship observed at the aggregate level. A reliable method for estimating individual-level information from aggregate data can be of significant value in geographic targeting. It would help us to understand true individual-level relationships, and it would allow for the estimation of disaggregate data from district-level totals. We will return to this issue below.

The lack of homogeneity within aggregate socioeconomic units also has implications for data integration. An example is the integration of village-level or survey cluster data referenced by using points and census data by region. GIS point-in-polygon operations allow us to perform this data integration where the resulting village data set will record for each village the variable values for the district into which it falls. Essentially this involves drawing a point sample from the polygon data set. Since the district values are not, in reality, homogeneous, the derived indicator for a village is the district mean, which is the true value for the village plus an unknown deviation. This is essentially a form of the well-known errors-in-variables problem in econometrics (see Griliches 1983).

Surveys

The second and more common type of socioeconomic data is based on sample surveys, which collect information about a representative part of a population in order to make inferences about the entire population.[8] The validity of the resulting survey data set depends critically on the sample design. Most socioeconomic samples are purely population based and ignore the distribution of spatial parameters in stratification. In natural resource or agricultural applications, by contrast, it is now common to use GIS data layers of generic biophysical, infrastructure, and related variables to obtain a sample that truly reflects geographic variation. This may often also be desirable in socioeconomic studies where individual behavior or characteristics are likely to be influenced by geography.

A serious problem with surveys is consistency and comparability over time. Surveys that are conducted repeatedly are often not designed to use the same sample selection procedures, size, coverage, and definitions. "Improvements" in sample design can thus seriously hinder comparisons across space, such as cross-national evaluations or the analysis of changes over time. Lanjouw and Ravallion (1996), for example, showed that two poverty assessments in Ecuador indicated a decline in the poverty rate between 1994 and 1995 despite an unfavorable economic environment and an absence of significant poverty alleviation policies. Further research revealed that the decline was solely due to a change in the definition of a key consumption variable. Correcting for this change of survey design showed that the poverty rate had actually increased significantly.

Furthermore, spatial analysis is often made difficult by the fact that few socioeconomic surveys are georeferenced before or during data collection. Determining the geographic coordinates of sample clusters after data collection is tedious, costly, and error-prone (see Croft and others 1997). The additional cost of using a global positioning system (GPS) to collect the geographic location of each sampled unit during field work is, in contrast, quite small. GPS receivers are relatively inexpensive handheld devices about the size of a pocket calculator. Using information broadcast from a set of navigation satellites, these systems are able to calculate the latitude and longitude of their position with acceptable accuracy (see Hightower, Chapter 9 of this volume, for application of a GPS in field data collection). This location information greatly supports integration of survey data with other spatial data sets, and thus easily recoups the added equipment costs. All current and future Demographic and Health Surveys (DHS) are using GPS to collect the exact sample cluster location. The same approach would also significantly improve the utility of economic surveys such as the Living Standards Measurement Surveys (LSMS).

A significant difference exists between sampling in geographically oriented natural resource applications—such as soil, climate, or vegetation surveys—and sample surveys in socioeconomic applications. In the latter, samples are usually used to provide an overall value at an aggregation level for which the sample size and design is deemed adequate (the DHS and LSMS surveys are examples). Natural resource studies usually sample with the objective of subsequently deriving a complete surface of the sampled indicator. Geostatisticians have developed an impressive array of interpolation methods for this purpose. Interpolation is made possible by the fact that many physical parameters vary in a predicable way, often changing smoothly or in coincidence with another, easily observed variable (for example, temperature declines steadily with higher elevation). Social science data, in contrast, tend to display much less predictable spatial variation. The reason, of course, is that socioeconomic variables depend on a multitude of complex elements including behavioral, political, ethnic, and economic factors. In addition, they are influenced by the geographic context, which includes biophysical conditions such as the ecological and agricultural endowment of an area (which in turn influences the standard of living), and physical infrastructure–related information such as access to input and output markets as well as public services (see Bigman and Deichmann, Chapter 6 of this volume). Despite the likely presence of neighborhood effects, we therefore cannot estimate, for example, a variable from the Demographic and Health Surveys for a village which was not sampled simply as a distance-weighted function of the values found at sampled clusters in the vicinity. Rather, to exploit the information about spatial variation that is present in the survey data, we need to use more indirect approaches as outlined in the following section.

The Use of Survey and Census Data

In the absence of data on individuals that can be observed and verified, it is necessary to determine criteria for targeting on the basis of observed data, aggregate information, and sample surveys. However, as noted earlier, the use of survey data may create a number of problems in spatial analysis. There are two statistical methods of addressing these problems: small area estimation and ecological inference.

Small Area Estimation

The sampling density of socioeconomic surveys is usually too sparse to yield reliable estimates for small geographic areas. Data from sources like the Demographic and Health Surveys or the Living Standards Measurement Surveys can only be aggregated to the national level or, at best, to a small number of regions within the country. Aggregation at smaller administrative levels, such as provinces or districts, would yield unacceptable standard errors due to the small sample sizes. Driven in part by the increasing need for reliable small area statistics by local governments and businesses in industrial countries, this problem has led to the development of techniques that "borrow strength" (Ghosh and Rao 1994) from related areas and additional data sets to generate reliable statistics for small areas (see also Patek and others 1987, and Pfeffermann and Barnard 1991). Small area estimation techniques range from simple Kendricks-Jaycox type synthetic estimators to more complex statistical estimation models.

The goal of small area estimation is to estimate a variable for target units, such as villages or districts, based on the relationship of that variable to a number of explanatory factors. These explanatory variables must be available in the survey as well as in the data set available for all target units such as a census. After estimating the relationship using statistical techniques, the resulting coefficients are applied to the explanatory data to derive an estimated value for each target unit.

In poverty related studies, the variable of interest is usually a consistent measure of well-being such as income or consumption. Such information is generally not available from a census, but only from surveys. In Hentschel and others (Chapter 3 of this volume), the statistical relationship between a measure of consumption and a large number of explanatory variables is estimated using household-level survey information. The target units are administrative units of Ecuador. Estimates were derived for each of the 2.5 million households in the country and subsequently aggregated. In studies where micro-data are not available, estimates for administrative areas would be generated directly using aggregate data (see Ghosh and Rao 1994).

In Bigman and others (Chapter 4 of this volume), the target units are villages for which no measure of well-being was available. The required parameters for prediction were derived using a subset of these villages in which a household survey of income and expenditures had been conducted. In each case, the result is a detailed spatial data set of well-being, which can be related to coordinates or boundaries and integrated in a GIS for visualization and further analysis in combination with other geographic data layers. In other small area estimation studies, the problem may be that a variable is collected only at large time intervals, such as a decennial or quintennial census. For example, Isaki (1990) estimated an annual time-series of retail sales at the county level from a survey that is conducted only every five years. For this estimation he used information from another county level survey conducted annually, but which does not collect retail sales information. Here the problem is interpolation in time rather than in space.

As pointed out above, the census is usually the only consistent, exhaustive source of data at the individual, household, or small area level. The number of questions included in the census varies by country, but in many instances, and especially in Sub-Saharan Africa, the census questionnaire is very brief. As a result, the number of potential explanatory variables available is often small and the scope of available data—for example, on health, education, or household facilities—might be limited. In data-poor applications it can be beneficial to augment the census data with other information. Information on agriculture, agro-ecological endowment, or access to services and infrastructure can be estimated indirectly, especially in rural settings, using satellite remote sensing or GIS techniques. Such spatially referenced data can be derived for the entire region or country and are therefore natural candidates for inclusion in small area estimation.

Ecological Inference

The problem of inferring individual-level behavior from aggregate data has recently attracted renewed attention. In many instances, successful targeting depends on an understanding of individual-level relationships among variables in the economic, health, education, or agricultural sectors. Often, however, we do not have sufficient information on these indicators at the individual level and must instead work with aggregate information on, for instance, the number of literate females of reproductive age within each of a number of districts, and the aggregate number of women using modern contraceptive techniques. In this case, we only have the total number of literate and illiterate women, and the total number of women using or not using contraceptives. In order to draw reliable conclusions about the relationship between literacy and contraceptive use, the cells in the corresponding two-way table must be filled in so that the number of women who are literate *and* who use modern contraceptives is known. This problem is called the *ecological inference problem*.

Solutions to the ecological inference problem have so far been largely unsatisfactory (see Cleave and others 1995). Available methods often give answers that are inconsistent with other evidence, or these methods might even generate impossible solutions, such as percentages larger than 100. King (1997) presents an alternative method. He combines a statistical regression model that estimates separate parameters for each small area (similar to variable parameter models in econometrics) with the method of bounds, which limits the resulting parameters to those that generate solutions that are consistent with the available data. In addition, King's method—much like the small area estimation approach—uses information from all other small areas to improve the plausibility of the estimates. By replicating a large number of studies where individual-level information was available to evaluate prediction success, King concluded that, compared to other techniques, his new method generated much-improved individual level estimates.

Clearly, improved ecological inference can have large benefits for targeting. Instead of relying solely on results of analysis at an aggregate level, which may be subject to aggregation bias, more detailed and relevant variables can be constructed that describe relationships at the individual level.

For instance, aggregate district or community level census data may be available on the proportion of households with access to safe drinking water and the proportion of female-headed households. King's method allows derivation of a more useful variable that indicates the proportion of female-headed households without access to safe drinking water for each community or district, as well as corresponding confidence intervals for each estimate. This variable can be mapped, combined with other relevant information, and used for targeting or further spatial analysis. If gender-specific intervention is the policy objective, the newly derived variable permits more accurate targeting than the aggregate information only.

Another example, reported in King (1997), concerns estimation of the fraction of men and women in poverty in each of 3,187 census blocks in the U.S. state of South Carolina, using aggregate data on gender and the proportion of the population below the poverty line. Output is a two-way table of poverty status by gender for each block group. Despite the fact that the gender ratio varies only slightly across the census blocks, the resulting estimates turn out to be very close to the observed fractions.

Although not explicitly spatial, ecological inference also addresses the modifiable areal unit problem discussed earlier. Because estimates are given at the individual level, overall results across a number of reporting zones will be very similar regardless of the aggregation determined by the boundaries of geographic units.

Integrating Additional Information

Small area estimation and ecological inference allow a change in the scale of analysis, from a limited number of survey points to a complete coverage of small areas, or from aggregate data sets available for small areas to individual-level data. In each method, statistical estimation is involved, which is, of course, not free from error. Neither method can completely eliminate the problems of missing data and of aggregation bias. Sensitivity analysis and an interpretation that is in line with the uncertainty associated with the estimates are thus mandatory (see the discussion of the standard errors of statistical estimates in Hentschel and others, Chapter 3 of this volume).

Apart from these statistical issues, there are other more general issues that should be considered in geographic targeting. Too often, the analysis is constrained to only one data set—for example, a survey or a census. This constraint ignores the significant gains in explanatory power that can be obtained by combining several data sets (see also Henninger 1998). For example, in developing countries, economic and social factors are often strongly influenced by others, such as the natural resource endowment, infrastructure, or access to local services. Another example is epidemiological studies, which are by definition interdisciplinary. Malaria research requires information on climate, elevation, and other natural factors that determine the distribution of the disease vector (see Hightower, Chapter 9 of this volume). Social information such as the adoption of bednets or the education level may be relevant in explaining the success of intervention programs. An example in the agricultural sector is the targeting of improved planting varieties. Adoption of new seeds depends as much on the farmer's education level, extension service availability, and other social indicators, as on the agro-ecological endowment of the region that influences the success or failure of a new plant. Much of the information required in such studies can be obtained from secondary sources such as remotely sensed images or existing GIS databases that may have been compiled for other purposes, or they can be constructed using standard GIS functions for data integration and modeling.

This leads to the issue of explicit versus implicit treatment of space. Cross-sectional data sets of spatial units such as villages or districts are used in numerous studies. It is surprising, however, that maps are often absent in the relevant reports. Geographic relationships are often not considered explicitly, and issues such as neighborhood effects, spatial interaction, or other geographic processes are ignored. A simple ranking of areal units to determine the allocation of resources may suffice for broad policy analysis, but treating space explicitly and mapping all relevant input and output data helps us to better understand causes and relationships between policy relevant variables.

Notes

David Bigman was at the World Bank while this work was done and is currently at the International Service for National Agricultural Research (ISNAR); Uwe Deichmann is with the Development Research Group of the World Bank.

1. A division of the localities according to certain broad characteristics, such as rural, urban, agro-climatic conditions, and so forth, can assist in establishing the impact of these characteristics of the place of residence on the households' decisions. A division into smaller areas is, however, not possible.

2. For a comprehensive discussion on targeting poverty alleviation programs, see Baker and Grosh (1994), and Besley and Kanbur (1993). See also Besley and Kanbur (1988), Besley (1990), Besley and Coate (1992), Ravallion (1989 and 1991), Datt and Ravallion (1993), Nichols and Zechhauser (1982), Ravallion and Chao (1989), Glewwe and Kanaan (1989), and Glewwe (1992).

3. This illustration is after Glewwe (1992).

4. In some countries, the Household Survey has been complemented by a community survey that includes much of this information. For a variety of reasons, little use has so far been made of the information contained in these surveys.

5. A second type of spatial effect, usually referred to as *spatial heterogeneity*, relates to patterns of a more discrete nature. We have discussed spatial outliers previously. Groups of such outliers may form clusters, and significant clusters of similar values—sometimes called hotspots—may indicate distinct subsets within a data set, where statistical relationships may follow a different form. Spatial heterogeneity can be addressed using standard statistical approaches such as dummy variables or Analysis of Variance.

6. The 2000 census in the United States is estimated to cost more than US\$6 billion. One dollar per person is an estimate that has been used in the past in planning censuses in developing countries.

7. However, statistical institutes sometimes make micro-data (also called unit-record data) available for in-house research or for academic purposes. Micro-data samples are sometimes also released without identifying information, but this usually means that the spatial referencing information is lost.

8. As Kish points out in his classic 1965 textbook, a census is, strictly speaking, also a sample: due to unavoidable error in data collection, any census data set is just one of many possible census outcomes. Also, the population is usually selected from a universe of many such populations that exist, for example, in the time dimensions—that is, the census is conducted on an arbitrary day within a ten-year period and any other census date would result in a different outcome.

References

Alderman, Harold. 1993. "Intercommodity Price Transmittal—Analysis of Food Markets in Ghana." *Oxford Bulletin of Economics and Statistics* 55(1): 43–64.

Anselin, Luc. 1988. *Spatial Econometrics. Methods and Models.* Dordrecht, the Netherlands: Kluwer.

———. 1998. "Interactive Techniques and Exploratory Spatial Data Analysis." In P. Longley, M. Goodchild, D. Maguire, and D. Rhind, eds., *Geographical Information Systems: Principles, Techniques, Management and Applications.* Cambridge: Geoinformation International.

Anselin, Luc, and A. Bera. 1998. "Spatial Dependence in Linear Regression Models with an Introduction to Spatial Econometrics." In A. Ullah and D. Giles, eds., *Handbook of Applied Economic Statistics.* New York: Marcel Dekker.

Anselin, Luc, and Arthur Getis. 1992. "Spatial Statistical Analysis and Geographic Information Systems." *Annals of Regional Science* 26(1): 19–33.

Baker, J.L., and M.E. Grosh. 1994. *Measuring the Effects of Geographic Targeting on Poverty Reduction.* Living Standards Measurement Study Working Paper 99, World Bank, Washington, D.C.

Besley, Timothy. 1990. "Means Testing versus Universal Provision in Poverty Alleviation Programs." *Economica* 57: 119–129.

Besley, Timothy, and R. Kanbur. 1988. "Food Subsidies and Poverty Reduction." *The Economic Journal* 98: 701–719

———. 1993. "Principles of Targeting." In M. Lipton and J. van Der Gaag, *Including the Poor*. Washington, D.C.: The World Bank.

Besley, Timothy, and Stephen Coate. 1992. "Workfare versus Welfare: Incentive Arguments for Work Requirements in Poverty Alleviation Programs." *American Economic Review* 82: 249–261.

Case, Anne C. 1991. "Spatial Patterns in Household Demand." *Econometrica* 59(4): 953–965.

———. 1992. "Neighborhood Influence and Technological Change." *Regional Science and Urban Economics* 22(3): 491–508.

Cleave, N., P.J. Brown, and C.D. Payne. 1995. "Evaluation of Methods for Ecological Inference." *Journal of the Royal Statistical Society. Series A—Statistics in Society* 158(1): 55–72.

Cleveland, W.S., and M.E. McGill. 1988. *Dynamic Graphics for Statistics*. Pacific Grove, CA.: Wadsworth.

Cressie, Noel. 1991. *Statistics for Spatial Data*. New York: Wiley.

Croft, T., S. Rutstein, J. Brunner, and N. Abderrahim. 1997. "West Africa Spatial Analysis Prototype: Development of a Georeferenced Regional Database." Paper presented at the Population Association of America Annual Meeting, Washington, D.C.

Datt, G., and M. Ravallion. 1993. "Regional Disparities, Targeting, and Poverty in India." In M. Lipton and J. van Der Gaag, *Including the Poor*. Washington, D.C.: The World Bank.

DeMers, M.N. 1996. *Fundamentals of Geographic Information Systems*. New York: John Wiley.

Ghosh, M., and J.N.K. Rao. 1994. "Small Area Estimation: An Appraisal." *Statistical Science* 9(1): 55–93.

Glewwe, Paul. 1992. "Targeting Assistance to the Poor: Efficient Allocation of Transfers When Household Income Is Not Observed." *Journal of Development Economics* 38: 297–321.

Glewwe, P., and O. Kanaan. 1989. "Targeting Assistance to the Poor: A Multivariate Approach Using Household Survey Data." Discussion Paper 94, Development Economics Research Center, University of Warwick, U.K.

Goodchild, Michael F. 1987. "A Spatial Analytical Perspective on GIS." *International Journal of Geographical Information Systems* 1(4): 327–334.

Griffith, Daniel A. 1988. *Advanced Spatial Statistics*. Dordrecht, the Netherlands: Kluwer.

Griliches, Zvi. 1983. "Economic Data Issues." In Z. Griliches and M.D. Intriligator, *Handbook of Econometrics*, Vol. III. Amsterdam: Elsevier.

Haining, Robert P. 1990. *Spatial Data Analysis in the Social and Environmental Sciences*. Cambridge: Cambridge University Press.

Haslett, J., R. Bradley, P. Craig, A. Unwin, and G. Wills. 1991. "Dynamic Graphics for Exploring Spatial Data with Application to Locating Global and Local Anomalies." *The American Statistician* 45(3): 234–242.

Henninger, Norbert. 1998. "Mapping and Geographic Analysis of Poverty and Human Welfare—Review and Assessment." Report prepared for the

UNEP/CGIAR Initiative on GIS, World Resources Institute, Washington, D.C.

Isaki, C.T. 1990. "Small-area Estimation of Economic Statistics." *Journal of Business and Economic Statistics* 8(4): 435–441.

Jalan, J., and M. Ravallion. 1997. "Spatial Poverty Traps?" Working Paper, Development Research Group, World Bank, Washington, D.C.

Jelinski, D.E., and J.G. Wu. 1996. "The Modifiable Areal Unit Problem and Implications for Landscape Ecology." *Landscape Ecology* 11(3): 129–140.

Jones, C. 1997. *Geographical Information Systems and Computer Cartography*. Harlow, U.K.: Longman.

Kanbur, R. 1987. "Measurement and Alleviation of Poverty." *IMF Staff Papers* 34: 60–85.

King, Gary. 1997. *A Solution to the Ecological Inference Problem*. Princeton: Princeton University Press (http://GKing.harvard.edu).

Kish, L. 1965. *Survey Sampling*. New York: John Wiley.

Lanjouw, Peter, and Martin Ravallion. 1996. "How Should We Assess Poverty Using Data from Different Surveys?" *Poverty Lines* No. 3, World Bank, Washington, D.C.

Lewis, B.D., and E. Thorbecke. 1992. "District-Level Economic Linkages in Kenya: Evidence Based on a Small Regional Social Accounting Matrix." *World Development* 20(6): 881–897.

Mason, A. 1996. "Targeting the Poor in Rural Java." IDS Bulletin.

Nichols, A., and R. Zeckhauser. 1982. "Targeting Transfers through Restrictions on Recipients." *American Economic Review, Papers and Proceedings* 72: 372–377.

Patek, R., J.N.K. Rao, C.E. Saernal, and M.P. Singh, eds. 1987. *Small Area Statistics*. New York: John Wiley.

Pfeffermann, D., and C. Barnard. 1991. "Some New Estimators for Small Area Means with Applications to the Assessment of Farmland Values." *Journal of Business and Economic Statistics* 9: 73–84.

Ravallion, Martin. 1989. "Land-Contingent Rural Poverty Alleviation Schemes." *World Development* 17: 1223–1233.

———. 1991. "On the Coverage of Public Employment Schemes for Poverty Alleviation." *Journal of Development Economics* 34: 57–79.

———. 1996. "Issues in Measuring and Modeling Poverty." *Economic Journal* 106: 1328–1343.

———. 1998. "Poor Areas." In A. Ullah and D. Giles, *The Handbook of Applied Economic Statistics*. New York: Marcel Dekkar.

Ravallion Martin, and K. Chao. 1989. "Targeted Policies for Poverty Alleviation Under Imperfect Information: Algorithms and Applications." *Journal of Policy Modeling* 11: 213–24.

Repetto, Robert. 1994. *The Second India Revisited*. Washington, D.C.: World Resources Institute.

Robinson, William S. 1950. "Ecological Correlation and the Behavior of Individuals." *American Sociological Review* 15: 351–357.

Scholten, H.J., and J.C.H. Stillwell. 1990. *Geographical Information Systems for Urban and Regional Planning*. Dordrecht, Netherlands: Kluwer.

Shepherd, I.D.H. 1991. "Information Integration and GIS." In D.J. Maguire, M.F. Goodchild, and D.W. Rhind, eds., *Geographical Information Systems: Principles and Applications*, Vol. 1: 337–360.

Snow, John. 1855. *On the Mode of Communication of Cholera*. London: John Churchill.

Tobler, Waldo R. 1970. "A Computer Movie Simulation of Urban Growth." *Economic Geography* 46: 234–240.

United Nations. 1998. *Principles and Recommendations for Population and Household Censuses*. Statistical Papers, Series M, No. 67/Rev. 1, Department of Economic and Social Affairs, Statistics Division, New York.

World Bank. 1986. *Poverty in Latin America: The Impact of Depression*. World Bank Country Study. Washington, D.C.: The World Bank.

2

Applications of a GIS in Program Impact Evaluation: Lessons from the U.S. Agency for International Development (USAID) Experience

Glenn Rogers

THE IMPORTANCE OF GEOGRAPHY and the spatial scale of socioeconomic interaction have been underappreciated in development assistance activities. Awareness of spatial structure in data and tools for statistical inference based on spatial data is rare in development assistance agencies. Applications and use of these analytical tools have been almost invisible. It is not surprising, therefore, that analysis of data is rarely structured in the most geographically relevant ways.

It is critically important to improve the geographic use of data for three reasons. First, the geographic unit of analysis chosen partly determines the analytical result. False policy conclusions may result from improperly structured data, and subsequent targeting efforts based on this analysis will also be faulty. Second, ignoring the geographic structure of data limits the uses of new survey data in combination with existing data. Data is available for testing a far broader range of development questions than are currently the subject of most evaluation efforts. As a result, many critical development questions are simply not tested, even though data has already been collected that could be used geographically to better respond to these questions. Third, limited analytical uses of data means that expensive data are collected but used for only few analyses. A higher proportion of current funding could be allocated to data analysis rather than data collection if existing data were better utilized geographically.

U.S. development assistance activities are designed with specific development models in mind. From a targeting perspective, these models are used to define necessary and sufficient conditions for development assistance to have an impact. GISs can help geographically identify population groups or areas with these conditions. From a program impact perspective, development models provide hypotheses that are testable using sample data on population groups that have received assistance and those that have not. The record of development assistance clearly shows the need for more testing and refining of development models for location-specific circumstances.

Unlike geographical targeting applications, impact evaluation can rely on a sample of locations. Geographical targeting generally relies on comprehensive coverage of descriptive statistics for an entire population or complete universe of locations. Targeting models rely on coefficients for weighting multiple criteria or GIS data layers. A comprehensive data set for all locations is needed to choose among locations. Impact evaluation uses real-world experiments to estimate weights for factors that result in specific outcomes. Through estimation of appropriate criteria weights, successful targeting is built upon successful impact evaluation. Successful impact evaluation is built upon empirically testing multivariate models and estimating the association between development interventions and impacts in a sample of locations. Geographically combining data allows more fully specified models to be used and more rigorous inferences to be drawn from fewer observations (Anselin 1988). Important classes of models can only be tested by compiling data geographically with the help of a GIS.

This chapter reviews applications of spatial analysis using a GIS as a tool for evaluation of U.S. development assistance in West and Central Africa. In Zaire, the emphasis was on moving from sectoral project evaluation to a country program level of impact evaluation. In West Africa, the emphasis was on moving from country program evaluation to a regional, multicountry program level of impact evaluation, targeting, and reporting. However, the approaches and challenges in data compilation, analysis, and definition of beneficiary groups were common to both cases. In Zaire and West Africa the approaches emphasized drawing useful inferences from existing spatial data about benefits that selected target groups received from U.S. assistance. A GIS was an indispensable tool for spatially referencing data, compiling databases for analysis, and presenting results.

Institutional Changes Leading to Broader Use of GISs in USAID

Before 1988 there was little interest in using geographic information systems to analyze the impact of U.S. development assistance programs in West and Central Africa. Evaluation tended to focus on project implementation within geographic project areas. Two fundamental shifts in management of development assistance began in the late 1980s. The first was the adoption of a "program impact evaluation" strategy of institutional reform. The second was an increasing emphasis on "performance based budgeting," formalized with the U.S. Government Performance and Results (GPRA) Act of 1993 (see also Pietrobelli and Scarpa 1992). These political decisions and subsequent institutional changes indirectly encouraged the adoption of GIS-based tools for program evaluation.

Impact Evaluation Strategy of Institutional Reform and Performance Budgeting

The U.S. Government is currently using what Taylor (1984, pp. 296, 316–317) called an "impact statement strategy" to improve the performance of USAID as a public organization and the foreign assistance programs it delivers. Taylor identified two key elements of this strategy of reform in his earlier study of other U.S. government agencies. The first is an external demand for increased data collection, analysis, and reporting on program impacts by agency staff and contractors. The second is more analytical competition between analysts inside the agency and those outside the agency in local governments, universities, and nonprofit organizations. New programming ideas and realistic feedback on program effectiveness are expected to come from more open and informed decisionmaking involving beneficiaries and partners outside the agency.

The combination of these two elements of reform were strengthened for USAID in 1988 when the U.S. Congress began separately funding bilateral development assistance to Sub-Saharan Africa as a budget line item called the Development Fund for Africa (DFA). Annual reporting requests under the Development Fund for Africa and now under the GPRA represent an external demand for USAID to improve its knowledge base and analysis. This annual analysis and reporting on results is leading USAID to formally set new goals, reorganize, and change the mix of its program portfolios. USAID's New Partnership Initiative is leading to more open decisionmaking involving beneficiaries' and partners' organizations. GIS databases and geographic analyses are tools to help achieve this reform through disseminating multisectoral data, communicating impact evaluation results, and building evaluation capacity among partner institutions.

The DFA allowed more flexible programming procedures for USAID field missions and encouraged performance-based allocation of funding. From 1993 to 1997, USAID was a pilot agency for implementing performance planning and reporting under the GPRA. The DFA and GPRA have led to reporting on expenditures by strategic objectives, which now serve as program budgeting categories. Impacts are increasingly measured and reported by these strategic objective budget categories that provide the link between budgeting and performance. A GIS is a tool for strengthening program performance budgeting through estimating cost ratios, combining data to evaluate impacts, and mapping the complex effects of budgeting alternatives.

Performance Reporting Requirements and Funding Stability That Encourage Use of GISs

Features of the DFA and GPRA led to an accelerated use of GISs for impact evaluation of U.S. assistance programs. First, both the DFA and GPRA increased the external demand for more rigorous quantitative reporting of impacts of government programs on human welfare indicators. Second, the DFA led to reporting on the impacts of country *programs* of assistance rather than impacts of individual *projects* in isolation. Under the DFA, a country program of assistance was defined by USAID as the "combination of all project, non-project, policy dialogue, and other activities using USAID human and financial resources" in a given country (USAID/W 1989). Third, the DFA provided increased stability in funding for development programs in Africa. These three changes coincided with the appearance on the market of affordable computers, GPS (global positioning system) equipment, and GIS software. These features encouraged the use of a GIS in impact analysis for the following four reasons.

First, evaluation efforts increasingly focused on the effects of assistance programs on the economic and physical welfare of target population groups, rather than tracking expenditures or trends in population charac- teristics. This meant that emphasis shifted from measuring changes in aver- age population statistics to the association between program expenditures and changes in population statistics, either in space or time (Schmid 1989 and Schick 1993). Databases structured around relevant geographic areas were often the easiest way to obtain a large enough set of observations for comparative purposes.

Second, effects of multiple projects, sometimes in different sectors such as health and agriculture, needed to be aggregated to report program rather than project impacts. Since individual projects overlapped geographically in a complex manner, a GIS was the best way to identify target population groups benefiting from multiple projects. A GIS also made mapping a more cost-effective tool for communication about programs of assistance.

Third, investments in a GIS are particularly sensitive to timeframe and funding stability, because start-up costs are high and marginal operating costs are low. In the five-to-ten-year timeframe provided for programs by the DFA, GIS-based approaches to monitoring and impact evaluation are cheaper and can provide higher-quality analytical results than alternatives. In a time horizon of only a few years, approaches with low startup costs make sense because there are no expected long-term cost savings. The shift to a program focus rather than a project focus lengthened the investment timeframe, since programs were generally viewed as having a longer life span than individual projects.

Fourth, a program rather than project focus facilitated sharing overhead startup costs for using a GIS across projects. Even though USAID increased expenditures on monitoring and evaluation to between 5 and 10 percent of total assistance program cost, sharing of GIS overhead costs was required to make a GIS feasible for programs with a set of small projects.

In summary, DFA and GPRA reporting requirements and their longer timeframe encouraged the use of geographically structured databases. These databases have been used to identify population groups targeted by existing programs and for analysis of changes in human welfare indicators across locations with and without development assistance.

Framework for Analysis of Program Impact

In most developing countries, the shortage of well-organized and accurate longitudinal data makes it difficult to examine impacts and changes over time. Data are often fragmented and used for single purposes. Numerous household cluster surveys with samples drawn at a community, regional, and national level are often only analyzed at an individual or household level, or used to produce aggregate national statistics. Potential uses of the same data at the household cluster level or across national boundaries (when comparable surveys exist in multiple countries) have generally been ignored. Secondary data collected by administrative authorities for local-area populations are generally aggregated up for national ministries, and the geographic content is lost. Under these circumstances, it is useful to employ a more spatially oriented approach in which the juxtaposition of services (such as roads and health clinics) is analyzed to explain variation in the welfare status of the surrounding population. A GIS is a technology that is inherently spatial in terms of its data organization and analysis capabilities, and it therefore provides an ideal tool for supporting spatial analysis and the management of spatially referenced data.

Development of geographic databases and subsequent geographic analysis for program-impact evaluation can be divided into the four steps explained below: (1) identify spatial units of observation; (2) identify spatial units of analysis; (3) develop typologies of local-areas; and (4) analyze the variance of population characteristics and covariance of population indicators with assistance provided.

Identifying Shared Spatial Units of Observation in Existing Data Sets

Local-area socioeconomic data are often submerged in the aggregation of national statistics, with the result that local-area data for a developing country are not available in any single archive for cross-sectional analysis. Local-area socioeconomic data are also not often geographically referenced, which means they cannot be used jointly with satellite imagery or infrastructure maps. In many countries the geographic boundaries of health service areas and administrative areas do not match. Data for local areas publicly reported from different ministries often cannot be combined due to these types of mismatch. For all these reasons it is difficult to bring together existing data into a single database for joint analyses.

In West and Central Africa socioeconomic sample survey data tend to be geographically representative of administrative areas, health service areas, and population census enumeration areas. These geographic categories used for sample stratification or census data collection provide three building blocks for geographically structuring socioeconomic data and merging them with biophysical data from maps or satellite imagery. A frequent problem is that agricultural production data are available for large subregions of a country while socioeconomic survey data are representative both of a smaller community level and at levels larger than the agricultural statistical areas. This mismatch means that the national level is the only common unit of observation for published agricultural production and socioeconomic data. In order to merge these different types of data geographically at a subnational level, data from original sampling areas may need to be recombined to geographically restructure the data. Good documentation of coding and sampling procedures are critical for meaningfully restructuring data geographically.

Since the 1980s round of population censuses, most household sample surveys are based on a systematic multistage sampling. First, primary sampling units (PSUs) of geographic clusters of households (often census enumeration areas) are chosen. Enumeration areas are often designed for ease of access during the census reference period, and in rural areas of Africa they may be between ten and fifty square kilometers with 700–1,500 people. Second, households within each PSU are selected with probability proportional to the size of the PSU based on a comprehensive listing of all households in the cluster. On this basis, the cluster-level random sample of 20 to 30 households provides an unbiased estimate of population statistics for all households in the geographic cluster. This means that these surveys have the household, PSU cluster level, subnational region, and national level as "units of observation" that can potentially be matched geographically with other data sets.

In normal survey jargon, these surveys are not considered representative at the cluster level because they are not considered to have usefully small standard errors at that level. However, if cluster-level estimates are unbiased, then they can be used at the cluster level for covariance analysis across multiple clusters. This makes cluster survey data potentially useful for impact evaluation using the PSU cluster as the unit of analysis. A sufficiently large number of relevant clusters need to be geographically matched with complementary data, such as on development interventions. Some readers may find it difficult to switch to thinking of cluster level data as useful units of observation, or as subsequent units for statistical analysis across clusters. MACRO International completed an analysis of the standard errors of a wide range of Demographic and Health Survey (DHS) cluster-level variables and concluded that this unit of observation was statistically useful. On this basis, MACRO compiled a cluster-level data set for West Africa as part of the USAID-funded West Africa Spatial Analysis Prototype (WASAP) effort (see MACRO, Intl. 1997, and McGuire 1998).

Even when local-level data that provides unbiased estimates are available, the critical problem is that most of these local-level data are not geo-referenced for a village, census area, or health clinic service area. This means they cannot be linked with other data geographically and thus cannot be analyzed jointly. The major task in creating geographic databases in the case studies reviewed in this chapter was georeferencing existing secondary data at the level of a health clinic service area and census enumeration areas (Rogers 1991a, BUCEN 1996). These cluster data were not previously used at this level in West Africa because of limited awareness of the spatial structure of the surveys that resulted in the lack of georeferencing. Greater flexibility in how data are geographically analyzed is critical to GIS use in impact evaluation, but this flexibility requires georeferenced data.

In Zaire, the geographic coding and secondary data were reviewed, including census data, household survey data, and project field records (Leirs 1990 and Rogers 1991b). Rural health clinic archives were examined and clinic data collection procedures were assessed. Specific villages had been assigned to each health clinic, so the service areas did not overlap and were roughly the same size. Child weighing was done monthly in each village, so time series and spatial cross-section data on malnutrition were based on the entire clinic service area population of children under age five, within a total population of 5,000 to 15,000. Malnutrition data was available by health zones, health clinic service areas within health zones, and villages. Clinic service areas fit geographically within a structure of larger health zones, so it was possible to analyze variance by health zone, as well as health clinic areas or villages, to guide the choice of relevant units of analysis. However, data for health zones was often not representative of the population due to incomplete coverage of services. Administratively and in the population census coding, villages have been organized into "groupements," "collectivities," and "subregions," so these groupings defined the units of observation that could potentially be matched for analysis of variance using census mortality (indirect methods with census data) and male migration data.

In West Africa hundreds of millions of dollars' worth of population censuses and sample surveys have collected data that provide unbiased estimates for census enumeration areas. However, none of these cluster samples (such as the USAID funded Demographic and Health Surveys, Living Standards Measurement Surveys, and UNICEF Multiple Indicator Cluster Surveys) were mapped during fieldwork before 1995. This means the data could not be brought together without georeferencing them first. If household clusters are georeferenced with an error of only a few kilometers, then data may be usefully matched geographically with satellite imagery, natural resource maps, or infrastructure maps for multivariate analysis.

Useful units of observation should represent a spatial unit that is homogeneous enough to pool data from a variety of sources, and that should not be larger than the desired spatial unit of analysis. Identifying the spatial structure of existing data sets is an important first step in assessing what data are available, how representative the data are for specific geographic areas, and what is needed to organize disparate data geographically.

Identifying Independent and Relevant Geographic Units of Analysis

A unit of analysis must be feasible in terms of available data, meet criteria for credible statistical tests, and be relevant in terms of the spatial processes assumed in the model being tested. To be feasible, a spatial unit of analysis must be at least as large as the smallest common unit of observation at which data can be merged from different sources. Often analysts simply adopt the most obvious unit of observation for the unit of analysis, giving little thought to the implications for the analysis. In the United States, the county is often used as a convenient unit of analysis, although this may not always be appropriate (see Rogers, Shaffer, and Pulver 1988). Choice of the geographic unit of analysis partly determines the analytical result because of the implicit assumptions about spatial processes that determine the observed outcome. False policy conclusions may result from improperly structured data. There is a large literature on the modifiable areal unit problem or ecological fallacy problem that may lead to false statistical conclusions and subsequently misleading policy recommendations (Openshaw and Taylor 1979 and Arbia 1989).

To have credible statistical conclusions, the units should be roughly similar in size, be independent observations in terms of the dependent variable, be numerous enough to identify data patterns, and have a sufficiently small intra-unit variance for the parameters of interest for inter-unit analysis. Anselin (1992, pp. 2–3) concludes that "a major consequence of the dependence in a spatial sample is that statistical inference will not be as efficient as for an independent sample of the same size. This may result in larger variances for estimates, lower significance levels in tests of hypotheses and a poorer fit for models estimated with data from dependent samples, compared to independent samples of the same size. The loss in efficiency may be remedied by designing a sampling scheme that spaces observations such that their interaction is negligible." This design was the approach used for the spatial analysis in West and Central Africa, but it required significant initial analysis of existing spatial structures and processes.

To be relevant, the units must be related to the spatial processes that determine outcomes. The analyst needs to consider which processes cause the outcomes under study and over what size geographic area these relationships are important (see Rogers, Shaffer, and Pulver 1990, and Case 1992). Anthropological, marketing, and historical studies are valuable in understanding these relationships. Haining (1990, p. 24) identifies four spatial processes that may underlie outcomes being studied:

(1) *Diffusion processes* in which information, behavior, disease, or technology is adopted by or reaches population groups,

(2) *Exchange and transfer* of production, income, or services,

(3) *Interaction*, in which events at one location influence and are influenced by events in other locations, such as market prices, social group behavior, or political consensus building, and

(4) *Dispersal* such as the spread of population within a land tenure structure ranging from national borders to village-level group lands.

In Zaire, statistical analysis of rural clinic records and local-area groupement census data were used to establish that significant variation in death rates and malnutrition occurred across very local areas within rural Zaire. Health zones serving hundreds of thousands of people were found to be too large a geographic unit of analysis because access to natural resources, markets, and health services varied significantly within health zones. Grouping communities by administrative subregions of several million people explained significant variation in the value of agricultural production, because this grouped related areas with a similar natural resource base and market access. Rapid rural appraisals, satellite imagery, and preliminary analysis of census data led to the conclusion that rural health clinic service areas were the most appropriate unit of analysis for program impacts on malnutrition. One limitation of this approach was that malnutrition data was available only for areas with a functioning clinic. Use of this type of cross-sectional data may result in substantial biases in the estimates of program effects because of the evident nonrandom spatial allocation of public programs (Pitt, Rosenzweig, and Gibbons 1993). Without careful analysis, preexisting factors that determined the location of public programs may be interpreted as impacts of those programs.

Health clinic service areas and villages were the smallest unit for which representative malnutrition data, information on project services provided, and landcover statistics from satellite imagery could be put together in Zaire. However, villages did not meet the criteria for statistical analysis and did not reflect the spatial processes determining outcomes. Villages varied by orders of magnitude in population size, land resource access across villages was not independent due to the structure of land tenure, and access to health care varied because distance to the health clinic varied systematically across villages.

When villages in Zaire are grouped by health clinic service areas, however, the population size only varies by a factor of two, average distances between villages and clinics are similar, land access tends to be limited to areas within the clinic service area, and by definition the quality of health care across villages served by the same clinic is the same. The geographic area served by a health clinic was often large enough to capture diffusion processes for information, the exchanges related to services, and interactions related to marketing. For these reasons, the health clinic service area was chosen as a primary unit of analysis for malnutrition.

In rural West Africa, census enumeration areas were chosen as the unit of analysis because they were similar in size, could be considered independent observations given the distance between rural sample sites, thousands of observations were available, and each observation had a sufficiently small variance for the parameters of interest. On this basis the West Africa Spatial Analysis Prototype (WASAP) was initiated in 1992 by USAID's Regional Economic Development Services Office for West and Central Africa (REDSO/WCA) in Abidjan, Côte d'Ivoire. WASAP was designed to georeference cluster household survey locations, conduct spatial analysis using these clusters as a unit of analysis, and make the data publicly available. WASAP was a US$600 thousand cooperative effort with funding provided by USAID to MACRO, Intl. (for DHS work), the World Resources Institute (WRI), the Famine Early Warning System (FEWS), and the U.S. Bureau of the Census (BUCEN) to develop a prototype for using GIS technology to integrate diverse socioeconomic data sets and to facilitate spatial analysis of those data. (Note that all dollar amounts in this paper are U.S.) Since 1997 this activity has been supported by the USAID-funded FEWS project and referred to as the West Africa Spatial Analysis Project (see the WASAP website at http://edcintl.cr.usgs.gov/adds/data/wasa/wasa.html).

Developing Typologies for Local Units of Analysis to Classify Population Groups

Typology development classifies local units of analysis into sets that are relevant for the analysis or implementation of development programs. If there are already commonly accepted groupings of the local areas chosen for analysis, then it may be helpful to adopt these to facilitate comparison with previous analytical results (see the USDA website at http://www.econ.ag.gov/epubs/other/typolog/). The local units that are grouped will generally not be geographically adjacent, though there may be clustering of local areas with similar characteristics.

Development of typologies for local geographic areas is necessary to identify and compare population categories with and without development assistance. The concept of groups receiving or not receiving new infrastructure assistance, such as a road, is fairly clear. However, even if policy reform is taken at a national level, the preexisting conditions make the impacts vary geographically by community. Communities without the preexisting conditions that enable them to benefit from a policy reform can be classified as not having received assistance. Conceptually this parallels the vulnerability analysis of FEWS in which certain baseline conditions make certain communities more or less vulnerable to climatic, political, or market changes (McGuire 1998, p. 7). Geographic identification of population groups benefiting from multiple programs, or with similar capacity to benefit from existing programs such as policy reforms or agricultural technology development, is a result that can be used for targeting, extrapolation of case study results on impacts, interpolation of missing data for small areas, and aggregation of beneficiary groups.

In Zaire, typologies of local areas were developed on the basis of total cost of the USAID assistance program per capita. Using a combination of project reports, census data, and community household registrations, the total population served by USAID projects was mapped. These maps were then overlaid to identify categories of program beneficiaries. Based on the geographic overlap, four categories of beneficiary were identified and combined with project expenditure data to estimate total program cost per beneficiary during the 1986–1990 five-year period. A population of 2.8 million was receiving only child immunizations at a total cost of $7 per capita. A population of 1.1 million received immunizations and improved access to potable water at a total cost of $19 per capita. A population of 400,000 received immunizations and improved access to water, as well as road access, at a cost of $45 per capita. In the fourth category, a population of 700,000 received immunizations, road access, and agricultural extension services at a total cost of $60 per capita.

In West Africa, WRI (1996) developed typologies of local administrative areas based on categories of access to economic opportunities, such as road access to metropolitan areas and aridity zones reflecting the natural resource base. Their report contains a detailed description of the database developed by WRI, including the georeferenced household survey clusters. McGuire (1998) developed typologies of household survey sample clusters in West Africa using an approach similar to Rogers and others (1988), and found that principle component analysis captured over 80 percent of the variation with four categories of variables. The four principal components identified were:

PC1—Education/literacy/household income status
PC2—Biophysical or resource base status
PC3—Demographic and fertility status
PC4—Children's nutritional status.

Groups of clusters can be identified based on combinations of their rankings on these principal components. For example, household clusters with high educational and income status, but low nutritional status, may benefit more from cost recovery and selected educational efforts than communities with low educational and income status. Categories of geographic areas were defined drawing on PC1 and PC3 elements during design of USAID's regional family health and HIV-AIDS project. This helped focus debate on policy issues and the types of communities where assistance impacts were expected. A different set of geographic areas was defined drawing on PC2 and PC4 during design of USAID support for West Africa regional trade. The geographic zones with greater potential for regional horticultural exports were found to have high malnutrition rates, suggesting that export-based income growth might have strong health effects.

Analysis of Variance of Population Characteristics and Covariance with Assistance Provided

Impact evaluation using geographic databases tests hypotheses related to the covariance between program expenditures and changes in population outcomes using a quasi-experimental design. This use of statistical inference requires the development and testing of models. Development of conceptual models based on an understanding of the spatial processes is necessary to interpret the conclusions of any subsequent analysis.

Although specialized statistical tools are increasingly being used, they are rarely available for impact evaluation in Africa (for an exception, see Deichmann 1993). Simpler techniques such as mapping residuals from regression analysis are useful for identifying problems with definition of units of analysis and missing variables. For example, these simpler approaches led to the inclusion of deforestation and land degradation as a key control variable for the second round of impact evaluations in rural Zaire. Currently available GIS packages should not be regarded as a substitute for statistical and regression analysis packages, but rather as another complementary analytical tool (Anselin and Hudak 1992).

Analysis of impact can be done in three stages. First, characterize and compare geographic population groups by typology categories. Second, estimate specific impact coefficients using time-series or cross-sectional data in such a way that differences can be interpreted as a temporal change related to assistance provided. Third, use a multivariate analysis that incorporates impact coefficients from findings in the second stage and decomposes the total variation described in the first phase. This sequence of analyses was used for impact evaluation at a country program level in Zaire and on a multicountry regional basis in West Africa. In practice, a series of rapid appraisals, carefully selected location-specific before and after studies, and broader testing of whether expected impact coefficients can explain spatial and temporal variation were used to establish whether any impact occurred, the number of beneficiaries, and a plausible magnitude of change associated with the assistance provided.

USAID Program Impact Evaluation in Zaire, 1988–1991

Under the DFA, monitoring and evaluation was increasingly expected to identify the contributions of sectoral projects and policy reform to overall cumulative program effects on human welfare indicators. A new GIS-based program impact evaluation system, initiated in response to the DFA, did allow the USAID/Zaire field mission to fully and systematically address these questions of higher-level impact at a lower cost (Rogers 1991a, 1991b).

Four categories of indicators were identified to measure program achievement at the strategic objective and goal levels: (1) per capita consumption, (2) labor productivity, (3) nutritional status, and (4) child survival. These were considered key economic welfare and physical quality of life indicators, provided information for those concerned with ultimate impact, were useful indicators of goal level achievement, and ultimately were used to provide criteria for selecting country assistance program elements. Secondary data or primary data already being processed was available on specific indicators in each of these four categories.

In the first phase several independent sources of data for the same population groups were compared to identify shared units of observation. USAID/Zaire developed geographic databases that combined existing data from the population census, rural health clinics, satellite imagery, and agricultural development projects to examine the effects of assistance programs on child malnutrition. The objective was to report cost-effectively on the association between program expenditures and changes in "people-level impacts." A conceptual model was developed as the foundation for setting priorities in data compilation, and for testing hypotheses related to impacts of development assistance (see Larson and others 1996). Primary data was also collected in six health zones to evaluate data quality (see Toko 1989 and USAID/Zaire February 1989).

Characterizing and Comparing Population Groups by Typology Categories

Typologies of areas were developed based on per capita assistance provided, and case studies of population characteristics in these zones were completed. The observed association of malnutrition with deforested areas while mapping regression residuals led to the processing of satellite imagery to identify long-term change in forest cover. A surprisingly high rate of malnutrition in areas with low death rates led to an increased focus in subsequent analysis on the independent causes of mortality as opposed to causes of malnutrition.

Estimates of Specific Program Impact Coefficients

In this phase, a series of individual studies were completed using different geographic units of analysis. Variation in life expectancy as a function of agricultural income, holding access to health care constant, was analyzed at an administrative subregion level to estimate the effect of agricultural extension and improved road access. To estimate the impact of agricultural extension without a change in road access, changes over time in malnutrition were compared in villages receiving agricultural extension services with villages in the same health clinic service areas that did not receive these services. Through analysis of small-area data, multiyear cycles in malnutrition were found to be associated with four-to-five-year agricultural cycles reflected in manioc prices.

Case studies of five health zones indicated that child malnutrition is caused by natural resource degradation—directly through declining agricultural labor productivity and indirectly through reducing the labor allocated to child care. It was not possible to separate these two effects, but the net effect associated with cross-sectional and time-series variation was estimated. In later rounds of analysis, 30-year historical time-series data on deforestation was collected to improve the analysis.

Synthesizing Available Evidence on Program Impacts

An area stretching from 16 to 21 degrees longitude (south) and from 2.5 to 7 degrees latitude (east), in the Kwilu Subregion of the Bandundu Region, was chosen for more detailed multivariate analysis as it had a relatively complete set of local-area data. This phase of the analysis examined three development interventions (immunizations, road access, and agricultural extension) and the impact that these have had on nutrition, mortality, and labor productivity, controlling for forest cover.

The analysis of variation in malnutrition was broken into three categories: chronic, which was common to all areas, cyclical changes, and transitional. Cyclical changes included an annual marketing cycle and a five-year price cycle for manioc. Transitional factors included improved road access, a deteriorating natural resource base, and rapid improvements in child survival due to immunization programs. When the impact coefficients estimated separately in the individual studies described above were combined, it was confirmed that they could jointly explain much of the extreme variation in malnutrition rates over time and across locations in rural Bandundu (Rogers 1990).

The next step was to refine the spatial database to statistically test the joint set of relationships identified in the set of individual studies. Attribute data for 162 health centers (Centres de Sante) were compiled and the geographic location of each clinic was recorded on a 1:200,000 scale map. Although some locations of clinics were identified on existing maps, these were cross-checked and completed with the help of a GPS during field visits. For each clinic service area, information was obtained on malnutrition rates, long-term change in forest cover, whether road and agricultural extension services were received, and how many years had passed since health services (immunization programs) had been initiated in the health zone. Seasonal factors were excluded by using annual data rather than monthly data, but the multiyear agricultural cycles were more difficult to control for because of the complex spatial structure of the effect and limited time-series data.

Impact evaluation is iterative and initial analysis usually suggests the need for new data. The problem with analyses based on a single survey is that all variables to be included in the analysis need to be decided upon before the survey is started. A GIS provides an excellent framework for sequentially incorporating new data as analysis proceeds. The analysis of malnutrition in rural Bandundu, Zaire, described below is a good example of this sequential approach that a GIS made possible.

An initial analysis of malnutrition in five health zones showed significant variation at a local level within health zones. A map of regression residuals showed unexplained spatial patterns in malnutrition after accounting for variation associated with road access and agricultural extension services. Most surprising was the fact that the Vanga health zone, with perhaps the best health care and immunization coverage, also had the highest malnutrition rates. To confirm these cross-sectional results, a longitudinal study of malnutrition in seven health clinic service areas within the Vanga Health Zone was initiated using archive data. From 1980 to 1984 the percentage of children under age five that were two standard deviations below standard weight for age was constant at about 25 percent. Between 1984 and 1990 this category of malnourished children increased to approximately 35 percent. Because the health clinic service areas were mapped, it was possible to examine change in forest cover for these health service areas during the preceding decade. No significant change in forest cover was identified in land-cover change analysis based on the satellite imagery.

At this point, a rapid rural appraisal was conducted among women farmers in the same area. The women said that the forests had been cut down in the 1960s (before our baseline satellite images in the 1970s), and that with growing population and shortening of fallow cycles they had run out of good forest soils in 1985. In 1985 they started farming the poorer savanna soils where yields were much lower per unit area and per day of labor invested. They recognized that because of better health care their children no longer died, but now the problem was hunger. Based on this information, landcover maps from the 1950s were collected for incorporation into the next round of analysis, using landcover change since 1950 as a control variable. A pilot analysis using a longer time period for landcover change was completed (Fowler and Barnes 1992 and Fowler 1993).

Due to civil unrest and evacuation of the USAID/Zaire staff in 1991, the sequential improvement in analysis of program impacts ended. However, without the GIS-based approach to program impact evaluation, the importance of incorporating changes in resource base over the last 30 years, pinpointing relevant communities in which to conduct rapid rural appraisals, and the confounding effect that multiyear cycles in agricultural prices have in overwhelming measurement of impacts of health services would not have been identified.

Spatial Analysis to Estimate Program Cost-Effectiveness in Zaire

In many sectoral programs there are useful estimates of project impacts on target beneficiaries. For example, agricultural development projects may estimate their impact on production or even farm income. Project-level analysis of agricultural development assistance estimated that the USAID/Zaire provision of roads and agricultural extension had increased agricultural income by 25 percent (Poulin, Appleby, and Quan 1987. pp.12–13). Health projects may estimate their impact on mortality, morbidity, or malnutrition rates. For example, a number of health program evaluations estimated a reduction of between 20 and 60 child deaths per thousand due to immunization programs, similar to the findings of Koenig, Fauveau, and Wojtyniak (1991). Given a five-year program cost in Zaire of $7 per capita, this suggests an expected reduction in death rates of 6 per 1,000 of population per dollar of assistance.

Impacts of increased agricultural income on health outcomes (or impact of health outcomes on agricultural productivity) are rarely addressed in project evaluations. These cross-sectoral impacts are a critical foundation of program budgets based on results. Two cross-sectoral questions to be answered for the Zaire program impact evaluation were the following:

(1) What are the per-unit costs of improvements in child mortality from agricultural development programs compared to health programs?
(2) What are the per-unit costs of improved nutritional status from agricultural development compared to health programs?

The key to estimating cross-sectoral impacts in Zaire was analysis of the geographic structure of the data and potential units of analysis. Several potential units of analysis were identified, including health clinic service area, health zone, and administrative areas including village, groupement, collectivity, and subregion. The use of existing data to estimate per-unit costs of the effects of agricultural development on child survival or life expectancy (using indirect methods based on population census data) is a good example of how the choice of unit of analysis was critical.

Child mortality and life expectancy were assumed to be a function of agricultural production and access to health care. It was known that agricultural production per capita varied significantly across administrative subregions with several million people due to differences in access to land, markets, and forest resources. It was also known that child mortality varied significantly across health zones with several hundred thousand people, and even across clinic service areas containing five to fifteen thousand people within a health zone. However, there was no agricultural production or income data by health clinic service area, so estimates of impact could not be obtained using this unit of analysis.

Examination of the health zone data by subregion showed that each subregion had the same proportion of population living in operational health zones, meaning the same proportion of the population had access to health care. This was an important finding, because it meant that a bivariate analysis of mortality rates or life expectancy as a function of agricultural production at the subregion level "controlled" for access to health care through choice of the unit of analysis. The regression coefficient of life expectancy as a function of agricultural production per capita at the subregion level could be interpreted as the impact of increased agricultural production on life expectancy, holding access to health care constant. Agricultural development and road rehabilitation programs were estimated to have together increased life expectance by two to four years. Given a five-year program cost of $52 per capita for roads and agricultural extension, these programs were estimated to increase life expectancy at birth (to mothers 25–30 years old) by up to one month per dollar of assistance provided per capita. In the project areas this roughly translated into a reduction of child death rates by 10 to 30 per thousand or 0.4 per dollar of assistance per capita.

Under conditions prevailing in rural Zaire in the mid-1980s, five years of assistance for immunization programs was more cost-effective in reducing death rates, while agricultural extension programs were more cost-effective in reducing malnutrition. In selected areas, improved access to potable water was found to be the most cost effective intervention to increase labor productivity (directly through time saved and indirectly through better health). These results might well be different after two years or after ten years, depending on the sustainability of the technologies transferred. However, a GIS-based approach made it possible to understand the per-unit costs for achieving similar improvements in human welfare indicators through alternative interventions and combinations of projects. This is a necessary foundation for meaningful, performance-based budgeting that must rely on comparative cost-effectiveness of alternative means to achieve common goals (see Schmid 1989).

Regional Program Impact Evaluation in West Africa, 1992–1997

In the 1990s USAID was closing country field offices in West Africa and reconsidering expansion of multicountry programs based on political commitment to long-term funding for the region, which is one of the poorest in the world. A growing emphasis on multicountry programs and cross-border health and trade issues increased the need for understanding of the geography of regional development in new ways. The GPRA led to efforts to aggregate results across country programs, and these efforts encouraged use of standardized welfare indicators and redefinition of beneficiary populations. This context encouraged the development and use of regional (multicountry) GIS databases for analysis of program impacts and targeting.

In West Africa sequential efforts have been made to pool multisectoral data in regional GIS databases. These include the USAID-financed FEWS Project, which was the first regional impact evaluation effort to support local-area targeting; the Sahelian Permanent Interstate Committee for Drought Control (CILSS-AGRHYMET) efforts to strengthen biophysical data analysis for planning; the Club du Sahel–supported West Africa Long-Term Perspective Study (WALTPS), which incorporated extensive demographic and infrastructure data with existing data sets for long-term trend analysis; and the REDSO/WCA West Africa Spatial Analysis Prototype, which incorporated health data with these earlier data sets for regional impact evaluation and targeting of development assistance.

A key weakness of regional GIS databases in the 1990s was the lack of comparable local-area data on quality of life, such as health and vital statistics, and human capital indicators, such as education levels. The basic units of observation for data in rural West Africa are agricultural/statistical or local administrative areas (such as counties and sous-prefectures), health or marketing service areas, and census enumeration areas, which form the sampling frame for a growing number of cluster sample surveys. The last two categories of data are neither well-delineated on basemaps nor georeferenced, and computer coding does not use any standard location codes to allow geographic linking of these data.

In response to this situation, in 1993 USAID began to support the development of methods to incorporate the wealth of cluster survey data into existing GIS databases in West Africa (Rogers 1993 and 1994). Initial cluster-mapping efforts, using basemaps and existing coding schemes in several countries such as Guinea and Ghana, were not successful. In some cases geographic codes or village names had not been keypunched as part of the data set, even though they were included on survey forms. Though census enumeration area maps existed for West African countries as they did in Zaire, they were not georeferenced. A critical initial priority was to identify the most cost-effective methods for georeferencing new survey data as well as previously collected household cluster survey data.

Methods combining existing basemaps and GPS equipment proved successful, as they did in Zaire for mapping health clinics and new survey data. In Côte d'Ivoire georeferencing was done with handheld GPS equipment during fieldwork for the DHS in 1995—the first time this worldwide survey was georeferenced in this manner. Subsequent surveys in Mali and Benin completed with USAID funding were also georeferenced using a GPS at less than $20 per cluster. The Chad survey funded by several U.N. agencies and the Nigeria survey are the only DHSs in West Africa since 1995 not georeferenced during fieldwork, which reflects the difficulty of collaboration to meet regional data needs at the same time as short-term national-level data needs.

However, using GPS equipment, which required field visits, was too expensive a method for georeferencing surveys already completed. To address this problem USAID funded the U.S. Bureau of the Census to evaluate the cost of alternative approaches for mapping cluster survey sites, devise codes for national administrative areas, and to locate and georeference over 2,000 cluster survey sample sites across West Africa (BUCEN 1996). On the basis of this experience, it costs between $20 and $40 per cluster to georeference survey data after the survey has been completed. Of the total of 2,594 clusters, BUCEN georeferenced 85 percent from the U.S. Defense Mapping Agency gazetteers using degrees and minutes. For clusters BUCEN could not find in the gazetteers, they used maps to locate them and then read the coordinates in degrees, minutes, and seconds off the maps. The location of almost all clusters is based on a populated place, whether from the gazetteers or the maps. A populated place in the DMA gazetteers is defined as a "city, town, village, settlement," including "some seasonal and shifting agricultural settlements."

To facilitate integration of the sampling cluster data in a GIS environment, BUCEN used U.S. Federal Information Processing Standards codes for first-order administrative areas and devised a uniform coding scheme for the second and third administrative divisions. For some countries, such as Côte d'Ivoire and Senegal, BUCEN used codes contained in census publications. For other countries BUCEN had to devise codes. What this shows is the importance and the need for standardized geographic codes and use of these codes when cluster survey data sets are keypunched.

Human welfare indicators based on DHS data were used as dependent variables, so the primary unit of analysis selected was the area represented by a DHS sample cluster or group of clusters in urban areas. Rather than using small-area data from sample clusters to represent larger areas, the statistical analysis was structured to test whether, on average, sample clusters located in areas with specific characteristics were significantly different from clusters located in areas without those characteristics. This allowed incorporation of other spatial data and enabled the analysis to avoid assumptions about the homogeneity required for using point data to infer conditions in broader geographic areas.

More detailed descriptions of how cluster data can be analyzed is described in WRI (1996) and McGuire (1998). The DHS is a standardized household-cluster survey that has been completed in almost every country in West Africa. In some countries two surveys have been completed at least five years apart. As the second round of these surveys become available, it will be possible to complete joint time-series and cross-sectional analyses. However, since the survey clusters cannot always be the same over time, it will be necessary to use typology categories of clusters for time-series analysis. This means that change over time can be estimated for categories of local areas (though not one specific local area) by grouping survey clusters from different points in time into sets of comparable typologies of local areas. A wide range of hypotheses about changes in DHS indicators by typology of local area can be evaluated by using data from non-DHS sources to classify survey clusters into appropriate categories. As the second round of DHS surveys is just now becoming available for much of West Africa—and possibly a second UNICEF–Multiple Indicator Cluster Survey—this type of time-series analysis has not yet been accomplished.

Conclusions on Broader GIS Use in Program Evaluation

GIS has been a critically important tool and process in the evolution of USAID impact evaluation and targeting efforts. As a donor agency, USAID chose, under the WASAP effort, to allocate funding to make existing data more usable to a broad audience of analysts in a regional GIS framework for West Africa. This has lowered the cost of subsequent analyses and helped shift the type of questions which analysts are addressing (see references in McGuire, Chapter 7 of this volume). In a review of data available on the Internet, including the WASAP data, the International Food Policy Research Institute concluded that once having obtained the data from Internet sources, an analyst would be able to indicate, with less than one hour of desk-based research in some cases, which areas of a particular country could be targeted for various projects. This has the potential to revolutionize NGO and donor project design and proposal evaluation by increasing analytical competition and access to information.

Multicountry programs are part of an organizational solution for donors, but progress will require political or senior management decisions to address the lack of country project–level incentives to better use existing data geographically. On a regional level in West Africa, investments in improving the fundamentals of geographic data coding, compatible data standards, and joint analysis of existing data in a geographic framework offer far higher returns than increased collection of new data.

There are tens of millions of dollars in surveys that have been completed across West African countries in the last decade using a cluster sampling method. Most remain inaccessible to use in a GIS or to use in combination with one another because they are not georeferenced. Under existing organizational arrangements, surveys may not be georeferenced in the future since much of the benefit accrues in the future to those outside the institution or country funding the survey. For this reason, donor funding for enabling and facilitating geographic analysis of existing cluster sample data by a broad range of analysts should be a high priority.

Over the past decade, availability of multisectoral data within individual USAID country programs facilitated the construction of geographic databases for analysis at the country level. In Zaire, as well as across West Africa, USAID country programs focused on socioeconomic as well as biophysical data collection. In West Africa the USAID-funded DHSs provided health data that could be combined with biophysical data compiled from numerous sources by the USAID-funded FEWS project (see McGuire 1998 or the WASAP and DHS websites). Individual donor programs are now tending to concentrate on fewer sectors and fewer countries. This means that in the future, blending of existing geographic data will require more collaboration across donors and multiple ministries in multiple countries. Increased collaboration and easier access to existing data in a georeferenced format is required to avoid spending the already limited research and evaluation funding on discrete analyses that independently spend an excessively large share of their budgets collecting incompatible data.

Political decisions regarding the timeframe of program funding and requirements for public reporting and debate on development impacts will continue to determine whether the use of GISs spreads rapidly in donor programs. Limited awareness of spatial processes that underlie development will continue to slow the adoption of low-cost use of existing data in a geographic framework. There is wide agreement that improving technical capabilities to extract statistical inferences from existing data requires improved awareness of spatial processes, broader access to data, and refinement of technical approaches used in program evaluation and design. However, technical capabilities are already far ahead of the institutional and organizational capabilities required to use a GIS as a tool to broaden input in the competition for better development ideas.

Bilateral and multilateral donors can best promote GIS applications through three actions. First, increase the demand for geographic data collection, analysis, and reporting on program impacts. Second, facilitate the supply of geographically referenced data sets. Third, continue opening up possibilities for more analytical competition between analysts inside donor organizations and those outside in host country governments, universities, and nonprofit organizations that can use this data. New programming ideas and realistic feedback on program effectiveness are expected to come from more open decisionmaking involving better-informed beneficiaries and partners. The primary constraints to increased benefits from GISs are institutional and organizational, not technical.

Notes

Dr. Rogers served as the USAID/Zaire Program Research Officer in Kinshasa from 1988 to 1991 and as the Regional Program Economist in the USAID Regional Economic Development Services Office for West and Central Africa (REDSO/WCA) in Abidjan, Côte d'Ivoire from 1992 to 1997. The author thanks John Bierke, who also served at the same time in USADI/Zaire and REDSO/WCA, for assistance in exploring and structuring the approaches presented. The views expressed in this chapter are those of the author and are not meant to represent official USAID policy.

References

Anselin, Luc. 1992. "Spatial Data Analysis with GIS: An Introduction to Application in the Social Sciences." NCGIA Technical Report 92-10, University of California, Santa Barbara, December.

————. 1988. *Spatial Econometrics, Methods and Models.* Dordrecht, The Netherlands: Kluwer Academic Publishers.

Anselin, Luc, and Sheri Hudak. 1992. "Spatial Econometrics in Practice." *Regional Science and Urban Economics* 22: 509–536.

Arbia, G. 1989. *Spatial Data Configuration in Statistical Analysis of Regional Economic and Related Problems.* Dordrecht, South Africa: Kluwer Academic Press.

BUCEN (U.S. Bureau of the Census), International Programs Center, Population Division. 1996. "Georeferencing Survey Clusters for Twelve West African Countries." Report prepared for USAID's REDSO/WCA office in Abidjan, Côte d'Ivoire, March.

Case, Anne. 1992. "Neighborhood Influence and Technological Change." *Regional Science and Urban Economics* 22: 491–508.

Deichmann, Uwe. 1993. "Issues in the Integrated Spatial Analysis of Socioeconomic and Environmental Data." Discussion paper prepared for UNEP IUFRO Workshop: Developing Large Environmental Databases for Sustainable Development. Nairobi, Kenya, July 14–16.

Fowler, Cynthia Ann. 1993. "Modeling the Relationship Between Deforestation and Malnutrition in Zaire Using a Geographic Information System (GIS) Approach." Masters Thesis, Ohio State University.

Fowler, Cynthia, and G. Barnes. 1992. "Modeling the Relationship between Deforestation and Malnutrition Using a Geographic Information System (GIS) Approach." ASPRS/ACSM/RT 92, Technical Papers Vol. 3, *GIS and Cartography*, American Society for Photogrammetry and Remote Sensing, Washington, D.C., 24–33.

Haining, Robert. 1990. *Spatial Data Analysis in the Social and Environmental Sciences.* Cambridge: Cambridge University Press.

IFPRI (International Food Policy Research Institute). 1998. "Strengthening the Household Food Security and Nutritional Aspects of IFAD (International Fund for Agricultural Development) Poverty Alleviation Projects: Developing Operational Methodolgies for Project Design and Monitoring." In Alison Slack and John Hoddinott, "Technical Guide #1: Food and Nutrition Security Data on the World Wide Web," February, draft.

Koenig, Michael, Vicent Fauveau, and Bogdan Wojtyniak. 1991. "Mortality Reductions from Health Interventions: The Case of Immunization in Bangladesh." *Population and Development Review* 17(1): 87–104.

Larson, Bruce, Grenville Barnes, Glenn Rogers, and Joy Green Larson. 1996. "Forests, Agriculture, and Child Health in Zaire: A Household Modeling Approach." *Forest Science* 42(1): 3–9.

Leirs, B. 1990. "Manuel d'usage de la banque de données géographique pour la région de Bandundu, Zaire." Unpublished report and annex prepared for USAID/Zaire, March.

MACRO, Intl. 1997. "West Africa Spatial Analysis Prototype (WASAP): Development of a Georeferenced Regional Database." Summary report by Trevor Croft and others at DHS/Macro International for the USAID/REDSO/WCA-funded WASAP. http://www.macroint.com/dhs

McGuire, Mark L. 1998. "Evaluation of Food Insecurity in West Africa: An Analysis Using Demographic and Health Survey Data (DHS) with a GIS." Report prepared for USAID/REDSO/WCA as part of the WASAP collaborative effort, April. (This report is an earlier version of his chapter included in this book).

Openshaw, S., and P. Taylor. 1979. "A Million or so Correlation Coefficients: Three Experiments on the Modifiable Areal Unit Problem. In N. Wrigley and R. Bennett, eds., *Statistical Applications in the Spatial Sciences*. London: Pion Press.

Pietrobelli, Carlo, and Carlo Scarpa. 1992. "Inducing Efficiency in the Use of Foreign Aid: The Case for Incentive Mechanisms." *Journal of Development Studies* 29(1): 72–92.

Pitt, Mark M., Mark R. Rosenzweig, and Donna M. Gibbons. 1993. "The Determinants and Consequences of the Placement of Government Programs in Indonesia." *The World Bank Economic Review* 7(3): 319–348.

Poulin, R., Appleby, and Quan. 1987. "Impact Evaluation of Project North Shaba." Report prepared for USAID/Zaire, Kinshasa.

Rogers, Glenn. 1990. "Evidence on Causes of Malnutrition in the Kwilu, Bandundu, and Quality of Data from Rural Health Clinic Archives." USAID/Zaire unpublished memo, September 11.

Rogers, Glenn. 1991a. "A Combined Geographic Information System and Social Accounting Matrix Approach to Program Impact Evaluation of U.S. Foreign Development Assistance." Paper presented at the North American meeting of the Regional Science Association International, New Orleans, November (available in USAID/Center for Development Information and Evaluation library.

Rogers, Glenn. 1991b. "USAID Program Impact Evaluation Research in Zaire." USAID/Zaire unpublished memo, July 26.

Rogers, Glenn. 1993. "Use of New Databases for USAID/Conakry Program Impact Analysis." USAID/REDSO/WCA, unpublished report, April 29.

Rogers, Glenn. 1994. "USAID/Conakry Support of Spatial Data Analysis in Guinea: Background and Proposed Action Plans." USAID/REDSO/WCA, unpublished report, March.

Rogers, Glenn, Ron Shaffer, and Glen Pulver. 1988. "The Identification of Rural Capital Markets for Policy Analysis." *Review of Regional Studies* 18(1): 55–66.

Rogers, Glenn, Ron Shaffer, and Glen Pulver. 1990. "The Adequacy of Rural Capital Markets for Rural Nonfarm Businesses." *Review of Regional Studies* 20(3): 23–32.

Schick, Allen. 1993. "A Performance-Based Budgeting System for the Agency for International Development." AID Program and Operations Assessment Report 4, USAID, Center for Development Information and Evaluation, June.

Schmid, Allan A. 1989. *Benefit-Cost Analysis: A Political Economy Approach.* Boulder: Westview Press.

Taylor, Serge. 1984. *Making Bureaucracies Think: The Environmental Impact Statement Strategy of Administrative Reform.* Stanford: Stanford University Press.

Toko, Alphonse. 1989. "Evaluation of the Causes of Low Birth Weight in the Kwilu Sub-Region, Bandundu." Review of data quality in rural clinics prepared for USAID/Zaire, October.

USAID/W. 1989. "STATE 283555." Official cable guidance for field missions, 3.

USAID/Zaire School of Public Health Project. 1989. "Review and Preliminary Analysis of Health Zone Data in Five Rural Health Zones in the Kwilu Sub-Region of Bandundu, Zaire." Report prepared for USAID/Zaire, February 21.

WRI (World Resources Institute). 1996. "Typology of Administrative Units in West Africa." Prepared for USAID/REDSO/WCA West Africa Spatial Analysis Prototype (WASAP).

Part Two

Alternative Methods of Geographical Targeting

3

Combining Census and Survey Data to Study Spatial Dimensions of Poverty: A Case Study of Ecuador

Jesko Hentschel, Jean Olson Lanjouw,
Peter Lanjouw, and Javier Poggi

POVERTY MAPS PROVIDE A DETAILED DESCRIPTION of the spatial distribution of poverty within a country. They can be of considerable value to governments, nongovernmental organizations, and multilateral institutions interested in strengthening the poverty alleviation impact of their spending. For example, poverty maps can be used to guide the division of resources among local agencies or administrations as a first step in reaching the poor. Poverty maps are currently being used in many developing countries for this purpose.

Poverty maps can also be an important tool for research. The empirical relationship between poverty or inequality and indicators of development, such as economic growth, is typically examined in a cross-country regression framework.[1] It is difficult, however, to control for the enormous heterogeneity which exists across countries—heterogeneity which may mask true relationships. There is also a limited universe of country experience to use in understanding the determinants and effects of the distribution of welfare. However, microstudies that use distributional variation across communities within a single country can improve research results.

But the development of poverty maps is hampered by the scarcity of disaggregated data. For example, while income or expenditure-based indicators are often favored, the information required for a finely disaggregated map based on income or expenditure is not generally available for a sufficient number of households. The World Bank's Living Standard Measurement Surveys (LSMS), variants of which have been fielded in many developing countries, collect the necessary information to construct comprehensive measures of income and consumption, but the LSMS surveys are too small to allow for disaggregation beyond a simple rural/urban breakdown within broad regions of a given country. Census data do not suffer from small sample problems, but they typically contain rather limited information. In many Latin American countries, but also in Africa and Asia, poverty maps used to rank regions have been based on indices of welfare constructed by combining, in some manner, basic census information such as access to public services, education levels, and so forth.[2] These are occasionally labeled "Basic Needs" (BN) indicators. They are generally constructed in an ad hoc manner and are restricted to the limited qualitative (and not quality-adjusted) data available in a census. As we demonstrate below, such indicators may be poor proxies for household consumption levels. Using detailed household survey data for Ecuador, we show that a crude BN indicator and a comprehensive consumption measure yield markedly different welfare rankings of households. We proceed to explore the extent to which census-based maps can be improved on when using an income- or consumption-based indicator of welfare.

In some situations there is a desire to look beyond a notion of welfare which only reflects access to resources and to examine explicitly nonincome components as well. For example, a welfare survey concerned with education programs might want to emphasize the intrinsic value of education beyond its instrumental role in influencing income or consumption levels. In this case the appropriate welfare indicator might give greater weight to education than would be implicit in a consumption or income indicator. If the focus of a welfare survey is the compensation of households for a general change in price levels, a welfare measure based on a fairly narrow consumption measure might be preferred. In general, a BN indicator can be constructed with weights chosen to reflect each available variable's relationship to total household resources as well as any direct contributions to welfare not captured in income. One would not expect rankings based on such a BN indicator to correspond exactly to those based on consumption, although it will almost certainly be desirable that broader measures reflect, to some extent, actual consumption levels. The results of this chapter, which demonstrate how actual consumption may be reliably indicated at a disaggregated level, are therefore useful even when one is concerned with a broader welfare measure. The broader, more accurate predictions of poverty based on consumption would simply need to be combined in some manner with the other indicators considered relevant given the policy issue of concern.

Our approach is as follows. Using an LSMS data set for Ecuador, we estimate models of consumption expenditure, restricting the set of explanatory variables to those which are also available in the most recent census for

Ecuador. We apply the parameter estimates from these models to the census data to predict the probability that a given household in the census is in poverty. We check the performance of our approach by estimating the incidence of poverty in six broad regions and comparing these with rates estimated from the household survey alone. The poverty rates coincide closely across data sets.

We consider some of the statistical issues which arise from the fact that the poverty figures have been predicted. The approach described above yields estimates of the incidence of poverty from the census which are unbiased, so that expected prediction errors are zero. However, the poverty estimates do have intrinsic standard errors and it is important that these are calculated alongside the poverty rates. We demonstrate that, for our Ecuador example, standard errors are encouragingly small at levels of regional disaggregation likely to be of practical relevance. However, we also show that these errors become quite sizeable when the poverty rates are calculated over particularly small groups of households. This serves as a warning against excessive spatial disaggregation of the poverty map.[3]

In the next section ("Targeting Poverty Based on a Basic Needs Indicator Versus a Consumption Indicator: Ecuador") we describe the data for Ecuador used to illustrate the analysis. We then consider the differences in targeting implied by an allocation based on a Basic Needs indicator, relative to an allocation based on consumption expenditures. In the third section ("Predicting Poverty") we estimate models of expenditure and then predict the probability of poverty for each household in the census. From this we estimate aggregate poverty rates and compare these with rates obtained from the household survey. The fourth section ("Province-Level Poverty in Ecuador: An Illustration") develops a simple province-level poverty map for Ecuador and illustrates that poverty in Ecuador varies markedly across provinces and between rural and urban areas. We also illustrate that as the poverty map is disaggregated further the confidence interval around each poverty rate widens. The last section offers concluding remarks and suggestions for further research.

Targeting Poverty Based on a Basic Needs Indicator Versus a Consumption Indicator: Ecuador

In this section we examine how effectively a BN indicator performs—judged in terms of its ability to identify the poor when the poverty indicator is consumption expenditure.[4] The BN indicator we are considering was developed in 1994 by the National Statistical Institute of Ecuador (INEC) in response to a specific request from the government to develop a directory of poor households. This directory was to be used to target compensatory transfers to poor households for a gas price increase that would result if the

government were to remove its gas subsidy. In the event, this program was
not implemented, and we do not wish to imply that the BN indicator was
regarded by INEC as anything other than a fairly crude measure developed
to meet an urgent government request at short notice. However, the
approach taken by INEC in constructing their BN indicator does resemble
that followed in many countries and therefore provides a useful example.

INEC's BN indicator was constructed at the household level and consists
of a weighted composite of five variables capturing access to water, access
to sanitation and waste disposal services, education (of the head of household), and a crowding index (the number of people per bedroom).[5] Each
service was assigned a certain number of points according to its availability
and its type or level. The points assigned to each service were based on estimates as opposed to being the result of our empirical analysis. The weighting scheme is presented in table 3.1. For each household, the BN indicator
value was simply taken as the total sum of points across services. The lower
the value of points per household, the poorer it was designated.

Using the data from a recent household survey we can examine how
well the BN indicator performs in identifying those who are poor in terms
of consumption. The Ecuador Encuesta Sobre Las Condiciones de Vida
(ECV) for 1994 is a nationally representative household survey modeled
closely on the World Bank's Living Standards Measurement Surveys. It provides detailed information for each household on a wide range of topics
including food consumption, non-food items, labor activities, access to services such as education and health, agricultural practices, and household
entrepreneurial activities. The survey was fielded by the Servicio
Ecuatoriana de Capacitacion (SECAP) in Ecuador from June through
September, 1994. Over 4,500 households were surveyed in total, and after

Table 3.1 Points by Services Included in the INEC BN Indicator

Service level	Water	Sanitation	Waste	Education	Crowding
1	100	100	100	100	100
2	50	50	50	50	75
3	25	25	25	25	50
4	0	0	0	0	25
5	—	—	—	—	0

— Not available.
Key:
Water: . . . . .1=public network; 2=water truck; 3=well; 4=other.
Sanitation: . . . . .1=flush, in house; 2=in house, no flush; 3=shared; 4=other.
Waste: . . . . .1=collection by truck; 2=burned or buried; 3=discarded; 4=other.
Education: . . . . .1=tertiary; 2=secondary; 3=primary or literate;
   (of head) . . . . .4=none or unknown.
Crowding: . . . . .1=one or less; 2=between one and two; 3=between two
   (persons per bedroom) . . . . .and three; 4=between three and four; 5=more than four.
Source: INEC.

cleaning and data consistency checks, information on 4,391 households was available for analysis.[6] The ECV data set was analyzed in a detailed study of poverty in Ecuador by the World Bank (World Bank 1996). Hentschel and Lanjouw (1996) constructed consumption totals for each household, and all comparisons of welfare across households in the World Bank Ecuador Poverty Report (World Bank 1996) were based on that criterion.[7]

In table 3.2 we compare poverty by region and area using the BN and consumption indicators. As no poverty line was developed specifically for the BN indicator, we must infer poverty rates. We do this by equating the national incidence of poverty (using the BN indicator) with the headcount rate that is obtained using per capita consumption and the consumption poverty line of 45,476 sucres per person per fortnight (approximately US$1.50 per person per day) developed in World Bank (1996). (Note: All dollar amounts in this chapter are U.S.)

Hence, we are asking how the regional ranking of poverty differs when poverty is defined using these two different indicators, but holding constant the total fraction of the population identified as poor. We distinguish only

Table 3.2 Poverty Incidence under Alternative Welfare Definitions

	Per capita consumption (percent population poor)	Indicator of "basic needs"
Costa (Costal)		
Urban	0.26	0.18
Rural	0.49	0.76
Total	0.35	0.39
Sierra (Highlands)		
Urban	0.22	0.04
Rural	0.43	0.50
Total	0.33	0.28
Oriente (Amazon)		
Urban	0.20	0.03
Rural	0.67	0.76
Total	0.59	0.65
National		
Urban	0.25	0.13
Rural	0.47	0.62
Total	0.35	0.35

Note: Calculations are based on two alternative welfare indicators applied to the ECV household survey data.
Source: Authors' calculations.

between rural and urban areas, and the three main agro-climatic zones of the country.

At this level of aggregation the rankings which derive from the two alternative definitions of welfare are the same, but regional differences are much more accentuated using the BN indicator. Rural areas appear poorer using the BN indicator than with consumption, and urban areas look less poor. Within rural areas, rural Oriente and rural Costa are poorer than rural Sierra and within urban areas, and the Costa region is poorest, followed by the Sierra and the Oriente respectively. As emphasized in the World Bank Ecuador Poverty Report (1996), under the consumption criterion the rankings within rural and urban areas between Costa and Sierra are highly unstable and easily overturned depending on where one draws the poverty line, and whether one chooses to work with a poverty measure other than the headcount ratio. Under the BN criterion the impression gained is that differences in well-being across regions are unambiguous.

Finally, we looked beyond regional comparisons to compare the performance of the two indicators at the household level. For this purpose we followed the design of the planned intervention by taking the bottom 20 percent of households as the intended beneficiaries of the program. The following experiment was conducted: We computed the total number of households represented by the ECV data and calculated that just under 450,000 households represented 20 percent of all households. Next, we calculated the total number of points for each household according to INEC's BN criterion and selected the 450,000 households with the lowest points. Finally we calculated the percentage of the beneficiary households falling into each household per capita expenditure quintile. Since the intended target group is the first quintile, the percentage of beneficiaries in the first quintile indicates how well the BN indicator identifies this particular target group. In addition, if all households were to receive the same amount of money, the percentage of beneficiaries represents the percentage of resources that would reach the targeted group. The results of this experiment are presented in table 3.3.

From table 3.3 we can see that only 41.4 percent of households identified under the BN criterion as constituting the bottom 20 percent of all households are, in fact, among the bottom 20 percent under a consumption criterion. Thus, the leakage of resources from an allocation based on this criterion would be very high: 60 percent of resources would go to non-intended beneficiaries, with almost 10 percent going to the top two quintiles.[8]

Predicting Poverty

To give a more analytical basis to the weighting scheme used to assess poverty, we consider here the possibility of imputing household consump-

Table 3.3 Distribution of Bottom 20 Percent under the BN Criterion across Consumption Expenditure Quintiles

Quintile of true per capita consumption (based on a BN indicator)	Percentage of beneficiary households	
	Percentage	Cumulative
Poorest 20 percent	41.4	41.4
20-40 percent	29.5	70.9
40-60 percent	19.5	91.4
60-80 percent	8.0	98.4
Richest 20 percent	1.6	100.0

Source: Authors' calculations.

tion levels using census data to form the basis of a poverty map.[9] This course of action can be pursued only if certain data requirements are met. First, a household survey such as the ECV in Ecuador must be available, and should correspond roughly to the same period as covered by the census. Second, unit record–level census data must be available for analysis. We were fortunate to have access to the 1990 census data for Ecuador, covering roughly 2 million households, for the purpose of this analysis. Although the 1994 ECV data were collected four years after the census, this period was one of relatively slow growth and low inflation in Ecuador, so it is reasonable to assume constant structures.

The underlying intention of the method proposed here is similar to that of small-area and synthetic estimation procedures applied in demography and area statistics.[10] There, the interest is with the derivation of (unobserved) local area attributes such as a mean or total, often in the form of proportions (Farrell and others 1997). For example, if population changes are known for a large area, small-area estimation techniques allow calculation of population changes at lower geographic levels based on postulated functional relationships. An important difference in the method proposed here is that we predict the variable of interest (consumption) at the unit (household) level, and base aggregate statistics on these predictions.[11]

Estimating Models of Consumption

To impute expenditures using the census, the first step is to estimate a model of consumption using household survey data. Of course, the only variables which can be used to predict consumption are variables which are also available in the census. In the case of Ecuador this set of potential predictors consists of various demographic variables such as household size and the age and sex of its members; education and occupation information for each family member; housing quality data (such as materials and size); access to public services such as electricity and water; the principal language spoken in the house; and location of residence. (See Appendix table 1 for comparative summary statistics from the two data sets.) After defining various dummy variables, interaction terms, and higher-order terms, the total number of explanatory variables available for the regressions was 48.

Separate models were estimated for each region (Costa, Sierra, and Oriente), and within these regions, urban and rural areas were distinguished. Separate estimates were also obtained for Guayaquil and Quito, as the ECV oversampled these two cities.[12] The dependent variable in each regression was the logarithm of per capita consumption expenditure for household i, $\ln y_i$:

$$\ln y_i = X_i' b + \varepsilon_i \quad \varepsilon_i \sim N(0, \sigma^2) \tag{3.1}$$

with the vector of independent variables X_i common to the ECV and the census, and ε_i a random disturbance term. The models were estimated using weighted least squares with household sampling weights as weights. The explanatory power of the eight models ranged from an R^2 of 0.46 for the rural Sierra, to an R^2 of 0.74 for the rural Oriente. The R^2's for the urban models ranged from 0.55 (Quito) to 0.64 (Urban Sierra).[13]

Before moving on to the second step, which involves applying the models to the census data, we tested whether predicting consumption (on the basis of the survey) would improve targeting as compared to the Basic Needs indicator discussed above. Although we obtained quite reasonable fits for cross-sectional regressions (as reported above), the coefficients of determination remained significantly lower than 1. To assess the performance of the model, we performed an analogous exercise to the one reported in table 3.3, in which the Basic Needs indicator was compared with actual consumption. Table 3.4 shows the results of comparing predicted with actual consumption levels.

From table 3.4 we see that prediction models do indeed perform better in identifying the poorest households, in terms of consumption, than the Basic Needs indicator. The first test consisted of using the full household sample in the prediction models and applying the parameter estimates to the full sample. In table 3.4 we can see an improvement in the targeting efficiency by almost 50 percent, with 59.9 percent of the bottom quintile according to predicted consumption also being found in the bottom quintile according to actual consumption. The second test was considerably more demanding. Here we split the household survey in half (randomly), estimated the model of consumption using only one-half of the survey data,

Table 3.4 Distribution of Bottom 20 Percent Using Predicted Consumption across Actual Consumption Expenditure Quintiles

Quintile of true per capita consumption	Percentage of beneficiary households (based on predicted consumption)		BN indicator (percent)
	Within-sample[1]	Outside-sample[2]	(From table 3.3)
Poorest 20 percent	59.9	51.0	41.4
20-40 percent	22.0	27.0	29.5
40-60 percent	13.8	13.1	19.5
60-80 percent	3.9	8.0	8.0
Richest 20 percent	0.2	0.9	1.6

Note:
1. The within-sample exercise derived predicted household consumption from models estimated using the full household survey, applying the parameter estimates again to the full sample.
2. The outside-sample exercise consisted of estimating the models for a subsample of the LSMS and then using the resulting parameter estimates to predict consumption for the remaining sample.
Source: Authors' calculations.

and predicted consumption for the other half (an out-of-sample prediction). As expected, the improvement over the Basic Needs indicator is less dramatic with this test. Nevertheless, if the goal is to target the bottom 20 percent of the population, this approach still improves the targeting efficiency from 41.4 percent (Basic Needs) to 51.0 percent.

Predicting Poverty

We now proceed to the second step in the imputation exercise, which consists of applying the parameter estimates from the regressions (using the full household sample) to the census data. For each household in the census, the parameter estimates from the applicable regression (determined by the location of residence) were multiplied by the household's characteristics in order to obtain an imputed value for (log) per capita consumption expenditure. We then estimated the household's probability of being poor taking into account the fact that consumption was not perfectly explained by the model (the R^2's were never 1) and that predicted consumption was based on sample data. Finally, the incidence of poverty was calculated as the mean, over the population in a given region of the census, of the household-specific estimates.[14]

More formally, given a poverty line z, the indicator of poverty P_i for each household i is shown in equation 3.2:

$$P_i = 1 \text{ if } \ln y_i < \ln z; \ P_i \text{ otherwise.} \tag{3.2}$$

Using the model of consumption in equation 3.1 above, the expected poverty of household i with observable characteristics X_i is shown in equation 3.3:

$$E[P_i \mid X_i, \boldsymbol{\beta}, \sigma] = \Phi\left(\frac{\ln z - X_i'\boldsymbol{\beta}}{\sigma}\right) \tag{3.3}$$

where Φ is a cumulative standard normal distribution. Given that we are dealing with the headcount poverty indicator in equation 3.2, the value in equation 3.3 is simply the probability that a household with observable characteristics X_i is poor.[15] We estimate equation 3.1 to obtain estimates of $\hat{\beta}$, the vector of coefficients, and $\hat{\sigma}$. Thus, our estimator of the expected poverty of household i in the census is

$$P_i^* = \hat{E}[P_i \mid X_i, \hat{\boldsymbol{\beta}}, \hat{\sigma}] = \Phi\left(\frac{\ln z - X_i'\hat{\boldsymbol{\beta}}}{\hat{\sigma}}\right) \tag{3.4}$$

which, as a continuous function of consistent estimators, is itself a consistent estimator of $E[P_i]$.

P, regional poverty, is

$$P = \frac{1}{N} \sum_{i=1}^{N} P_i \tag{3.5}$$

where N is the number of households in the region, and expected poverty is

$$E[P \mid X, \boldsymbol{\beta}, \sigma] = \frac{1}{N} \sum_{i=1}^{N} E[P_i \mid X_i, \boldsymbol{\beta}, \sigma]. \tag{3.6}$$

The predicted incidence of poverty, P^*, given the estimated model of consumption, is thus

$$P^* = \hat{E}[P \mid X, \hat{\boldsymbol{\beta}}, \hat{\sigma}] = \frac{1}{N} \sum_{i=1}^{N} \Phi\left(\frac{\ln z - X_i'\hat{\boldsymbol{\beta}}}{\hat{\sigma}}\right). \tag{3.7}$$

Note that we calculate the incidence of poverty as a mean of household-level probabilities of being poor, rather than simply counting up those households whose predicted expenditure is below the poverty line, z. The latter approach would give biased estimates of poverty rates (see below).[16] Given the random component of consumption, ε, no household has a zero probability of being poor or non-poor given its observed characteristics.

In table 3.5 we report the estimated incidence of poverty from the census data, using our imputed consumption values, for each of the eight geographic regions. We compare these rates with those obtained from the ECV household survey using the consumption figures actually in the data. In the ECV data the estimated incidence of poverty in Ecuador as a whole is 35 percent. The poverty rates calculated on the basis of consumption imputed from the census data are reasonably close to those based on the survey. In general, poverty rates in the survey are somewhat lower than those from the census (except Rural Oriente, which is unchanged across the two data sources). This is likely due to changes in the exogenous variables underpinning the consumption regressions over the four-year period between the 1990 census and the 1994 ECV survey. For example, reductions in poverty are most apparent for the Sierra region in table 3.5. As is shown in Appendix

Table 3.5 Regional Poverty Rates For Ecuador

Comparing Rates from the 1994 ECV to Rates from the Census Using Imputed Expenditures Based on a Model Calibrated from the ECV Survey

ECV Ranking	Poverty incidence (percent below poverty line) (estimated standard errors in brackets)		
	ECV	Census	Rank
1. Rural Oriente	0.67 (0.02)	0.67 (0.004)	(1)
2. Rural Costa	0.50 (0.02)	0.52 (0.002)	(3)
3. Rural Sierra	0.43 (0.02)	0.53 (0.001)	(2)
4. Guayaquil	0.29 (0.02)	0.35 (0.002)	(4)
5. Quito	0.25 (0.02)	0.33 (0.002)	(5)
6. Urban Costa	0.25 (0.02)	0.29 (0.002)	(6)
7. Urban Oriente	0.20 (0.02)	0.25 (0.009)	(8)
8. Urban Sierra	0.19 (0.02)	0.29 (0.003)	(7)

Source: Authors' calculations.

table 1, mean years of schooling of the household head appears to have risen most sharply in this region between 1990 and 1994. At the regional level, standard errors on the poverty rates calculated from the Census are remarkably low.[17] Rankings of the eight regions are not identical across the two data sources, but in both cases rural areas are clearly identified as poorer than urban areas, with rural Oriente emerging as clearly the poorest of all regions. The World Bank report on poverty in Ecuador (1996) indicated that orderings of regions, based on the ECV data, were generally non-robust in the sense that the use of alternative poverty lines and poverty rates often resulted in re-rankings of regions. The only exception in this regard was the rural versus urban ranking, which was found to be highly robust (first-order stochastic dominance held with rural Ecuador consistently poorer than urban Ecuador). The comparison of regional rankings across the ECV and census data is quite consistent with these dominance results.

Standard errors on the ECV-level poverty rates in table 3.5 are such that we cannot reject the hypothesis that within sectors (urban and rural, respectively) poverty rates across regions are the same (although we can statistically distinguish urban from rural sectors). In the Census, our estimates are sufficiently precise to permit meaningful comparisons across regions within sectors.[18]

Province-Level Poverty in Ecuador: An Illustration

The purpose of the methodology outlined in the previous sections is to allow us to construct a poverty map, based on consumption expenditures, at a level of disaggregation below the eight broad regions for which the ECV is suitable. For example, there are nearly 400 cantons in Ecuador, each with some degree of local autonomy and administration, and these cantons themselves can be divided into a total of well over 1,000 parroquias ("parishes"). Working with the census data, one could easily calculate canton-level or parroquia-level expected poverty rates to determine where poverty is concentrated. In fact, as we have seen in the example described in the second section of this paper, the census-level information can, in principle, be used to identify poor households and to target transfers to these households directly.

However, the standard errors on poverty estimates are a function of the degree of disaggregation of the poverty map (see final term in the second equation of note 19). This warns us against attempting to employ our methodology to identify, for instance, individual households that are poor.[19] Moreover, these objections are in addition to the well-known arguments against targeting in this way, which focus on the impact that such policies could have on the behavior of potential beneficiaries.[20]

Despite the caution against microtargeting, it may still be desirable to develop a poverty map at a degree of disaggregation below broad regions. Ultimately, the optimal degree of disaggregation will depend on a number of factors. One is the precise purpose that the poverty map is expected to fulfill. Is it, for example, intended to identify government administrative areas so that the desired level of disaggregation is some level of local government? Or is it intended to identify poor villages or neighborhoods so that community-level project interventions (such as public infrastructure) can be better targeted? A second important consideration is whether the parameter estimates from a regression model estimated, say, at the regional level, can be assumed to apply to subregional breakdowns. Throughout this exercise we are implicitly assuming that within a region, the model of consumption is the same for all households irrespective of which province, county, or community they reside in.[21] This is an assumption we cannot test, and at very fine levels of disaggregation it might be less appealing. The desired degree of disaggregation will also depend on the availability of other sources of information on the poverty of individuals that might become available locally. Finally, other methods of local targeting, such as self-targeting, will become more important and effective at certain levels of disaggregation. Constructing a poverty map is thus likely to be a sequential process of gradual disaggregation until it seems there is no further insight to be gained from further disaggregation. At all stages it will be very important to keep in mind the purpose of the poverty map.

In table 3.6 we present a breakdown of the headcount rate of poverty in Ecuador by province, distinguishing between rural and urban areas in each. It is clear from table 3.6 that poverty rates across provinces vary considerably. We can also see that at the level of provinces the standard errors on the poverty rates remain low, so that disaggregating to the province level has not come at a significant cost in terms of statistical precision. In fact, a poverty map would have to be constructed at quite a high degree of spatial disaggregation before the standard errors increase significantly due to small populations. We demonstrate this in figure 3.1, by plotting the standard errors associated with the headcount rates for each of the 1,000-odd parroquias in Ecuador against their populations. Only when the parroquia population falls well below 500 households does the corresponding standard error rise to levels which could compromise comparisons.[22]

Concluding Remarks

In many developing countries poverty maps play an important role in guiding the allocation of public spending for poverty alleviation purposes. A poverty map is essentially a geographical profile of poverty, indicating in

Table 3.6: Ecuador Poverty Map: Urban and Rural Provinces

Region	Sector	Province	Expected poverty rate	Standard error
Oriente	**Rural**		**0.67**	**0.004**
		Pastaza	0.65	0.005
		Sucumbios	0.65	0.005
		Morona Santiago	0.66	0.005
		Zamora Chinchipe	0.67	0.005
		Napo	0.69	0.004
Sierra	**Rural**		**0.53**	**0.001**
		Tungurahua	0.45	0.002
		Pichincha	0.46	0.002
		Azuay	0.50	0.002
		Canar	0.52	0.003
		Bolivar	0.55	0.003
		Imbabura	0.56	0.003
		Loja	0.57	0.003
		Carchi	0.58	0.004
		Chimborazo	0.59	0.003
		Cotopaxi	0.63	0.003
Costa	**Rural**		**0.52**	**0.002**
		el Oro	0.45	0.003
		Guayas	0.48	0.002
		Los Rios	0.55	0.002
		Manabi	0.56	0.002
		Esmeraldas	0.59	0.003
		Galapagos	0.14	0.008

which parts of a country poverty is concentrated, and thus in which locations policies might be expected to have the greatest impact on poverty. A poverty map is most useful if it can be constructed at a fine level of geographical disaggregation.

To achieve such fine levels of disaggregation it is essential to be able to work with very large data sets. However, it is rare to find survey data that are both large in sample size but detailed in terms of the information they collect on household welfare. In general, there is a tradeoff between size and quality because both goals are costly in financial and administrative terms.

In this chapter we have explored the possibility of combining the best of two different sources of data in order to construct a disaggregated poverty

Region	Sector	Province	Expected poverty rate	Standard error
Costa	**urban**	**Guayaquil**	**0.35**	**0.002**
Sierra	**urban**	**Quito**	**0.33**	**0.002**
Costa	**other urban**		**0.29**	**0.002**
		el Oro	0.24	0.003
		Esmeraldas	0.27	0.004
		Manabi	0.29	0.003
		Guayas	0.30	0.003
		Los Rios	0.32	0.003
Sierra	**other urban**		**0.29**	**0.003**
		Azuay	0.23	0.003
		Tungurahua	0.25	0.004
		Chimborazo	0.25	0.004
		Cotopaxi	0.28	0.004
		Loja	0.31	0.004
		Canar	0.31	0.006
		Imbabura	0.33	0.004
		Carchi	0.33	0.005
		Pichincha	0.33	0.003
Oriente	**urban**		**0.25**	**0.009**
		Pastaza	0.24	0.011
		Zamora Chinchipe	0.24	0.013
		Morona Santiago	0.28	0.013

Source: Authors' calculations.

map which is also based on an income or consumption measure of welfare. We illustrated first that constructing a poverty map based on census data, but using an ad hoc weighting scheme, may not be a good approach to targeting those households which are poor in terms of consumption. Transfer programs to alleviate poverty, based on such a map, might reach only a subset of the intended beneficiaries and might entail considerable leakages to the non-poor.

We then suggest an alternative approach: Using household data in a high-quality, but small, living standards survey for Ecuador (ECV 1994), we directly modeled consumption as a function of explanatory variables which

Figure 3.1 Standard Errors on Headcount Rates and Population Disaggregation

Parraquoia-level estimates

Households per parroquia

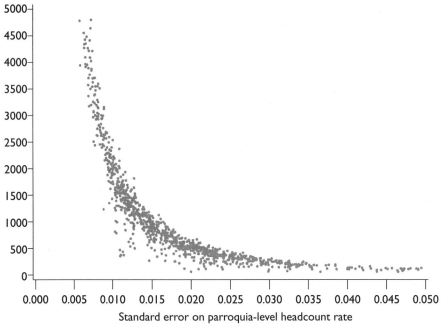

Standard error on parroquia-level headcount rate

Source: Authors' estimates.

are also present in the census. Because even the relatively few explanatory variables common across the census and the ECV were able to explain much of the variation in household consumption in the ECV, the incidence of poverty calculated from the census, based on this imputed consumption figure, was quite close to that calculated from the ECV. We also demonstrated that in Ecuador the poverty rates calculated in the census were generally calculated with a high level of statistical precision. This precision inevitably declines as the degree of spatial disaggregation increases. While one might be tempted to use the methodology developed here to identify individual poor households, we have demonstrated that such an application would be highly inappropriate. We argue, instead, that the approach developed here can be taken quite some distance in the direction of disaggregation, but it should be supplemented with complementary sources of information and investigation.

Probably the most useful practical application to which this methodology can be devoted lies in comparisons against regional patterns of *other* indicators of well-being, opportunity, and access. For example, one could overlay a map documenting regional patterns of access to primary health care centers against our map illustrating where poverty is concentrated. Such an exercise could be of considerable use to policy makers for a number of reasons. It might help policy makers decide *where* to prioritize efforts to expand access to primary health centers. It could also help in thinking about *how* to expand access to primary health—for example, subsidizing access in poor areas, but experimenting with cost-recovery methods in the less poor ones. Furthermore, a close correlation between, say, regional patterns of rural poverty and road access, might also offer clues as to possible *causes* of poverty. This type of exercise could be undertaken with respect to a wide range of indicators: levels of health and education; ethnicity and indigeneity; access to infrastructure and other public services; land quality and ecology; environment, and so on.

Finally, as mentioned in the introduction, an ability to construct finely disaggregated poverty maps might also inform broader research questions. One approach could be to analyze the spatially varying relationship between distributional outcomes and economic performance within a country, in a manner analogous to the cross-country analysis that currently receives much attention among researchers. This approach may well avoid some of the methodological concerns that the cross-country approach raises. There are also other research questions that could be tackled. For example, underlying some of the current arguments in favor of decentralizing poverty alleviation efforts is a notion that local communities themselves are best placed to identify the kinds of interventions which are most beneficial to the poor within those communities. This position hinges somewhat on the contention that at the local community level public resources are less likely to be captured by a subset of non-poor households. This is probably linked to the degree of inequality at the community level; something which has traditionally not been easy to investigate. With the methodology presented here, household-level consumption inferred from the census could be analyzed to assess the extent of inequality within smaller geographic areas.

Appendix

Table A.3.1 Comparative Descriptive Statistics

Selected Variables from the 1994 LSMS against the 1990 Census

	Rural Sierra		Urban Sierra		Quito		Rural Costa	
	LSMS	Census	LSMS	Census	LSMS	Census	LSMS	Census
Years of schooling of HH head								
mean	4.48	4.33	8.75	8.11	10.67	9.52	3.63	4.12
(s.d.)	(3.36)	(4.18)	(5.15)	(5.19)	(5.25)	(5.23)	(3.16)	(4.01)
Male HH head								
mean	0.84	0.78	0.81	0.77	0.82	0.79	0.96	0.87
Persons per bedroom								
mean	3.04	3.28	2.42	2.59	2.21	2.45	3.74	3.73
(s.d.)	(1.78)	(2.05)	(1.49)	(1.66)	(1.32)	(1.52)	(1.98)	(2.29)
Connection to public water network								
mean	0.31	0.52	0.94	0.89	0.90	0.83	0.08	0.21
Garbage collection by truck								
mean	0.25	0.19	0.80	0.81	0.89	0.88	0.05	0.12
Flush toilet								
mean	0.37	0.24	0.69	0.68	0.79	0.68	0.27	0.33
Telephone connection								
mean	0.04	0.07	0.31	0.27	0.43	0.36	0.00	0.03
Years of schooling of HH head								
mean	6.64	6.91	8.88	8.65	5.82	5.16	8.27	8.29
(s.d.)	(4.42)	(4.98)	(4.89)	(4.96)	(3.94)	(4.08)	(4.50)	(4.79)
Male HH head								
mean	0.83	0.80	0.77	0.78	0.89	0.85	0.83	0.78
Persons per bedroom								
mean	3.16	3.12	3.01	2.99	3.54	3.49	2.54	2.64
(s.d.)	(2.08)	(1.96)	(1.87)	(1.92)	(1.89)	(2.26)	(1.50)	(1.63)
Connection to public water network								
mean	0.55	0.71	0.72	0.62	0.16	0.29	0.92	0.87
Garbage collection by truck								
mean	0.57	0.56	0.75	0.54	0.10	0.20	0.81	0.83
Flush toilet								
mean	0.66	0.71	0.76	0.75	0.23	0.18	0.66	0.60
Telephone connection								
mean	0.12	0.13	0.25	0.23	0.01	0.03	0.24	0.14

Source: Authors' calculations.

Notes

The authors are very grateful to the Instituto Nacional de Estadistica y Censos (INEC) in Ecuador for access to the unit record data of the 1990 Census. We have benefited from discussions with Uwe Deichmann, Stefan Dercon, Joanna Gomulka, Vassilis Hajivassiliou, Jeffrey Hammer, Berk Ozler, and Martin Ravallion. Useful comments were received from three anonymous referees as well as participants at a seminar at the Suntory Toyota International Centre for Economics and Related Disciplines (STICERD), London School of Economics, in May, 1997, and a workshop on Geographical Targeting for Poverty Reduction and Rural Development at the World Bank in November 1997. Thanks also to Jim Shafer for assistance. The views in this chapter are our own and should not be taken to represent the views of the World Bank or any of its affiliates. All remaining errors are our own.

This chapter is based on the paper of the same title published in WBER, January 2000.

The authors are from the World Bank, Yale University, the World Bank, and Superintendencia Banco y Seguros, Lima, Peru, respectively.

1. Deininger and Squire (1996) have recently compiled a large international database for this purpose. Bruno, Ravallion, and Squire (1997) utilize this database to explore the relationship between economic growth and inequality. See also Alesina and Rodrik (1994), and Fields (1989).

2. For recent descriptions of the derivation of such maps see World Bank (1996) for Ecuador, Government of El Salvador (1995) for El Salvador, and Fondo de Compensacion y Desarollo Social (FONCODES) (1995) for Peru. Other Latin American countries in which such maps are used to guide the allocation of public social-sector spending include Colombia, Honduras, and Venezuela.

3. For example, attempting to identify individual poor *households* on the basis of our methodology would be quite inappropriate.

4. Consumption is an imperfect indicator of the standard of living, but a comprehensive measure of expenditure comes reasonably close to the goal of capturing a household's *achievement* of well-being; that is, to what extent the household acquires its own chosen bundle of goods and services. The choice between income and consumption also merits attention. For developing countries probably the most compelling argument in favor of consumption is that it is typically easier to measure accurately. Its relative smoothness across seasons or even from year to year may make consumption a better indicator of long-term living standards than a measure of current income (see, however, Chaudhuri and Ravallion 1994). For more discussion see Atkinson (1989), Ravallion (1994), and Sen (1984). Hentschel and Lanjouw (1996) and Lanjouw and Lanjouw (1997) also discuss further the attractions of a *comprehensive* indicator of consumption expenditures as an indicator of welfare

5. In other poverty-mapping exercises for Ecuador, INEC has experimented with wider ranges of variables. In El Salvador, the government has constructed a poverty map using 12 different variables (Government of El Salvador 1995).

6. The survey design incorporated both clustering and stratification on the basis of the three main agro-climatic zones of the country and a rural/urban breakdown.

The survey design also included an oversampling of Ecuador's two main cities, Quito and Guayaquil. Some 1,374 rural households were surveyed in total. Household expansion factors were added to the data set so that inferences could be made about population aggregates.

7. Expenditures were also adjusted to take into account regional cost of living variation based on a Laspeyres food price index reflecting the consumption patterns of the poor.

8. The BN indicator might not perform so poorly if the targeting scheme was aimed, say, only at urban areas, or if an alternative cut-off point was applied in the distribution.

9. While imputation of missing observations within a sample is a common procedure (see, for instance, Paulin and Ferraro 1994), out-of-sample imputation that combines different data sets is less frequent. In a recent article, Bramley and Smart (1996) combine the British Family Expenditure Survey with census information to estimate local income distributions. However, Bramley and Smart did not have access to unit-level data from both data sources. They derived local income distributions not from predicted household incomes but from estimates of mean incomes and distribution characteristics.

10. See Purcell and Kish (1980) for an overview and Isaki (1990) for an application of small-area estimation to obtain economic statistics.

11. The combination of information of different data sets has sparked a recent interest in the literature (see, for example, Arellano and Meghir 1992, Angrist and Krueger 1992, Lusardi 1996, Imbens and Hellerstein 1998). These studies generally combine several household surveys, rather than census and survey data, and have not addressed spatial poverty estimation.

12. Note how the BN weights in table 3.1 relate to those implied by the regression coefficient estimates. Quito is a typical example. In the BN classification, a decrease in persons per bedroom from four to three is associated with a welfare improvement *equivalent* to a move from primary to secondary education for the household head. From the consumption regression, the point estimates suggest that an increase in the education of the household head from primary to secondary level is associated with an increase in consumption of 30 percent, while a decline in persons per bedroom from four to three is associated with an increase in consumption of just 6.7 percent. An increase in education from secondary to tertiary is also associated with an increase in consumption of 30 percent. However, in this case a decrease in persons per bedroom from three to one, which has the equivalent welfare effect of a university education according to BN weights, is associated with a much bigger increase consumption of 47.6 percent The same pattern holds across regions. This would suggest that at high levels of crowding and low education, more weight is given in the BN system to reductions in crowding relative to increases in education than would be appropriate as a reflection of their relationship to consumption, and vice versa. If, as discussed in the introduction, the BN weights are intended to reflect both variables' relationships to overall consumption as well as an adjustment for their intrinsic value, the system of weights implicit in the BN classification seem to suggest a value judgement that literacy, or attending primary school, are of less importance than reducing crowded bedrooms.

13. Full sets of parameter estimates, standard errors, and diagnostics from the eight regression models are not reported here for reasons of space, but are available

from the authors upon request. Correctly specifying the precise functional form of the disturbance term in the consumption regression is important when calculating the second-stage poverty estimates. Thus, we tested the normality assumption made in equation 3.1. In three of the eight regions we could not reject normality of the disturbance terms based on Shapiro-Wilk and joint skewness and kurtosis tests (all p-values > 0.15). Closer inspection of the residuals revealed that, in the other regions, failure of normality was due to just a few outliers in one or both tails. These may well be due to mismeasurement. (For example, in one case, the top consumption was six times higher than the one just below.) After trimming these few observations, a total of only 13 out of 4,635, we could not reject normality at conventional levels of significance in any region. Such small deviations from the assumed normality of the disturbance term should have a negligible effect on the accuracy of the results that follow. Further, with the exception of Guayaquil, we could not reject (at $\alpha = 0.10$) the null hypothesis of homoskedasticity against the alternative of heteroskedasticity related to the full set of independent variables.

14. Our discussion will be in terms of a single poverty criterion—the incidence of poverty—and a single poverty line. One could, however, rank regions on the basis of a large range of alternative poverty or inequality measures, and experiment with a range of possible poverty lines (see Elbers, Lanjouw and Lanjouw 2000). It is also in terms of the incidence of poverty of households. To calculate incidence at the level of individuals it is necessary to weight each household-level observation by its corresponding household size (see note 17). The poverty figures provided in the tables are such weighted totals.

15. That is, if one were to take infinite draws from a population of households, the resulting poverty rate among households with observables X_i would be that given in equation 3.3. Note that this value will not, in general, be the same as the actual poverty rate that is a *sample* from this infinite population, and depends on the particular realization of e_i.

16. This has been noted in the context of errors in individual welfare measurement due to inequality in intra-household distribution (Haddad and Kanbur 1990). See also Ravallion (1988). The Peruvian statistical institute INEI (1996) has developed a model very similar to the one described above but derived poverty rates from direct estimation of the headcount rate and not from the predicted poverty probabilities.

17. For the census poverty incidence, the standard error of our indicator around the true poverty rate can be calculated as follows (see Elbers, Lanjouw and Lanjouw, 2000, for details):

$$P^* = \sum_{i=1}^{N} \frac{m_i}{M} \left(\frac{\ln z - X_i'\hat{\beta}}{\hat{\sigma}} \right)$$

$$\text{var}\left(P^*\right) = \left(\frac{\partial P^*}{\partial \hat{\beta}} \right)' \text{Var}\left(\hat{\beta}\right) \left(\frac{\partial P^*}{\partial \hat{\beta}} \right) + \left(\frac{\partial P^*}{\partial \hat{\sigma}^2} \right)^2 \frac{2\hat{\sigma}^4}{n-k-1} + \sum_{i=1}^{N} \frac{m_i^2 P_i^* \left(1 - P_i^*\right)}{M^2}$$

where n is the sample size for the consumption model with k parameters, estimated using the LSMS survey. N is the number of households in the census population in the region of interest, m_i is the number of individuals in household i, and M is the total number of individuals in the census population.

$$\frac{\partial P^*}{\partial \hat{\beta}_j} = \sum_{i=1}^{N} \frac{m_i}{M} \left(-\frac{x_{ij}}{\hat{\sigma}} \right) \phi \left(\frac{\ln z - X_i'\hat{\beta}}{\hat{\sigma}} \right)$$

where ij indicates the jth element of the vector of explanatory variables for the ith household.

$$\frac{\partial P^*}{\partial \hat{\sigma}^2} = -\frac{1}{2} \sum_{i=1}^{N} \frac{m_i}{M} \left(\frac{\ln z - X_i'\hat{\beta}}{\hat{\sigma}^3} \right) \phi \left(\frac{\ln z - X_i'\hat{\beta}}{\hat{\sigma}} \right)$$

18. Because the eight regions being compared are based on different regression models in the ECV, the parameter estimates underlying the predicted expenditures are independent across regions. In this case one can test for statistical significance of the difference in poverty rates between region r and region u based on the formula:

$$\text{var}\left(P_r^* - P_u^* \right) = \text{var}\left(P_r^* \right) + \text{var}\left(P_u^* \right)$$

19. Suppose the predicted probability of poverty for a given household was 48 percent. For a single household a lower-bound estimate of the standard error on that household's poverty rate would be: $0.49 \approx \sqrt{[0.48(1 - 0.48)]}$.

20. Van de Walle and Nead (1995) provide a clear and thorough discussion of these issues.

21. Partly this depends on whether ε_i is viewed primarily as a household fixed effect or whether most variations are idiosyncratic shocks to income. We assume that ε_i has mean zero at the level of estimation. Moving to subgroups, however, this will, in general, no longer be true if ε_i is a household fixed effect. In this case, households in one subgroup may have relatively high incomes, given their observable characteristics, compared to those in another subgroup with similar characteristics. The expected poverty measure would then tend to be biased, understating the wellbeing of the first group and overstating that of the second.

22. The standard error on the difference in poverty rates between two parroquias in different regions would be calculated as was described earlier. However, because the parameter estimates determining the imputed expenditure figures are the same for all parroquias within a given region, the standard error on the difference in the incidence of poverty between two parroquia in a given region

$$\text{var}\left(P_1^* - P_2^* \right) = \left(\frac{\partial \left(P_1^* - P_2^* \right)}{\partial \hat{\beta}} \right)' \text{var}\left(\hat{\beta} \right) \left(\frac{\partial \left(P_1^* - P_2^* \right)}{\partial \hat{\beta}} \right) +$$

$$\left(\frac{\partial \left(P_1^* - P_2^* \right)}{\partial \hat{\beta}^2} \right)^2 \frac{2\hat{\sigma}^4}{n-k-1} + \sum_{i=1}^{N_1} \frac{m_i^2 P_{1_i}^* \left(1 - P_{1_i}^* \right)}{M_1^2} + \sum_{h=1}^{N_2} \frac{m_h^2 P_{1_h}^* \left(1 - P_{1_h}^* \right)}{M_2^2}$$

where N, M and m are defined as in note 17 for parroquias 1 and 2 which are subscripted by i and h respectively, and

$$\frac{\partial\left(P_1^* - P_2^*\right)}{\partial\hat{\boldsymbol{\beta}}_j} = \sum_{i=1}^{N_1} \frac{m_i}{M_1} \left(-\frac{x_{ij}}{\hat{\sigma}}\right) \phi\left(\frac{\ln z - \boldsymbol{X}_i'\hat{\boldsymbol{\beta}}}{\hat{\sigma}}\right) - \sum_{h=1}^{M_2} \frac{m_h}{M_2} \left(-\frac{x_{hj}}{\hat{\sigma}}\right) \phi\left(\frac{\ln z - \boldsymbol{X}_h'\hat{\boldsymbol{\beta}}}{\hat{\sigma}}\right)$$

and

$$\frac{\partial\left(P_1^* - P_2^*\right)}{\partial\hat{\sigma}^2} = -\frac{1}{2}\sum_{i=1}^{N_1} \frac{m_i}{M_1} \left(\frac{\ln z - \boldsymbol{X}_i'\hat{\boldsymbol{\beta}}}{\hat{\sigma}^3}\right) \phi\left(\frac{\ln z - \boldsymbol{X}_i'\hat{\boldsymbol{\beta}}}{\hat{\sigma}}\right) - \frac{1}{2}\sum_{h=1}^{N_2} \frac{m_h}{M_2} \left(\frac{\ln z - \boldsymbol{X}_h'\hat{\boldsymbol{\beta}}}{\hat{\sigma}^3}\right) \phi\left(\frac{\ln z - \boldsymbol{X}_h'\hat{\boldsymbol{\beta}}}{\hat{\sigma}}\right)$$

with j the jth element of the given vector.

References

Alesina, A., and Rodrik, D. 1994. "Distributive Policies and Economic Growth." *Quarterly Journal of Economics.* 109: 465–490.

Angrist, J.D., and A.B. Krueger. 1992. "The Effect of Age of School Entry on Educational Attainment: An Application of Instrumental Variables with Moments from Two Samples." *Journal of the American Statistical Association* 87: 328–336.

Arellano, M., and C. Meghir. 1992. "Female Labour Supply and on the Job Search: an Empirical Model Estimated Using Complementary Data Sets." *Review of Economic Studies* 59: 537–559.

Atkinson, A. 1989. *Poverty and Social Security.* Hemel Hempstead, U.K.: Harvester Wheatsheaf.

Bramley, G., and G. Smart. 1996. "Modelling Local Income Distributions in Britain." *Regional Studies* 30: 239–255.

Bruno, M., M. Ravallion, and L. Squire. 1997. "Equity and Growth in Developing Countries: Old and New Perspectives on the Policy Issues." In Vito Tanzi and Ke-Young Chu, eds., *Income Distribution and High Quality Growth.* Cambridge: MIT Press.

Chaudhuri, S., and M. Ravallion. 1994. "How Well Do Static Welfare Indicators Identify the Chronically Poor?" *Journal of Public Economics* 53(3): 367–394.

Deininger, K., and L. Squire. 1996. "A New Data Set Measuring Income Inequality." *The World Bank Economic Review* 10: 565–91.

Elbers, C., J.O. Lanjouw, and P. Lanjouw. 2000. "Welfare in Villages and Towns: Micro-Measurement of Poverty and Inequality." Free University of Amsterdam, Netherlands. Processed.

Farrell, P., B. MacGibbon, and T. J. Tomberlin. 1997. "Empirical Bayes Estimation Using Logistic Regression Models and Summary Statistics." *Journal of Business and Economic Statistics* 15: 101–108.

Fields, B. 1989. "Changes in Poverty and Inequality in Developing Countries." *World Bank Research Observer* 4: 167–185.

Fondo de Compensacion y Desarollo Social (FONCODES). 1995. *Mapa de Pobreza en Peru.* Lima.

Government of El Salvador. 1995. "Priorizacion de Municipios a Partir de Datos Censales." Direccion General de Politica Economica y Social, Ministerio de Coordinacion del Desarollo Economico y Social.

Haddad, L., and R. Kanbur. 1990. "How Serious is the Neglect of Intra-Household Inequality?" *The Economic Journal* 100: 866–881.

Hentschel, J., and P. Lanjouw. 1996. "Constructing an Indicator of Consumption for the Analysis of Poverty: Principles and Illustrations with Reference to Ecuador." LSMS Working Paper 124, Policy Research Department, The World Bank, Washington, D.C.

Imbens, G., and J. Hellerstein. 1998. "Imposing Moment Restrictions from Auxiliary Data by Weighting."' NBER Technical Working Paper 202. *Review of Economics and Statistics*. Forthcoming.

National Statistical Institute of Ecuador (INEI). 1996. *Metodologia Para Determinar el Ingreso y la Proporcion de Hogares Pobres.* Lima.

Isaki, C.T. 1990. "Small-Area Estimation of Economic Statistics."*Journal of Business and Economic Statistics* 8: 435–441.

Lanjouw, J., and P. Lanjouw. 1997. "Poverty Comparisons with Noncompatible Data: Theory and Illustrations." Policy Research Working Paper 1709, Policy Research Department, the World Bank, Washington, D.C.

Lusardi, A. 1996. "Permanent Income, Current Income and Consumption: Evidence from Two Panel Data Sets." *Journal of Business and Economic Statistics* 14(1).

Paulin, G. D., and D.L. Ferraro. 1994. "Imputing Income in the Consumer Expenditure Survey." *Monthly Labor Review* (December): 23–31.

Purcell, N.J., and L. Kish. 1980. "Postcensal Estimates for Local Areas (or Domains)." *International Statistical Review* 48: 3–18.

Ravallion, M. 1988. "Expected Poverty Under Risk-Induced Welfare Variability. *The Economic Journal* 98: 1171–1182.

Ravallion, M. 1994. *Poverty Comparisons.* Chur: Harwood Academic Publishers.

Sen, A.K. 1984. *Resources, Values and Development.* Oxford: Blackwell.

Van de Walle, D., and K. Nead, eds. 1995. *Public Spending and the Poor: Theory and Evidence.* Baltimore: Johns Hopkins University Press.

World Bank. 1996. "Ecuador Poverty Report." World Bank Country Study, The World Bank, Washington, D.C..

4

Community Targeting for
Poverty Reduction in Burkina Faso

David Bigman, Stefan Dercon, Dominique Guillaume,
and Michel Lambotte

BUDGETARY AND SOCIAL PRESSURES to increase the impact of health, education, and rural development projects and programs on the poor have given strong impetus to improving the targeting of public assistance. Undifferentiated transfers that cover the entire population, such as general food subsidies, have exceeded the budget constraints of most developing countries, and the benefits from such transfers go disproportionately to the non-poor.[1] In many developing countries, particularly in Sub-Saharan Africa, targeting criteria that cover large geographical areas or large population groups are also likely to be too costly and too ineffective; a program that is targeted on the entire rural population of a country, for example, will actually reach the majority of the total population—poor and non-poor.

More accurate targeting requires the choice of criteria that can effectively identify eligible recipients. Such criteria can be narrowly defined—at the level of individual households, or they can be more broad-based—for example, at the level of the region or province—by identifying the geographical areas or the population groups that have a higher than average incidence of poverty (van de Walle 1995, pp. 1–5). Narrow targeting at the household level is very data-intensive, and the necessary information is very costly. Identification of eligible households requires complex and expensive means testing, and even in many industrialized countries it is only partly successful—despite the wide range of data available in these countries on individual households—and a large portion of the benefits leaks to non-eligible

125

households. In most developing countries, data on individual households—particularly poor households—which is necessary for means testing is not available, and the scope for narrow targeting at the household level is therefore very limited. If direct means testing is not possible and general coverage of the entire population is not feasible, the only alternative is to identify the target population on the basis of some general criteria. Toward that end, the standard household income and expenditure surveys can be used to identify the more general characteristics of the poor, thereby determining a set of indicators that establish eligibility without resorting to direct means testing. Examples of possible criteria include the number of children, the number of persons per room in a household, and a person's age.

The usefulness of these targeting criteria, as indicated by the capacity of a program to reach a large number of the country's poor, must be weighed against the direct costs of collecting the necessary data, as well as the costs of leakage to the non-poor due to targeting errors. Using data of the World Bank's Living Standard Measurement Surveys (LSMS) in Côte d'Ivoire, Glewwe (1991) examined the tradeoff between the use of a refined and exhaustive set of indicators for narrow targeting at the individual or the household level, and the costs of collecting the information on these indicators. He concluded that, in the case of Côte d'Ivoire, a rather limited set of community and household indicators proved to be quite effective in identifying the poor households. However, the incentives for households to change or misrepresent their characteristics to qualify for the program, once these indicators are determined as eligibility criteria, can significantly reduce its effectiveness and inflate budgetary costs.[2] This, together with the high costs of administering a program, and the danger that the eligibility criteria will leave out too many of the country's poor, has deterred the governments of most developing countries from targeting social welfare programs on individual households.

Geographical targeting may offer an effective approach for reaching the poor in countries where there are substantial disparities in living conditions between geographical areas, and where administering these programs is relatively straightforward (for example, because the local administration is already in place). In India, the allocation of central government disbursements across states has long been determined, in part, by the large disparities between states in their levels of poverty. Indeed, the decision to locate rural development projects in backward regions has become the center of India's poverty-oriented agricultural development strategy. However, even in countries where the poor are concentrated in certain regions or provinces, geographical targeting at the level of large administrative areas is likely to entail considerable leakage of benefits to the non-poor that live in the target areas, while failing to cover the poor that live in other areas. Although targeting at the large geographical areas of the state, the region, or the province is likely to be more effective in reducing leakage and enhancing coverage than general, non-targeted programs, quantitatively the effectiveness of these programs tend to be rather small (Ravallion 1993, Baker and Grosh 1994, and Ravallion 1996).[3] Ravallion (1993) evaluated the costs and effects of geographical targeting at the province level in Indonesia, and concluded that province-level targeting offers clear, but rather small, reductions in poverty. Baker and Grosh (1994) analyzed geographical targeting in Venezuela, Mexico, and Jamaica and concluded that targeting priority regions can be an effective mechanism of transferring benefits to the poor. With a given budget constraint, however, poverty reduction is greater the more narrowly defined and the smaller the target areas are, and the greatest reduction in poverty is achieved when the target areas are individual municipalities or villages.

Narrow geographical targeting at the level of the village or the urban community can reduce the leakage of benefits to the non-poor in countries or regions where, as an effect of agro-climatic or socioeconomic conditions, the standard of living in the majority of the households in most villages and urban communities is similar. The households in these villages often have similar sources of income, and they are all affected by the same agro-climatic and geographic conditions—including road conditions, the distance to the nearest town, and the availability of public facilities for health, education, water supply, and so forth. Consequently, the overall income inequality in these countries or regions is primarily due to income differences between villages, and only to a lesser degree to income differences between individuals within villages.

Targeting at the lower geographical level of the district or the village requires, however, much more information on the spatial distribution of poverty across districts or villages and on the characteristics of the poor population in these areas. Information on the standard of living provided by the household survey is not suitable, however, for small-area targeting since the sample size in the standard survey is far too small to estimate the incidence of poverty at the level of the village or the district. The LSMS are designed to provide a map of the spatial distribution of poverty only at the country or the region levels. Some countries that use geographical targeting apply an alternative, readily available set of indicators to estimate the geographic distribution of poverty and establish criteria for targeting. These indicators include access to public services, the percentage of school-age children in an area that attend school, the prevalence of certain illnesses that are associated with malnutrition, and so forth. All too often, however, these indicators are not sufficiently correlated with the income or expenditure indicators of welfare, and they may lead to targeting errors in determining eligibility and the ineffective use of resources (Hentschel and others 1998). On the other hand, the income or expenditure indicators are not always the proper indicators of the standard of living when it also depends significantly on access to public services; more direct indicators such as the rate of child mortality may be more suitable.

The objective of this chapter is to present a method for narrow geographical targeting at the level of rural villages and individual urban communities. The method is based on the construction of a very large data set from a wide variety of sources in the form of a geographic information system and the use of these data to provide a mapping of poverty at the community and the province levels. This data set includes several strata of information: first, demographic and socioeconomic information at the household level from a variety of surveys; second, village- and community-level information, including demographic information from the population census, the distance to the urban centers, the condition of the road infrastructure, the availability and quality of public services, the sources of drinking water, and so forth; third, department- or region-level information on agro-climatic and geographic conditions, including the location of the main towns and main transport routes. The entire data set was integrated at the level of the village or the urban community using georeferencing, and organized in the form of a GIS database. The second step is to use this data set in an econometric analysis that also uses the detailed data of a household survey to construct a prediction model of households' welfare—using household-, community-, and department-level variables. However, these variables were selected from the GIS database, and they include, therefore, only variables for which mean values were available for all communities in the country. The third step is to apply the predictions of this model to derive estimates of the average level of well-being of the households in a community for all the communities in the country. These estimates were derived on the basis of the community and department data that were available for all communities. The estimates were then used to determine the spatial distribution of poverty in the country at the village level.[4] This method has been applied for Burkina Faso, using the relatively detailed household data of the Priority Survey (PS) conducted by the Institut National de Statistique (INSD).

The plan of this chapter is as follows. The next section ("Methodology") describes the method and econometric model used to estimate households' well-being from the sample of the PS, and the method of applying these estimates to predict poverty levels in the communities outside the sample. A third section ("The Data") details the different data sources and presents their organization in a geographical information system; it is followed by a section discussing the specification of the prediction model ("The Empirical Model"). A fifth section ("Estimating Poverty within the Sample") presents the results of the econometric analysis of the household survey. A sixth section ("Predicting the Geographical Distribution of Poverty in Burkina Faso") demonstrates the application of these estimates to predict the incidence of poverty in the villages outside the sample of the PS, and presents some simulation results that indicate the effectiveness of the targeting system. The last section offers some concluding remarks.

Methodology

The econometric analysis in this study has two parts. In the first part, a prediction model for household consumption is estimated, using the PS household data and community data from all other sources, to determine the variables that best explain households' consumption levels and households' poverty. The explanatory variables in that model are selected such that only variables for which data were available for all villages outside the PS sample are included. In the second part, the prediction model is used to determine the levels of welfare at the village level for all the villages outside the sample of the PS, using the village-level data of the explanatory variables from the GIS database. In line with similar studies on this subject, we use consumption per "standard adult" ("adult equivalent") as our welfare indicator at the household level, and focus on the poverty incidence, measured by the Headcount index, as the measure of poverty.[5]

Let c_{ij} denote the level of consumption per standard adult in household i, residing in community j. Let z denote the poverty line and let $y_{ij} = c_{ij}/z$ be the normalized welfare indicator per standard adult. The analysis will be conducted in terms of the natural logarithms of y_{ij}.[6] The Headcount index H_j measures the relative size of the poor population in community j; the individual poverty indicators H_{ij} indicates the probability that the household ij is poor. The individual poverty indicator is determined by the normalized welfare function as shown in equation 4.1:

$$H_{ij} = 1 \ \text{ if } \ \ln y_{ij} < 0$$
$$H_{ij} = 0 \ \text{ if } \ \ln y_{ij} \geq 0. \tag{4.1}$$

In the construction of the prediction model, the individual welfare indicator is modeled as a function of a vector of household and community explanatory variables X_{ij} and a residual term u_{ij}, which is assumed to be normally distributed with $u_{ij} \sim N(0, \sigma_j^2)$—thereby allowing for village level heteroscedasticity. The prediction model is thus given by equation 4.2:

$$\ln y_{ij} = \beta' X_{ij} + u_{ij}. \tag{4.2}$$

As noted earlier, the explanatory variables were selected only if their mean values were available for all villages in the GIS database. They include community characteristics as well as mean values of household characteristics for all households in the community, such as average household composition, average literacy rates, and so forth. Equation 4.2 can be estimated by means of maximum likelihood, with $u_{ij} \sim N(0, \sigma^2 \cdot \exp(\gamma X_j^V))$, where X_j^V represents the mean values of the explanatory variables in community j, to correct for the heteroscedasticity, and to obtain the estimators b and s_j of the parameters β and σ_j. These estimators and the set of explanatory variables can be used to predict the community's mean consumption for all communities outside the PS sample. Mean consumption in a community is, however, not necessarily a good predictor of poverty, since the poverty measure is a function not only of mean consumption, but also of the distribution of consumption in the community. The term s_j represents one part of that distribution, since the within-community variance is the sum of the variance of the regression and the deviation of the predicted household level consumption from the predicted mean level of consumption. Both components are therefore part of the overall measure of the within-village distribution of consumption.[7]

Using these estimators and the set of explanatory variables, a consistent estimate of the probability that household ij with characteristics X_{ij} is poor can then be expressed as equation 4.3:

$$E\left(H_{ij} \mid X_{ij}, b, s_j\right) = \mathrm{Prob}\left(u_i < -b'X_{ij}\right) = \Phi\left(-b'X_{ij} / s_j\right) \qquad (4.3)$$

where $\Phi(.)$ is the cumulative normal distribution. The predicted level of the incidence of poverty per community j is determined from this equation as shown in equation 4.4:

$$E\left(H_j \mid X_{ij}, b, s_j\right) = E\left(\Phi\left(-b'X_{ij} / s_j\right)\right). \qquad (4.4)$$

If complete information on the variables X_{ij} was available for *all* households and all villages in the country, this prediction would be fairly straightforward: equation 4.3 would then be used to estimate the probability that each of the households in the village is poor, and equation 4.4 would be used to predict the incidence of poverty in the community across all villages outside the sample.[8] However, in Burkina Faso the only data available for all the villages outside the PS sample are the mean values of the explanatory variables per community. Since equation 4.4 is nonlinear, these variables cannot be used to predict the village-level poverty incidence. Using Taylor expansions, it is nevertheless possible to obtain an approximation. For this purpose, equation 4.4 can be expanded around $(-b'X_j^V/s_j)$. Using the property that $E(b'X_{ij} - b'X_j^V) = 0$, we obtain equation 4.5 (Maddala 1983):

$$E\left(H_j\right) = E\left(\Phi\left(-b'X_{ij} / s_j\right)\right)$$
$$\approx \Phi\left(-b'X_j^V / s_j\right) + \tfrac{1}{2} \cdot \left(b'X_j^V / s_j^3\right) \cdot \phi\left(-b'X_j^V / s_j\right) \cdot E\left(b'X_{ij} - b'X_j^V\right)^2 \qquad (4.5)$$

where $\phi(.)$ is the normal density function and $E(b'X_{ij} - b'X_j^V)^2$ is the variance of the predicted household-level consumption around the predicted mean consumption within each village. In other words, the predicted level of poverty for villages outside the sample is a function of the mean level of consumption per adult and of its variance around that mean. Equation 4.5 can therefore provide a prediction of the incidence of poverty in communities outside the sample, using the estimates b and s_j of the parameters of the household consumption function and the community-level characteristics X_j^V of the villages outside that sample.

Note that the regression analysis is used to predict consumption levels for all households. The latter approach would be equivalent to estimating equation 4.1 directly. This is often referred to as a multivariate "poverty profile" (Ravallion 1996). The individual poverty indicator in equation 4.1 is binary, so one could use a probit (or alternative) model to construct a prediction model. As pointed out by Ravallion, a puzzling feature of this approach is that the estimation techniques used were typically developed for situations in which the observed data were dichotomous or truncated at zero. The standard way of writing the solution to this estimation problem is then to define a regression model in which a continuous latent (unobserved) variable is regressed on a set of observed explanatory variables (Maddala 1983). A particular error structure (for example. the normal distribution for the probit) is then assumed, allowing the parameters of inference to be estimated. These parameters can then be used for inference related to the explanatory variables and the observed limited dependent variable. If this procedure is used on a poverty indicator, such as the Headcount, then the latent variable is in fact an observed variable that was used to calculate the limited dependent variables. Since the latent variable is observed, limited dependent variable estimation of the poverty indicators is not necessary and will be less efficient, since some information actually available is not used in constructing the prediction model.

The Data

Data for this study were collected from a large number of sources and brought together at the level of the village, according to the name of the village and the geographical coordinates that indicate its location. Some of the data, most importantly the census, cover all the villages in the country or the entire population; other data cover only a sample of villages and a sample of households within each village. Table 4.1 lists the different sources of data collected as well as their coverage. Not all data could be used in the econometric analysis, however; some of the data did not cover all provinces, while other data, most notably the Agriculture Survey, did not contain the information that was necessary to incorporate the data in the GIS database.

Table 4.1 Data Sources

Level of aggregation	Data source	Acronym	Coverage
Household	Priority Survey (1994): provides data on income and expenditure for 8,642 households	PS	Survey sample (473 villages)
Village	Priority Survey (1994): community component of the PS which covers infrastructure and communal services	PS	Survey sample (473 villages)
Village	National census (1985): demographic data	NC	National
Village	Ministry of Water Management and Infrastructure (1995): data on health and water infrastructure, distances to infrastructure, public administration, and social groupings	DGH	25 out of 30 provinces
Village	Ministry of Education (1995): data on primary school infrastructure and teacher/pupil ratios	EDU	National
Department	Ministry of Agriculture (1993): data on various indicators ranging from average literacy rates to vegetation indices	ENSA	National
Department	Directorate of Meteorology (1961–1995): data on temperature (31 locations), evapo-transpiration (15 locations) and rainfalls (160 locations)	METEO	National
Province	Ministry of Agriculture (1993): data on cattle per household	ENSA	National

Source: Authors' calculations.

After collecting all the data, they were standardized and integrated within a common data set. At the conclusion of this stage of the work, the database contained more than 60 tables that included data on the geographical coordinates of all of the country's villages, towns, markets and public facilities; data on the entire road network; socioeconomic and demographic data from a variety of surveys and the population census; and a large data set on the agro-climatic conditions in the country's main provinces. The data were organized as a geographical information system.

As an illustration of the type of information that was extracted from the GIS for the community study, figure 4.1 shows the location of water points and their proximity to the villages in the Department of Karangasso-Vigue. The points in the map that indicate the locations of the villages are scaled

Figure 4.1 Water Point Proximity

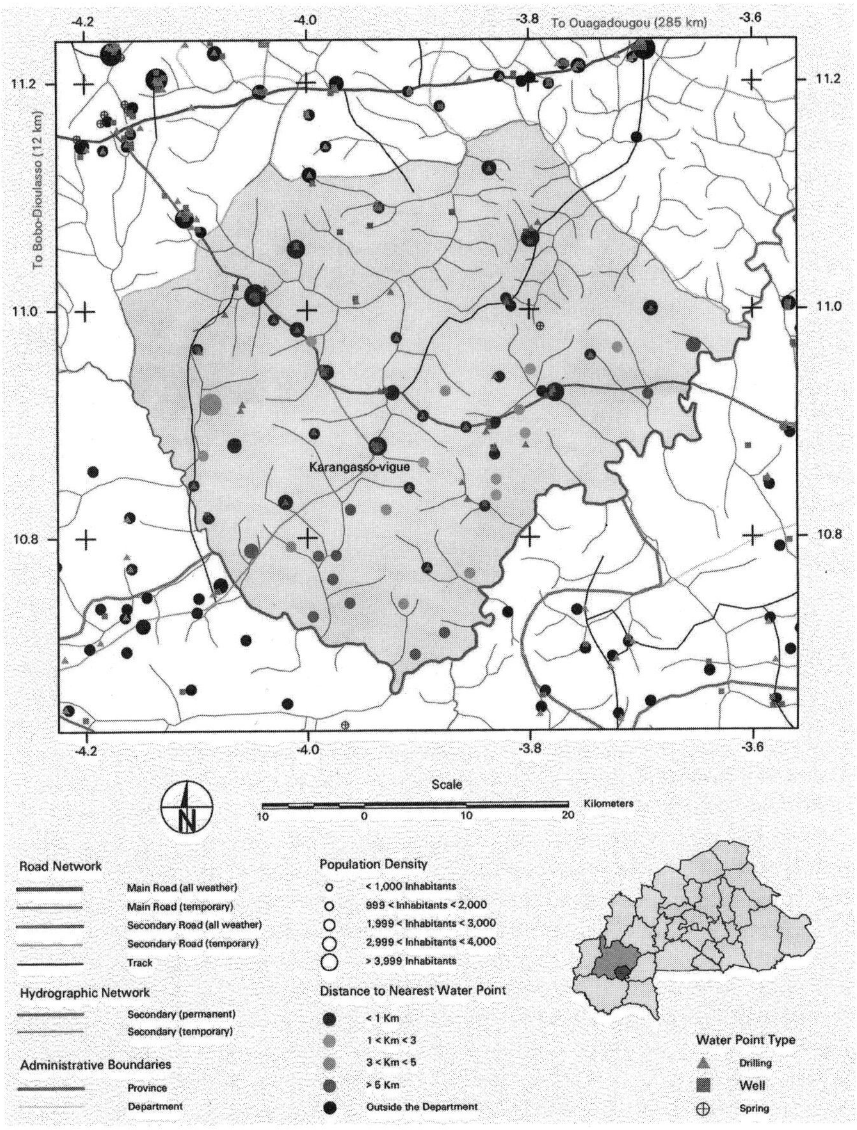

Scale

Road Network

	Main Road (all weather)
	Main Road (temporary)
	Secondary Road (all weather)
	Secondary Road (temporary)
	Track

Hydrographic Network

	Secondary (permanent)
	Secondary (temporary)

Administrative Boundaries

	Province
	Department

Population Density

○	< 1,000 Inhabitants
○	999 < Inhabitants < 2,000
○	1,999 < Inhabitants < 3,000
○	2,999 < Inhabitants < 4,000
○	> 3,999 Inhabitants

Distance to Nearest Water Point

●	< 1 Km
●	1 < Km < 3
●	3 < Km < 5
●	> 5 Km
●	Outside the Department

Water Point Type

▲	Drilling
■	Well
⊕	Spring

Source: Data from Province of Houet, Department of Karangasso-Vigue.

Figure 4.2 Schools Proximity and Characteristics

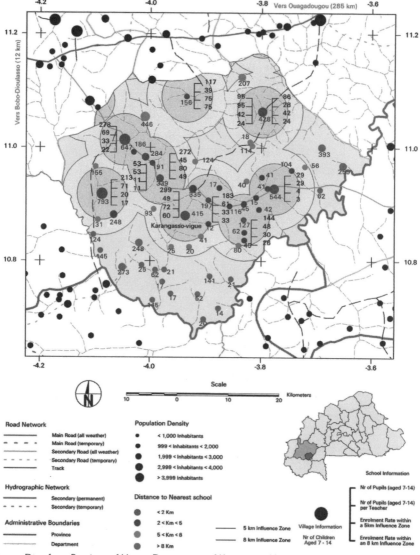

Source: Data from Province of Houet, Department of Karangasso-Vigue.

according to the size of their population, thus showing the demand pressures on each water point. The map also contains information on the road infrastructure, including the quality of the roads, and on the hydrographic networks. Figure 4.2 shows the location of schools and the communities that are covered by these schools within a distance of 5 kilometers and with a distance of 8 kilometers.

The application of these data for predicting poverty across communities in Burkina Faso had to be constrained in this study to a smaller data set, since not all information was available for all villages at the time the data were collected. In particular, Table 4.1 indicates that the data obtained from the Ministry of Water Management were limited to 25 provinces, or 5,207 out of the country's 6,821 villages. Data for the remaining 5 provinces were subsequently collected from the Ministry of Water Management, but these data were collected in another survey and there were very few variables that were comparable between the two surveys. In some villages there were also missing data on other variables and, for this reason, the number of villages in the final prediction analysis had to be reduced to 3,871, or 57 percent of the country's total number of villages. Tables 4.2 and 4.3 provide the details of the variables used in the final analysis, also emphasizing the limited coverage of some of these variables The lack of sufficient data for all of the country's 6,821 villages is, of course, a cause of concern. Some of the missing data are available in the archives of the different ministries and, in principle, could be retrieved. However, if a significant number of villages still do not have all the necessary data, targeting will have to be made at higher levels of geographical aggregation of the department or the provinces. Targeting at these levels would still have to use the predictions of the village levels of poverty, which were obtained in this study for all the villages

Table 4.2 Descriptive Statistics on Variables Used in the Estimation

| | | | URBAN | | | RURAL | | |
| | | | | Number | | | Number | |
Aggregation level *	Variable	Mean∞	Standard Error∞	of observ*	Standard Error∞	Mean∞	of observ*	Data source**
Household	Children 0–6 per adult (15–50 years) in household	0.530	0.495	2,671	0.779	0.598	5,508	PS
Household	Children 7–14 per adult in household	0.618	0.590	2,671	0.748	0.640	5,508	PS
Household	Elderly (50+) per adult in household	0.183	0.343	2,671	0.313	0.426	5,508	PS
Household	Literate head in household	0.477	0.499	2,736	0.134	0.341	5,906	PS
Household	Percent male adults literate in household	0.562	0.422	2,736	0.177	0.313	5,906	PS
Household	Percent female adults literate in household	0.373	0.397	2,736	0.053	0.174	5,906	PS
Household	Livestock units per capita	0.123	0.909	2,736	0.442	0.943	5,906	PS
Village	Distance to nearest rural primary school	—	—	—	2.29	5.64	4,412	DGH
Village	Teachers per child 7–14 years	0.014	0.002	2,736	0.005	0.006	5,760	EDU
Village	Distance to nearest health facility	—	—	—	4.79	7.77	4,434	DGH
Village	Whether nearest facility has safe water	0.82	0.39	2,416	0.034	0.18	4,434	DGH
Village	Number of pumps per rural community	—	—	—	7.35	10.64	5,241	DGH
Village	Existence of an all-weather road	—	—	—	0.57	0.50	4,434	DGH
Department	Cultivated area in department per capita	0.211	0.221	2,736	0.507	0.301	5,760	FEWS
Department	Average rainfall 1980–94	65.80	10.07	2,736	62.50	14.84	5,760	METEO
Department	1994 absolute value of deviation of rainfall from average	19.45	14.49	2,736	22.58	12.96	5,760	METEO
Department	Average length rainy season 1982–92	9.52	1.34	2,736	9.53	2.00	5,760	FEWS
Department	Average vegetation index 1982–92	0.114	0.034	2,736	0.136	0.051	5,760	FEWS
Department	Homogeneity rainy season 1982–92	0.162	0.019	2,736	0.161	0.036	5,760	FEWS

— Not available.

* For community level variables, the same value is assumed for all the households of the community.

** Acronyms are given in table 4.1 on data sources.

∞ Weighted using sampling weights.

Source: Authors' calculations.

Table 4.3 Descriptive Statistics on Variables Used in the Prediction

			URBAN				RURAL	
Aggregation Level *	Variable	Mean∞	Standard error∞	Number of observ.*	Mean∞	Standard error∞	Number of observ.*	Data source **
Village	Children 0–6 per adult (15–50 years) in household	0.656	0.110	300	0.645	0.227	6,818	NC
Village	children 7–14 per adult in household	0.593	0.120	300	0.563	0.280	6,818	NC
Village	elderly (50+) per adult in household	0.320	0.076	300	0.348	0.351	6,818	NC
Province	Literate head in household	0.450	0.181	191	0.113	0.075	6,711	PS
Province	Percent male adults literate in household	0.522	0.147	191	0.141	0.079	6,711	PS
Province	Percent female adults literate in household	0.323	0.149	191	0.044	0.034	6,711	PS
Province	Livestock units per capita	0.147	0.090	191	0.492	0.263	6,711	AGRI
Village	Distance to nearest rural primary school	—	—	—	4.39	5.04	4,556	DGH
Village	Teachers per child 7–14 years	0.023	0.032	295	0.003	0.011	4,753	EDU
Village	Distance to nearest health facility	—	—	—	6.79	7.46	4,393	DGH
Village	Whether nearest facility has safe water	0.15	0.35	219	0.005	0.073	4,390	DGH
Village	Number of pumps per rural community	—	—	—	2.350	2.765	5,425	DGH
Village	Existence of an all-weather road	—	—	—	0.43	0.50	4,618	DGH
Department	Cultivated area in department per capita	0.669	0.605	300	0.751	0.717	6,821	FEWS
Department	Average rainfall 1980–94	65.52	15.34	300	69.16	16.34	6,821	METEO
Department	1994 absolute value of deviation of rainfall from average	18.90	11.54	300	18.61	13.95	6,520	METEO
Department	Average length rainy season 1982–92	10.19	2.31	300	10.77	2.44	6,520	FEWS
Department	Average vegetation index 1982–92	0.126	0.054	300	0.121	0.051	6,821	FEWS
Department	Homogeneity rainy season 1982–92	0.152	0.038	300	0.153	0.036	6,821	FEWS

— Not available

* For department or province level variables, the same value is assumed for all the households of the community.

** Acronyms are given in table 4.1 on data sources.

∞ Weighted using total population relative to village population.

Source: Authors' calculations.

outside the sample since it cannot make direct use of the LSMS survey. The reason is that the sampling frame and the sample size do not provide an adequate representation of all departments and provinces.

Similarly to the LSMS surveys, the sampling for the Priority Survey used in the estimation of the consumption model was semi-stratified (INSD 1996). The survey was designed to be representative at both the national and regional levels. First, the country is divided into seven regions: five rural regions that represent five agro-climatic areas; and two urban regions, one comprising Ouagadougou and Bobo-Dioulasso, the two main cities, and the other one comprising all the other remaining cities. A total of 434 enumeration areas were selected from all seven regions on the basis of socioeconomic characteristics. In each of the 434 enumeration areas, 20 households were randomly selected. In the econometric estimation, however, the sample size had to be reduced to 5,618 households and 201 enumeration areas as a result of the missing data for 5 provinces and the incomplete data on certain variables in a few other villages.

The Empirical Model

As discussed in the "Methodology" section, the econometric analysis has two parts. First, a consumption model is specified for the households included in the Priority Survey. Second, this model is used to predict for poverty levels by community, for all communities included in the GIS database. Table 4.2 presents the data used in the econometric analysis. The corresponding community-level variables used for the prediction are presented in table 4.3. To estimate household consumption levels, we used a standard reduced-form framework in which income (measured in terms of household consumption) is regressed on household characteristics, including human and physical capital, as well as on community-level characteristics.[9] Some community characteristics are specified at the village level, whereas others, primarily the agro-climatic conditions, are specified at the department or region levels.

The Priority Survey contains a limited but important set of variables that can be used to explain households' consumption levels. In this study, the household-level explanatory variables had to be selected to allow aggregation at the community level, and thus be used for the prediction. This limited the choice of explanatory variables to only those household-level variables for which the corresponding mean values at the community level were available for all communities in the country. Consequently, several variables that are usually found to be significant in a consumption model, such as the education level of household members (as opposed to the literacy of the household's head), could not be included in the estimation. Furthermore, data on household assets and land holdings, which are also significant explanatory variables in most consumption models, were not available in the Burkina Faso PS. This reduced the explanatory power of the model, and very likely created also a standard missing variable problem. Moreover, since the underlying data are cross-section, household heterogeneity—a common problem affecting any regression of welfare indicators—is also hard to address. Despite these reservations, we were able to collect data on most of the important explanatory variables and include them in the model (see table 4.2). They include demographic variables, variables that characterize the household's human capital such as literacy rates, and the household's physical capital such as livestock.

Table 4.2 also lists the village- and department-level variables included in the econometric estimation. Department-level variables are primarily climatic data and department-level means of certain household variables (for example, average area of cultivated land in the Department) which were obtained from the Ministry of Agriculture. In the analysis of the impact of climatic factors, we distinguished between the impact of the long-term climatic characteristics and the impact of temporary fluctuations by including among the explanatory variables the average level of rainfall during the past 15 years, as well as the absolute value of the deviation of the past year's level of rainfall from the long-term average. The village-level explanatory variables include also data on the distance to schools and health facilities, the quality of the access road, the quality of these facilities, and water supply in the community.

Estimating Poverty within the Sample

Table 4.4 provides some descriptive statistics on poverty and consumption per adult equivalent by agro-ecological zones in rural and urban areas of Burkina Faso. The poverty line in these estimations was equal to two-thirds of the country's mean level of consumption per adult equivalent. The table emphasizes the large difference in the incidence of poverty between urban and rural households and the much higher standard of living in the country's two main cities. In rural areas, the western region has relatively lower rates of poverty, whereas in the other regions, poverty rates are higher and the differences between these regions are rather small.

In the econometric analysis, consumption per adult equivalent was regressed on the explanatory variables listed in table 4.2, according to the linear model in equation 4.2. The model was estimated via the maximum likelihood method, in which the regression coefficients and the heteroscedastic errors were jointly estimated.[10] By allowing for heteroscedasticity by community, the community-level information can be used for predicting the mean level of consumption per standard adult as well as the variations of consumption around this mean level. This estimated variance within a community may provide some information on the extent of inequality in the distribution of consumption within that community. The regression analysis was conducted separately for households in rural and urban areas.[11] The results for the consumption regression are reported in table 4.5a, and the results for the error regression are reported in table 4.5b.

Table 4.4 Poverty and Consumption in Burkina Faso: Estimates of the Priority Survey (1994)

Level of aggregation	Consumption per adult equivalent[a]	Headcount[b]
Ouest	7,573	0.56
Sud/Sud-Est	5,699	0.67
Centre-Nord	4,952	0.74
Centre-Sud	5,240	0.75
Nord	6,122	0.64
Other urban	12,173	0.39
Bobo/Ouaga	20,768	0.14
Whole country	8,766	0.58

a. In CFA francs per month.
b. Poverty line is set at two-thirds of mean consumption.
Source: Authors' calculations.

Table 4.5a Regression Results—Dependent Variable Is Log (Consumption per Standard Adult)

Variable	Rural		Urban	
	Coeff.	T-value	Coeff.	T-value
Constant	7.71	52.48**	10.82	21.99**
Children 0–6 per adult (15–50 years) in household	0.02	1.55	0.01	0.40
Children 7–14 per adult in household	−0.03	−1.67+	−0.04	−1.60
Elderly (50+) per adult in household	0.03	1.24	−0.13	−2.91**
Literate head in household	0.18	3.66**	0.33	7.63**
Percent male adults literate in household	0.13	2.48*	0.16	3.18**
Percent female adults literate in household	0.55	8.41**	0.42	10.11**
Livestock units per capita(/10)	0.93	11.06**	0.31	1.49
Distance to nearest rural primary school(/100)	−0.48	−2.80**	—	—
Teachers per child 7–14 years (*10)	0.21	1.07	−0.39	−0.22
Distance to nearest health facility(*100)	0.18	1.58	—	—
Whether nearest facility has safe water	0.14	2.92**	0.92	5.24**
Number of pumps per rural community(/100)	0.34	3.27**	—	—
All-weather road?	0.10	4.83**	—	—
Cultivated area in department per capita	0.01	0.32	1.66	5.29**
Average rainfall 1980–94(/100)	0.53	3.39**	−1.64	−2.28*
1994 absolute value of deviation from average (divided by 100)	−0.22	−2.78**	−0.44	−2.03*
Average length rainy season 1982–92	−0.01	−0.69	−0.06	−0.98
Average variable: vegetation index 1982–92	−0.54	−1.81+	8.17	3.24**
Homogeneity rainy season 1982–92	2.50	8.38**	−12.26	−3.63**
F-joint significance regression	F[19,4107]	=34.58**	F[15,2346]	=53.70**
Number of valid observations	4,119		2,362	

** = Significant at 1 percent; * = Significant at 5 percent; + = Significant at 10 percent
Source: Authors' calculations.

In the regression results for both urban and rural areas, multiplicative heteroscedasticity cannot be rejected at 1 percent.[12]

Because maximum likelihood estimation was used to jointly determine the coefficients in the model and the heteroscedasticity structure, no simple R^2 can be reported. The first step, Ordinary Least System (OLS) estimates of the model, indicate, however, that the adjusted R^2 is quite low, with R^2 equal to 0.28 for the urban population and equal to 0.17 for the rural population. These low levels are primarily due to the restrictions on the choice of variables included in the model, restrictions assuring that these variables are available for all communities outside the sample. When all the household- and community-level variables available in the PS were used in the estimation, the value of R^2 in the regression for rural households rose to 0.50. The low values of the adjusted R^2 with the more limited set of explanatory variables required us to make significant adjustments in the application of the results in the prediction model. These adjustments are discussed in the next section. The results show, however, that the variables included in the model have strong joint significance, and that a substantial number of household-

Table 4.5b Regression Results: Estimated Variance with Multiplicative Heteroscedasticity

Variable	Rural		Urban	
	Coeff.	T-value	Coeff.	T-value
Constant	0.12	5.03**	0.03	1.75+
Children 0–6 per adult (15–50 years) in household (community mean)	0.40	2.85**	–0.86	–3.68**
Children 7–14 per adult in household (community mean)	0.79	6.27**	1.12	5.08**
Elderly (50+) per adult in household (community mean)	–0.29	–1.64+	0.47	1.53
Literate head in household (community mean)	0.49	3.86**	0.09	0.91
Percent male adults literate in household (community mean)	–0.26	–1.96*	0.12	1.12
Percent female adults literate in household (community mean)	0.11	0.90	0.05	0.70
Livestock units per capita (community mean)	–0.05	–0.94	0.00	0.04
Distance to nearest rural primary school	0.00	0.07	—	—
Teachers per child 7–14 years (*100)	0.20	4.70**	2.00	4.95**
Distance to nearest health facility	0.00	–0.97	—	—
Whether nearest facility has safe water	–0.38	–3.28**	–1.47	–3.63**
Number of pumps per rural community	0.01	2.16*	—	—
All-weather road?	0.20	4.03**	—	—
Cultivated area in department per capita	0.33	3.05**	–1.03	–1.33
Average rainfall 1980–94	0.02	4.20**	0.02	1.38
1994 absolute value of deviation from average	0.00	1.14	0.00	–0.38
Average length rainy season 1982–92	0.09	2.78**	0.00	–0.01
Average variable: vegetation index 1982–92(*10)	0.31	4.36**	–3.19	–5.56**
Homogeneity rainy season 1982–92(*10)	–0.16	–2.25*	4.35	5.65**
Breusch-Pagan LM heteroscedasticity	=603.35**	(19 d.f.)	=158.33	(15 d.f.)
Glesjer-test multiplicative heteroscedasticity	F[19,4107]	=3.66**	F[15,2328]	=3.66**

** = significant at 1 percent; * = significant at 5 percent; + = significant at 10 percent
Note: A positive coefficient of the explanatory variable indicates that this variable has the effect of raising the variance; a negative coefficient indicates that this variable has the effect of lowering the variance.
Source: Authors' calculations.

and community-level variables are highly significant. The following results stand out:

- The household-level variables that are most closely correlated with the level of consumption in both rural and urban areas are the literacy rates of the adult members of the household.[13]
- The dependency rates, namely the number of children and elderly persons per adult in the household, do not seem to have a clear effect on consumption of rural households, whereas for urban households, dependency rates, particularly the number of elderly persons per adult in the household, have a significant impact by reducing the level of consumption per adult equivalent.
- Livestock units per capita—the only proxy for the household's physical assets available in the Priority Survey—are found to be significantly and positively correlated with consumption in rural areas.

- The community-level variables in rural areas that characterize agro-climatic conditions have a strong impact on consumption. In rural areas that have relatively high levels of long-term average rainfall, relatively normal rain in the survey year, and low rainfall variability over the rainy season, consumption per capita is typically higher.
- Interestingly, however, in the urban consumption function, agro-climatic variables that indicate the average level of rainfall and the homogeneity of the rainy season seem to have a negative effect on consumption. A possible explanation is that the consumption basket of these households includes, in normal years, commodities that were not recorded in the PS survey (which tracks only a small number of consumption items); the reduction in consumption during the normal years recorded in the survey is therefore spurious. Another possible explanation is that these variables are correlated with certain significant missing variables that have a negative impact on the consumption of urban households. The data we had at our disposal did not allow us, however, to make a further analysis of these effects, however intriguing.
- In rural areas, the level of consumption in villages that are further away from schools is generally lower. No similar effect is revealed with respect to the distance to health facilities. A possible explanation is that in some regions, villages located further away from the health facility receive services from mobile health clinics.
- In both urban and rural areas, the quality of the services in the health facility—approximated by the variable that indicates the availability of safe drinking water in the facility—is significantly correlated with the level of per capita consumption in the surrounding villages and urban neighborhoods. Only about one-third of the health facilities in Burkina Faso have safe drinking water.
- In rural areas, the quality of the infrastructure, indicated by the availability of safe drinking water in the village (measured by the number of functioning pumps),and the quality of the access road to the village, has a significant and positive impact on consumption. In villages that have access to an all-weather access road, mean consumption is nearly 10 percent higher than in villages that do not. The greater opportunities to trade, rather than produce for own-consumption, and the better alternatives for nonagricultural work that access to an all-weather road provides, are the main reasons for this effect.
- The coefficients that determine the pattern of the village-level error terms indicate that in villages with a relatively high proportion of literate heads of households, the distribution of per capita consumption is less equal than in villages with a low proportion of literate heads of households—possibly because in a village with more literate adults,

the income differences between households with less educated heads and households with more educated heads are relatively larger.

- In villages with relatively high average levels of rainfall, there are larger differences between households in their levels of per capita consumption, possibly because in these villages some households are better equipped and more capable to take advantage of the better conditions for agriculture.
- Villages with higher average land holdings per household have a larger variability of per capita consumption.

Several of the above interpretations of the results suggest possible causal relationships between the explanatory variables and the dependent variable. However, these interpretations are intended primarily as background for a more thorough evaluation of the possible policy implications of the results, and they are made under the usual caveat of possible endogeneity of the community-level variables, which means that correlation need not be an indication of causality. For example, the government policy of locating relatively more public education facilities in the relatively poor villages as part of an anti-poverty program will lead to high negative correlation between the average level of per capita consumption and the proximity of the village to school (Rosenzweig and Wolpin 1986). The availability of a large number of water pumps in a village, to take another example, need not be the cause of a relatively high standard of living of the households in that village, but rather the effect of the larger demand for safe drinking water of the more affluent villagers.

In the present analysis, however, the objective of the regression estimates is to construct a prediction model that can identify the very poor and the least poor villages. The quality of these predictions depends only on the degree of correlation between the explanatory and the dependent variables, irrespective of whether or not this high correlation indicates causality. If, for example, health facilities are systematically placed in the poorer villages, then the variable that indicates the distance from the village to the health facility can be useful for predicting the standard of living of the households in these villages.[14] Nevertheless, the possibility of endogeneity requires special care in the interpretation of the results for policy purposes.[15] While the significance and size of the coefficients are suggestive, more work would be needed for designing appropriate poverty-reduction policies.

Predicting the Geographical Distribution of Poverty in Burkina Faso

The next step is to apply the regression results obtained for a sample of communities to the data available in the GIS database for all communities in Burkina Faso, in order to predict the distribution of poverty across all communities. As noted earlier in this analysis, we had to focus on the 3,871 out of a total of more than 6,000 villages for which all the necessary information was available to us. The Headcount index of a community is calculated by means of equation 4.5, using the estimates of the parameters that were obtained in the regression analysis. To apply this equation, it was necessary to provide estimates for the level of mean consumption per adult in the community and for the variance of consumption. For the term $E(b'X_{ij} - b')^2$ in equation 4.5, we used the average value per region (rather than per community) in the survey data, while s_j was obtained using the coefficients given in table 4.5b. Mean consumption per standard adult in the communities outside the sample was predicted from the mean values of the explanatory variables for each of these communities, using the coefficients given in table 4.5a.

Before applying these predictions for all the communities outside the sample, we assessed the quality of the predictions by comparing them with the direct estimates of poverty in the sample of 201 communities which were included in the PS. Toward that end, we calculated the correlation coefficients of the predicted and calculated poverty levels for these villages. The value of the Pearson-correlation coefficient was 0.51 and it was strongly statistically significant. For policy decisions, the more relevant criterion is the relation between the order of villages on the poverty scale according to the incidence of poverty determined by the predictions, and the order determined by the direct estimates from the PS survey. To test this aspect of the prediction model, we calculated the Spearman-rank correlation coefficient between the order established by the direct estimates of poverty and the order established by the model's predictions. That correlation coefficient was also strongly significant at 0.43. Table 4.6 provides another illustration of the quality of the predictions by comparing the estimated and the predicted values of the Headcount measure of poverty for selected communities in three provinces. Although the predicted values of the Headcount measures per community often fall outside the confidence interval of the calculated levels of poverty, the rank order of communities from the richest to the poorest in each province is quite similar.

Despite these results of the tests, the low levels of R^2 in the regression analysis of equation 4.5 and the low quality of the data prevented us from making a direct use of these predictions. Moreover, these predictions rely on the assumption of normality of the error term. One common test for normality is the Jarque-Bera test; our estimate of the Jarque-Bera statistic was 11.8, and the normality hypothesis therefore had to be rejected.[16] As a result, we did not use the prediction to establish a complete order of the communities on the poverty scale. Instead, we divided the 3,871 villages and urban communities for which predictions were made into four categories of poverty, ranging from the poorest to the least poor, according to the predicted

Table 4.6 Comparison of the Model's Predictions of the Headcount Measure of Poverty and the Direct Estimates for Villages in the Sample for Three Provinces

Province	Village ID #	Within sample estimates*	Outside sample predictions
Kossi	4,426	0.28 (0.01)	0.24
	3,786	0.33 (0.01)	0.67
	512	0.54 (0.01)	0.64
	2,936	0.54 (0.04)	0.65
	5,266	0.57 (0.02)	0.56
	5,117	0.64 (0.02)	0.69
	1,626	0.68 (0.02)	0.70
	1,556	0.69 (0.01)	0.61
	1,290	0.78 (0.01)	0.70
	50	0.80 (0.01)	0.57
Kouritenga	744	0.64 (0.03)	0.66
	6,233	0.72 (0.03)	0.66
	657	0.75 (0.01)	0.57
	1,627	0.80 (0.03)	0.74
	2,943	0.83 (0.01)	0.65
	3,213	1.00 (0.00)	0.64
	3,828	1.00 (0.00)	0.76
Mouhoun	1,278	0.23 (0.01)	0.32
	790	0.36 (0.02)	0.52
	6,753	0.48 (0.03)	0.57
	4,982	0.48 (0.02)	0.56
	740	0.50 (0.02)	0.52
	5,149	0.57 (0.02)	0.52
	5,635	0.72 (0.01)	0.60
	6,674	0.72 (0.01)	0.65

*Standard errors in brackets (Deaton 1997, p.47). The figures are weighted by household size.
Source: Authors' calculations.

levels of poverty. Despite the errors in these predictions, our results suggest that the majority of the villages in the lowest category of the poorest villages are likely to have a higher incidence of poverty than the majority of the villages in the highest category of the least poor villages. The villages in the poorest category are therefore candidates for targeted poverty alleviation programs, and the villages in the least poor category are candidates for cost-recovery program. Given the data limitations in Burkina Faso, effective targeting would have to focus only on these two extreme categories to reduce the leakage as much as possible and keep within budget constraints. In the present circumstances, further improvements in targeting when the available data are rather limited and their quality quite low can be achieved by dividing the villages into a larger number of categories and focusing on the villages in the two extreme categories. Future research aimed at improving targeting would have to focus, however, on efforts to improve the quality of the data as well as generating additional series of georeferenced data.

Table 4.7 presents the geographical distribution of the rural and urban communities across these categories of well-being in the different provinces of Burkina Faso. The table was constructed by dividing the villages into the four categories—ranging from the poorest to the least poor—using the

Table 4.7 The Distribution of the Population in the Provinces of Burkina Faso into Four Poverty Categories according to the Classification of Their Communities (Percent)

Province	Poorest	Lower middle	Upper middle	Least poor	Total	Percent of total population
Bam	0	10	36	54	100	0.90
Bazega	13	36	35	16	100	4.85
Boulgou	37	22	32	9	100	7.04
Boulkiemde	41	36	15	7	100	5.99
Ganzourgou	47	33	19	2	100	2.74
Gnagna	24	13	21	41	100	3.73
Gourma	34	17	23	25	100	5.55
Kossi	26	30	29	14	100	6.22
Kouritenga	7	25	43	25	100	3.11
Mouhoun	41	39	18	2	100	6.06
Nahouri	23	29	40	8	100	1.71
Namentenga	4	25	18	52	100	2.16
Oubritenga	9	24	40	27	100	4.73
Oudalan	24	36	19	21	100	1.69
Passore	11	2	18	68	100	3.77
Sanguie	31	23	25	21	100	4.64
Sanmatenga	17	11	25	46	100	7.64
Seno	26	29	19	26	100	4.70
Sissili	41	43	16	0	100	3.69
Soum	3	14	21	61	100	2.54
Sourou	12	12	12	64	100	5.31
Tapoa	60	17	22	1	100	2.12
Yatenga	24	24	31	21	100	6.72
Zoudweogo	3	59	30	8	100	2.40

Note: Poverty line is set at two-thirds of mean consumption.
Source: Authors' calculations.

predicted values of the poverty incidence, and allocating the entire population in each of the villages to the corresponding category. These categories
were determined so that, in the country at large, the population in each category represents 25 percent of the total population. Table 4.7 highlights the
large differences between provinces that make a targeted program even at
the district level quite effective. In nearly 14 percent of the provinces less
than 10 percent of the population were classified in the poorest category,
while in nearly 21 percent of the provinces more than 40 percent of the population were classified in the poorest category.

Targeting at the village level can be much more effective, however, than
targeting at the province level, because within each province there are villages that were classified in the poorest category and villages that were classified in the least poor category. For example, 41 percent of the population
in the province of Boulkiemde live in villages that were classified in the category of the poorest villages, and only 7 percent of the population in this
province live in villages that were classified in the least poor category.
Consider, as an illustration, the five provinces in which at least 40 percent of
the population live in villages that were classified in the poorest category.
Only 3 percent of the population in the four target provinces (which account
for less than 5 percent of the province's total population) live in villages that
were classified in the least poor category—suggesting that leakage is likely
to be quite small. Nearly 43 percent of the population in the target provinces
live in villages that were classified in the poorest category, and they account
for 36 percent of the country's total population that live in the poorest villages. At the other extreme, a cost-recovery program targeted on seven of
the provinces in which more than 40 percent of the population live in villages that were classified in the least poor category will cover 26 percent of
the country's total population but only 13 percent of the country's population that live in the poorest villages. Targeting anti-poverty programs at the
province level is likely, therefore, to be less effective than targeting at the village level, because each province includes villages in which the incidence of
poverty is quite low, thereby raising the leakage. Targeting on villages of the
poorest category is likely to cover a larger share of the country's poor population, entail less leakage relative to a program targeted at the province
level, and imply that in each and every province there will be villages that
will be targeted by the program.

In urban areas, most of the communities were classified in the least poor
category. This result is largely due to the much higher standard of living
and much lower incidence of poverty in urban areas. There are several other
more technical reasons, however, for this classification:

- In urban areas the distinction between poor and non-poor communities is less clear than in rural areas—first, because, in many developing

countries, it is not uncommon to have poor households that reside in relatively affluent urban communities and vice versa, and second, because the communities—as defined in the household surveys—are, in fact, enumeration areas that have been determined by the local authorities for administrative purposes, and their borders are often quite arbitrary. Whereas in rural areas the enumeration areas are generally limited to one or two neighboring villages which tend to have similar living standards, in urban areas, where the distance between neighborhoods is small, enumeration areas often include communities with very different living standards. In our study, we had access to community-level data in urban areas only in the household survey.

• In all other data sources, the towns, including Ougadougou and Bobo-Dioulasso, were considered as single points in the GIS data set. In the econometric analysis, all enumeration areas from each of the large towns had the same community characteristics and thus had to be considered as a single entity.

The main advantages of community targeting are demonstrated in figure 4.3, which shows all the villages in the Province of Sanguie divided into the four categories of well-being. The map shows that in this area, most of the poorest villages are located further away from the urban centers and they are not connected to an all-weather road. The map also highlights the fact that targeting an anti-poverty program on the entire population of the Sanguie province is bound to include many non-poor villages, whereas excluding this province from the program will leave out a considerable number of poor villages.

Finally, to evaluate the effectiveness of community targeting of anti-poverty programs, we conducted a simple simulation experiment. For this experiment, we used the consumption data in the 201 communities for which we had information from the Priority Survey. The simulation design follows closely the framework of Baker and Grosh (1994). It is assumed that the government has a given budget for income transfers to the target population. The effects of the income transfers on poverty are evaluated using the actual household consumption data. The selection of the villages for targeting is determined, however, by the predicted levels of the village poverty determined by the model. The simulations can thus evaluate how effective were these predictions in identifying the poor, by estimating the leakage (the number of non-poor included in the scheme) and the undercoverage (the proportion of poor not reached by the program). The estimates are made for the households included in the survey, but we use the individual sampling weights to measure the impact on the total population at the regional and national levels. The reliability of the regional and national results is therefore affected by the sampling errors that are due to the

Figure 4.3. Poverty Index at Village Level

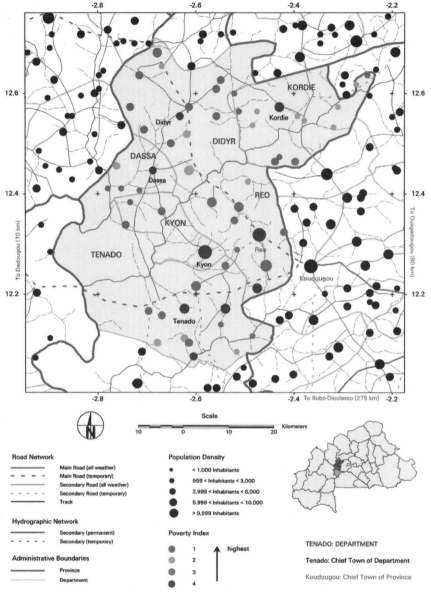

Source: Data from Province of Houet, Department of Karangasso-Vigue.

sampling frame of the PS survey. To evaluate the program, its outcomes are compared with an untargeted uniform transfer scheme, in which all the individuals in the country receive an equal transfer. The targeted program is designed to include only 30 percent of the population, by setting the poverty line accordingly.[17]

Selection of the villages targeted by the program is as follows. All the villages in the sample are first ranked according to the estimated levels of poverty. The villages are selected for targeting starting from the poorest village until (at least) 30 percent of the population is being included in the program.[18] With village-level targeting using the predicted poverty levels per community, the undercoverage is 56 percent and the leakage is slightly over 50 percent. By design, the undercoverage of the untargeted transfers is zero, but the leakage is high. For the untargeted program, the leakage, namely the share of the non-poor covered by the program (in the total population) is 70 percent (since the poverty line has been set so that 30 percent of the population are poor). The targeted program reduces leakage by 20 percent, but this is achieved by a program that leaves more than 50 percent of the poor uncovered.

Conclusion

Geographical targeting of anti-poverty programs can effectively reach the poor while keeping the costs of such programs in check in countries where the information on individual households is incomplete or unavailable and a practical individual or household targeting is therefore not possible. By identifying the geographical areas in which the poor concentrate, these programs can reduce the leakage to the non-poor so that, compared with a non-targeted program, a larger share of the poor population can be reached with a given budget. However, in most countries where geographical targeting is applied, the target areas are the region, the state, or the entire rural area. Although targeting even at these levels can offer considerable savings compared with a non-targeted program, they necessarily involve substantial leakage to non-poor households that reside in the target areas. Narrow targeting at the level of the community or the administrative department may offer a more effective alternative of reaching the poor, reduce leakage, and lower the costs in countries or regions where the communities are relatively homogeneous in terms of the standard of living of their population. Narrow targeting can be effective when poverty tends to be concentrated in a relatively small number of villages and urban communities. It is often more effective than other methods of targeting because it requires relatively low costs to administer the programs. In addition, by relying primarily on the local authorities, narrow targeting has the potential of ensuring that a larger portion of the benefits will reach the target population.

This chapter presents a methodology of using data from a wide variety of different sources to establish criteria for targeting poverty-alleviation programs at the levels of the village, the urban community, or the local administrative department, and illustrates its application for Burkina Faso. The methodology is based on the construction of a detailed database with information collected from a large number of sources and brought together at the village level as a GIS. Data on the population were collected from several socioeconomic and demographic surveys as well as the population census; data on the road infrastructure, public facilities, and the location of central towns and markets were collected from several government ministries and public administrations; and agro-climatic data were collected from local and international research institutes. An econometric analysis was then conducted with the data of the household survey to identify the variables that best explain the households' consumption levels. The explanatory variables in this analysis included important characteristics of the community—such as the distance to the urban center and the public facilities, the quality of the access road, and the agro-climatic conditions—together with key characteristics of the households in that community—such as literacy levels or dependency ratios. The explanatory variables at the household level were selected so that their mean values per community were available for the majority of the communities in Burkina Faso and not only those covered by the household survey. This made it possible to use the model that has been estimated in the regression analysis with the data of the PS to predict the incidence of poverty in all the villages outside the PS sample, and thereby identify the spatial distribution of poverty at the community level.

In the present analysis for Burkina Faso, constraints on the availability and quality of the data led to considerable prediction errors and prevented us from using the complete ordering of the villages according to their incidence of poverty as was predicted by the econometric analysis. We used a simple method to reduce the impact of these errors by dividing the villages into several categories and focusing only on the categories of the poorest and the least poor villages. Indeed, practical considerations in the application of anti-poverty programs and tight budget constraints are likely to reduce the use of complete ordering. Instead, poverty alleviation programs are likely to focus on villages at the lower end of the distribution, and cost-recovery programs are likely to focus on the villages at the higher end. The limited availability of georeferenced data and the low quality of the data currently available reduced the predictive power of our econometric analysis, and further work would be necessary to augment and improve the stock of relevant data.

Targeting poverty alleviation or cost-recovery programs at lower-level administrative areas of the village or the department have other advantages as well. First, budget constraints are likely to restrict programs that are targeted on larger geographical areas of regions or states, and, as a result, the errors of inclusion and exclusion are likely to be quite high. Targeting on smaller geographical areas can, with the same budget constraints, reach many more of the country's poor. Second, lower-level targeting is likely to include villages and districts in all regions or states and thus be less divisive and contentious on ethnic, social, or political grounds. Third, whereas the differences in the incidence of poverty between regions are primarily due to differences in their agro-climatic conditions, differences in the incidence of poverty between villages within the same region often reflect past biases in policies that led to differences in the quality of their access road or their public services; targeting future policies in light of these criteria can remedy these past biases.

Notes

David Bigman was at the World Bank while this work was done and is currently at ISNAR; Stefan Dercon is at the Catholic University of Leuven, Belgium, and at Oxford University—Centre for the Study of African Economies; Michel Lambotte is at I-Mage, Mons, Belgium; Dominique Guillaume was at the Catholic University of Leuven, Belgium, and at Oxford University—Centre for the Study of African Economies while this work was done and is currently at the International Monetary Fund (IMF). This chapter does not necessarily represent the views of the IMF or its board of directors.

1. For simulated examples from Latin America, see Baker and Grosh (1994).
2. See also Besley and Kanbur (1991), pp. 69–90.
3. These programs may also provide incentives to households to move to the targeted areas, thereby defeating the purpose of the program and raising its costs.
4. Due to data limitations discussed below, the complete data set necessary for the predictions was available only for 3,871 out of the country's 6,821 villages.
5. Simple nutritional adult equivalent scales were used, using 0.7 for a child 5 to 15 years old and 0.3 for younger children. Each adult counted as one.
6. For a poor person, therefore: $y_{ij} < 1$, or $\ln y_{ij} < 0$.
7. Note that the within-village variance of consumption can be written as:

$$E[(Y_{ij} - E(Y_j))^2] = E[(b'X_{ij} - b'X_j^V)^2] + s_j^2$$

in which Y_j is the mean level of consumption in the village. In other words, the variance of consumption is the sum of the squared deviation of predicted household consumption from predicted mean consumption per village and the village-level variance of the prediction model.

8. Hentschel and others (1998) use this property to predict regional poverty from census data.
9. Examples are Glewwe and Kanaan (1989), or Coulombe and McKay (1996). Glewwe (1991) has a useful discussion on the justification for including particular

variables in this type of approach. We will return to the problems related to this specification below.

10. The regression was weighted with individual sampling weights derived from the original sampling frame used by the World Bank/INSD.

11. Pooling tests convincingly rejected running one national regression.

12. The Breusch-Pagan LM test convincingly reject homoskedasticity (see table 4.5a). The Glesjer (1965) test indicates that in both urban and rural areas, the null hypothesis of multiplicative heteroscedasticity cannot be rejected at the 1 percent level.

13. Note that the variables describing the literacy of adults in the households also include the household head.

14. Note that this also requires that the same program-placing rule is used both outside and inside the sample. Since the sample is nationally representative, this may be an appropriate assumption.

15. There are other sources of endogeneity. For example, our approach assumed that location is not a choice variable. Migration is therefore not explicitly considered, requiring further care in the interpretation of the results.

16. This statistic is distributed a Chi-square with two degrees of freedom and the normality hypothesis had to be rejected at 0.997 probability. One should note, however, that the Jarque-Bera test is not robust to the presence of heteroskedasticity, which could not be rejected by the Breusch-Pegan LM test and the Glesjer test. We are not aware of a test of normality in the presence of heteroskedasticity, but the high value of the Jarque-Bera statistic suggest that it is highly probable that the residuals are not distributed normally.

17. The simulation thus sets the poverty line at a lower level than in the previous section of this chapter ("Estimating Poverty within the Sample").

18. Further details, including on the inter-regional distribu tion of leakage and undercoverage, is given in a longer, working paper version of this paper (Bigman and others 1999).

References

Baker, J., and M. Grosh. 1994."Measuring the Effects of Geographic Targeting on Poverty Reduction." LSMS Working Paper 99, The World Bank, Washington, D.C..

Besley, T., and R. Kanbur. 1991. "The Principles of Targeting." In V. Balasubramanyam and S. Lall, eds., *Current Issues in Development Economics.* New York: St. Martin's Press.

Bigman, D., S. Dercon, D. Guillaume, and M. Lambotte. 1999. "Community Targeting for Poverty Reduction in Burkina Faso." *CES Discussion Paper Series,* DPS 99.10, Center for Economic Studies, Leuven.

Coulombe, H., and A. McKay. 1996. "Modeling Determinants of Poverty in Mauritania." *World Development* 24: 1015–1031.

Deaton, A. 1997. *The Analysis of Household Surveys: A Microeconometric Approach to Development Policy.* Washington D.C.: Johns Hopkins University Press.

Glesjer, H. 1965. "A New Test for Heteroscedasticity." *Journal of the American Statistical Association* 60: 539–547.

Glewwe, P. 1991. "Investigating the Determinants of Household Welfare in Côte d'Ivoire." *Journal of Development Economics* 35: 307–337.

Glewwe, P., and O. Kanaan. 1989. "Targeting Assistance to the Poor Using Household Survey Data." Policy, Planning and Research Working Papers, WPS 225, World Bank, Washington. D.C.

Hentschel, J., Lanjouw, J., Lanjouw, P., and J. Poggi. 1998. "Combining Survey Data with Census Data to Construct Spatially Disaggregated Poverty Maps: A Case Study of Ecuador." World Bank, Washington, D.C. Processed.

Institut National de Statistique (INSD). 1996. "Le Profil de pauvrete au Burkina Faso." Ouagadougou, Burkina Faso..

Maddala, G.S. 1983. *Limited Dependent and Qualitative Variables in Econometrics.* Cambridge: Cambridge University Press.

Ravallion, M. 1993. "Poverty Alleviation through Regional Targeting: A Case Study for Indonesia." In K. Hoff, A. Braverman, and J. Stiglitz, *The Economics of Rural Organization.* Oxford: Oxford University Press.

Ravallion, M. 1996. "Issues in Measuring and Modeling Poverty." *Economic Journal* 106 (September): 1328–1343.

Rosenzweig, M., and K. Wolpin. 1986. "Evaluating the Effects of Optimally Distributed Public Programs." *American Economic Review* 76(3): 470–482.

van de Walle, D. 1995. "Public Spending and the Poor: Theory and Evidence: Introduction." In D. van de Walle and Kimberly Nead, eds., *Public Spending and the Poor: Theory and Evidence.* Baltimore: Johns Hopkins University Press.

5

Applying Household Expenditure Survey Data to Improve Poverty Targeting: The Case of Ghana

Hippolyte Fofack

HOUSEHOLD SURVEYS, WHICH HAVE TRADITIONALLY provided the basis for poverty studies and the design of targeted programs, are conducted rather infrequently. The frequency of these surveys was originally planned at five-year intervals; over the past decade, however, very few countries in the developing world have followed this course in their statistical program and analysis plan. This irregularity has made it difficult to assess the effects of macroeconomic reforms on poverty and income inequality in the short and medium term. The major constraint in conducting household surveys more regularly and frequently is their high cost, which is increasingly difficult to meet in the context of limited budget.

The need to have reliable poverty maps to assess changes in poverty and allocate scarce resources to the most needy is fully recognized by policy-makers.[1] To regularly update these maps, several surveys have been designed and proposed as short-term alternatives to integrated surveys. These alternatives are generally defined as light monitoring surveys (LMS), because they are a subset of much broader comprehensive surveys and are designed to provide quick and regular identification of groups on which targeted interventions should be focused. These broader surveys include Rapid Appraisal methods (see Narayan and Srinivasan 1994) and Priority Surveys (PS) (see Marchant and Grootaert 1991). More comprehensive surveys include Living Standards Measurement Surveys (LSMS) (see Grosh and Glewwe 1998) and Integrated Surveys (IS) (see Delaine and others1992).

Integrated Surveys and the similar Living Standards Measurement Surveys are broad in scope and were specifically designed for integrated poverty analysis;[2] they are known to be more appropriate for policy analysis (see Ravallion and Gaurav 1993, Ravallion 1996, and Deininger and Squire 1996). More specifically, the IS and LSMS questionnaires are more comprehensive than other surveys (Demery and others 1992); they provide extensive information on household income, credit, and savings; household enterprise; valuation of durable, productive, and financial assets; agricultural livestock; food processing and consumption of own produce; food and non-food consumption; and other expenditures. The turnaround time is particularly long for these surveys, since the enumeration is spread over a year, with multiple visits to households in order to capture seasonality. Reduction in nonsampling errors is achieved through low recall periods. However, a much smaller sample size is recommended for IS and LSMS surveys to contain the costs and limit the time lag between data collection and production of results for policy analysis. This constitutes a major constraint on both the application of the survey for poverty analysis in a country's different geographic areas, and also for geographical targeting, because the sample size at the subregional level is too small to provide the minimum data required for sound inference.

Light monitoring surveys in contrast are administered very quickly and are less broad in the scope of data collected, but much broader in terms of geographical coverage. Their questionnaires are designed to collect information to construct key socioeconomic indicators and are much shorter. Moreover, unlike integrated surveys, LMS instruments collect a limited set of information on single visits to households, and can neither capture seasonality of consumption pattern nor provide an accurate estimate of consumption and income. However, from the design standpoint, a short questionnaire and a single visit to households reduces the time allocated to data collection, and allows for a larger sample size with a better representation of the different geographical areas.

The limited coverage of expenditure items in LMS does have some major drawbacks for policy analysis. Short questionnaires focus data collection of household expenses on a few sets of goods, and consumption aggregates based on subsets are likely to provide total expenditure estimates that are lower than estimates from more integrated type surveys (see Deaton and Grosh 1998). Moreover, it is highly unlikely that underestimation of total consumption will be uniform across households, causing a simple shift in the Engel curve, and thus preserving the ranking for policy analysis. Rather, the degree of bias in estimating household expenditure aggregates varies significantly across households and regions, in part because changes over time and regional differences in consumption patterns, which are determinants of the overall distribution of income and expenditure, are not taken into account. The representation of distributions of income and expenditure under integrated and light monitoring surveys differ significantly.

Despite the differences between integrated surveys and LMS, and evidence that the latter might provide inaccurate estimates of aggregated expenditure, LMS instruments have been used extensively as tools for policy design. Particularly in Sub-Saharan African countries, major recommendations made in Poverty Assessments are drawn from these surveys (see World Bank 1997). This chapter shows that welfare indicators estimated from LMS are biased, and the bias affects not only representation of the magnitude of poverty, but also its apparent spatial distribution. Dispersal rates are not maintained under the LMS design, in part because household per capita expenditure, which is the basis for targeting, underestimates aggregate expenditure and may yield inaccurate poverty maps. Any targeted program based on LMS might cause leakage in income transfer schemes. In the past, attempts have been made to circumvent these limitations and provide more accurate welfare estimates for improved policy analysis in the absence of appropriate data. These include proxy means tests (see Ravallion 1989, Ravallion and Gaurav 1993, and Grosh and Baker 1995) and combining household surveys for optimal household ranking (see Fofack 1997).

The objective of this chapter is to investigate how comprehensive surveys can be combined with LMS to improve geographical targeting, achieve efficient transfers for poverty alleviation, and improve inference on welfare measures drawn from LMS. The paper is organized as follows. The next section ("Limits of Light Monitoring Surveys as Instruments for Targeting") assesses the limits of LMS when they are used for poverty analysis. In particular, it is shown that poverty maps constructed from these surveys do not reflect the spatial distribution of poverty. A method for designing more efficient targeted schemes that combines comprehensive surveys and LMS to derive poverty predictors for imputing consumption is proposed in the section titled "Estimating Total Expenditure for Improved Targeting." Results and policy implications of the proposed method on targeting and poverty mapping are assessed in the section titled "Results and Implications for Geographical Targeting." In particular, it is shown that imputing consumption significantly reduces the error of inclusion and improves inferences about welfare drawn from LMS. The final section provides some concluding remarks.

Limits of Light Monitoring Surveys as Instruments for Targeting

This section looks at the implications of errors in measurement in poverty mapping when light monitoring surveys are used as a basis for poverty analysis. Error frequency and impact is ascertained by comparing welfare indicators estimated from LMS with the ones derived from the more comprehensive LSMS. In order to allow full comparability, we extract LMS-aggregated expenditure from LSMS. In that regard, this study can be viewed as a counterfactual experiment, since estimates of total expenditures are actually known, and the study aims at assessing the variation in poverty measures through cross-sectional analysis.

There are several benefits in adopting the construction described above when comparing these two surveys. In a country where both light monitoring and comprehensive surveys have been carried out, the absence of reliable regional price indices and national consumer price indices has been a major impediment for cross comparison. Therefore, adjusting for seasonality and changes over time, monitoring inflation is essential for cross comparison and trends analysis. Moreover, in addition to the implied seasonal variation, changes over time in the sampling frame and design make it difficult to assess the performance of these surveys in light of household welfare estimates. Under the method used here, comparisons are made on the same households for which expenditure aggregates have been suitably constructed under both the full LSMS assumption and hypothesized LMS assumption. There is no time lag in data collection between the two surveys, and errors in measurement associated with variation in the sampling design are completely eliminated because the comparisons are made on the same unit of analysis.

Distribution of Expenditure from LSMS and LMS

The present study is based on the last Ghana Living Standards Survey (the GLSS 3, conducted in 1992), which is similar to the standard LSMS survey. The GLSS 3 was the third round of a series of living standards surveys initiated in Ghana. This was a nationally representative household survey, based on the master sample of enumeration areas defined by the 1984 population census.[3] The data collection was spread over a whole year. A high response rate was achieved, and this survey design provided a total sample size of about 4,500 households. GLSS 3 differs from the two previous rounds of household surveys carried out in Ghana because it collects data on all dimensions of household welfare and economic behavior. The sections on household income and expenditure are comprehensive and much more disaggregated than previously.[4] Overall, estimates of this third round are considered more accurate (see GSS 1995), in part because they are based on much shorter bounded recall periods—seven recalls at two-day intervals in rural areas, and 10 recalls at three-day intervals in urban areas.

Although LSMS and IS surveys collect extended information on both household income and expenditure, the data on the latter variable are used as a measure of economic welfare. In part because nonsampling errors due to underreporting of income create large biases in reported household income, there are strong theoretical reasons for the use of an expenditure variable (see Deaton and Muellbauer 1980). For this study, therefore, expenditure data is retained and serves as the basis for differentiating poor from non-poor households, for constructing poverty maps to design improved targeted programs.

Estimates of household total expenditure on food and non-food constructed from the GLSS 3 data uses six aggregates and seventeen subaggregates. These estimates account for all household expenses including total household expenditure on rent, with imputed rent calculated from owner-occupied, rent-free, or subsidized dwellings; consumption of home-produced food; and the value of wage income received by household members in the form of food. Other imputed expenditures include total wage income paid in kind to household members, the value of non-farm enterprise produce consumed by households itself, and the use value of durable goods. The value of remittances made by the household, and all other expenses, such as for education and household amenities, were also included in the overall total expenditure aggregates. Missing values and outliers were imputed on each variable (see GSS 1996).[5] Since the survey was carried out over one year, all expenditure data were adjusted to take account of inflation over the survey period, and the monetary values are based on March 1992 prices. However, no adjustment for seasonal effects on household expenditure was made.

The aggregate total household expenditure is obtained by summing up across all household expenditure items, subaggregates, and aggregates on food and non-food items. We first sum across items and subaggregates to obtain intermediate values for expenditure aggregates at the household level, as shown in equation 5.1:

$$S_k^h = \sum_{j=1}^{N} \lambda \delta_j^h P_{jk}^h Q_{jk}^h \qquad (5.1)$$

where h stands for households varying from 1 to the total sample size, and $j = 1,2, \dots , N$ is the total number of items. The total household expenditure for LSMS surveys is obtained by summing across expenditure aggregates, as shown in equation 5.2

$$\hat{Y}_{LSMS}^h = \sum_{k=1}^{A} S_k^h = \sum_{k=1}^{A}\sum_{j=1}^{N} \lambda \delta_j^h P_{jk}^h Q_{jk}^h \qquad (5.2)$$

where $k = 1,2, \dots , A$ is the total number of subaggregates, and $\hat{Y}_{LSMS}^h$ is the total household LSMS expenditure aggregates for a given household h. P_{jk}^h and Q_{jk}^h are price and quantity of item j, the component of aggregate k consumed by a given household h. The multiplicative factor δ_j^h is the frequency of purchase (recall period) of a given item within household h, and λ is the seasonality factor or frequency of visits to the households.

Estimates of household total expenditure from LMS design are obtained by similar aggregation, except that the number of items and subaggregates are much smaller. The components of total household aggregated expenditure are selected following the recommendations of the standard PS, which suggest limiting the collection of expenditure data to key food items and a few non-food items (see Demery and others 1991). The total expenditure aggregate constructed for this experiment is based on three subaggregates: two non-food which include expenditure on education and health, and a food expenditure aggregate containing 10 key food items.[6] The total household expenditure from the hypothesized PS is constructed by summing up across these three subaggregates, which of course have already been adjusted to account for inflation over time. The adjustment is necessary because the PS design recommends a single visit to the households, and inference on welfare is drawn assuming no seasonal variation in the consumption pattern. In fact, the relatively short time period devoted to data collection reduces the range of price fluctuations. Estimates of total household expenditure from the hypothesized PS can be provided by equation 5.3:

$$\hat{Y}_{PS}^h = \sum_{k=1}^{a<A} S_k^h = \sum_{k=1}^{a<A} \sum_{j=1}^{n<N} \delta_j^h P_{jk}^h Q_{jk}^h \qquad (5.3)$$

Note that in the PS estimate, the number of subaggregates is much smaller ($a < A$), and the number of items is much smaller as well ($n < A$). The seasonality factor λ does not appear in the PS aggregates because the data are collected in a single visit to households. Since the number of items and subaggregates is smaller in the PS design, this value is generally underestimated and one would expect the following ordering between the two constructed variables: $\hat{Y}_{PS}^h < \hat{Y}_{PS}^h$. In the remaining of this chapter, these two variables are adjusted for the effects of household size to produce the household per capita expenditure data used for analysis.

Table 5.1 provides summary statistics relative to these two variables. Note that the variance of the distribution of total household per capita expenditure from LMS is relatively high, because the coefficient of variation of the LMS per capita expenditure is higher than the LSMS estimates across all regions, despite the fact that the PS mean per capita expenditure is uniformly smaller.

While the ratio of regional estimates of mean per capita expenditure to national estimates shows less variations in the LSMS design—the ratio oscillates around 1, indicating that these values do not differ markedly from the national estimate—large fluctuations are observed when these ratios are estimated from LMS. While the mean per capita expenditure in rural areas

Table 5.1 Summary Statistics Distribution of Per Capita Expenditure by Survey Type and across Region

Regions	Priority survey			LSMS survey			*PS LSMS
	Share of national mean PCE	CV	Max	Share of national mean PCE	CV	Max	t-test stat
Accra	2.1651	181.3	698520	1.2097	155.69	2557883	12.79
Other urban	1.8803	175.1	369300	1.0467	155.88	1647617	20.1
Rural forest	0.6578	231.05	197760	1.0123	147.4	2731410	18.17
Rural coastal	0.4961	269.86	194700	0.9928	178.55	3412836	20.58
Savannah	0.4907	350.34	229500	0.8769	150.81	1391917	19.72
All urban	1.9506	179.13	698520	1.0869	157.68	2557883	23.5
All rural	0.5285	285.52	229500	0.9569	166.1	3412836	32.6
National	—	278.5	698520	—	163.87	3412836	40.2

— Not available

* Comparison of the distributions of total expenditure from the two surveys.

Source: Author's calculations.

represents approximately 95 percent of national mean per capita in the full GLSS 3 survey, the bias is more pronounced in the PS setting, where the mean per capita expenditure in rural areas represents only 52 percent of the national estimate. On the other hand, the mean per capita expenditure is much higher in urban areas, where it represents nearly twice the national estimate. In other words, the disparities between urban and rural areas are more pronounced in LMS. As a result, effective targeted programs for poverty alleviation drawn from LMS-based poverty maps are likely to require more resources than actually required to improve living standards in rural areas and reduce regional disparities.

Similar variations are observed in the regions when the regional mean per capita expenditure is expressed as a percentage of national mean estimates. The estimated mean per capita expenditure in Rural Coastal and Savannah regions are the lowest and represent about 50 percent of the LMS national estimate. On the average per capita expenditure, these two regions are the poorest in Ghana. However, the difference that exists between these regions does not show up in the PS design, especially in rural areas where important disparities are known to exist. In fact, while Savannah and Rural Coastal regions are both poor, poverty is more acute in the Savannah where the ratio of per capita household expenditure to national level estimates is the lowest in the GLSS 3 design (88 percent), and the magnitude of the difference between the two poorest regions is close to 12 percent.

Since the value of household total expenditure is based on few items, the downward bias in mean per capita expenditure is likely to cause the distribution to shift to the left, which better reflects the low level of consumption reported. However, while the scope of items and subaggregates might explain large absolute difference between these two distributions—the LMS mean per capita expenditure is 17,678 cedis and represents less than 8 percent of LSMS estimate of 21,5185 cedis—the variation in the structure of these distributions, and the large urban/rural difference might be largely due to the nature of the consumption items in the overall aggregate. Although own consumption represents a large share of household consumption in rural areas, it is not accounted for in the total PS aggregate, partly because of low-level of monetisation of the rural economy, but also because the key consumption items are more tradable in urban areas.

Important variations are also observed in the overall distribution of income across income groups. The distribution of income across income group is not maintained in the LMS design, where the concentration of income tends to be much larger in the uppermost quintile, and substantially smaller in the lowest quintile—implying that the distribution of income is highly unequal in the PS survey. Figure 5.1 shows the distribution of household per capita expenditure across expenditure quintiles under the two designs. This figure shows the share of expenditure quintiles. Note that the distributions of income across income groups are significantly different in the two surveys. The bottom two expenditure quintiles (40 percent of

Figure 5.1 Distribution of Household Per Capita Expenditure by Quintile

Per capita expenditure share

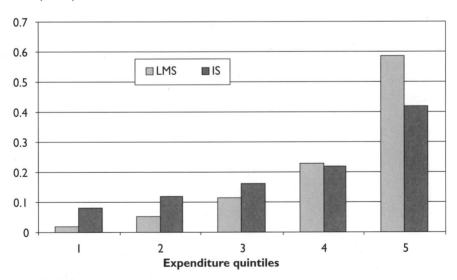

Expenditure quintiles

Source: Author's calculations.

population) accounts for less than 8 percent of total expenditure declared in the PS; the LSMS estimates are over 20 percent. However, a reverse scenario is observed in the upper quintiles where expenditure shares are overestimated in the hypothesized PS design. These differences in distribution of income across income groups suggest that poverty maps constructed from LMS may not be accurate, partly because poverty maps are constructed from these distributions. Moreover, since ranking across expenditure quintiles is a mere reflection of individual welfare, a small income share in the income group is inversely proportional to the poverty rate in the group. The degree of inaccuracy is further illustrated by the scope of underestimation in the lowest quintile. LMS tends to overestimate the living standards of the non-poor and underestimate the living standards of the poor—the income share is relatively high in the upper quintile, and extremely low in the lowest quintile, suggesting that the poor might be even poorer than the data indicates.

Implications for Policy Analysis and Poverty Mapping

In the latest Ghana poverty profile (World Bank 1995), the upper and lower poverty lines are defined as one-half and two-thirds of national mean per capita expenditure respectively.[7] The upper poverty line is 132,230 cedis per person per annum, and the lower line is 107,188 cedis. In this chapter, the lower poverty line is used as the cutoff point, because maximum targeting is easily achieved at the lower and upper end of the distribution where the within-group variance and the probability of household misclassification are lower. The lower poverty line is also used because total household expenditure aggregated from light monitoring surveys shows a large difference between urban and rural areas; the rural expenditure aggregate is substantially lower, and using an upper poverty line would have exacerbated the scope of rural poverty. Similarly, a relative poverty line is defined as fraction of the hypothesized PS mean per capita expenditure for comparison in a cross-section analysis where we look at variations in the poverty rates across regions, in the two designs and for the same reference period. The choice is partly dictated by the fact that poverty profile constructed from LMS use relative poverty lines defined as fraction of total per capita expenditure aggregated from few items (see World Bank 1997 and 1998).

In order to assess the performance of LMS when used as targeting instruments, welfare indicators and poverty indices are estimated from the two distributions.[8] The results are provided in table 5.2, where the Headcount, poverty gap, and severity indices are estimated from the hypothesized PS and the full GLSS 3. The performance of the PS as an instrument for targeting is also assessed by the size of type I and type II error probability, as well as the rate of mistargeting.

Formally defined as $\varepsilon_I = (P(y_j \in P \mid y_j \in \bar{P}))$,[9] type I error probability is also termed as the error of inclusion because it gives the probability of classifying households or individuals as poor, while they are actually non-poor. On the other hand, type II error probability, formally defined as $\varepsilon_{II} = (P(y_j \in P \mid y_j \in \bar{P}))$, is generally termed as the error of exclusion because it gives the probability of classifying individuals as non-poor while they are actually poor. The rate of mistargeting depends on the size of these two errors. Perfect targeting is achieved when the rate of mistargeting is equal to 100 percent, implying that the number of individuals classified as poor under the hypothesized PS design are also ranked as poor in the GLSS 3 or LSMS design. This successful rate of targeting occurs when the errors of inclusion and exclusion are both close to zero. Let $\zeta_{RM}(\varepsilon_I, \varepsilon_{II})$ be the rate of mistargeting expressed as function of the error of inclusion (ε_I) and the error of exclusion (ε_{II}). This rate is a number between 0 and n, where $n < \infty$ $\zeta_{RM}(\varepsilon_I, \varepsilon_{II}) > 1$ when mistargeting results mostly from a large error of inclusion. However, when the error of exclusion is much larger than the error of inclusion, the rate of mistargeting is confined between 0 and 1, that is, $\zeta_{RM}(\varepsilon_I, \varepsilon_{II}) < 1$.

When household per capita expenditure aggregated from the hypothesized PS is used as the basis for constructing poverty maps, Rural Coastal and Savannah remain the poorest regions of Ghana. However, variations in the scope of differences across regions are important. While the magnitude of differences across regions is slim as measured by GLSS 3—a 4-percentage point difference exists between urban and rural areas—the scope of urban-rural difference is more significant in the hypothesized PS design (55 percent). Similarly, while over 68 percent of the population residing in the Savannah region is classified as extreme poor, the poverty incidence in Rural Forest is less than 56 percent, and these proportions are much smaller in urban areas (8 percent) and Accra (6 percent). When the poverty map is constructed from GLSS 3, the Headcount in urban areas is much higher, in part because accounting for consumption of own produce in rural areas during the GLSS 3 implementation reduces the urban/rural discrepancy and increases the overall national mean per capita expenditure, and therefore the extreme poverty line. Therefore, LMS surveys underestimate the scope of urban poverty and reduce the prospect of effective targeting for poverty alleviation. Under the full GLSS 3 design, however, targeting is more justified in urban areas where the number of intended beneficiaries is more important.

Poverty in Sub-Saharan Africa is generally much higher in rural areas where the prospects of income-generating activities are much more limited and aggregate expenditure is much lower. However, while one might expect extreme poverty to be more acute in rural than urban areas in most Sub-Saharan African countries, we rarely expect the large difference in magnitude found in Ghana, where over 65 percent of the rural population lives under extreme poverty, compared with less than 8 percent in urban areas. The differences in scope of extreme poverty reflect the magnitude of the error of inclusion, which is relatively low in urban areas (0.04) and much higher in rural areas (0.47). Note that the size of this error is directly proportional to the rate mistargeting, and the larger the probability of error, the higher the rate of mistargeting. However, a low error of inclusion does not always imply perfect targeting, especially if the corresponding error of exclusion is much higher, as in the present scenario.

In urban areas where the error of inclusion is low and the error of exclusion is much higher (0.11), mistargeting results from a large error of exclusion—which is a consequence of undercoverage of poor households in the sample of intended beneficiaries. On the other hand, a large error of inclusion in rural areas results from oversampling of the poor population in the hypothesized PS design, which causes households normally classified as non-poor to be surveyed as intended beneficiaries for targeted interventions. Table 5.2 shows that mistargeting is relatively high under the PS design, where the population identified for targeted intervention is nearly 2.5 times larger than the true population estimate. This high rate of poor targeting is certainly inflated by the rural rate of mistargeting, which is even higher. For instance, the total number of extreme poor estimated from LMS in rural areas is over three times the actual number of intended beneficiaries. The variations in the rate of mistargeting across other rural regions are not significant; these rates have the same order of magnitude in Rural

Table 5.2 Indices of Extreme Poverty and Rate of Mistargeting across Regions: A Comparison of the Priority Surveys and Living Standards Measurement Surveys

Regions	Priority Survey			LSMS Survey			PS-LSMS comparison		
	PO	PI	P2	PO	PI	P2	Type I error probability	Type II error probability	Rate of mistargeting
Accra	0.0678	0.0274	0.0158	0.1429	0.0259	0.0072	0.0369	0.1121	0.47
Other urban	0.0865	0.0325	0.0180	0.1657	0.0350	0.0118	0.0423	0.1214	0.52
Rural forest	0.5543	0.3029	0.2060	0.1673	0.0324	0.0097	0.3978	0.0108	3.31
Rural coastal	0.6731	0.3722	0.2493	0.1887	0.0409	0.0135	0.4889	0.0045	3.57
Savannah	0.6810	0.4236	0.3082	0.2471	0.0546	0.0173	0.4752	0.0414	2.76
All urban	0.0819	0.0313	0.0175	0.1600	0.0327	0.0106	0.041	0.1191	0.51
All rural	0.6506	0.3753	0.2604	0.2043	0.0438	0.0141	0.4648	0.0186	3.18
National	0.4621	0.2612	0.1799	0.1897	0.0401	0.0129	0.3243	0.0519	2.44

Source: Author's calculations.

Forest, Rural Coastal, and Savannah.

The amount of leakage is directly proportional to the rate of mistargeting and will be lower in urban areas where differential rates are smaller. While the total number of the extreme poor population mistargeted in the LMS design is about half the actual targeted population in urban areas, the size of the population that are wrongly classified is over three times the number of primary beneficiaries in rural areas. In terms of resource allocation, the dollar amount of leakage that results from poor targeting associated with the LMS stratification is over three times the monetary value actually required to alleviate extreme poverty in rural Ghana.

The estimated amount required to eradicate extreme poverty $(nz\hat{p}_1)$ is proportional to the poverty gap, and the larger the poverty gap, the larger the amount. Hypothetically, the poverty gap estimated from the PS is about six times higher than the full GLSS estimate, at the national level. As a result, the amount required to eradicate extreme poverty if the PS is used as the basis for poverty analysis is about six times higher, other things being equal. More precisely, to fill the gap so as to ensure that there is no extreme poverty in Ghana requires about 27,997.5 (0.2612*107188) cedis per annum and per person in the PS design, instead of 4,298.5 (0.0401*107188) cedis according to the GLSS estimate.[10] The potential costs and losses for central government and local authorities are considerable, in part because poor targeting and improper identification of intended beneficiaries increases the amount of leakage and the estimated amount of resources allocated for poverty alleviation. The following section proposes a method for correcting light surveys for improved targeting.

Estimating Total Expenditure for Improved Targeting

To motivate the use of LMS instruments that have limited data on expenditure, but good data on social and access indicators, location of infrastructure, and large coverage for poverty analysis and targeting, we consider using poverty predictors—which are correlates of expenditure to impute for household consumption. In Fofack (1997), a methodology for deriving national poverty predictors was proposed, and this exercise can be viewed as a model calibration for improved targeting. By combining LMS with more general LSMS and IS surveys (which are comprehensive on income and expenditure), poverty predictors and their corresponding weights are estimated from the latter two surveys and are used to impute for household total expenditure, which then serves as the basis for poverty analysis and for constructing poverty maps in the LMS setting.

As core components of national statistical programs, LMS and LSMS are both household-level surveys, with important similarities. Similarity in the sampling frame and sampling design, as well as the geographic proximity in the implementation of these surveys, make their combination extremely appealing for poverty and policy analysis. In an early empirical study, the poverty predictors and their corresponding weights were estimated from GLSS 3 (see Fofack 1997). In order to assess the stability over time of these predictors and their corresponding weights, they were applied to earlier surveys, GLSS 1 (1987) and GLSS 2 (1989), to predict the standards of living. The expected average discrepancy based on the error of prediction was relatively small, as a result of the small absolute deviation between sampled household expenditure and predicted values. Successful rates of household classification across expenditure quintiles were achieved when the predicted values were compared with the actual welfare measure reported. Rates as high as 95 percent were attained in the extreme quintiles, and 90 percent in the intermediate ones, when based on GLSS 2.

When applied to GLSS 1 (1987), the stability of these regressors and coefficients was preserved as well: absolute deviation between predicted value and actual welfare measure reported was still relatively small. The rate of successful classification across expenditure quintiles remained high, despite the time lag between the GLSS 3 (1992) and GLSS 1 (1987). Rates as high as 92 percent were attained in the extreme quintiles, and 83 percent in the intermediate ones. The precision of welfare measure prediction is further highlighted by the fact that mistargeted households were located in neighboring quintiles, hence limiting leakage in targeting for poverty reduction.

Recently, attempts have been made to exploit the large coverage of population censuses to construct poverty maps for poverty and policy analysis, by combining the census with household surveys (see Hentschel and others 1998). While such a combination might be appealing, especially given its scope for geographical targeting, the data requirements to capture the large proportional variance observed in welfare could be enormous. Moreover, the frequency of census implementation is relatively low in Sub-Saharan Africa, which may prevent timely update of weights and welfare correlates whose precision can decline over time. While the method proposed by Hentschel and others uses a large number of regressors from the census to predict household welfare, the method used in this study draws on a different approach based on data reduction. The poverty correlates to predict welfare for poverty analysis are reduced to a set of minimum core variables that can be collected easily on a single household visit with a low level of nonsampling errors.

To impute household consumption for poverty analysis, the best correlates of welfare are first derived in the broad GLSS 3 survey using correlation analysis and regression models. The model assumes that the conditional expectation $E(y \mid x_1, \ldots, x_k)$ of the response given the covariates is related to the linear predictors by the response link function $h(x, \theta)$. Since the variance of total household expenditure across regions and within regions is large, a logarithmic transformation is applied to the response to make the relationship between the y and the xs linear. This transformation stabilizes the error variance, reduces asymmetry in the distribution of error terms, and improves prediction. The structural form of the correcting model is specified by equation 5.4:

$$Y = X'\beta + \varepsilon \qquad (5.4)$$

where Y is total household expenditure transformed to the log scale, β is the vector of estimated parameters relative to continuous and discrete level variables, and $\varepsilon \approx N(0,\sigma^2)$ is the distribution of error terms. The set of poverty predictors is mostly discrete-level variables. Most continuous variables with strong predictive capabilities are dichotomized to discriminate between poor and non-poor households. These dummy regressors were constructed and included in the model to capture the effects of qualitative independent variables.

In order to account for selection bias in the choice of the predictor variables, a conditional maximum likelihood (CML) estimation method is used to select predictors. Unlike other selection criteria,[11] the CML method is based on the expected overall discrepancy and produces an unbiased estimation of the discrepancy, since the omission bias in the fixed model becomes additional residual variation. The best poverty predictors were the ones that contributed to a significant marginal increase in the explanatory power of the model. That is, if $(x_1, x_2, \ldots, x_j)$ is the initial set of poverty correlates, and x_{j+1} x_{j+k} for $k \neq 1$ are potential poverty predictors candidates, the variable x_{j+1} will often be selected over x_{j+k} if the conditions in equation 5.5 are true:

$$\sum \left(y_j - E\left(\hat{y} \mid x_1, x_2, \ldots, x_j, x_{j+1} \right) \right)^2 < \sum \left(y_j - E\left(\hat{y} \mid x_1, x_2, \ldots, x_j, x_{j+k} \right) \right)^2 \quad (5.5)$$

Initially, we assumed that all predictor variables were available for inclusion in the model. We then proceeded by elimination using the stepwise selection method, with a minimum level of significance. A given independent variable was removed from the model only when a marginal increase of the percentage variance of the response explained by the model as a result of its inclusion was smallest (equation 5.6):

$$\Delta \left(R^2 \left(y \mid \sum_{j=1}^{k} \lambda_j x_j \right) - R^2 \left(y \mid \sum_{j=1}^{k-1} \lambda_j x_j \right) \right) < \varepsilon \qquad (5.6)$$

Applying this selection procedure to the model iteratively produces an optimal model with 10 core poverty predictors. The resulting set of poverty predictors actually has very few continuous variables and has essentially either dichotomized or discrete-level variables. This reduces errors due to long recall periods and increases the accuracy of targeting based on a pre-

diction function, because the poverty predictors and the weighted coefficients are estimated from full LSMS and IS surveys, and are imputed using
information collected at the household level during the implementation of
light surveys. Therefore, the poverty indices are no longer just a function of
the aggregated household total expenditure, but also depend on the estimated regression coefficients, as shown in equation 5.7:

$$P_k = f(\hat{y}, z), \text{ for } k = 0, 1, 2, \text{ where } \hat{y} = \Phi^{-1}\left(\sum_{j=1}^{n} \beta_j x_j\right) \qquad (5.7)$$

where z is the poverty line. Using this methodology, the poverty predictors
are derived at the national and regional level and used in conjunction with
the corresponding weights to impute total expenditure. The predicted
expenditure is then used as a basis for constructing poverty maps, and for
classifying regions for poverty analysis and targeting. The poverty predictors were able to explain over 65 percent of proportional variance observed
in the actual welfare measure reported. The proportional variance explained
by the model was high at the national level, but also at regional level when
the models were calibrated to derive poverty predictors for each agro-climatic region. Table 5.3 provides a complete listing of the derived poverty
predictors. These predictors are derived at the national and regional level to
account for regional differences in the pattern of consumption.

Results and Implications for Geographical Targeting

To assess the accuracy of poverty maps constructed from improved LMS,
the incidence of poverty and other poverty indictors are computed for different agro-climatic regions using the predicted expenditure constructed
from the model, estimated as the weighted sum of the poverty predictors.
These estimates are compared with the poverty indicators derived from
actual GLSS 3 data. Table 5.4 reports these values and the corresponding
error of inclusion (type I error probability) and error of exclusion (type II
error probability).

The differences in the poverty estimates decrease substantially in both
urban and rural areas when the poverty predictors are used to model household expenditure. The error of inclusion is now confined between
$(0 < P(y_j \in P \,|\, y_j \in \bar{P}) \leq 13)$, from a rate as high as 0.48 in the hypothesized
Priority Survey setting. It is worth pointing out that the significant decrease
in the error of inclusion, which translates into improved poverty maps, is
not at all compensated for by increased errors of exclusion; this error
remains low across all agro-climatic regions.

The poverty indicators calculated on the basis of full GLSS data and the
LMS with predicted expenditure are quite close. At the national level, the
absolute relative error is less than 0.081 ($ARE < 0.08$), in part because the

Table 5.3 National and Regional Poverty Predictors for Poverty Analysis

National level	Urban areas	Rural areas
Expenditure on soap	Expenditure on soap	Expenditure on soap
Number of spouses	Number of spouses	Number of spouses
Assets score	Assets score	Assets score
% school age kids enrolled	% school age kids enrolled	% school age kids enrolled
Expenditure on meat	Expenditure on meat	Expenditure on meat
Land ownership	Land ownership	Ownership of poultry
Consumption of bread	% household members employed	Ownership of goats and sheep
Ownership of poultry	Use of tooth paste	Number of members per room
Export crops	% children enrolled in public school	Ownership of farm
Number of member per room	% household member literate	Ownership of cattle

Accra region	Other urban	Rural forest
Assets score	Expenditure on soap	Expenditure on soap
Expenditure on meat	Number hh member employed	Consumption of bread
% household members employed	Expenditure on meat	Assets score
Expenditure on rice	Assets score	Use of tooth paste
Number of hh members completed secondary	% school age children	Number of spouses
Expenditure on soap	Expenditure on bread	Expenditure on meat
% of school age children	% hh member completed secondary	% hh member completed secondary
Number of under-five	Use of tooth paste	Expenditure on rice
Use of paper toilet	Ownership of land	Number of members per room
% children enrolled in public school	Use of paper toilet	Use of paper toilet

Rural coastal	Savannah	
Expenditure on soap	Expenditure on soap	
Assets score	Number of spouses	
% school age children	Consumption of bread	
Number of spouses	Ownership of sheep and goats	
% children enrolled in public school	Use of tooth paste	
Consumption of bread	Expenditure on meat	
Use of paper toilet	Assets score	
Ownership of poultry	Use of paper toilet	
Number of under-five	Gender of head	

Source: Author's calculations.

Table 5.4 Indices of Extreme Poverty and Rate of Mistargeting across Regions: A Comparison of LSMS and Imputed Expenditures

Regions	Poverty Predictors (PP)*			LSMS type survey			PP-LSMS comparison		
	P0	P1	P2	P0	P1	P2	Type I error probability	Type II error probability	Rate of mistargeting
Accra	0.0878	0.0163	0.0040	0.1429	0.02587	0.0072	0.0212	0.0763	0.615
Other urban	0.1344	0.0274	0.0076	0.1657	0.03495	0.01175	0.0623	0.0936	0.811
Rural forest	0.0988	0.0159	0.0039	0.1673	0.0324	0.0097	0.0537	0.1220	0.591
Rural coastal	0.1868	0.0357	0.0103	0.1887	0.0409	0.0135	0.1036	0.1056	0.990
Savannah	0.2787	0.0461	0.0116	0.2471	0.0546	0.0173	0.1261	0.0946	1.128
All urban	0.1229	0.0247	0.0067	0.16	0.0327	0.0106	0.0522	0.0894	0.768
All rural	0.1999	0.0351	0.0094	0.2043	0.0438	0.01407	0.1008	0.1053	0.978
National	0.1743	0.0317	0.0085	0.1897	0.0401	0.0129	0.0847	0.1001	0.919

* Poverty Predictors refer to LMS with imputed consumtion.
Source: Author's calculations.

difference in Headcount indices estimated from reported LSMS expenditure and predicted welfare function figures is slim. The relatively small deviation between the predicted poverty rates and the actual rates estimated from the GLSS 3 survey is largely due to the sample size effects. The sample size at the subregional level is the smallest in the Accra and Rural Forest regions, where the magnitude of the difference is the largest. However, the error in prediction is inversely proportional to the sample size, and one would therefore expect this error to decrease substantially in the actual LMS design, where the large sample size allows a much higher representation at the regional and subregional levels. Part of the prediction error could also be attributed to random noise affecting values of expenditure reported. These prediction errors are associated with the design, and could be reduced if sampling and nonsampling errors were controlled during the survey implementation.

This section assesses the implications of large reductions of both errors of inclusion and exclusion on the poverty map. Figure 5.2 provides the spatial distribution of poverty measured using the Headcount index, across agro-climatic regions under the three types of surveys: LSMS, LMS with imputed consumption, and the Priority Survey. While the predicted poverty indices are quite close to those estimated from GLSS 3, a large discrepancy exists between these rates and PS-based estimates.

The differences between Headcount indices are maintained when the predicted expenditure is used for poverty analysis. The bias towards higher rural poverty is preserved in the regional ranking, and ranking of five agro-climatic regions is consistent across the two ranking criteria: LSMS-based data and LMS with predicted expenditure. Thus, although poverty is generally widespread in rural areas, there are some variations across rural regions reflected by the difference in their poverty indices. In terms of extreme poverty, the Savannah remains the poorest region, followed by Rural Coastal and Forest regions, while Accra is the least poor region in Ghana.

The performance of the proposed method is also assessed by the size of errors of inclusion and exclusion, as well as the rate of mistargeting. Figures 5.3 and 5.4 provide estimates of errors of inclusion and exclusion relative to the PS and the LMS with predicted expenditure for comparison. Note that while the error of inclusion is generally much higher in the PS setting, when estimated across agro-climatic regions, the error of exclusion, in contrast, is often much lower. However, the magnitude of difference between the error of exclusion estimated from the PS and the LMS with predicted expenditure is small, in part because mistargeting is largely due to the high error of inclusion.

Figure 5.2 Spatial Distribution of Poverty across Agro-Climatic Regions: Comparison of Priority Survey, LMS with Imputed Consumption and LSMS Surveys

Headcount index

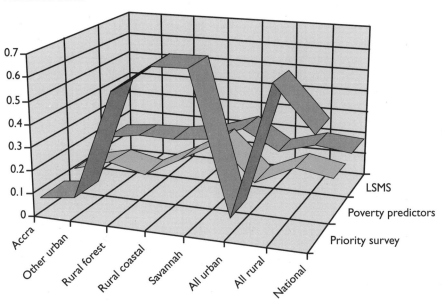

Source: Author's calculations.

Figure 5.3 Type I Error Probability Estimate across Agro-Climatic Regions: A Comparison of PS and LMS with Imputed Consumption

Error probability

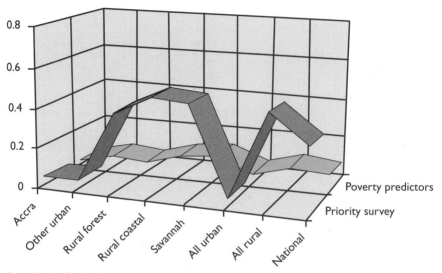

Source: Author's calculations.

The rate of mistargeting, which reflects the gap between the true population of intended beneficiaries and the population estimate based on LMS with predicted expenditure reduces substantially, as shown in table 5.3. Except the Rural Forest region, where the rate of misclassification is slightly different from unity (perfect targeting), targeting is almost perfect in all other regions. In particular, perfect targeting is achieved in all Rural and Rural Coastal areas when the predicted expenditure variable is used as the basis for household ranking and constructing poverty maps. Compared with the LMS ranking, the gains in accuracy achieved in the spatial distribution of poverty are significant, especially if one considers the fact that mistargeting under the hypothesized PS design increases the population of intended beneficiaries by a factor of three. Even in the Rural Forest region, where the error of inclusion is relatively high (0.12) and the rate of misclassification is slightly different from unity, the gap is less than 40 percent. Moreover, the rate of mistargeting is less than one, implying that poor targeting is largely due to the high error of exclusion (undercoverage of the population of intended beneficiaries), and does not necessarily translate into increased resources for poverty alleviation.

This rate of mistargeting reflects the size of both errors of inclusion and exclusion and is expressed as the ratio of estimated population of beneficiaries

Figure 5.4 Type II Error Probability Estimate across Agro-Climatic Regions: A Comparison of PS, LMS with Imputed Consumption, and LSMS

Error probability

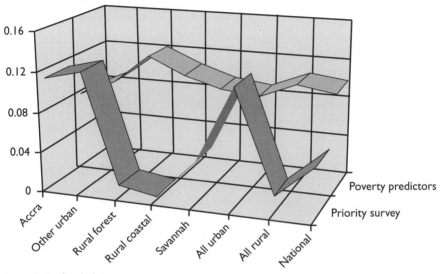

Source: Author's calculations.

to the exact population of beneficiaries in each region. As indicated earlier, these rates vary between 0 and $n < \infty$, and $0 < \zeta_{RM}(\varepsilon_I, \varepsilon_{II}) < 1$ reflects the undercoverage resulting from a large error of exclusion, whereas $\zeta_{RM}(\varepsilon_I, \varepsilon_{II}) > 1$ reflects a large error of inclusion of unintended beneficiaries in the target population. Note that the rates of mistargeting $\zeta_{RM}(\varepsilon_I, \varepsilon_{II})$ are relatively high: especially in rural areas, $\zeta_{RM}(\varepsilon_I, \varepsilon_{II}) > 1$ when the hypothesized PS is used to construct the poverty map. These high rates are largely attributed to a large error of inclusion and could increase leakage and the cost of poverty reduction programs. However, significant improvement is achieved when LMS with predicted expenditure is the basis for targeting.

The objectives of the method outlined are twofold: first, to improve accuracy of poverty maps constructed from LMS, and second, to draw on the large samples provided by the design of these surveys, as well as the nature of poverty predictors, to achieve geographical targeting at levels below administrative regions. In the counterfactual experiment presented in this chapter, the hypothesized PS is constructed from the more comprehensive GLSS 3 survey, and the sample size corresponding to the hypothesized PS is dictated by the GLSS 3 design—just as the level of disaggregation is determined by the actual GLSS 3 sample size.

The geographic profile of poverty provides living-standard indicators at the level of agro-climatic regions. However, it has been demonstrated that greater gains in efficiency and significant reduction of leakage in transfers for poverty alleviation can be achieved from fine-tuning targeting to smaller geographic units (see Baker and Grosh 1994). This is because finer disaggregation creates homogeneous groups and reduces leakage in transfers to the poorest population. The actual PS design recommends a large sample size for targeting smaller administrative units (see Grootaert and Marchant 1992).[12] Predicting household expenditure using poverty predictors should strengthen PS analytical capabilities and enable researchers to exploit its large coverage to achieve geographical targeting, with minimum leakage, at a level of disaggregation well below agro-climatic regions.

The causes and determinants of poverty, as well as sources of large disparities across agro-climatic regions are variable.(The Savannah and Rural Coastal regions are the poorest.) While at the aggregate level, differences in potential for income-generating activities and wage inequality might constitute important factors, at the regional and district level, human capital, access indicators, and location of infrastructure might be more critical. LMS have good data on access indicators—location of schools, health centers, and water supply—and its relatively large sample size may provide opportunities for georeferencing information at subregional levels, thus improving the potential for analysis beyond fixed geographical boundaries. Moreover, overlaying poverty maps with improved spatial distribution on maps of local infrastructure (schools, health clinics, hospitals, water supplies, and roads), and presenting both maps at the same level of disaggregation, may provide a better understanding of poverty dynamics. More light may be shed on the constraints to growth and poverty reduction, and prioritizing, impact assessment, and policymaking may be improved.

Glewwe (1992), Kanbur and others (1994), and Bigman and Fofack (2000) provide a survey of targeting methods with applications to developing countries. The methods of targeting that provide criteria of eligibility for poverty alleviation programs fall into the following categories: targeting by household income, targeting by other indicators, targeting by commodities, self-targeting, and geographical targeting. While successful implementation of geographical targeting requires large data sets to achieve high levels of disaggregation and reduce induced leakage, the needs and requirements for targeting by income, commodities, and indicators are somehow different.

A successful implementation of targeting by indicators is based on the ability to easily identify a few key indicator variables that are highly correlated with household income and expenditure. Using this scheme in Côte d'Ivoire, Glewwe (1992) found that the correlates of poverty identified were essentially household amenity variables; Ravallion (1989) showed that substantial gains in targeting can be achieved if land ownership is used as the criterion for discriminating poor from non-poor. The poverty predictors are strong correlates of welfare varying across regions, and poverty alleviation programs as well as targeting schemes can suitably be designed using these indicators. Since household amenity variables are strong correlates of poverty, indirect measures to alleviate poverty can be implemented by designing programs that use these variables to maximize transfers to the most needy.

The poverty predictor's variables include food and non-food consumption items, and can well serve as a basis for commodities-based targeting. This targeted scheme draws on the differences observed in the consumption basket of the poor and non-poor. Its objective is to reduce the cost of those commodities that are heavily consumed by the poor through targeted subsidies. Although poverty predictors are not derived along the poverty dimension, but rather by agro-climatic regions, the methodology presented is flexible and can be used in multiple steps—first by predicting household expenditure using the poverty predictors, and then using the predicted variable to differentiate between poor and non poor. A cross-sectional analysis which focuses on the variation in the consumption pattern of the poor by agro-climatic regions could be a starting point to investigate the causal link between variation in the depth of poverty and the nature of poverty correlates. Future research will involve exploring the association between these correlates and poverty dimension at the regional and district level, and investigating how a better understanding of that association could be used to effectively channel scarce resources to the most needy.

Concluding Remarks

Many developing countries are confronted with widespread poverty and limited resources for poverty alleviation. In most of these countries, however, broad-based poverty reduction is often an overarching economic objective and can be achieved only if the limited resources are allocated to the beneficiaries with minimum leakage. This requires that the country's economic and poverty profiles elaborated from survey data be consistent with the spatial distribution of poverty. Effective targeting of poverty reduction also requires that the profile carefully differentiate between the poorest and the least poor regions at a fine level of disaggregation.

In the past, financial costs and logistics have led some of these countries to use LMS, which have a large sample size and are much cheaper than comprehensive surveys, as a basis for constructing disaggregated poverty maps to design antipoverty programs. The present study shows that the cost of mistargeting associated with the use of light monitoring surveys is significant for targeting purposes, and can in certain circumstances outweigh the saving made by not implementing full LSMS and IS surveys. In fact, aggregated total expenditure, which is the basis for differentiating between poor and non-poor, is underestimated in the PS design. Since underestimation of total household consumption is not uniform across regions, welfare indicators and poverty maps derived from LMS may not always be consistent with the actual spatial distribution of poverty. There are variations in the dispersal rates, and ranking is not preserved across agro-climatic regions.

The present study shows that by combining more detailed surveys, which have more comprehensive income and expenditure data, with LMS, which have relatively large samples, improved poverty maps disaggregated at a level below agro-climatic regions can be constructed. This chapter shows that a substantial reduction in the rate of mistargeting, and improved poverty maps resulting from a much higher reduction of the errors of inclusion and exclusion, can be achieved by modeling LMS-based total expenditure using poverty predictors which are carefully derived from more comprehensive surveys. These poverty predictors are household-level variables available in both the much broader LSMS and IS surveys and LMS, and can be collected during the implementation of the latter in a single household visit with relatively low error in reporting.

Over the past few years, the request for poverty maps disaggregated down to levels as low as districts has been growing in developing countries in general, and in Sub-Saharan African countries in particular. These demands have been prompted by the need to have a more accurate distribution of poverty over space, but even more so by decentralization policies which are increasingly used in these countries to channel resources more efficiently to the communities. As the demand for more disaggregated information continues to grow under increasing budgetary and resource constraints, methods that optimize the use of LMS instruments which are less expensive, but have potential for geographical targeting, will be increasingly in demand. The method proposed in this chapter recommends using expenditure proxies to improve poverty mapping and geographical targeting, and is one useful way of getting more values from the LMS-limited data sets.

The accuracy of household welfare predicted from the targeting model depends on the base point of the prediction, the stability of the poverty predictors, and their corresponding weights. While modeling consumption significantly reduces the errors of inclusion and exclusion, the level of targeting attained in the various agro-climatic regions is less than perfect due to unavoidable prediction errors. These errors in prediction can be attributed in part to noise affecting actual expenditure reported and result in part from sampling and nonsampling errors. Reducing this noise will greatly improve the accuracy of prediction and the poverty maps. The stability of the predictors over time is another important question. Stability was assessed using surveys conducted under the same sampling frame, and it would be worthwhile investigating how this stability is affected by variation of the sampling frame, as well as its possible implications on poverty mapping. Finally, while disaggregated poverty maps and overlaying of these maps may shed some light on the constraints to poverty reduction and the determinants of poverty, improved efficiency in transfers and allocation of resources could be achieved if geographical targeting is combined with some other form of targeting—for instance, targeting by commodities or indicators. The poverty predictors are correlates of expenditure, and could serve as a vector of transfers if we have a better understanding of the dynamic between these correlates and poverty. Future research will focus on investigating the association between these proxies and poverty.

Notes

The author of this chapter, Hippolyte Fofack, is at the World Bank.

1. Poverty maps show spatial distribution or geographical profiles of poverty and are used by policymakers as a basis for allocating resources for poverty reduction.

2. For more details on the design and implementation of Integrated Surveys and Living Standards Measurement Surveys, see Demery and others (1992), and Grosh and Glewwe (1998).

3. A multistage stratified random sampling was used: initially, 407 clusters were enumerated and households were selected with probability proportional to size. There were 15 households drawn in each urban cluster, and 10 households in each rural cluster.

4. During the GLSS 3 implementation, the data was collected on about 107 food items, and the scope of non-food items sampled was relatively important as well.

5. A team from the Department of Economics Research Center at the University of Warwick developed a methodology for estimating imputed values for outliers and missing values used in the context of GLSS 1 and GLSS 2 survey. In the last survey, a team from the same university worked with the Ghana Statistical Services to refine the methodology and adapt it to the GLSS 3.

6. Components of food subaggregates include corn, rice, cassava, plantains, beans, groundnuts, palm oil, sugar, salt, and meat.

7. The same definitions were used in the 1987–88 poverty profile, and the 1988 base values were adjusted for inflation change over time and expressed in 1992 constant price for the latter profile. It is worth pointing out that the lower poverty line is sensibly equal to the same fraction of national mean per capita expenditure estimated from the full GLSS 3.

8. The welfare indices are selected from the P_α class of poverty indices (Foster, Greer, and Thorbecke 1984), which measure different dimensions of poverty depending on the value of α. For $\alpha = 0$, the P_α indices represent the Headcount index; when $\alpha = 1$, it measures the poverty gap index. The indices provide estimates of severity of poverty when $\alpha > 1$.

9. The symbol P represents the set of poor households or individuals (y_j) and $\bar{P}$ represents the set of non-poor households or individuals.

10. This is a hypothetical scenario for illustrative purpose because direct income transfers are not the cornerstones of anti-poverty policy in Sub-Saharan African countries, where the cost of such measures would be enormous and further deteriorate fiscal deficits.

11. Other criteria used to select subset of predictors include the S_p and the Mallow C_p criteria. For more detail on the rationale and criteria for model selection, see Linhart and Zucchini (1986).

12. LMS conducted in Sub-Saharan Africa over the past three years have collected data on a relatively large sample: the Kenya Welfare Monitoring Survey (1994) was based on a sample of 12,000 households, and the Ghana Core Welfare Indicators Survey (1997) was based on a sample of 15,000 households.

References

Baker, Judy L., and Margaret Grosh. 1994. "Measuring the Effects of Geographical Targeting on Poverty Reduction." Living Standards Measurement Study Working Paper No. 99. The World Bank, Washington, DC.

Besley, Timothy, and Ravi Kanbur. 1993. "The Principles of Targeting." In Michael Lipton and Jacques Van Der Gaag, eds., *Including the Poor*. Washington, D.C.: The World Bank.

Bigman, David, and Hippolyte Fofack. 2000. "An Overview of Targeted Schemes for Poverty Reduction in Developing Countries." In D. Bigman and H. Fofack, eds., *Geographical Targeting for Poverty Alleviation: Methodology and Applications*. Washington, D.C.: The World Bank. Forthcoming.

Deaton, Angus, and John Muellbauer. 1980. *Economics of Consumer Behavior*. Cambridge: Cambridge University Press.

Deaton, Angus, and Margaret Grosh. 1998. "Consumption." In M. Grosh and P. Glewwe, eds., *Designing Household Survey Questionnaires: Lessons from Ten Years of LSMS Experience for Developing Countries*. Manuscript. Washington, D.C.: The World Bank.

Deininger, Klaus, and Lyn Squire. 1996. "A New Data Set Measuring Income and Inequality." *The World Bank Economic Review* 10: 565–91.

Delaine, Ghislaine, Lionel Demery, Jean-Luc Dubois, Branko Grdjic, Christiaan Grootaert, Christopher Hill, Timothy Marchant, Andre McKay, Jeffery Round, Christopher Scott, eds. 1992. "The Social Dimensions of Adjustment Integrated Survey: A Survey to Measure Poverty and Understand the Effects of Policy Change on Households." Social Dimensions of Adjustment in Sub-Saharan Africa (SDA) Working Paper 14. The World Bank, Washington, D.C.

Demery, Lionel, John-Luc Dubois, Christiaan Grootaert, and Tim Marchant. 1992. "Annotated Integrated Survey Questionnaire." In G. Delaine and others, eds., "The Social Dimensions of Adjustment Priority Survey: A Survey to Measure

Poverty and Understand the Effects of Policy Change on Households." SDA Working Paper 14. The World Bank, Washington, D.C.

Demery, Lionel, Christiaan Grootaert, and Christopher Hill. 1991. "Annotated Questionnaire and Listing Forms." In G. Delaine and others, eds., "The Social Dimensions of Adjustment Priority Survey: A Survey to Measure Poverty and Understand the Effects of Policy Change on Households." SDA Working Paper 14. The World Bank, Washington, D.C.

Demery, Lionel, and Jeffery Round. 1992. "Objectives of the Integrated Survey." In G. Delaine and others, eds., "The Social Dimensions of Adjustment Integrated Survey: A Survey to Measure Poverty and Understand the Effects of Policy Change on Households." SDA Working Paper 14. The World Bank, Washington, D.C.

Fofack, Hippolyte. 1997. "Using Poverty Predictors as Expenditure Proxies for Ranking Households for Poverty Analysis." *Proceedings of the International Statistical Institute 1997*. Ankara: State Institute of Statistics.

Foster, James E., Joel Greer, and Erik Thorbecke. 1984. "A Class of Decomposable Poverty Measures." *Econometrica* 53: 173–77.

Ghana Statistical Services. 1995. "Ghana Living Standards Survey Report on The Third Round (GLSS 3)." Ghana.

———. 1996. "Measuring Household Income and Expenditure in the Third Round of the Ghana Living Standards Survey (1991/92): A Methodological Guide." Ghana.

Glewwe, Paul. 1992. "Targeting Assistance to the Poor: Efficient Allocation of Transfers when Household Income Is Not Observed." *Journal of Development Economics* 38: 297–321.

Grootaert, Christiaan, and Timothy Marchant. 1992. "SDA Socioeconomic Information System." In G. Delaine and others, "The Social Dimensions of Adjustment Integrated Surveys: A Survey to Measure Poverty and Understand the Effects of Policy Change on Households." SDA Working Paper 14. The World Bank, Washington, D.C.

Grosh, Margaret, and Judy Baker. 1995. "Proxy Means Tests for Targeting Social Programs: Simulations and Speculation." Living Standards Measurement Study Working Paper 118. The World Bank, Washington, D.C.

Grosh, Margaret, and Paul Glewwe P. 1998. "The World Bank's Living Standards Measurement Household Surveys." *Journal of Economic Perspectives* 12(1): 187–196.

Hentschel, Jesko, Jean Lanjouw, Peter Lanjouw, and Javier Poggi. 1998. "Combining Census and Survey Data to Study Spatial Dimensions of Poverty." Policy Research Working Paper 1928. The World Bank, Washington, D.C.

Kanbur, Ravi, Michael Keen, and Matti Tuomala. 1994. "Labor Supply and Targeting in Poverty Alleviation Programs." *The World Bank Economic Review* 8(2): 191–211.

Linhart, Heine, and Walter Zucchini. 1986. *Model Selection*. Willey Series in Probability and Mathematical Statistics. New York: John Wiley.

Marchant, Timothy, and Christiaan Grootaert. 1991. "The Social Dimensions of Adjustment Priority Survey: An Instrument for the Rapid Identification and

Monitoring of Policy Target Groups." SDA Working Paper 12. The World Bank, Washington, D.C.

Narayan, Deepa, and Lyra Srinivasan. 1994. "Participatory Development Tool Kit: Materials to Facilitate Community Empowerment." The World Bank, Washington, D.C.

Ravallion, Martin. 1989. "Land-Contingent Poverty Alleviation Scheme." *World Development* 17(8): 1223–1233.

———. 1996. "How Well Can Method Substitute for Data? Five Experiments in Poverty Analysis." *The World Bank Research Observer* 11(2): 199–221.

Ravallion, Martin, and D. Gaurav. 1993. "Regional Disparities, Targeting, and Poverty in India." In Michael Lipton and Jacques Van der Gaag, eds., *Including the Poor*. Washington, D.C.: The World Bank.

The World Bank. 1995. "A Poverty Profile for Ghana, 1987–1988." Social Dimensions of Adjustment in Sub-Saharan Africa Working Paper 5, Washington, D.C.

———. 1997. "Status Report on Poverty in Sub-Saharan Africa 1997: Tracking the Incidence and Characteristics of Poverty." Institutional and Social Policy AFTI1. Washington, D.C.

———. 1998. *African Development Indicators*. Washington, D.C.

6

Spatial Indicators of Access and Fairness for the Location of Public Facilities

David Bigman and Uwe Deichmann

THE EASE, SPEED, AND COMFORT with which the public can access facilities such as hospitals and schools are among the most important variables determining the benefits that individuals can obtain from the services at these facilities. The design of the sites of the public facilities that provide these services must therefore take into account not only the direct monetary costs of accessing the facilities, but also variables that indicate the ease, speed, and comfort of access. The goals that determine the location configuration of public facilities are therefore fundamentally different from the ones set up for private facilities. They include goals such as the provision of a minimum package of services to all households within a certain distance from their place of residence, or equal access to health services by all households. These goals must then be translated into decisions on the sites of the public facilities and on the services that each facility will provide by taking into account the access costs for all households and the ease, speed, and comfort of access.

Quantitative measures of accessibility can have a wide variety of uses in descriptive, explanatory, and normative studies:

- As a means for base-line characterization. In combination with detailed, geographically referenced census data, accessibility indicators can be used to compute the proportion of any subgroup of the population living beyond an acceptable threshold from a service center, thereby identifying imbalances in service provision between regions.

- As explanatory variables, for example, to investigate the reasons for spatial differences of health indicators.
- For determining the size of the population that would benefit from additional health facilities or from improvements in access roads.

Studies on public facility location and accessibility have been conducted in the disciplines of geography, economics, and regional sciences. Early studies date back to the works by Stewart and Warntz (1958); see also Pooler (1995). In the context of public services, there has recently been a renewed interest in questions of *equity* and *fairness* as criteria for determining the location of public facilities. This interest is due, in large measure, to the ease with which a wide variety of the rather complex accessibility indicators can be computed when all relevant information is organized as a geographical information system. A second line of research focuses on the wider issue of using accessibility measures in applying *spatial equity* as a criterion for the provision of public services (Truelove 1993, Marsh and Shilling 1994). Accessibility indicators in this context provide criteria for comparing the quality of the services provided in different geographic areas or for different social groups. For this analysis, geographic indicators of distance and access time must be complemented with indicators that characterize the need for the public service by the various social subgroups. Accessibility is then evaluated within the framework of the analysis of the demand for these services. Examples include the number of school-age children that attend schools in an educational sector study, or the number of women of childbearing age that come to health clinics in a family planning application. The analysis of spatial equity within the framework of these studies will then focus on the degree of inequality in access, or on the maximum distance between the point of demand and the point of provision that can be accepted within the society's norms.

Studies of *spatial equity* in public facility locations have generally concentrated on the comparison of accessibility indicators between population groups using common measures of inequality such as the mean absolute deviation (MAD), the standard deviation, or the Gini coefficient. This chapter suggests an alternative set of summary measures as criteria of social fairness in accessibility that have the form of measures of *poverty*. The next section ("Approaches to the Measurement of Accessibility") provides a brief overview of common approaches to the analysis of service provision and a review of existing accessibility measures. The third section ("Criteria of Social Fairness in the Location of Public Facilities") discusses the shortcomings of these measures in the context of spatial equity analysis. The fourth section ("Accessibility Indicators Based on Poverty Measures") presents an alternative set of measures and discusses their interpretation in the context of welfare analysis. Finally, we present an illustrative application of these measures in an analysis of family planning service centers in Madagascar in the fifth section ("An Illustration"). This chapter concentrates largely on the geographic aspects of public service provision and is thus most concerned with the effects of the spatial distribution of public services, the distance from the points of demand to the public facility, and the quality of the access road. Equally important in this evaluation are nonphysical aspects of service provision such as access to information about service availability, personal preferences for different types of services, and the economic means of the users of these services. We will briefly discuss these issues in the conclusions.

Approaches to the Measurement of Accessibility

The starting point in the spatial analysis of public service provision is to estimate demand for the services in the facilities by determining the service area for each facility, namely the geographical area from which the demand for these services will gravitate to the facility. Once that area has been determined, the potential demand for the services in the facility can be estimated. Census or survey data on the size and the socioeconomic characteristics of the population residing in the service area can be used to determine the required capacity of the facility and the type of services that it will provide. This approach is closely related to the design of market areas in economic analysis.

The simplest way to determine the service area for a given facility is to define a circular region with the facility located at the center and the radius chosen to reflect a *target* travel distance (or time) for the population served. National health plans often state planning goals in terms of the *target* distance such that all persons in the country should have access to medical or educational facilities that are located within the *target* distance from their place of residence. Health sector studies in Niger (Wane and others 1995) and Kenya (DSA 1997), for example, chose the target distance to be 5 kilometers. Circular service areas of a given radius obviously imply that travel in all directions takes a similar effort or the same time. In areas where terrain or dense vegetation make travel more difficult in some directions this is not a reasonable assumption, since the time required to access the facility from different points in that area may vary considerably.

If the population is sparsely spread across large areas, achieving similar access as defined by circular service areas will either require a large number of facilities or it will leave large segments of the population uncovered. In this case, an alternative approach is to partition the regional territory into an exhaustive set of nonoverlapping service areas. This can be done by means of so-called *Thiessen* polygons, which assign each point in a study area to the closest facility based on straight-line proximity. This purely geometric approach has the same drawbacks as the circular areas, however, in that it assumes equal travel time in all directions. Moreover, in sparsely populated areas, services may be provided in different ways and by different means, such as mobile health clinics.

A more accurate description of the service areas can be achieved by incorporating information on the transport routes, the terrain, and so forth. This information is used, for example in a GIS analysis, to determine for each demand point the travel time to the nearest facility. Clearly, travel time to a facility that is determined by the existing road network and the quality of the access roads can be significantly different from the straight-line distance to the facility, and assigning each demand point to the nearest center so as to minimize the travel time will yield a set of irregularly shaped service areas which more accurately reflect the conditions on the ground. Figure 6.1 illustrates the large differences in the shapes of service areas for hospitals in eastern Nepal when the analysis is based on a straight-line distance only, and when the analysis incorporates information on transportation infrastructure and natural barriers (see United Nations 1997).

An alternative approach in the analysis of public service provision concentrates on the individuals or the households requiring the services, and the exact places in which they reside, rather than on the entire geographical area that surrounds the facility. This analysis typically applies the data provided by a census along with data from a variety of surveys at the household or village level that often include questions about access to services and the means of transportation. The community profile section of the Demographic and Health Surveys (DHS), for instance, contains questions about distance to the nearest health and family planning facilities as well as questions on the mode of transportation. This information can either be measured on road maps based on the actual location of the facilities and the villages or it can be based on the questionnaire responses. The latter source, however, often creates problems of consistency and reliability that may limit comparability across a larger study area and may require, in addition, independent estimates of travel time using consistent sources.

The most consistent independent source of data are digital geographic databases of transport networks and the location of service centers.[1] These can be used to measure the shortest distance from any demand point in the study area to the closest facility. Formally, the shortest distance measure can be denoted as shown in equation 6.1 (see, for instance, Anselin 1995, Talen and Anselin 1998):

$$E_i = \min_j \left(d_{ij} \right) \tag{6.1}$$

where E_i is the shortest-distance index for location i, and d_{ij} is the distance from the point of origin i to the location of facility j. This indicator is derived

Figure 6.1 Service Area Delineation Source: United Nations (1997)

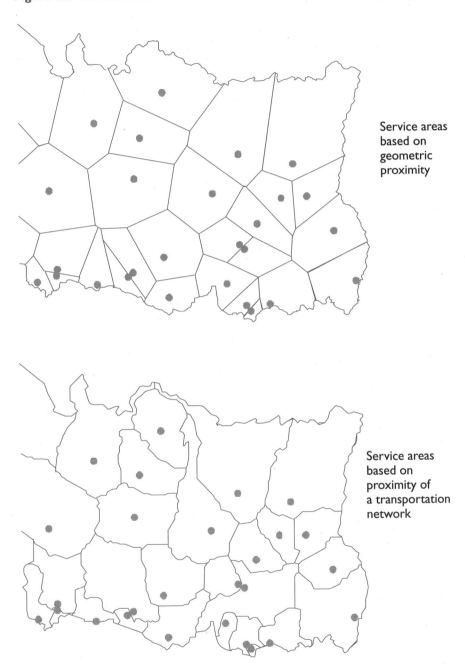

Service areas
based on
geometric
proximity

Service areas
based on
proximity of
a transportation
network

Source: Authors' calculations.

using standard shortest path algorithms which are implemented in many commercial mapping packages. Distance may not be the most appropriate measure, however, where the quality of the transport network is highly variable or where the cost of using public transport must be taken into account. A measure of travel cost or travel time can provide a more realistic measure. For these reasons, the more generic terms "impedance" or "friction" are sometimes used in the geographical literature rather than the term "distance."

The shortest-distance index has two drawbacks when used to determine the demand for and location of public facilities: First, this indicator considers only the spatial relationship between a given location and the service center, but not the services provided at that center. In most cases there are large differences between the services that each facility provides, and the more advanced or expensive services are typically provided only in a small number of central facilities. In that case, separate indicators should be computed for each type of service. Second, the shortest-distance index has an underlying assumption that people will use the closest facility. In general, this is indeed the decision of most people who tend to use the closest facility if the required service is provided there (Mayhew and Leonardi 1982). For example, a study by the Medical Research Council in South Africa on the use of public health facilities in a region of northern Natal province, which is characterized by a poor population and sparse infrastructure, found that more than 96 percent of the people use the nearest clinic (LeSueur and others 1997). In some cases, however, people may opt to go to a facility located farther away if the quality of the service in the more distant facility is deemed better. This may specifically apply in more urbanized areas where the density of service centers is higher (Amer and Thorborg 1996). Low-income households are more likely to use the closest facility, but quality considerations are likely to become more significant the higher the person's income. Additional considerations for the selection of the service center include government versus privately run services, and whether there are any costs for the services in the public facility (see, for example, Amer and Thorborg 1996).

When there are two facilities or more in an area, two alternative accessibility measures can be used: One is the *average* distance (or travel time, or travel costs), and the other is the *covering index*. The first is simply the average distance from a given demand point to all facilities in the area, as shown in equation 6.2:

$$T_i = \sum_{j=1}^{k} d_{ij} / k \qquad (6.2)$$

where T_i is the average distance (or travel time or travel costs) index, d_{ij} is the distance between demand point i and the location of facility j, and k is the number of facilities. This index can also be calculated only for the k nearest facilities, that is, the facilities that are located within a predetermined distance from the demand point. In this case the indicator will reflect the local density of facilities. The covering index, in contrast, is simply the number of facilities that are located within a predetermined threshold distance from the demand points. If the different facilities have different sizes or capacities, this index can also be calculated as the sum of a *size attribute* of all facilities that are located within a specified threshold distance or travel time. Formally, as shown in equation 6.3,

$$C_i = \sum_j \delta_{ij} S_j \qquad (6.3)$$

where C_i is the covering index, δ_{ij} indicates whether or not a destination is within the threshold distance δ ($\delta_{ij} = 1$ for $d_{ij} \leq \delta$ and $\delta_{ij} = 0$ otherwise), and S_j is the size attribute for each facility j. The *size attribute* can indicate the number of hospital beds, nurses, classroom spaces, teachers, or employment opportunities. In contrast to the shortest and average *travel time indicators*, which consider only the geographical distance between the demand point and the location of the facility, the *covering index* can also incorporate information on the size of the demand points and the quality of the services in the facility as expressed by its size attributes.

The information on size can also be incorporated into the *measure of accessibility* by assuming that accessibility decreases in proportion to the distance or travel time to the facility, but increases with the size of the facility. The well-known family of gravity models, which has found widespread application in fields such as transportation and migration analysis, is the best example of incorporating this information. In its original form, the gravity model states that interaction between, say, two cities, is proportional to the size of their populations and inversely proportional to some measure of distance between them (equation 6.4):

$$I_{ij}^g = k \frac{P_i P_j}{d_{ij}^b} \qquad (6.4)$$

where I_{ij}^g is the magnitude of interaction between cities i and j, k is a constant to be estimated, P_i and P_j are the population totals for the cities, d_{ij} is the distance between the two cities, and b is the distance exponent which, in the original formulation, was set equal to 2. The model parameters can be estimated using observed interaction data (see Fotheringham and O'Kelly 1989). The gravity model gives rise to a large family of spatial interaction models (Wilson 1971) that use different pieces of information to estimate the interaction between two points—for example, information on all flows, on outflows only, or on inflows only. These models are frequently used in health services analysis where data on the patients' place of residence are available (Taket 1989, Thomas 1992). Incidentally, gravity models have also received renewed attention in development economics in the context of the "new economic geography" (see, for example, Krugman 1995).

Although the formulation of the gravity models is intuitively appealing, it is necessarily ad hoc since it is not derived from standard consumer theory. For a more comprehensive formulation of the measure of accessibility, the starting point must be the basic theory of consumer behavior and the most general specification of the utility function. In consumer theory, that function is given by a Von Neuman—Morgenstern (VNM) function in which consumers' utility is a monotonic, strictly increasing, and strictly concave function of income. The implicit assumption in the standard geographical analysis is that utility is a function of two variables: the *distance* between the consumer's place of residence (the *demand point*) and the facility (along the road network), and the *size* of the facility, where the *size* can be a composite variable representing the variety and quality of services provided in that facility. These two variables are the basic building blocks in the gravity model. The utility function can thus be written as equation 6.5:

$$U_i = U(d_{ik}; M_k) \qquad (6.5)$$

where d_{ik} is the distance from the place of residence of household i to the public facility k and M_k is the "size" of that facility, which stands as a proxy for the variety of services provided. With K public facilities, d_{ik} and M_k are both K-dimensional vectors. To represent the *inverse* relations between the distance to the facility and the level of utility, the utility function can be written as equation 6.6:

$$U_i = U(1 / d_{ik}); M_k \qquad (6.6)$$

That utility function is assumed to be monotonically increasing in the two variables $(1/d_{ik})$ and M_k. The gravity model combines these two variables into a single variable, M_k/d_{ik}, and determines a specific functional form of the utility function.

To make this formulation less general, other assumptions must be added with respect to the structure of the utility function. In the literature on risk bearing, individuals are assumed to have no "money illusion." Changing the monetary units of a given prize from, say, dollars to cents should not change their utility from that prize. In the geographic context, the equivalent assumption is that a change in the units of measurement of the distance from kilometers to miles will not change the "disutility" from the public facility. This assumption implies that the utility function—as a function of distance—is similar to a Cauchy equation, that is, an equation that satisfies the following equality: $U(x \cdot y) = U(x) \cdot U(y)$. For a positive x and y and when $U(x)$ is monotonically increasing, the only solution of that equation is:

$$U(x) = U(1) \cdot x^{\delta} \quad \text{for} \quad \delta > 0$$

and

$$U(x) = \log_e(x) \quad \text{for} \quad \delta = 0.$$

The utility function U_i can thus be written as equation 6.7:

$$U_i = U(M_k) / (d_{ik})^{\beta} \quad \text{for} \quad \beta > 0. \tag{6.7}$$

This presentation of the utility function emphasizes that the underlying assumption in the gravity model is that the utility from the size of the public facility is simply proportional to the size. It implies therefore that the *marginal* utility from the size of the facility remains constant. In utility theory it is generally assumed, however, that the marginal utility from each factor is declining, and this assumption may also be reasonable with respect to the size of the public facility. If we assume, in addition, that individuals have no "illusion" with respect to the units of measurement of the size of the public facility, then the utility function will have the following form:

$$U_i = (M_k)^{\varepsilon} / (d_{ik})^{\beta}: \quad \text{where} \quad \beta > 0 \quad \text{and} \quad 0 < \varepsilon < 1. \tag{6.8}$$

Under these constraints on the parameters β and ε, the utility function will be a monotonic strictly increasing and strictly concave function of the two variables. In the case of a single facility of a given size the utility function for a single demand point i can be simplified and written as equation 6.9:

$$U_i = M^{\varepsilon} / (d_i)^{\beta} \quad \text{for} \quad \beta > 0 \quad \text{and} \quad 0 < \varepsilon < 1. \tag{6.9}$$

The constraint, $\varepsilon < 1$, implies that the marginal utility from the size of the facility (or the quality of its services) is positive but decreasing. We can now compare this representation of a consumer's utility from his spatial interactions, which has been derived from a general utility function, with the representation in the gravity model: First, the gravity model assumes that the marginal utility from size is constant. Second, the gravity model implicitly assumes a specific value of the elasticity parameter β, which determines the percentage decline in utility with an increase in the distance by one percent. The assumption of the gravity model for the value of this elasticity, $\beta = 1$, may unduly restrict the analysis to a specific type of consumers.

Gravity models can be generalized to yield so-called *potential models*. Rather than narrowing the computation to a specific demand point i and a specific destination j, the general measure of interaction can be extended to all possible or relevant destinations of a given demand point. The measure would then be the sum of the size attributes at all these destinations divided by a weighted sum of the distances to these destinations (Weibull 1976). Arentze and others (1994), and Geertman and Ritsema van Eck (1995) present recent applications. In the original formulation the measure of accessibility in the potential model is given by equation 6.10:

$$I_i^c = \sum_j \frac{S_j}{d_{ij}^\beta}$$
(6.10)

where I_j^c is the "classic" accessibility indicator, S_j is a size indicator at destination j, d_{ij} is the distance between origin i and destination j, and β is a distance exponent—which, along the lines of the earlier analysis of the consumer's decisions over space, represents the increasing marginal disutility from distance. The elasticity parameter can be estimated from actual data on consumers' interaction patterns. Several alternative models have been suggested, however, to characterize the interactions of consumers in space and the decline in their utility with the rise in distance (sometimes referred to as the "distance decay function"). One of the most popular is a negative exponential model:

$$I_i^{ne} = \sum_j S_j \cdot e^{\left(-d_{ij}^\beta / 2a^2\right)}$$
(6.11)

where I_i^{ne} is the potential accessibility indicator based on the negative exponential distance decay function, most other parameters are defined as before, and the parameter a is the distance to the point of inflection of the negative exponential function. The main difference between this formulation and the one derived earlier from the consumer's utility function is that in the present formulation the elasticity itself is no longer constant but is rising with the rise in the distance.

The choice among the alternative formulations of the gravity model must be based on empirical evidence. In empirical studies these models were shown to describe migration flows, trade, and consumers' travel choices very well. There is often a practical problem, however, in obtaining sufficient data in order to estimate the model's parameters. All too often, therefore, the parameters of the distance decay function are "borrowed" from other studies or set at some "reasonable" value. Moreover, the gravity model itself—in practically all its formulations—is ad hoc and the parameters are arbitrarily restricted to specific values rather than estimated.

Criteria of Social Fairness in the Location of Public Facilities

Early geographical studies that developed models for determining the "optimal" location of public facilities departed from the models that have been developed to determine the location of private facilities—such as the *p-median* problem which seeks to minimize the overall transport costs—by emphasizing the significance of the distribution of travel time or distance of the potential users. The *p-center* problem, for example, seeks to minimize the maximum distance from any demand node to its nearest facility. In economic analysis of income inequality, the equivalent formulation is the Rawlsian Max-Min principle in which the objective is to maximize the income of the poorest individual. (In the geographical context the criterion of the p-center problem thus represents a Min-Max principle.) When all instruments of redistribution are available without restrictions, the solution to that problem is equal income to all. In the context of the p-center problem, however, there are strict limitations on the policy instruments, since the demand points cannot be moved and the *p* public facilities can be placed only in the predetermined *q* locations which are available for that purpose.

There are other potential problems with the objective of the p-center problem. First, it gives very large weight to the needs of very remote households (or communities) regardless of their weight in the population. Second, it seeks to minimize the maximum distance regardless of what that distance is. The maximum distance may still be very manageable and there may thus be no justification for changing the location of public facilities to reduce this distance still further. Third, it seeks to minimize the maximum distance regardless of cost. As we shall see later, the Max-Min criterion for determining the location of public facility represents a very unique form of the underlying social evaluation function.

Closely related to this approach is the *covering problem* (Church and ReVelle 1976, ReVelle 1987). The *set covering location problem* (SCLP) determines the minimum number and location of facilities that are necessary to ensure that the *entire* population is covered within a certain distance. In cases where the available resources limit the number of new facilities that can be added to the system, the problem can be stated as *a maximum covering location problem* (MCLP) which seeks to find the optimal location of a specified number of facilities that will maximize the size of the population that can be served within a certain "acceptable" distance. The solution to this problem may benefit, however, first and foremost those individuals or communities that reside very close to the acceptable distance from a facility (just outside the covering range) while leaving uncovered those who reside farther away. An alternative strategy may be one that seeks to ensure first the coverage of those who reside furthest from a facility. This alternative highlights a fundamental problem with these optimization approaches:

Although the objectives that they establish are appealing, they are based on ad hoc criteria of social fairness.

Later geographical studies that evaluated the location configuration of public facilities from the point of view of social fairness have also focused on *distributional equity* as the main criterion of fairness (Taket 1989, Mandell 1991, Erkut 1993, Hay 1995, Talen and Anselin 1998; see Marsh and Shilling 1994 for a review of the relevant geographic literature). There are, however, differences between the use of equity as a criterion of fairness and social justice in economics and its use in geographical studies. In economic analysis, equity is measured in terms of money income and the policymakers have the instruments of taxes, subsidies, and income transfers at their disposal to change the existing income distribution and thereby achieve greater equity. The guiding principle in this process—and one of the axioms that the measure of inequality is required to satisfy—is the "principle of transfers," which states that a (regressive) transfer of income from one person to a more affluent person would increase income inequality and thereby worsen the overall welfare, however measured. In the context of geographical studies, this principle of (regressive) transfers can be stated as follows. Let $S_1 = (d_1,..., d_i, d_j,...d_n)$ be the distribution of the distances of n individuals from the public facility, where $d_1 \geq ... d_i \geq d_j \geq ... \geq d_n$. A distribution S_2 which represents a relocation of the public facilities that shortens the distance to individual j while increasing the distance to individual i, without changing the distance to any of the others—that is, $S_2 = (d_1,..., d_i + e, d_j - e,..., d_n)$—will be less equitable than S_1.[2]

In the context of spatial analysis, the policy instruments available for achieving greater equality in access to public facilities are far more limited than the policy instruments available for achieving greater income equality. First, these instruments are limited to the relocation of existing public facilities or the addition of new facilities whereas a relocation of the demand points is, in most cases, not feasible. Second, in many cases the location of new public facilities is limited to specific areas only—for example, areas where enough space is available. Third, the decision is often restricted to the location of one or few additional facilities due to budget constraints, and the location of existing facilities must be taken as given. These restrictions make the goal of achieving or even enhancing equality much more complex and expensive.

Several accessibility indicators that reflect equity considerations have been used in the geographic literature. They include the mean absolute deviation (MAD), the standard deviation, the Rawlsian maximum deviation (Erkut, 1993), and a host of inequality measures that have been developed for the analysis of income inequality, ranging from the Gini, to Theil's and Atkinson's measures. Each of these measures gives different weight to the individuals that are served by public facilities, depending on their distance from the facility. Berman and Kaplan (1990) used the MAD measure, given by equation 6.12, as the performance measure for equity considerations:

$$\sum_i \sum_j |d_{ij} - \bar{d}| \tag{6.12}$$

In this measure, the weight of each individual is equal to the distance from the place of residence to the facility. The Min-Max measure is given in equation 6.13:

$$MIN\left(\underset{ij}{MAX} |d_{ij} - \bar{d}| \right) \tag{6.13}$$

and it gives all the weight to the single individual who is furthest from the facility while the weight of all other individuals is zero.

In these measures, the "reference" point is the *average* distance to the facility, and the indicators measure the deviation from the *ideal* solution $(\bar{d}, \ldots, \bar{d})$ in which all individuals are located at an equal distance from the facility. The theory of welfare economics suggests, however, a different reference point for that evaluation which, in the present context, can be termed the "equally distributed equivalent" (EDE) distance. The EDE distance is defined as follows: If all households were equally distant from the facility at the EDE distance, the level of *social* welfare would have been the same as that with the actual distances of these households. Symbolically, the EDE distance d_E is defined as the distance for which:

$$W(d_1, \ldots, d_n) = W(d_E, d_E, \ldots, d_E) \tag{6.14}$$

where W is the social welfare function and n is the number of households (or consumers, or demand points) in this society. With an additive social welfare function and concave individual utility function with respect to distance, this definition implies:

$$\sum_j U(M, d_E) = n \cdot \frac{M^{\varepsilon}}{d_E^{\beta}} = \sum_j U_j(M, d_j) = \sum_j \frac{M^{\varepsilon}}{d_j^{\beta}} \tag{6.15}$$

From this equality we can solve:

$$d_E = \left\{ \frac{1}{n} \cdot \sum_j (d_j)^{-\beta} \right\}^{-1/\beta} \tag{6.16}$$

The reference point would then be the solution $(d_E, \ldots, d_E)$, and a reduction in the EDE distance to the facility represents a rise in social welfare. The concavity of the individual utility function implies that $d_E < \bar{d}$, indicating that the weights given to individuals are rising with the rise in their distance to the facility. The parameter β represents the sensitivity of the social evaluation function to the individual distances from the facility. From this specification of the EDE distance we can conclude that, other things being equal, a reduction in the distance to the facility for any individual will lead to a reduction in the distance d_E and a rise in social welfare, and that reduction is proportional to the distance of the individual from the facility. The rise in social welfare will therefore be larger the larger the distance of the individual from the facility.

Accessibility Indicators Based on Poverty Measures

An alternative approach to the evaluation of the location configuration of public facilities is closely related to the approaches in the economic literature on the measurement of poverty. In what follows, we review the possible application of the axiomatic approach to poverty measurement in order to develop criteria for evaluating access to public facilities. We then proceed to present the spatial analogs of some of the common poverty measures, and discuss their use as performance criteria in location analysis.

In the economic analysis of poverty, the starting point is the definition of the *poverty line*, defined as the minimum income or consumption level which is necessary to provide certain essential needs.[3] In spatial analysis, the equivalent of the poverty line would be the maximum distance to the public facility, beyond which the services provided would not be adequate. For health clinics or hospitals, this would be the maximum response time in which patients with certain illnesses must be reached or brought to the hospital without risking their life. For schools, this would be the maximum distance from the child's place of residence to the school; beyond this distance the child is likely to drop out of school. Similar criteria can be established for other public services and other public facilities. To illustrate these criteria, we consider the specific case of public health clinics, and the poverty line will be defined as the *safety threshold*, or the maximum response time that can be permitted in order to secure an adequate treatment.[4] Once the maximum response time has been determined, the next step is to measure the effectiveness of the system, namely its capacity to meet all demands within this response time. In an analogy to poverty measures, the performance criterion would be the *ineffectiveness* (rather than the effectiveness) of the system, and the principal difference between this measure and the one considered earlier is that the measure of the ineffectiveness focuses only on those households that cannot be served within the maximum response time.

The most common measure of *income* poverty in the economic literature is the *Headcount index*, which measures the proportion of the population with income per-person (or per "standard adult")[5] that is lower than the poverty line income. In location analysis, this would be the percentage of the population that the public facilities fail to serve within the maximum response time. The main deficiency of the Headcount index is that it is not sensitive to the actual distance to the facility of those that reside outside the maximum response time. A household that resides just outside the area covered within the maximum response time—that is, just beyond the safety threshold—has the same weight in this measure as a household that resides farther away. A location of a new facility aimed at reducing the Headcount measure would thus tend to cover individuals just outside the area covered within the maximum response time rather than those that reside farther away. This measure thus does not reflect the extent to which the system of public facilities fails to meet the necessary levels of safety. The Headcount measure of ineffectiveness remains unchanged with a rise in the distance to the facility of any of the households that reside outside the safety threshold.[6]

Another common measure of poverty is the *Poverty Gap*. In location analysis, the "gap" refers to the difference between the actual travel time or distance to the public facility and the maximum acceptable response time, and it is measured only for those households that reside outside the safety threshold. The mathematical specification of this measure is given in equation 6.17:

$$P(d,z) = (1/n) \cdot \sum_{g>0}(g_i / z) \tag{6.17}$$

where d_i is the actual distance from the household's place of residence to the facility; z is the safety threshold (the maximum response time), $g_i = (d_i - z)$ is the difference (the distance above the safety threshold) of the *ith* household, and n is the total number of households in the community. $P(d, z)$ is the measure of *ineffectiveness* when $d = (d_1, ..., d_q)$ is the vector of the actual distances to the facility of the households that reside outside the safety threshold, and z is the safety threshold. This measure can be written as equation 6.18:

$$P(d,z) = H \cdot (1/q) \cdot \sum_{g>0}(g_i / z) = H \cdot G \tag{6.18}$$

where $H = (q/n)$ is the Headcount measure, q is the number of households that reside outside the safety threshold, and G is the average time/distance to the facility above the maximum response time/distance. Figure 6.2 shows the parameters of these measures in a spatial analysis.

The disadvantage of this measure is that it fails to reflect the rising marginal *disutility* with the rise in the distance to the facility. On these grounds, Foster, Greer, and Thorbeke (1984) (see also Sen 1974, Foster and Shorrocks 1991, Ravallion 1994 and 1996) suggested a class of poverty measures that have the following general structure:

$$P_\alpha(d;z) = (1/n) \cdot \sum_{g>0}(g_i / z)^\alpha: \text{ where } \alpha \geq 0. \tag{6.19}$$

Figure 6.2 Computation of Accessibility Indicators

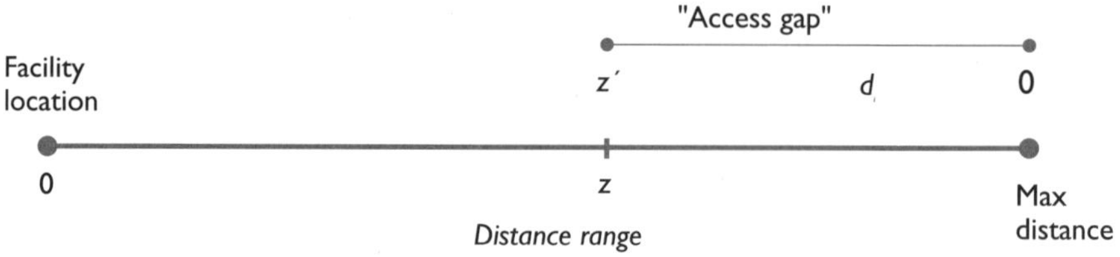

Source: Authors' calculations.

For $\alpha = 0$, $P_0(d; z) = H$ is simply the Headcount measure; for $\alpha = 1$, $P_1(d; z)$ is the Poverty Gap. For $\alpha = 2$, the measure can be written as follows:

$$P_2(d;z) = H \cdot \left[G^2 + \left(1 - G^2\right)C_p^2 \right] \tag{6.20}$$

where C_p^2 is the coefficient of variation of the distances to the facility of the households that reside outside the safety threshold, given by equation 6.21:

$$C_p^2 = (1/q) \cdot \sum \left[\left(d_i - d_p\right)^2 / d_p^2 \right] \tag{6.21}$$

and $d_p = (1/q)\sum d_i$ is the average distance to the facility of these households. The advantage of the latter index is that it is more sensitive to the safety needs of the households that reside farther away from the facility and reflects the rising *disutility* of these households from the location configuration of the public facilities.

An Illustration

This section provides an illustration of the use of these indicators of social fairness. Figure 6.3 shows the shortest distance indicator for a set of family planning service centers in two Faritany (province or first subnational level) of Madagascar. Travel times were computed using a road network database produced by the USAID-sponsored ANGAP (National Association for the Management of Protected Areas) project. Travel speed in off-road areas is assumed to be equivalent to an average walking speed of 5 kilometers per hour. Road quality information was converted into average travel speeds, which we used to compute travel times measured in minutes for each road segment in the transportation network. A standard shortest-path algorithm, as implemented in many GIS packages, was used to determine the distance from every 1-kilometer cell in a regular raster grid draped over the two provinces to the closest facility.

Figure 6.3 Shortest Distance Indicator for Two Provinces in Madagascar

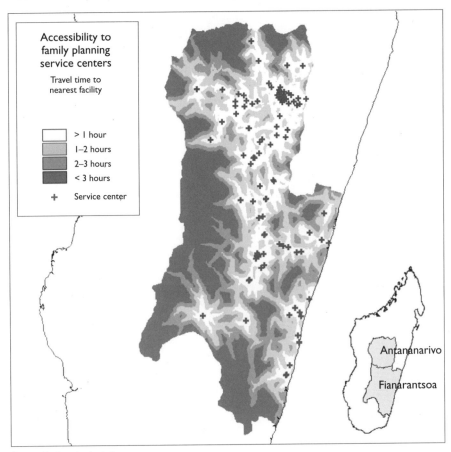

Source: Authors' calculations.

The underlying assumption is that a person living at a given location in the study area will travel directly to the nearest road access point and continue travel to the closest facility using, for instance, a bus or collective taxi. The travel speed estimates chosen for this analysis thus assume that every person has access to public transportation. In practice that may not be the case, and it may even be unlikely in many developing countries. One could therefore carry out a second analysis with lower travel speed estimates to complement these best-case estimates with a worst-case scenario.

Information on the location of family planning service centers was collected using global positioning systems (GPS) by the APROPOP/PF family planning/reproductive health (FP/RH) program in an ongoing project that is also supported by USAID. In the future, this project intends to also compile information on the types of services available and the capacity of each facility. Since not all services are provided at each facility, an accessibility analysis can then be conducted for each type of service using only those facilities at which the service is available.

By itself, the shortest distance indicator provides only limited information about the quality of the service delivery system. In order to get a full picture, we need to compare the information on travel times with effective or estimated demand. Data on effective demand requires a comprehensive monitoring program at the service centers which records the number of patients, their characteristics, needs, and, ideally, their place of residence. Such data could also be collected in a patient survey or a more general household survey such as a DHS. However, this information is not always readily available in developing countries, and comprehensive surveys tend to be expensive. Prospective demand therefore usually needs to be estimated. The most complete information available is the national population and household census, which provides a complete enumeration of the population and its main demographic characteristics, and is compiled by aggregating the information collected for small enumeration areas up to the district, province, and national level. While in the past small area statistics have often been difficult to obtain, the growing demand for such data and access to new technology has enabled many countries to compile data at a level of geographic detail that is useful for spatial analysis and targeting of policy interventions.

A spatially referenced database of population data by Firaisana (commune or third subnational level) from the 1993 census of Madagascar was produced by the Direction de la Démographie et Statistiques Sociales (DDSS) in Antananarivo in collaboration with the U.N. Population Fund-supported Software Development (POPMAP) Project of the United Nations Statistics Division. For the two provinces studied, there are 587 communes with an average population size of 10,529. The population within each commune is assumed to be distributed homogeneously. This may not always be the case in areas where terrain leads to a fragmented habitation pattern, but in light of the small administrative units, constant densities are a reasonable approximation for this illustrative application. Due to the nature of the service centers in this study, we chose the number of women in reproductive age (15–49) as the reference group rather than total population. Each commune has on average 2,483 women in reproductive age. In a purely family planning–oriented study this will, of course, not provide actual demand at the service centers. Ideally one would estimate the number of women in this age group who do not want additional children, using information, for example, from a DHS. However, population programs are increasingly oriented towards providing more comprehensive reproductive health services, which broadens the prospective user base significantly.

Using standard GIS functions, we cross-tabulated the total number of women in childbearing age by travel time to their closest facility (figure 6.4). After specifying a maximum acceptable travel time, this information, in turn, can be used to compute FGT-like accessibility indicators (Foster, Greer, and Thorbecke 1984). In this application, the threshold travel time was set to 60 minutes, the time in which an average person can cover about five kilometers on foot and a correspondingly larger distance by public or private transport. Obviously the choice of the threshold distance is as crucial in accessibility studies as the definition of a poverty line is in poverty analysis. The ability and willingness of people to travel to a facility will vary depending on age, health, economic means, the cost and quality of service at the target facility, and other factors. People in rural areas may be willing to travel farther than persons in urban areas. Amer and Thorborg (1996), for instance, found in a study of health facility use in Dar Es Salaam that patients were willing to travel about two kilometers or approximately 30 minutes. More than 90 percent traveled on foot, and people were willing to walk somewhat farther to a private or voluntary health facility than to a government clinic.

Figure 6.4 shows that approximately 57 percent of the women in reproductive age in the two provinces of Madagascar for which service center locations are available live within 60 minutes of the nearest facility. We can now summarize this information by political, administrative units using the

Figure 6.4 Number of Women in the Reproductive Age Group by Travel Time to the Closest Service Facility

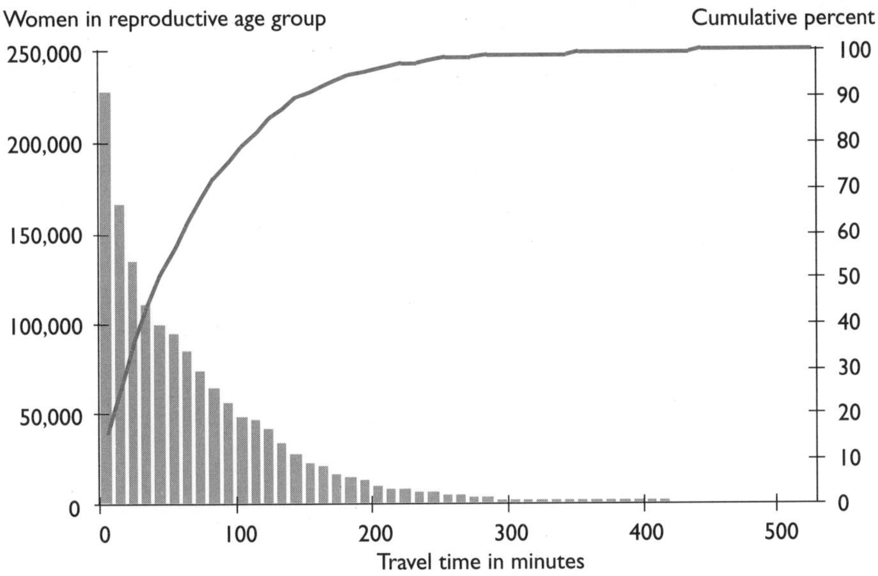

Source: Authors' computations.

indicators outlined above. To avoid the undue influence of a small number of very large travel times, we used a maximum (reference) travel time that covered 99.9 percent of the population and 99 percent of the total area— 517 minutes—rather than the maximum estimated travel time of 705 minutes. Table 6.1 shows the Headcount, the Access Gap, and the weighted Access Gap (severity) measures for the two provinces. To complement the Headcount index, we also computed each province's share of the total number of women in reproductive age who live beyond an acceptable distance. As can be easily verified, the indicators satisfy the additivity or subgroup consistency requirement; that is, the population-weighted average of the Access Gap and severity measures for the two provinces corresponds to the measures for the entire region.

Looking at the province-level figures, Fianarantsoa province has poorer overall accessibility by any measure. However, a more complex picture emerges when we compute the indicators at the Firondronana (district or second subnational) level. The results at this geographic level are shown graphically in figure 6.5 rather than in tabular form. The maps show the percentage of all women in the region living beyond the threshold distance, as well as the Headcount index, the Access Gap, and severity (P2) measures. Districts are shaded using a quintile classification whose ordinal ranking, while leading to class ranges of unequal size, highlights the different policy options very clearly. Assuming that the district is the level at which decisions about service delivery are made, we see that the geographic units that would be targeted—that is, those with the highest indicator scores—vary depending on which indicator is used.

- If the objective is to reach the largest absolute number of women that currently live beyond the predetermined distance, resources would be

Table 6.1 Accessibility Indicators—Women in Reproductive Age Groups (WRA)

Province	Numbers of WRA 15–49	Numbers of WRA living beyond 60 min. travel time	Percent of total WRA living beyond 60 min. travel time	Headcount index (percent)	Access Gap index*	Severity index*
Antananarivo	870	266	42.7	30.6	4.0	1.1
Fianarantsoa	588	358	57.3	60.9	9.8	3.0
All districts	1,458	624	100.0	42.8	6.3	1.9

* Using 517 minutes as a reference maximum travel time which covers 99 percent of the total area (99.9 percent of the population).

Source: Authors' computations.

Figure 6.5 Accessibility Indicators—Women in Reproductive Age Groups (WRA)

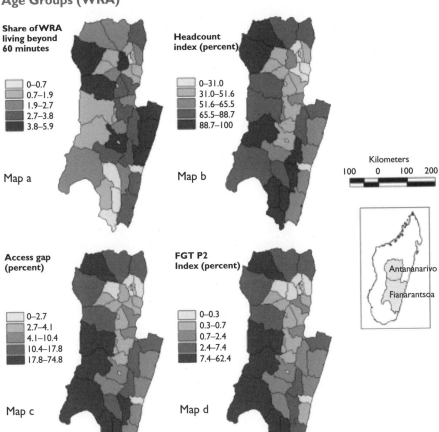

Source: Authors' computations.

allocated to the districts that are shaded in the darkest color in map a of figure 6.5. These districts are primarily located along the northern coastal region of Fianarantsoa province and in the northwest of Antananarivo province.

- If the objective is to improve access in those districts where the largest proportion of the district's women in reproductive age live beyond the predetermined distance, resources would be channeled to districts within the highest category in the Headcount index (map b of figure 6.5). Most of the target districts in this case are located in the south of Fianarantsoa province and in the northwest of Antananarivo province.

- Severity of the lack of access to services is best shown in maps c and d of figure 6.5. These two maps show a fairly similar pattern. In both cases, resources would be allocated to districts in the southwest of Fianarantsoa province, although one district in the northwest of Antananarivo province would also be the target of these allocations.

This example also shows how decisions about geographic targeting of resources and policy interventions can be improved by incorporating high-resolution, spatially referenced information. More precise allocation of funds reduces the chance that communities most in need will be ignored and that leakage of funds to less needy communities will occur. In the illustration in this section, we considered only a limited amount of information regarding the demand for services and the quality of the services provided at each facility. In a realistic application the analysis should also include data for various population groups, primarily about the effects of income and the quality of service. The macroeconomic conditions in the country, the national health policy, and the institutional arrangements may also be relevant (see, for example, Smith 1993).

Conclusions

This chapter suggests a new set of indicators for evaluating the *social fairness* of a location configuration of public facilities. These measures are the spatial analogues to measures of poverty in economic analysis, and are designed to satisfy a set of axioms that describe criteria of fairness. These indicators are easy to interpret and, similar to poverty measures, they have the property of subgroup consistency. The clear interpretation and the ease of computation of these measures make them suitable for a wide range of applications. The results can be represented in graphical form, thus clarifying the interpretation still further, and the analysis of alternative policy options in terms of their effects on these measures is straightforward. An important use of indicators of social fairness is to establish priorities in determining the location of *additional* public facilities; the indicators that have the form of poverty measures focus on the needs of the population that is not covered by the existing facilities within the acceptable standards of distance or travel time. An illustration of the application of these indicators measures the effectiveness of family planning centers in Madagascar and shows that the choice of an indicator can greatly influence the priorities between districts for the location of new centers. These different priorities reflect, in turn, different underlying approaches to the concept of fairness in spatial analysis: Whereas the Headcount indicator focuses on the *number* of persons who currently do not have access to the facilities within the acceptable standard, the Access Gap focuses on the persons who are the most distant from the facility. The Headcount index thus gives priority to the more dense, semi-urban areas, whereas the Access Gap index gives priority to the more remote rural areas.

The conceptual and computational simplicity of these indicators—particularly in comparison to many of the indicators that have been derived from location/allocation models in operations research—make them suitable for immediate application. These applications may require, however, additional data on the population and on the services provided by the facilities. These data are available in most developing countries and their presentation as a GIS database can greatly facilitate the analysis. The incorporation of additional data may also allow proper adjustments in the structure of the indicators themselves in order to introduce additional criteria of fairness and effectiveness. Thus, for example, indicators of access to family planning service centers may focus on the access of *poor* women or women in a specific age group rather than the access of *all* women. A proper adjustment of the indicators may also establish different accessibility criteria for the different services provided by these centers. These adjustments are straightforward, and they make these indicators particularly suitable to incorporate a wider variety of criteria in addition to distance.

Notes

A previous version of this chapter was presented at the workshop on "Geographical Targeting for Poverty Reduction and Rural Development," conducted at the World Bank on November 11, 1997.

We were fortunate to have access to a number of data sets for the Madagascar sample application, which were produced by the Direction de la Démographie et Statistiques Sociales (DDSS), and the APPROPOP/USAID and ANGAP/USAID projects. We are grateful to Jim Allman, Eric Ribaira, Jean-Michel Dufils, and Vu Duy Man for making the data sets available and to Norbert Henninger and the three reviewers for comments on an earlier draft of this chapter. The opinions expressed in this chapter are those of the authors and do not necessarily represent those of the World Bank.

David Bigman is at the International Service for National Agricultural Research (ISNAR). He was at the Africa Region of the World Bank when this chapter was written. Uwe Deichmann is with the Development Research Group of the World Bank.

1. It should be noted, though, that published maps and digital data sets of transportation networks are often incomplete and may include roads that have become unusable or that have been planned but were never completed.

2. The reason for specifying the Transfer Axiom for *regressive* rather than *progressive* transfers is that, with a progressive relocation of the facility the two individuals may just "trade places" in the distribution as an effect of the relocation so that $d_i \geq d_j$ before the relocation, but $d_i - \varepsilon < d_j + \varepsilon$ after the relocation.

3. These needs can be specified, for example, in terms of the food expenditures needed to provide the minimum necessary caloric intake.

4. In risk analysis, the comparable concept is the *safety first* criterion. This criterion is concerned only with the risk of failing to achieve a certain minimum target or secure prespecified safety margins. The risk can then be expressed as a probability statement: $P_r(x \leq z) \leq \beta$ where x is the random variable of, say, profits; z is the minimum profit target, often referred to as the "disaster level" or the "safety threshold;" $P(\ )$ is a probability statement; and β is an acceptable limit on the probability of failing to reach that target.

5. To take account of the difference in consumption between children and adults, the consumption of children younger that 13 years old is calculated as a fraction of the consumption of adults.

6. It should be noted that when the MCLP is stated in its inverse form of minimizing the proportion of the population that resides outside the threshold, it has the same objective.

References

Amer, S., and H. Thorborg. 1996. "Health Coverage in Urban Dar es Salaam. Users, Interaction Patterns, Under-Serviced Areas." International Institute for Aerospace Survey and Earth Sciences. Enschede, The Netherlands.

Anselin, Luc. 1995. *SpaceStat Version 1.80 User's Guide.* Morgantown: Regional Research Institute, West Virginia University.

Arentze, T.A., A.W.J. Borgers, and H.J.P. Timmermans. 1994. "Multistop-Based Measurements of Accessibility in a GIS Environment." *International Journal of Geographical Information Systems* 8(4): 343–356.

Berman and Kaplan. 1990. "Inequality Maximizing Facility Location Schemes." *Transportation Science* 24(2): 137–144.

Church, Richard L., and Charles S. ReVelle. 1976. "Theoretical and Computational Linkages between The P-Median, Location Set-Covering and Maximal Covering Location Problem." *Geographical Analysis* 8: 406–415.

Development Solutions for Africa (DSA). 1997 "Health and Family Planning in Kitui District: A Geographic Information Systems Analysis." Report prepared for U.N. Population Fund, Development Solutions for Africa, Nairobi, Kenya.

Erkut, E. 1993. "Inequality Measures for Location Problems." *Location Science* 1(3): 199–217.

Foster, J.E., J. Greer, and E. Thorbecke. 1984. "A Class of Decomposable Poverty Measures." *Econometrica* 52(4): 761–766.

Foster, J.E., and A.F. Shorrocks. 1991. "Subgroup Consistent Poverty Indices." *Econometrica* 59(3): 687–709.

Fotheringham, A. S., and M.E. O'Kelly. 1989. *Spatial Interaction Models: Formulations and Applications.* Dordrecht, The Netherlands: Kluwer Academic Publishers.

Geertman, S.C.M., and J.R. Ritsema van Eck. 1995. "GIS and Models of Accessibility

Potential: An Application in Planning." *International Journal of Geographical Information Systems* 9(1): 67–80.

Hay, A.M. 1995. "Concepts of Equity, Fairness and Justice in Geographical Studies." *Transactions, Institute of British Geographers* 20: 500–508.

Krugman, Paul R. 1995. *Development, Geography and Economic Theory*. Cambridge, MA: MIT Press.

LeSueur, David, and others. 1997. "Towards a Spatial Rural Information System." Medical Research Council, Durban, South Africa.

Mandell, M.B. 1991. "Modelling Effectiveness-Equity Tradeoffs in Public Service Delivery Systems." *Management Science* 37(4): 467–482.

Marsh, M.T., and D.A. Shilling. 1994. "Equity Measurement in Facility Location Analysis: A Review and Framework." *European Journal of Operational Research* 74: 1–17.

Mayhew, L.D., and G. Leonardi. 1982. "Equity, Efficiency, and Accessibility in Urban and Regional Health-Care Systems." *Environment and Planning* 14: 1479–1507.

Pooler, J.A. 1995. "The Use of Spatial Separation in the Measurement of Transportation Accessibility." *Transportation Research* 29(6): 421–427.

Ravallion, Martin. 1994. *Poverty Comparisons*. Chur, Switzerland: Harwood Academic Publishers.

———. 1996. "Issues in Measuring and Modelling Poverty." *Economic Journal* 106: 1328–1343.

ReVelle, Charles S. 1987. "Urban Public Facility Location." In E.S. Mills, ed., *Handbook of Regional and Urban Economics*, Vol. 2. Amsterdam: North Holland.

Sen, A.K. 1976. "Poverty: An Ordinal Approach to Measurement." *Econometrica* 46: 437–446.

Smith, K.A. 1993. "Accessibility, Ethics and Equity in Health Care." *Social Science and Medicine* 36(12): R3–R7.

Stewart, J.Q., and W. Warntz. 1958. "Physics of Population Distribution." *Journal of Regional Science* 1: 99–123.

Taket, A.R. 1989. "Equity and Access: Exploring the Effects of Hospital Location on the Population Served—A Case Study in Strategic Planning." *Journal of the Operational Research Society* 40(11): 1001–1010.

Talen, Emily, and Luc Anselin. 1998. "Assessing Spatial Equity: An Evaluation of Measures of Accessibility to Public Playgrounds." *Environment and Planning* A(30): 595–613.

Thomas, R. 1992. *Geomedical Systems. Intervention and Control*. London: Routledge.

Truelove, M. 1993. "Measurement of Spatial Equity." *Environment and Planning* B(11): 19–34.

United Nations 1997. *Geographical Information Systems for Population Statistics*. Studies in Methods, Series F, 68, New York, United Nations Statistics Division, Department of Social and Economic Information and Policy Analysis.

Weibull, J. 1976. "An Axiomatic Approach to the Measurement of Accessibility." *Regional Science and Urban Economics* 6: 357–379.

Wane, H.R., H. Kontongomde, and C. Kolars. 1995. "Population, Health and Environment in Niger. A Geographic Information Systems (GIS) Perspective." Niamey: Government of Niger, AGRHY-MET, CILSS, CERPOD/ INSAH.

Wilson, A.G. 1971. "A Family of Spatial Interaction Models, and Associated Developments." *Environment and Planning* A(3): 1–32.

Part Three

Applications of a Geographical Information System (GIS) for Geographical Targeting

7

Evaluation of Food Security in the Sahel: An Analysis Using the Demographic and Health Survey (DHS) Data with a Geographical Information System

Mark McGuire

THE PROCESS OF PREPARING A PLAN for the spatial distribution of health or education programs, selecting sites for economic development activities, or designing the road infrastructure, requires a wide variety of detailed data on the climate and geography of the target area, and on the socioeconomic characteristics of the population that lives in this area. In West Africa, a considerable amount of data has been collected over the last decade on geographic regions and economic sectors by different organizations, government ministries, and international organizations. However, these data collection efforts often are not followed by comparable analytical efforts, and even when analytical efforts have been made, they were not integrated into regional program planning. The objective of this work is to shift the focus from collecting new data to utilizing existing databases, to better respond to the needs of decisionmakers in the area of food security, vulnerability assessments, and regional planning. In these times of cutbacks and downsizing, the demand for information has not subsided and organizations and institutions are compelled to find ways to make more efficient use of existing resources and databases.

In recent years, there has been a concerted effort of USAID to extend spatial analysis in Sub-Saharan Africa, with the objective of improving the understanding of vulnerability to food insecurity. Another objective is to strengthen the linkage between the spatial data that has become available and analysis of these data to improve decisionmaking in this critical area.[1] This chapter will describe the databases collected under several USAID projects in Sub-Saharan Africa, review the basic vulnerability assessment model used by the Famine Early Warning System (FEWS), and evaluate the relations between the mapping of vulnerability to the food insecurity determined by these data, and poverty mapping.

The USAID study made use of the linkage established in previous work among the databases in West Africa under a project entitled "West Africa Spatial Analysis Prototype" (WASAP). This project had three main objectives:

1. Geocoding the Demographic and Health Survey (DHS) clusters from West and Central Africa,
2. Developing socioeconomic indicators from DHS data, and
3. Developing a georeferenced regional database, including socioeconomic and biophysical information.

The DHS program was created to provide an internationally comparable set of data to describe health and demographic characteristics of populations in developing countries. There are many publications describing the sampling characteristics of the DHS, individual country reports, and various comparative studies and analytical reports (see MACRO, Intl. 1997a, 1997b, 1996, 1994). The following is a brief description of the DHS database:

The DHS is a national sample survey designed to provide information on fertility, family planning, and health. The DHS involves interviewing a randomly selected group of women who are between 15 and 49 years of age. These women are asked about their background, the children they have given birth to, their knowledge and use of family planning methods, the health of their children, and other information that is important to understand their behavior.

Typically, the DHS sample is selected in two stages. Initially, a predetermined number of enumeration areas (EA) are chosen, usually stratified based on geographic region, or urban or rural residence, with equal probability. A complete household listing and mapping activity is next conducted in all chosen EAs. The second sampling stage is based on this listing of households. Households are selected from these lists for inclusion in the survey with probability proportional to the size of the EA. All women age 15 to 49 years in selected households are eligible for interview.

The DHS data in the WASAP database are aggregated to the cluster level, and various demographic and health indicators can then be calculated for each cluster. Each cluster contains approximately 30 households and the cluster-level indicators can then be aggregated to higher levels (for example, subregions within a country or user-specified geographic areas). The DHS indicators used in the WASAP database are grouped according to the following characteristics:

- Individual and household background characteristics
- Women's fertility and fertility preferences
- Family planning practices of currently married women
- Access to prenatal and delivery care
- Status of maternal and child nutrition
- Access to childhood immunization
- Prevalence of childhood morbidity and treatment
- Knowledge of and attitude towards HIV/AIDS
- Availability of services at the cluster level.

The DHS data are included as part of the WASAP database, as are other variables and geographic characterizations (for example, economic diversity, agro-ecological zones, and accessibility). Figure 7.1 illustrates the distribution of the DHS clusters in the WASAP database with an example of a geographic characterization used in this study, that is, aridity zones (which will be discussed in more detail in the fourth section of this chapter, "Results and Discussion"). The data are stored in a georeferenced format and are readily accessible for analysis in a geographic information system (GIS).[2] Among other results, the WASAP project demonstrated the benefits of georeferencing data to:

1. Examine the spatial distribution in the DHS data
2. Integrate different surveys for the same geographic area
3. Allow changing between geographic units of analysis
4. Integrate socioeconomic data with biophysical data.

Overview of the FEWS Project and Vulnerability Assessments

Since 1985, the USAID-funded FEWS Project has been collecting and analyzing secondary data related to food security in several Sub-Saharan African countries. A GIS has been an important tool for the storage, analysis, and presentation of FEWS products and information. The primary medium for disseminating this information is through monthly bulletins and via the Internet.[3]

In addition to the monthly FEWS bulletins, the project has also been conducting periodic Vulnerability Assessments (VA) that summarize the food security situation in a given country. Vulnerability is defined in the FEWS context as "relative susceptibility of households to various levels of food insecurity"—that is, food shortages that would have an impact on the health or physiological development of individuals. The VA analysis examines factors that affect *food availability* (for example, crop production, rainfall, pasture conditions, and imports and exports) as well as factors that affect *access to food* (such as prices, household income, and proximity to markets).

VAs are usually done country-by-country, but in 1994, FEWS conducted a Regional Vulnerability Assessment (RVA) as an attempt to describe the food security situation across multiple countries in the Sahel (Mali, Burkina Faso, Niger, and Chad). The RVA addressed such issues as how to select and analyze food security indicators that would be comparable across different countries, how to determine the most appropriate geographic unit of analysis, and how to deal with missing or incomplete data for certain countries (Wright and others 1994). The model differentiates vulnerability into the temporal dimensions of *baseline* and *current* vulnerability, defined as follows:[4]

- *Baseline* (or *chronic*) vulnerability to food insecurity is the result of poverty, riskiness of income sources, and limited access to alternative income sources. Baseline vulnerability indicators attempt to capture relative wealth and stability of income as a description of the general economic environment.
- *Current* (or *transitory*) vulnerability is the result of major changes in income or production for own consumption in the past three years, such as recent changes in growing conditions, crop production, general functioning of the cereal markets, and civil insecurity situations.

Factors that lead to chronic vulnerability can be further subdivided into those factors that affect the *resource base* (for example, length of growing season, variability of the growing season, variability in rainfall, and physical access to infrastructure, such as markets, schools, and health clinics), and those factors that affect the *income base* within the household (for example, as given by per capita production of cereals, livestock, and cash crops). Ideally, household surveys should be used to get a more complete picture of the income structure, but secondary, aggregated data were used as proxies for income in the RVA. However, when taken together as a whole, the chronic factors give an indication of the relative long-term vulnerability to food insecurity of a population in a given area or, conversely, the apparent resiliency of the population to deal with economic or climatic shocks that may disrupt the food security situation. The RVA was one of the first attempts by the FEWS project to compare vulnerability across multiple countries. Since this study was completed in 1994, there have been a number of developments in VA methodology, both within the project and outside, but not much in the way of regional analysis or cross-country comparisons.[5]

This brief overview of the FEWS and WASAP projects illustrates the utility of linking socioeconomic data with biophysical data using a GIS. The WASAP project was a significant step forward in that, in addition to demonstrating the utility of a georeferenced database to study cross-sectoral issues, the project also made these data more available and accessible to sector specialists interested in their operational use. The FEWS project has also made important contributions in studying and analyzing cross-sectoral issues, by combining socioeconomic and biophysical factors from a food security perspective. Other initiatives to make existing socioeconomic data more wide-ly available, accessible, and integrated across sectors are now underway.

One example of a project that combines socioeconomic data with bio-physical data is the poverty mapping being conducted by the World Bank and others. The purpose of poverty mapping is to identify populations that would be most affected by major economic disruptions, and to help guide policies and programs to alleviate poverty. Poverty mapping and vulnera-bility assessments have similar objectives. The next section discusses the assumptions underlying vulnerability and poverty mapping with the DHS variables.

Vulnerability and Poverty in the DHS Data

Henninger (1997) indicated that the baseline (chronic) data and indicators used in the FEWS vulnerability assessments could be adapted to meet the needs of a poverty analysis, and the results of poverty mapping could be incorporated in vulnerability and food security assessments. The various approaches presented at the World Bank–sponsored Geographical Targeting Workshop for poverty alleviation illustrated the overlap of data and indicators used in the different approaches for vulnerability assessment and poverty mapping (such as household income, consumption, expendi-tures, census data, health and nutrition, education, environmental, and accessibility). The largest difference is the scale and geographic coverage of the data and the level of effort required to get the desired results.

The various reviews of poverty mapping and assessment of vulnerabili-ty to food insecurity point out the difference between poverty and vulnera-bility, and note that poverty is not the same as vulnerability (Glewwe and Hall 1995).[6] There are, however, similarities between the basic goals of poverty mapping and the assessment of vulnerability to food insecurity.

Vulnerability assessments attempt to identify where the poorest people are, but they focus on those people who live in "risky" environments and would be most affected by a disruption to their livelihoods such as pro-longed drought, major crop failure, devastating livestock disease, or major macroeconomic shocks. The poorest tend to have not only low incomes, but also low and unstable resource base. Poverty mapping attempts to identify where the poor people, particularly the chronic poor, reside, taking into account their low income or low consumption, but not their low resource base. By focusing on the income components, poverty mapping may ignore the effects of biophysical factors such as the rainfall regime and soil type. Vulnerability mapping identifies more biophysical factors, but most meth-ods now assume that some measure of income is a critical component to characterizing susceptibility to food insecurity.

In our basic regional model of vulnerability, we assume that poor peo-ple tend to be more food insecure and that the major determinants of food security are income related. The data on the income-related components are, however, the most difficult and costly to gather. Direct or proxy indicators can therefore improve the mapping of poverty and vulnerability.

In general, the poorest people, as well as the people most vulnerable to food insecurity, tend to have similar demographic, socioeconomic, and health characteristics, such as low levels of education, high fertility rates and more children, limited access to health facilities and schools, and poor health and nutritional status. The data on these characteristics are included in the DHS data.[7] DHS data would allow the inclusion of these demographic and health factors in the basic model of vulnerability to food insecurity and to develop proxies for income-related measures. For example, access of women to prenatal care (a DHS variable) is partly a function of income, of the proximity of the health facility, and mother's level of education (also DHS variables).

Study Site Description

We first created several analysis scenarios, following the aggregation of certain DHS variables by various geographic characterizations, such as aridity zones or vulnerability classes. For this analysis we used the geographic information in the WASAP database, which included 14 West and Central African countries.

Subsequently, we focused on those countries that overlap between FEWS vulnerability assessments and the DHS variables, such as Mali, Niger, Burkina Faso, and Senegal. These selected countries are the study area to test various hypotheses between DHS variables and vulnerability characterizations. The resulting subset database comprised 1,023 DHS clusters as summarized in table 7.1.

Table 7.1 Study Site Summary of DHS Database.

Country	Administrative level	Number of clusters	Urban (%)	Rural (%)
Senegal	30 departments	258	132 (51)	126 (49)
Mali	47 cercles, including Bamako	300	118 (39)	182 (61)
Burkina Faso	30 Provinces	230	110 (48)	120 (52)
Niger	36 arrondissements, including Niamey	235	105 (45)	130 (55)
Total	143	1023	465 (45)	558 (55)

Note: Numbers in parentheses are percent of total.
Source: McGuire (1998).

Results and Discussion

The results of the analysis of DHS data, in relation to selected indicators of food security, are presented along the following three axes: (1) aggregating DHS statistics by broad geographic zones, (2) using multivariate analysis of DHS data at the cluster level, and (3) developing summary indicators by subnational administrative units.

Aggregated DHS Statistics by Geographic Zone

One way to represent and analyze the DHS indicators is to develop aggregated statistics for a given variable relative to some geographic characterization or geographic construct. A geographic construct could be national or subregional boundaries, or other geographic areas of interest, such as agroecological zones, FEWS vulnerability classes, or economic diversity zones. These geographic constructs can be thought of as ways to classify and organize data that are more explicit to a given sector than simple administrative units (such as the department, province, or arrondissement).

As part of the WASAP project, the relationship between selected DHS variables and various geographic constructs was examined (World Resources Institute (WRI) 1996a, 1996b, 1996c). One of the case studies examined the relationship between child nutritional status and the aridity of the child's place of residence. The anthropometric indicators of child nutrition included stunting (low height-for-age), wasting (low weight-for-height), and underweight (low weight-for-age). Aridity zones were taken from the International Center for Research in Agroforestry (ICRAF) in Nairobi, Kenya. The aridity index (AI) was used as given by the World Atlas of Desertification, in which AI is defined as the ratio of precipitation to potential evapotranspiration (table 7.2). The distribution of the DHS clusters in the WASAP database and the ICRAF aridity zones are shown in figure 7.1.

Results (figure 7.2) show a gradual decline in malnutrition indicators in the transition from the arid zones in the north to the more fertile and humid zones along the coast. The only exception is the percentage of children stunted, which is highest in the semi-arid zone. Further analysis shows a significantly higher incidence of malnutrition in rural areas compared with urban areas, with the highest proportion of stunted children in the dry sub-humid zone of the urban clusters.

The United Nations Environment Programme (UNEP) poverty-mapping project also examined malnutrition in the various aridity zones, as well as in land degradation zones, focusing primarily on the rural clusters (UNEP 1997). The UNEP study also used the DHS variables to approximate a Human Development Index (HDI), using child mortality, adult female literacy, primary school enrollment, and percentage of children stunted as surrogates

Table 7.2 Aridity Zones and Population Characteristics of the WASAP Database

Aridity zone code	Aridity zone	Aridity index (AI) range	Estimated population 1994 (millions)	Person/km2
1	Hyper arid	< .05	.4	.35
2	Arid	.005–.20	.8	9.57
3	Semi-arid .	20–.5	51.2	50.5
4	Dry sub-humid	.5–.65	15.4	41.3
5	Moist sub-humid	.65–1.0	30.7	35.6
6	Humid	> 1	47.1	65.1

Source: Adapted from World Resources Institute (1996c).

for poverty levels. The human development variables used in the UNEP study are summarized by aridity zones in table 7.3. These results show a clear north-south relationship for three of the four indicators: child mortali-

Figure 7.1 DHS Cluster Locations and ICRAF Aridity Zones

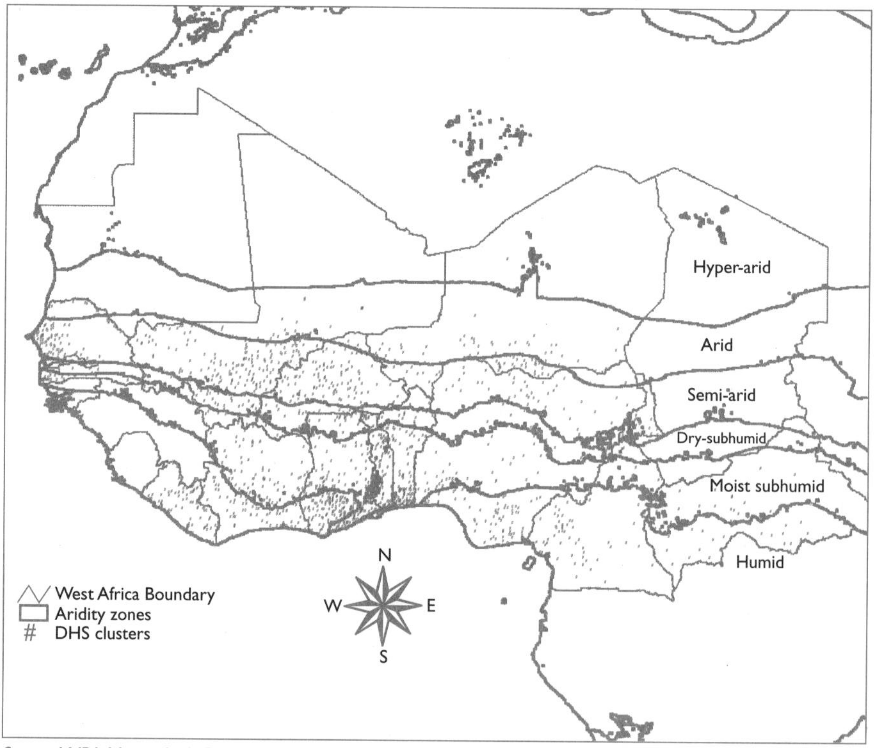

Source: WRI, Macro Intl., BUCEN, ICRAF; June 1997.

Figure 7.2 Child Malnutrition by Aridity Zone

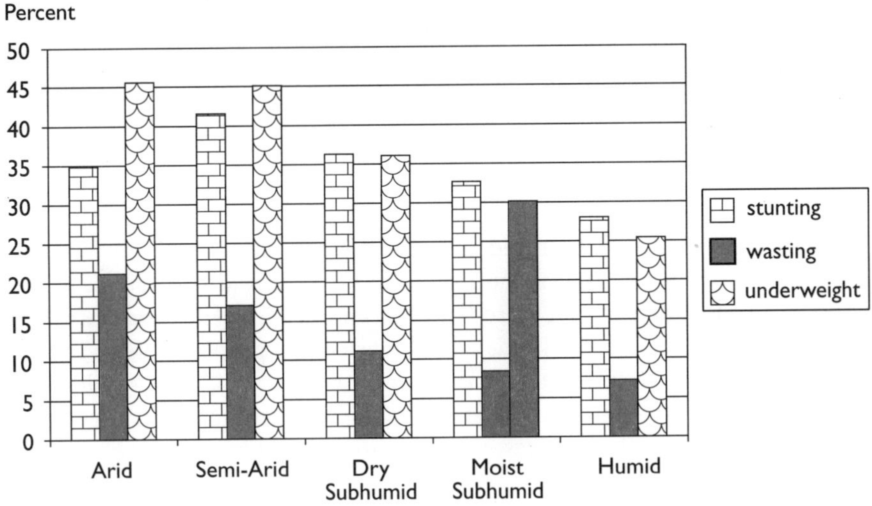

Percent

Source: Adapted from WRI, 1996a.

ty, adult literacy, and school enrollment, but were less clear for the stunted children index—although there is a slight peak in the semi-arid zone (similar to the WRI results).

The examples given above illustrate how information by different geographic zones can be used to study socioeconomic variables in the context of vulnerability to food insecurity. The data raise several questions however.

For example, why do the malnutrition data indicate a slight, but statistically significant peak in the semi-arid zone? Health data are not typically analyzed relative to environmental data and it is difficult to draw absolute conclusions. However, the analysis does provide a new way of looking at

Table 7.3 Proxy Variables Used by UNEP to Develop a Human Development Index (HDI) from the WASAP Database.

Aridity zone	Child mortality	Adult literacy	School enrollment	Stunted growth
Arid	31.7	4.1	13.1	36.9
Semi-arid	26.7	6.3	15.8	37.8
Dry subhumid	21.7	10.0	25.1	34.9
Moist subhumid	17.3	21.5	36.9	33.8
Humid	17.9	42.3	61.0	32.0

Note: Units are the average value (in percent) of the DHS variables by aridity zone.
Source: From UNEP (1997).

the question, and among the plausible explanations are the following. (1) The inherent variability in the DHS data is greater in the semi-arid zone than the arid zone. (2) The diet of the principally nomadic groups in the arid zone (that is, groups with more dairy products in their diet) is different from that of the populations in the semi-arid zone, where rain-fed agricultural systems are the most variable.

These examples illustrate how socioeconomic data (derived from the DHS database) can be analyzed with respect to biophysical data instead of simply aggregated by administrative units. The examples also illustrate the utility of having a georeferenced database, which, in addition to the new analytical capabilities, allows the results to be readily displayed in maps. These examples suggest that there are trends in certain DHS variables when aggregated across different kinds of biophysical geographic zones. To further examine the DHS data and determine which variables would contribute the most to the spatial characterization of vulnerability, we used multivariate analysis techniques, which are discussed in the next section.

Using Multivariate Analysis

To further explore the possibility of using the DHS cluster–level data to make inferences about the relationship between variables and the variability between clusters, we resorted to multivariate analysis techniques (such as principal components analysis, or PCA). The sample unit for the multivariate analysis was the cluster itself, as compared with the broad summary statistics by geographic strata described above. Our assumption was that indicators are valid estimates at the cluster level since each cluster actually comprises approximately 20 to 30 samples at the household level.

The first step was to select a subset of variables from the extensive DHS database, focusing on those variables we expected to be most appropriate in the basic model for describing vulnerability to food insecurity. The initial subset of variables included child mortality, child nutrition (wasting, stunting, underweight), education, and various household characteristics. We also selected a corresponding subset from the FEWS biophysical variables as presented in the *baseline* vulnerability assessment methodology. The FEWS income base indicator was not used in this analysis because it represented only agricultural income, and one of the underlying goals for exploring the DHS database was to find proxy variables that could be used to fill in the gaps in the income-related components.

The next step was to develop descriptive statistics for the DHS subset using the 1,023 clusters in the study site (as given in table 7.1). From the initial subset, only those variables that had a "quasi-normal" frequency distribution as given by the descriptive statistics and skewness measures were retained for further analysis. The descriptive statistics were developed for each selected DHS indicator using the SPSS statistical package and then mapped in ARCVIEW to examine the geographic coverage of the indicator. We also examined the correlation matrices and removed those variables that were not highly correlated. The final subset was then analyzed using PCA.

The results of the PCA indicate that the first four principal components explain over 81 percent of the variability among the clusters (table 7.4). The loadings of the first four components were interpreted as follows:

- PC1 —> Education/literacy/household income status
- PC2 —> Biophysical or resource base status
- PC3 —> Demographic and fertility status
- PC4 —> Children's nutritional status

Although the results of the PCA and the interpretation of the components do not provide a causative model for vulnerability, the results are not inconsistent with what has been indicated in previous studies: the relative importance of education and income in explaining the variability between the clusters, especially as it relates to poverty or vulnerability status. These findings lend support to the assumption that the cluster-level data can be used to characterize the relationship between education, fertility, access, and biophysical parameters as determinants of vulnerability to food insecurity.

DHS Indicators Summarized by Subnational Administrative Units

The final presentation of the results was designed to be more useful to policymakers and regional planners. Examining the DHS variables aggregated by geographic zones or as clusters may lead to better understanding of vulnerability and child mortality and malnutrition, but these techniques are too broad (or too detailed) to use in planning regional programs and interventions. To address this concern, we summarized the results of the DHS analysis at the second administrative level, which corresponds to departments (Senegal), cercles (Mali), provinces (Burkina Faso), or arrondissements (Niger), as given in table 7.1. However, often the data do not provide exhaustive coverage at these levels. Usually, data are available at higher administrative levels (level 1), but they do not contain sufficient detail at lower levels. For this reason, we extended the use of the DHS data slightly beyond its original design in order to provide reasonable estimates at the second administrative level, since the DHS sampling design is generally consistent across these countries and contains the same variables.

In order to represent the results at subnational level, we used several basic data manipulation techniques: spatial filtering, to increase the coverage of the DHS data, and rescaling and ranking, to develop indexes that could be compared across the four countries. Only the variables that were selected in the final stage to characterize vulnerability across this region were filtered, rescaled, and ranked. A brief description of the spatial filtering technique will be presented along with examples of the final indexes.[8]

Table 7.4 DHS Cluster-Level Principal Component Analysis

Total variance explained (rotated values for PCA)	PC1	PC2	PC3	PC4
Eigenvalues	3.921	2.387	1.733	1.713
Percent of variance	32.7	20.0	14.4	14.3
Cumulative percent	32.7	52.7	67.1	81.4
Average cumulative rainfall	0	.922	0	0
Average length of growing season	0	.939	0	0
Variability of growing season	0	−.808	0	0
Percent of HH with no education	.881	0	.322	.177
Percent of women who can read	−.838	0	−.376	−.164
Percent of HH attending primary school	−.859	0	−.225	−.138
Percent of HH with natural flooring	.839	0	.205	.261
General fertility rate	.304	0	.802	.164
Percent of HH below age 15	.248	0	.843	.104
Percent of women receiving prenatal care	−.812	0	0	−.258
Percent of children stunted	.264	0	.142	.866
Percent of children underweight	.319	0	.139	.844

Note: Units are factor loadings for the first four principal components.
HH = household, percent = proportion. See Appendix for detailed description of variables.
Source: McGuire (1998).

Spatial Filtering Technique

Originally, the DHS surveys were designed to provide statistically reliable estimates at the national level, or at the level of subnational units (1st administrative level) such as regions in Mali and departments in Niger. In many cases, at the second administrative level, there are not enough DHS clusters within the administrative unit to calculate a reliable estimate. However, we wanted to test the feasibility of extending the DHS data slightly by applying a spatial filter that would include neighboring clusters to increase the sample size and reduce the standard error of the estimate. The spatial filtering technique used in this study is similar to techniques used in image processing and for generating surfaces from points (such as rainfall surface images from point rainfall data). Filtering helps to smooth (or mask) some of the variability and can be used to fill in gaps in the data coverage, increase the sample size, and reduce the standard errors of the estimates. The basic assumption required to employ this type of filtering is that the neighboring points (that is, nearest neighbor clusters) sufficiently represent the administrative unit in question.

Two different administrative units were selected to illustrate this point—Soum, Burkina Faso, and Bakel, Senegal (figure 7.3). One of the DHS indicators, the proportion of children underweight, was calculated under several scenarios, as shown in table 7.5. For example, using only the original three clusters that fall within the Soum province, the value for proportion underweight was calculated and its value was 42.3. This was only based on 36 cases (weighted) and therefore has a large standard error (SE) of 8.76, and a relative error (RE) of 20.7 percent (RE = SE divided by indicator value). If we assume that the "nearest neighbors" are representative of this province, and select the four nearest clusters, we can increase the sample size to 7 clusters, which comprises 120 cases and reduces the SE to 1.60 and the RE to 3.8 percent. Adding the next two nearest clusters did not change the results significantly.

There are several limitations to this type of filter, especially in the context of DHS data. The nearest neighbors are not always the most appropriate to include in the extended sample. Sometimes the nearest cluster to a predominantly rural administrative unit may be urban. To prevent the bias, we avoided mixing urban and rural clusters across administrative units. Also, we did not take samples across international borders since there are implications regarding the impact of government policies on health, education, and the resultant DHS indicators. Finally, in some cases, the geographic context needs to be taken into account to select the most appropriate clusters. In the case of Bakel, the clusters along the river in Matam department, although further away, are likely to be more similar to Bakel than the nearest clusters in the "far away" Tambacounda department. This *contextual* filter was not used often and was fairly easy to implement with a basic understanding of Sahelian economic and cultural geography, but would be more difficult to implement as an automated program.

The spatial filtering routine used in this study is experimental, but it appears that the process works and yields reasonable results, allowing some of the DHS variables to be used at a more detailed level. This is an important consideration from a regional planning perspective, and some type of filtering or summarizing routine would be necessary to retain subnational detail for regional analysis, especially when combining data from different surveys or data sources. In this filtering example, if a *relative* indicator to

Table 7.5 Spatial Filtering Examples for Soum, Burkina Faso, and Bakel, Senegal

Administrative unit name and number of clusters	DHS indicator value in percent, e.g. proportion underweight	Number of cases in sample	Standard error (SE) indexes	Relative error = SE/indicator
Soum 3	42.3	36	8.76	20.7
Soum 7	41.1	120	1.60	3.8
Soum 9	41.5	182	1.45	3.5
Bakel 2	28.3	46	7.36	26
Bakel 6	32.6	95	3.19	9

Source: McGuire (1998).

Figure 7.3 Examples to Illustrate Spatial Filtering of DHS Clusters

a. Soum province, Burkina Faso

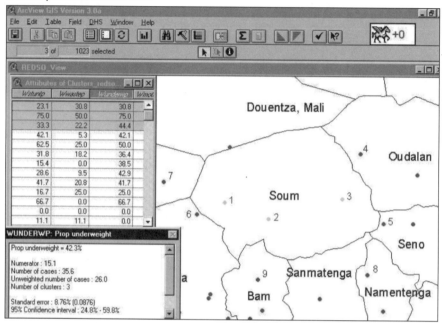

b. Bakel department, Senegal

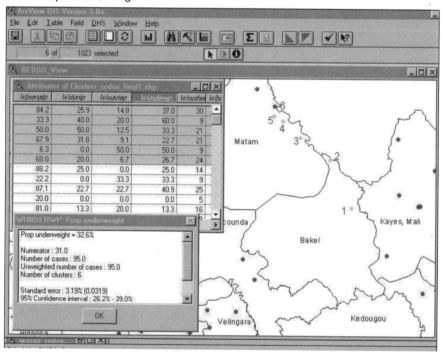

rank the different administrative units across the region is sufficient, then we will be confident in assigning a value of 41.5 for Soum and a value of around 32 for Bakel for the proportion underweight. However, the values of the filtered variables should be compared with more site-specific information at the national level (if it exists) and used appropriately.

The final step in the presentation at the subnational level uses an approach similar to that of the UN to develop the Human Development Index (HDI) and others.[9] Each of the final variables given in table 7.4 were scaled from 0 to 1 and then in most cases, using the results from the multivariate analysis, were grouped into meaningful composite indexes. We scaled the data so that 0 was "bad" and 1 was "good" from a food security perspective, across the four countries. The final indexes were grouped into the following categories:

- Biophysical = combining length, variability, and average cumulative rainfall
- Education = combining percent attending primary school with inverse of percent with no education
- Demographic = combining fertility with percent of household members less than 15 years old
- Nutrition = inverse of combining stunting and underweight
- Access = percent of women receiving prenatal care, used as proxy for access, in general
- Flooring = inverse of percent of household with natural flooring, used as income proxy.

Once all the selected indicators were aggregated, filtered, and rescaled at the 2nd administrative level, they could be studied individually or in various combinations or used to develop a composite index. Figure 7.4 shows a summary map of the biophysical index that was derived by rescaling the three image-based indicators: length, variability and average cumulative rainfall. This relative biophysical index corresponds to the well-known agro-ecological bands across the Sahel, but with slightly more detail than the broad bands used in the map of aridity zones, and each administrative unit now has a single value that can be compared to other types of data (for instance, the DHS variables).

Figure 7.5 illustrates the results for the final composite vulnerability index. The final composite index was a simple average of the six composite indexes described above. In a relative and chronic sense, and ranked across the four countries, the worst situation from a vulnerability to food insecurity perspective is in most of Niger, northern Burkina Faso, and in Mali along the border with Mauritania and Burkina Faso. The food security situation is better in coastal and northern Senegal and around the urban centers of Bamako, Ouagadougou and Bobo-Dioulasso, Burkina Faso. Again, these are not surprising results and confirm what would probably be surmised if the

Figure 7.4 Composite Biophysical Index

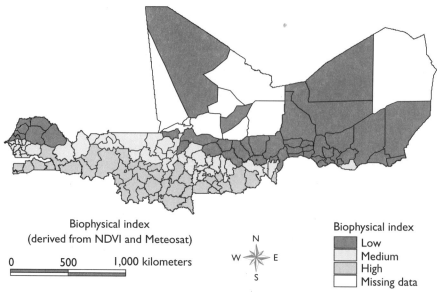

Biophysical index
(derived from NDVI and Meteosat)

0   500   1,000 kilometers

Biophysical index
- Low
- Medium
- High
- Missing data

Source: McGuire 1998.

Figure 7.5 Final Composite Vulnerability Index

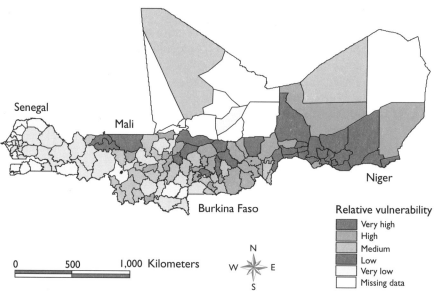

Relative vulnerability
- Very high
- High
- Medium
- Low
- Very low
- Missing data

0   500   1,000 Kilometers

Source: McGuire 1998.

individual DHS country reports were summarized for the different countries and combined with biophysical data. The difference here is that all of the data for the entire region (in this case, the four countries) is in the same database, and can more easily be analyzed and studied to draw inferences on regional perspectives. In general, those areas with a higher resource base, more education, fewer and healthier children, with good access, and *not* with natural flooring, are less vulnerable.

Two examples are offered to illustrate how the final composite indexes may be used from a regional planning perspective: graphically (in two-dimensional plots) and geographically (by querying the database to display only those regions that contain certain characteristics). First, one can examine the final tables to look for the most significant factors in any given region, or, to identify the anomalies and then determine why they are different. However, it is difficult to scan the entire summary table and interpret the regional significance. This technique would work to evaluate certain subnational areas or to verify the indicator values for a given region.

Another way to utilize the final results is by plotting the composite indicators, two at a time (figure 7.6, showing access and malnutrition). The trend

Figure 7.6 Access and Nutrition Index Derived from DHS Data

Nutritional index

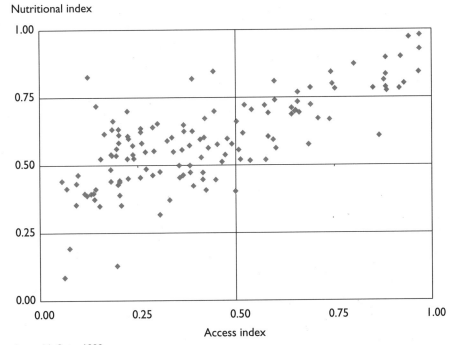

Access index

Source: McGuire 1998.

in the scatterplot is consistent with our assumptions: increased access to prenatal care is positively correlated with improved child nutritional status. From a food security perspective, we can use this relationship to show those areas with better (or worse) access and better (or worse) nutritional status, assuming that these areas would be less (or more) vulnerable to food insecurity. However, from a regional planning perspective, it may be more interesting to examine the anomalies and develop various what-if scenarios: For example, what if we wanted to isolate the worst cases (lower left quadrant in figure 7.6), or, what if we are most interested in those cases that have relatively good nutritional status but poor access (upper left quadrant in figure 7.6)? Conversely, for cost recovery programs, a regional planner may want to isolate those cases that already have good access and good nutritional status (upper right quadrant in figure 7.6).

To help visualize the results of this analysis the database can be queried using a GIS to isolate areas with certain characteristics, *and* display these on the map. Example queries (or what-if scenarios) are illustrated in figure 7.7, which shows the same two indicators discussed above—access and nutrition—but displayed geographically. The queries are essentially isolating three of the four major quadrants that are graphically displayed in figure 7.6. Using an arbitrary index value of 0.50 to delineate the quadrants into "good" and "bad," the maps show the following scenarios:

- Query 1 = areas with poor access and poor nutrition
- Query 2 = areas with good access and good nutrition
- Query 3 = areas with poor access and good nutrition.

Note that in figure 7.6 there are no cases in the lower right quadrant, which would be interpreted as good access to prenatal care and poor nutritional status. The results from this type of analysis can then be used to plan regional programs and intervention activities, depending on the question being asked and the relevant quadrant. Of course, these results should be verified with supporting information and detailed local knowledge from within the different countries, but they do provide a useful tool to help visualize where these different what-if scenarios exist across a broad geographic region.

Conclusions and Implications

This study had two primary goals—to improve understanding of vulnerability to food insecurity and to strengthen the linkages between information provided and analysis done by a wide variety of projects in West Africa. We did gain new insights into vulnerability issues and worked closely with other projects using existing data to strengthen the linkages between several West African activities. This final section will address some of the lessons learned from this study and implications for database development,

Figure 7.7 Example Queries with Final Indices

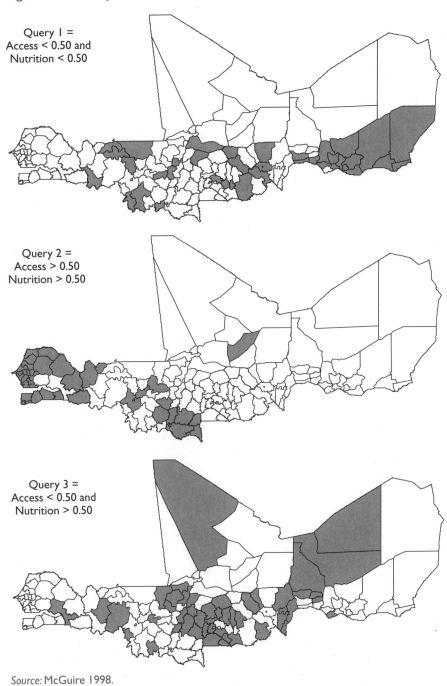

Query 1 =
Access < 0.50 and
Nutrition < 0.50

Query 2 =
Access > 0.50
Nutrition > 0.50

Query 3 =
Access < 0.50 and
Nutrition > 0.50

Source: McGuire 1998.

vulnerability assessments, and development planning from a regional perspective.

This study did encounter the persistent questions of what scale to use, what geographic regions to include, and what geographic units should be used in the analysis. Clearly, a compromise between the level of detail that can be obtained from detailed surveys and how that information is retained when aggregated to subnational levels is unavoidable.

With databases as extensive as the ones used in this study, there is usually no single answer to these questions. The very nature of having a complex database that is acquired from different sources with different objectives, and integrated across sectors and geographic regions, implies that there will be technical questions to address. In this study, we used a combination of analysis units and geographic regions, depending on the type of analysis. One of the advantages of using a GIS is that all the database components are already linked geographically by virtue of being in geographic format, and it is much easier to change between units of analysis.

However, some types of data lose their meaning and significance if the units of analysis are pushed too far. The DHS data is easily summarized at the country or subregional level, or by broad geographic constructs, but the next level of detail is problematic. The spatial filtering technique that was utilized in this study may offer one method to get around this, but this technique is experimental and still needs to be verified and automated. Even though this technique appeared to work in a *regional* setting, it is likely to mask important details in some areas. Again, this is the trade-off between retaining detail and striving for consistency across the region to enable regional analysis and cross-country comparisons to be made. The advantage of using a database such as the DHS is that it has already received international recognition and has been the basis of study and analysis by many researchers and scholars. The survey designs are consistent and compatible, which allows for cross-country comparison. This is not always apparent when attempting to combine surveys or results from different projects that have used different procedures and techniques.

From a food security perspective it is clear that many of the DHS variables are related to certain aspects of our basic model of vulnerability, at least for the chronic, long-term component. The final vulnerability map (figure 7.5), which was based on a combination of biophysical and socioeconomic variables, gives a reasonable characterization of those areas that are chronically vulnerable to food insecurity. It appears that the DHS data helped to fill in a major gap in our information base, that is, how to obtain proxy measurements for household income that we know are critical to describing vulnerability. The approach of ranking the 2nd level administrative units provides one method for retaining as much level of detail as possible, but summarized across the region.

This analysis also helped to clarify and question some of our basic assumptions and definitions of vulnerability; for example, the apparent anomalies encountered with the malnutrition data in the remote and arid zones may lead to redefining how these zones are characterized from a vulnerability perspective. Most vulnerability assessments have focused on the rural poor and mostly agricultural populations and have not properly assessed the pastoral and agro-pastoral communities. It is more difficult to assess the situation in pastoral and nomadic communities. but there is evidence that our basic assumptions about vulnerability do not necessarily apply in this situation and may need to be adjusted.

There should also be more follow-up on the similarities and differences between vulnerability assessment methodologies and poverty mapping. The major difference may simply be a matter of the scale and level of detail that is required to obtain the desired results. Poverty mapping is often part of a process designed to understand and attack the root causes of poverty; hence, it requires a more rigorous survey design and is less likely to be satisfied with the use of proxy values. Vulnerability assessments have historically used proxy indicators, which may have been sufficient from an early warning perspective, but more and more, there is a desire to add more details as to the nature and cause of the vulnerability to assist in preparing more efficient responses to a food security situation.

The examples presented in this report were primarily from the health and food security sectors, and were geared towards supporting regional planning for USAID in West Africa. Since this current study was initiated there have been major changes in USAID's regional structure and the findings from this study will need to be integrated into USAID's Regional Strategic Plan for West Africa. This will include linking with other USAID-funded regional programs and sharing the findings of this study with other international and regional institutions. The technical expertise is available within the region and other institutions are looking at similar issues regarding the integration of biophysical and socioeconomic data to help assess and monitor poverty, food security, health, and education issues.

There will most likely be a growing interest for others to use the WASAP and DHS database, not only for regional analysis and planning, but also as a training tool in creating such a database and using a GIS. Some of the results presented in this study could serve as a starting point to work with a regional planning team or strategic objective team to select the areas with the highest (or lowest) relative malnutrition levels. By using map queries, new scenarios could be developed to isolate areas that meet other criteria and identify their development planning needs.

The database queries could be done without a GIS, but it is much easier and the results can be directly displayed in map format to allow for a more powerful presentation of results. One simple example would be to design queries that summarize selected DHS variables for only rural clusters for certain countries, or within selected subregions. This would be a useful output and presentation tool for strategic planning of health and education programs.

Finally, this project utilized the extensive efforts that had already been made by others—in this case, the WASAP collaborative effort between MACRO, Intl., WRI, and BUCEN. One of the primary goals of this study was to illustrate how an existing database could be analyzed and exploited more efficiently. More efforts are required to look at the connections between vulnerability mapping and poverty mapping—to emphasize where they differ and where they converge and to develop synergy between the two approaches.

Appendix

Description of Variables Used in PCA Subset

Indicator	Description
1	Average cumulative rainfall from Meteosat rainfall estimates
2	Average length of season, from NOAA-NDVI historic average, 1982–1994
3	Average variability of cumulative NDVI (coefficient of variation), from NOAA-NDVI historic average, 1982–1994
4	Proportions of HH members 15 years of age or older with no years of education
5	Proportion of HHs with natural flooring, i.e., sand, earth, etc.
6	General fertility rate for the three year period preceding the survey
7	Proportion of HH members below age 15
8	Proportion of women aged 15–49 years that can read easily or with difficulty
9	Proportion of births in the last three years for which women received prenatal care from a doctor, nurse, midwife, or trained auxiliary midwife
10	Proportion of all children at the age of primary education currently attending school
11	Proportion of all children at the age of secondary education currently attending school
12	Proportion of children 3–35 months that are stunted; where height-for-age z-score falls below −2 standard deviations of the median height-for-age
13	Proportion of children 3–35 months that are underweight; where weight-for-age z-score falls below −2 standard deviations of the median weight-for-age
14	Proportion of women aged 15–49 who are currently employed

Note: See MACRO, Intl., 1997b for more detailed description of all DHS variables.
HH = households
Source: All are from DHS database, except the first three, which are image-based indicators from the FEWS project.

Notes

The author is under contract with Associates in Rural Development, Inc.

1. This chapter summarizes work in progress under a contract between USAID's Regional Economic Development Services Office for West and Central Africa (REDSO/WCA) in Abidjan, and Associates in Rural Development (ARD), Inc., in association with the FEWS Project.

2. The WASAP data are stored in ARCVIEW® format. All the necessary parameters required to aggregate the cluster-level data to higher levels, such as subnational administrative units, are provided in the WASAP database, including the numerator and denominator values used to compute the indicator and sampling weights for each cluster. Programs to calculate aggregated, weighted indicators at a user-specified level are also included in the database (for instance, ARC-VIEW script files written by Trevor Croft at MACRO, International). A more complete description of the WASAP and DHS databases can be found in reports by MACRO, Intl. and WRI (see MACRO, Intl. 1997a, 1997b, and WRI 1996c or the DHS website at http://www2.macroint.com/dhs).

3. USAID/FEWS website (www.info.usaid.gov/fews/fews.html).

4. Downing (1991).

4 See Vulnerability Assessments at the FEWS website (www.info.usaid.gov/fews/fews.html) and various FEWS publications—for example, FEWS/Malawi (1996). For reviews of vulnerability assessment techniques see Henninger, 1997; WFP (1996); Deichmann (1997); UNDP Poverty Guidebooks (1997); Ramachandran and Eastman (1996); Riely (1995); and Downing (1991).

6. For example, see footnote 3 and the World Bank Living Standards Measurement Study (LSMS) publications Nos. 88, 117, and 129.

7. See World Bank (1997).

8. See McGuire (1998) for more details on the idea of the spatial filtering of DHS clusters.

9. See also Pison and others (1995). This report examined recent changes in the demographic situation of Senegal, particularly those related to fertility and mortality rates.

References

Deichmann, Uwe. 1997. "Accessibility Indicators in GIS." UN Report, Department of Economic and Social Information and Policy Analysis, Statistics Division.

Downing, T.E. 1991. "Assessing Socio-Economic Vulnerability to Famine: Frameworks, Concepts, and Applications." FEWS Working Paper 2.1. Arlington, VA USA: USAID-FEWS Project.

FEWS/Malawi. 1996. "Quest for Causality, Vulnerability Assessment and Mapping (VAM)." FEWS Malawi in conjunction with the World Food Program and Government of Malawi. Arlington, VA USA: USAID-FEWS Project.

Glewwe, Paul, and Gillette Hall. 1995. "Who is Most Vulnerable to Macroeconomic Shocks? Hypotheses Tests Using Panel Data from Peru." World Bank Living Standards Measurement Study Working Paper 117. Washington, D.C.: The World Bank.

Henninger, Norbert. 1997. "Mapping and Geographic Analysis of Human Welfare Indicators—Review and Assessment." Washington, D.C.: World Resources Institute.

Josserand, H., and others. 1997. "Rural Poverty Analysis for Senegal as Part of a Agricultural Sector Investment Plan." Burlington, VT USA: Associates in Rural Development, Inc.

McGuire, Mark L. 1998. "Evaluation of Food Insecurity in West Africa Using Demographic and Health (DHS) Data with GIS." Final Report of USAID/West Africa contract under the FEWS Project with ARD, Inc., P.O. Box 1397, Burlington, Vermont 05402, USA.

MACRO, Intl. 1997a. "West Africa Spatial Analysis Prototype (WASAP): Development of a Geo-referenced Regional Database." Summary report by Trevor Croft and others. Calverton, MD USA: Macro, Intl.

———. 1997b. "Documentation for Demographic and Health Survey (DHS) Datasets." Calverton, MD USA: Macro, Intl.

———. 1996. "Nutrition of Infants and Young Children in Mali, 1995–1996." Calverton, MD USA: Macro, Intl.

———. 1994. "Children's Nutritional Status." DHS Comparative Studies No. 12. Calverton, MD USA: Macro, Intl.

Pison, Gilles, Kenneth H. Hill, Barney Cohen, and Karen A. Foote, eds. 1995. *Population Dynamics of Senegal.* Washington, D.C.: National Academy Press.

Ramachandran, M., and J. R. Eastman. 1996. "Applications of GIS to Vulnerability Mapping: A West African Food Security Case Study." The IDRISI Project. Winchester, MA USA: Clark University.

Riely, Frank. 1995. "Vulnerability Analysis in the FEWS Project." FEWS Working Paper 2.9. Arlington, VA USA: USAID-FEWS Project.

United Nations Environment Programme (UNEP). 1997. "Mapping Indicators of Poverty in West Africa. A Pilot Study to Examine the Relationship between the Location of Rural Poor Population and Land Use Quality in West Africa based on 'Best Available' Data using GIS Technology." UNEP/DEIA/TR.97-8. New York: United Nations.

United Nations Development Programme (UNDP). 1997. "Technical Support Documents. Five modules related to poverty mapping and selection of indicators." Available at http://www.un.org. New York: United Nations.

West Africa Long Term Perspective Study (WALTPS). 1995. "West Africa Long Term Perspective Study. Preparing for the Future: a Vision of West Africa in the Year 2020." OECD/ADB/CILSS. Paris.

World Bank. Various. Living Standards Measurement Study (LSMS). Series of Working Papers describing various aspects of LSMS. Washington, D.C.

———. 1997. "Nutritional Status and Poverty in Sub-Saharan Africa." *Findings* Report 108, April. Washington, D.C.

World Resources Institute (WRI). 1996a. "Fertility vs. Settlement Type in West Africa: Preliminary Results." Washington, D.C.: WRI.

———. 1996b. "Child Health vs. Aridity in West Africa: Preliminary Results." Washington, D.C.: WRI.

————. 1996c. "Typology of Administrative Units in West Africa." Prepared for USAID/REDSO West Africa Spatial Analysis Prototype (WASAP) project. Washington, D.C.: WRI.

Wright, J., F. Lee, M. McGuire, J. Johnson, and M. Mitchell. 1994. "A Model for Assessing Vulnerability to Famine in Burkina Faso, Chad, Mali, and Niger." Famine Early Warning System (FEWS) Project, Arlington, VA USA.

World Food Programme (WFP). 1996. "Senegal: The Structure of Vulnerability." A preliminary analysis for the World Food Programme. Rome.

8

Using a GIS to Target River Blindness Control Activities in Guatemala

Frank O. Richards

HUMAN ONCHOCERCIASIS IS A PARASITIC INFECTION that can result in severe skin disease, visual impairment, and blindness. The condition is caused by a parasitic worm (*Onchocerca volvulus*), and transmitted by the bite of a vector black fly of the species *Simulium*. Because black flies breed in rapidly flowing rivers and streams, onchocerciasis is often called "river blindness." The adult parasites (males and females) live and mate in human tissues, often just under the skin where they may become encased in a fibrous tissue reaction that manifests clinically as subcutaneous nodules. The adult females produce embryos (microfilaria) that leave the nodule and swarm underneath the skin. To survive, they must be ingested by black flies, develop in the fly to infectious stages, and then be inoculated back into humans, where they reach adulthood and so continue their life cycle. The microfilaria irritate tissues, and, when they enter the eye, cause loss of vision and sometimes blindness (WHO 1987, 1995).

An estimated 18 million persons are infected with *Onchocerca volvulus* in Africa and Latin America. The infection is focal in nature, stable (that is, not prone to explosive epidemics), and occurs in its worst forms in remote, rural regions, where more than 90 percent of persons can be infected. Most of the skin and eye involvement occurs in villages, where more than 40 percent of adults have nodules (hyperendemic onchocerciasis); communities with 20 to 40 percent nodule prevalence (mesoendemic onchocerciasis) are also at risk for severe manifestations of the infection (WHO 1987, 1995).

Until recently, the only two methods for controlling onchocerciasis were by surgical removal of the nodules containing the adult worms (nodulectomy) or by reduction of vector black fly populations through application of insecticides. In Guatemala and Mexico, the ministries of health have had long-standing programs in which communities in disease-endemic areas are visited once or twice per year by special medical teams that surgically remove the nodules. In West Africa, a large vector control program (the Onchocerciasis Control Program) has been operational since 1975, and uses fixed-wing aircraft and helicopters to apply insecticides to large rivers (WHO 1987, 1995). However, a new tool to control this affliction was introduced in 1987 when ivermectin (Mectizan® from Merck & Co.) was licensed for human use (Mectizan® Expert Committee 1990, Hopkins and Richards 1997, Taylor and Greene 1989). Ivermectin is a safe microfilaricidal drug that prevents skin and eye disease from onchocerciasis when provided to infected persons as a single oral dose annually or semiannually. It is safe enough to allow large-scale (mass) administration to eligible populations (persons greater than five years of age, nonpregnant women, or women not breastfeeding very young infants). The World Health Organization encourages mass treatment in communities with severe (meso- or hyperendemic) onchocerciasis. In 1987, Merck generously donated ivermectin free of charge for public health efforts against river blindness, and so it has become the cornerstone of a global control initiative. Community-based ivermectin delivery treatment programs have safely provided millions of treatments in Africa and in all six disease-endemic countries of Latin America over the last ten years (Hopkins and Richards 1997, Taylor and Greene 1989).

Targeting Communities to Be Treated with Ivermectin

One must identify quickly, economically, and accurately those hyperendemic and mesoendemic communities where ivermectin distribution would have its greatest benefit. A first step taken by all ivermectin distribution programs is to establish a "target" area (Taylor and others 1992, Ngoumou and Walsh 1993). As treatment is ultimately delivered at the community level, targeted areas (states, districts, provinces, and so forth) must be refined to the targeted communities, where the final implementation of the program occurs. Based on the targeting exercise, the program commits itself to treat the entire eligible population with ivermectin, for an indefinite period of time. It is important, therefore, that these targeted areas be carefully selected, based on available epidemiological information, knowledge of environmental factors that support dense black fly populations, and rapid field assessment surveys (Taylor and others 1992, Ngoumou and Walsh 1993, Mace and others 1997, Richards 1993).

The Use of GIS for Targeting

Guatemala is a country of about 9 million inhabitants located in Central America. Mexico borders it to the north, Belize to the east, the Pacific Ocean to the west, and Honduras and El Salvador to the south. Guatemala has four recognized onchocerciasis endemic areas and an estimated 400,000 persons at risk of infection with onchocerciasis (Richards 1993, Brandling-Bennett and others 1981, Tada and others 1979, WHO 1996, 1997, Yamagata and others 1986).

The most important endemic area in Guatemala (with the greatest numbers of infected persons and the most communities with meso- or hyperendemic disease) is known as the Central Endemic Zone (CEZ) (Yamagata and others 1986). This area is in a mountainous region on the slopes of the Pacific piedmont, near the central highlands, just south of the large volcanic Lake Atitlán. The CEZ has an estimated area of about 900 square kilometers, and spans four departments (states). The population consists primarily of poor, indigenous people of Mayan descent who mostly live and work on small (populations 75–1,500), privately owned coffee farms called *fincas*. These farms are scattered through the mountains, and generally lie at elevations between 500–1500 meters that favor both coffee cultivation and breeding of the vector black flies (Richards 1993, Ramirez 1986, Shelly 1988). The Guatemalan Ministry of Health (MOH) has provided nodulectomy services to the populations in the CEZ for decades, and has extensive files on nodule rates in communities in the area (Yamagata and others 1986).

The Guatemalan Ministry of Health adopted in 1989 the strategy of community therapy with ivermectin for onchocerciasis control. Along with this decision, it was resolved to carry out a comprehensive review of available epidemiological data and revise the maps of the endemic areas to establish a list and the locations of targeted communities. Despite the existence of an extensive MOH archive on onchocerciasis from the years of nodulectomy activities, it was also recognized that these data were incomplete, and that there were many fincas in the CEZ for which there were no data. How many was unknown. There were other questions: Would all villages of unknown endemicity falling in the elevation range of 500–1,500 meters have to be visited and evaluated for inclusion in the ivermectin program? Could villages with no data at any elevation be first stratified based on other environmental factors into those at greater and lesser risk?

To address these questions, the MOH launched a pilot project in partnership with the Centers for Disease Control and Prevention and the Universidad del Valle de Guatemala to apply new geographic technologies in parallel with the process of epidemiological data review and map revision. The primary goal of the project was to develop a GIS for targeting both communities known to have onchocerciasis, as well as those communities *suspected* of having significant (meso- or hyperendemic range) prevalences. The results of some of this work have been reported (Richards 1993). The project also sought to strengthen the overall health infrastructure and surveillance system by creating maps that could be used for many other disease-control efforts.

Geographical information systems (GIS), which combine rectangular database and spatial digital mapping functions, have an enormous potential for assisting in targeting activities. Powerful and relatively inexpensive GIS software is available for microcomputers, most notably MapInfo (MapInfo Corporation), Atlas*GIS (Strategic Mapping/Environmental Systems Institute Research) and ARCINFO ARCVIEW Environmental Systems Institute Research (ESRI). Most recently GISs have become tools used in planning operational phases of tropical disease research and control. The global positioning system (GPS), the digitizing tablet, and remotely sensed data (satellite images and aerial photography) are other new and important tools used to create multiple and rich data layers in the GIS. GIS maps can fill a common void in developing countries where large scale (1:250,000 or greater) maps are restricted, outdated, or nonexistent.

When the project was initiated in 1989, GIS consultation, specialized equipment (scanners and plotters), and digital or remotely sensed data were very expensive, so only a middle range vector-based geographic information system (Atlas*GIS® for DOS, and later, Windows® Atlas*GIS) and a small digitizing table (SummaSketch®, Summagraphics Inc.) were used. The four data components in the system design were (1) the community inventory, (2) the digital map, (3) the MOH epidemiology data set, and (4) the vector flight-range area. The community inventory and the MOH data sets were rectangular (tabular), georeferenced FoxPro® (Dbase®) data sets. The digitized map and data sets for the vector flight-range area were GIS-generated (vector-based) geographic files. In the process of executing this project, we also evaluated and used a GPS, evaluated two commercially available data sets, and produced large hard copy paper maps for field use.

Methodology

Permission was granted from Guatemalan military authorities to purchase the complete set of restricted 1:50,000 maps (dated 1974–1981) prepared by the Guatemalan Instituto Geographico, in collaboration with the U.S. Defense Mapping Agency. These maps became the principal source of information for the GIS. We selected those map sheets that overlayed the four Guatemalan disease-endemic areas and then identified all communities on those maps (Yamagata and others 1986), along with their latitude, longitude (read with a special transparency designed for this purpose), and elevation.

A FoxPro® file was created in which each community was entered as a unique record. Over 3,000 communities were identified on the maps and entered into the database (Richards 1993), which was called the community inventory. Community names in the database were frequently repeated, and some names appeared over ten times (table 8.1). Indeed, there were 28 communities named "La Esperanza." To avoid confusion, it was critical for geocoding purposes that each community is assigned a unique identification number. This identification number was used to link (using the relational database function) the community inventory with the MOH epidemiology database (see below). In all data entry activities we followed routine data quality assurance activities: we printed hard copies of the computer files and compared them with the data extraction forms, and we routinely backed up the hard disk.

The Digital Map

The "digital map" was an Atlas*GIS geographic file created from the same 1:50,000 maps used to create the community inventory. The basic feature data were derived from selecting important lines and regions to provide the substance of the disease-endemic area over which the points of community

Table 8.1 Examples of Repeated Names in the Community Inventory Data Set

Community name	Number of communities with shared name
Buena Vista	13
Buenos Aires	10
El Carmen	10
El Milagro	13
El Paraiso	10
El Porvenir	13
El Progreso	7
El Recuerdo	14
El Rosario	13
El Socorro	10
La Esperanza	28
La Providencia	17
La Reforma	7
La Trinidad	9
La Union	11
Las Delicias	14

Source: Data from Guatemalan Instituto Geographico, in collaboration with the U.S. Defense Mapping Agency.

inventory were plotted. Using a small (SummaSketch®) digitizing table, important features (roads, lakes and rivers, and 500 and 1,500 meter elevation contour lines) were created in their exact (at 1:50,000 scale) latitude-longitude positions (Richards 1993).

Unfortunately, the 1:50,000 maps did not show political or administrative boundaries of the departments or counties, which were critical elements for linking MOH data to the community inventory (see below). To obtain the political boundaries, we digitized the county and department boundaries from maps of a considerably smaller (1:1,000,000) scale (see map 8.1). Plotting the community inventory on the digital map allowed us to determine the county and department of each community. Differences in scale, however, resulted in a sacrifice of accuracy of administrative positions for communities located near the administrative borders.

The Epidemiology Data Set

A comprehensive retrospective review of MOH data for 11 years (1980–1990) was carried out from March to October 1992. A special office was assigned for the completion of this task at the MOH's Department of Onchocerciasis. All files produced during field visits to disease-endemic communities by nodulectomy teams were gathered and reviewed. Date of visit, community name, county, department, population size, number of persons examined, and nodule rates were coded on data extraction forms and then keyed into a FoxPro® file (the MOH epidemiology data set). A data entry software program was developed that first searched the community inventory data set to identify the name, county, and department of the entry community, and then, with a match, extract and write the appropriate ID to the newly generated MOH epidemiology file record entry. Since community inventory identification numbers were associated with latitude, longitude, and elevation, all such matches automatically georeferenced the MOH epidemiology data set. Those MOH records that did not match a record in the community inventory were assigned a new ID number by the program, and that community was automatically entered into the community inventory and labeled as "position unknown" (thus flagged for later GPS reading in the field).

The MOH epidemiology data set was analyzed by calculating community endemicity, based on the simple mean nodule rate (the ratio of persons with nodules to total persons examined) for all entries for a given ID number over the 11-year period. Nonendemic communities were defined as having a nodule prevalence of zero, hypoendemic communities a prevalence of 1–20 percent, mesoendemic 20–40 percent, and hyperendemic ≥ 40 percent.

The project purchased the least expensive global positioning system then available on the market, the Sony IPS-360, a handheld, nondifferential, four-channel GPS system. GPS units, by reading signals from navigational satellites on 12-hour elliptical orbits at 20,000 kilometers altitude, can calculate a latitude-longitude position and an elevation accurate to within 30–100 meters. (Calculations based on civilian frequencies are influenced by "selective availability," which is a random error placed in the satellite's time signal to reduce accuracy). The unit was set on a coordinate area for Central America (North America 1927) at the highest allowable precision setting (accepting only a dilution of precision < 6). The GPS then was tested at the Universidad del Valle de Guatemala against the (working) scale of 1:50,000 maps. Thirty-three GPS readings were taken at the same open site (the NE corner of the football field on the campus). Data were obtained on 16 different days, at different times over a 36-day period. Latitude-longitude (to the nearest 10th of a second), elevation in meters, and the unique ID numbers of the four satellites used to calculate the position were recorded. GPS readings were compared with a position read from the appropriate 1:50,000 map. The map is of large enough scale to show the corner of the football field where GPS readings were taken—longitude 90° 29′ 35″ W, latitude 14° 36′ 19″ N, elevation 1,490 meters above sea level.

After testing showed acceptable latitude and longitude readings at scale (see results), field reconnaissance was conducted together with MOH field staff to verify presence and locations of all meso- and hyperendemic communities in the MOH epidemiology data set that could not be identified on the maps.

GIS Analysis

GIS analysis of the data sets was based on the knowledge that the maximum flight range of the black fly vector of onchocerciasis (*Simulium ochraceum*) in the CEZ is 5 kilometers (Collins and others 1992). Using the GIS buffer function, we undertook two buffering exercises to create circular 5-kilometer vector flight ranges, (1) around hyperendemic and (2) around both hyper- and mesoendemic communities. By merging these buffers, we defined putative disease-endemic areas that captured or excluded other communities in the vicinity. We compared these two target areas for their ability to capture known and suspected communities in need of treatment. Suspected communities were defined based on their being positioned at an elevation between 500–1,500 meters elevation. The best strategy was used to generate a listing of targeted communities recommended for either ivermectin distribution or additional epidemiological assessment.

Evaluating the Data for Targeting

Two available digital sources of georeferenced community settlement data were compared with the databases we created. The first source was the Digital Chart of the World (DCW). The DCW, which can be found both in the public domain as well as in costly value-added formats adapted to different commercial software products, is primarily based on the U.S. Defense Mapping Agency Operational Navigational Chart series, the largest scale unclassified series available with complete global coverage. It contains layers that include international boundaries, settlements, roads, and elevation contours, along with 100,000 place-name entries. The second source of information was 1:500,000-scale data used to prepare the 1984 Gazetteer for Guatemala. These data (obtained from the U.S. Defense Mapping Agency) consisted entirely of points (not regions or lines) of latitude and longitude (rounded to the nearest minute), names of the position, and position type (for example, human settlements, rivers, mountain peaks, parks, and so forth).

To make the GIS project interesting and relevant to the MOH field workers, we produced hard copy, color thematic maps (the size of common tourist road maps) from which community names and their identification numbers could be read. Their production required considerable time given the need to adjust hundreds of labels to allow a legible printout. These maps were provided to field workers (who had previously relied upon hand drawn maps), and we noted if they found them useful in their operational activities.

Results

Figure 8.1 shows the CEZ community inventory (716 communities) plotted on the digital map for the Central Endemic Zone, along with the positions of supplemental GPS readings. The MOH epidemiology data set had 1,793 records, representing the visits to 517 communities in all four disease-endemic zones of Guatemala. Overall, there were 152 (29 percent) nonendemic communities, 196 (38 percent) hypoendemic, 111 (21 percent) mesoendemic, and 58 (11 percent) hyperendemic. The CEZ was clearly the most important onchocerciasis endemic area in Guatemala. Of the 365 endemic communities identified in the MOH data set, 308 (84 percent) where in the CEZ; more important, 55 (95 percent) of 58 hyperendemic communities and 89 (80 percent) of 111 mesoendemic communities were found there. Figure 8.2 shows the positions of the meso- and hyperendemic communities identified in the CEZ.

The MOH data analysis for the CEZ showed that 52 (17 percent) of communities visited were nonendemic, 112 (36 percent) were hypoendemic, 89 (29 percent) mesoendemic, and 55 (18 percent) hyperendemic. However, there were an additional 408 villages (57 percent of the total of 716 communities) in the CEZ community inventory without MOH data. These required targeting classification.

Thirty-eight (7 percent) of the communities on file with the MOH could not be matched in the community inventory. Field reconnaissance was

Figure 8.1 Central Endemic Zone for Onchocerciasis, Guatemala
The 1:50,000 digital map and community inventory

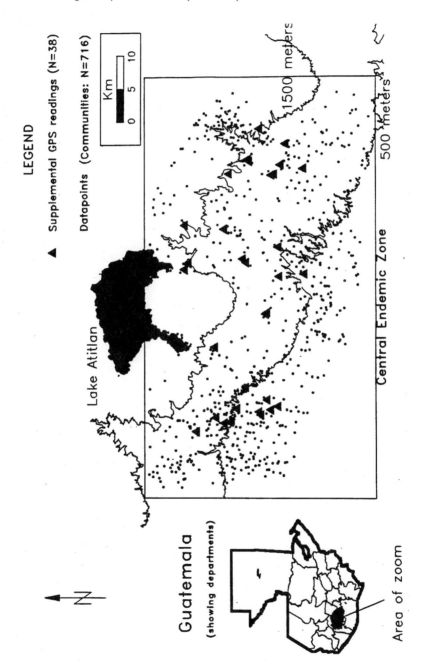

Source: Author's calculations.

Figure 8.2 Central Endemic Zone for Onchocerciasis

Hyper- and mesoendemic villages, MOH epidemiology data set

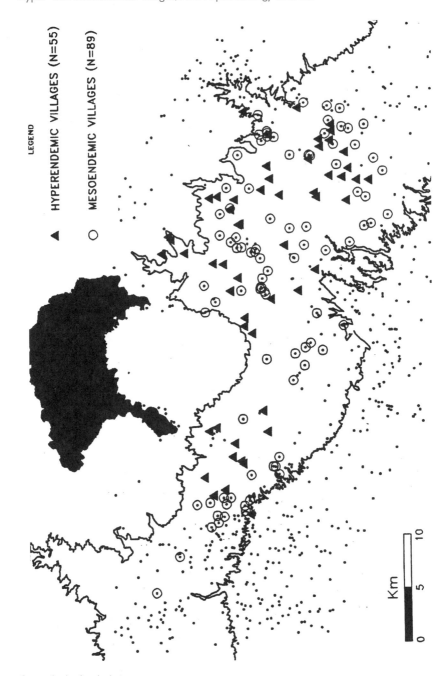

Source: Author's calculations.

needed to verify the presence of the missing communities (particularly the meso- and hyperendemic communities in the MOH data set), and to obtain a latitude and longitude reading to plot their location in the GIS.

We evaluated the GPS unit before field reconnaissance. During the testing period, the GPS unit fixed on signals from 13 different satellites. The most frequent readings were taken from satellites 29 (17 observations), 1 and 14 (each with 13 observations), 15, 18, 25, 28 (each with 12 observations). Figure 8.3 shows a spatial analysis (each tick = 100 meters) of the horizontal plain of the football field. The star in the figure indicates the position (90° 29' 35 W, 14° 36' 19" N) read from the map. The central position of the GPS readings ("central GPS position") was calculated to be 90° 29' 33.9" W, 14° 36' 21.6" N, which was 85 meters SSW from the map position. Figure 8.4 shows a plot of horizontal and vertical distances from the map position.[1] The mean GPS elevation was 1,525 meters, or 35 meters above that of the

Figure 8.3 Spatial Analysis of the Horizontal Plain

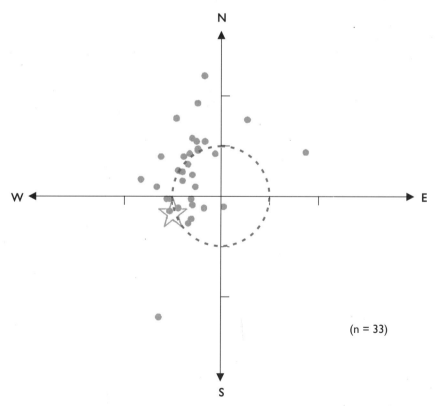

(n = 33)

Source: Author's calculations.

Figure 8.4 Horizontal and Vertical Distances from the Map Position

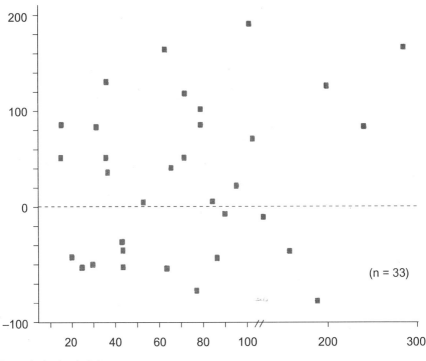

Source: Author's calculations.

map (range –96 to +204) and 48 meters above the field's actual elevation. Statistically, the mean GPS elevation was different from that of the map (1,490 meters, $z = 2.39$, $p < 0.05$). Similar to the findings on the horizontal plane, 79 percent (26) of elevation observations fell within 100 meters of the map position. In univariant analysis, the outlying GPS readings did not correlate with time of day, day of reading, or satellite fix.

All spot GPS readings were within a 300-meter sphere of the map position; the average horizontal and vertical GPS positions clustered 85 meters and 35 meters respectively from the map position. Nearly 20 percent of positions were beyond the stated accuracy range (30–100 meters) of the unit. On the horizontal plane, this GPS error was not a major concern at the operational scale requirements. However, a similar variance in GPS elevation readings could potentially result in misclassification of unacceptable numbers of communities. It was concluded that GPS readings of latitude and longitude, but not elevation, were acceptable in the targeting application.

Contour lines in the GIS derived from the 1:50,000 maps continued to serve as the guidelines for elevation of GPS points. Field surveys led by MOH field staff were successful in identifying all meso- and hyperendemic village positions in the CEZ.

Four hundred and eight (57 percent) of the 716 communities in the CEZ community inventory were without MOH data, and therefore required targeting classification. Of the 408 communities without data, 140 (34 percent) were found in an elevation of high risk (500–1500 meters), and so were classified as "suspect." The remaining 268 above or below that elevation were called "nonsuspect" (table 8.2). We defined a disease-endemic area for the treatment program to determine which of those 408 communities were to be targeted. In the first strategy, the series of 5-kilometer vector-flight ranges were drawn around the 55 hyperendemic communities (figure 8.5). Figure 8.6 shows the disease-endemic area that was created (GIS determined plane dimensions 143 kilometers perimeter, 837 square kilometers area, maximum east-west extent 48 kilometers, maximum north-south extent 30 kilometers). There were a total of 356 (50 percent of the CEZ community inventory) villages within the newly defined disease-endemic area (table 8.2). Of these, (1) 55 (15 percent) were hyperendemic communities used to create the flight range buffers, (2) 165 (46 percent) were communities for which there existed MOH data indicating less severe onchocerciasis, (3) 24 (7 percent) had already been determined to be nonendemic by the MOH survey, and (4) 111 (31 percent) were communities for which no MOH data were available.

We observed however, (figure 8.6) that seven of the mesoendemic villages, as well as 59 percent of suspect villages, fell outside of the hyperendemic zone, observations suggesting that this buffer area was not sufficient to

Table 8.2 GIS Buffering Exercise Communities to Be Assessed or Treated

	Total In CI* (percent total)	Program 1 Hyper (percent of category)	Program 2 Meso/Hyper (percent of category)
Hyperendemic	55 (8)	55 (100)	55 (100)
Mesoendemic	89 (12)	82 (92)	89 (100)
Hypoendemic	112 (16)	83 (74)	108 (96)
Not endemic	52 (7)	24 (46)	40 (77)
Suspect	140 (20)	57 (41)	112 (80)
Not suspect	268 (37)	54 (54)	78 (29)
Total	716 (100)	356 (50)	482 (67)

Note: *CI = Community Inventory of the Central Endemic Zone of Guatemala
Source: Guatemalan Instituto Geographico, in collaboration with the U.S. Defense Mapping Agency.

Figure 8.5 Central Endemic Zone for Onchocerciasis

Hyperendemic vector flight range buffering

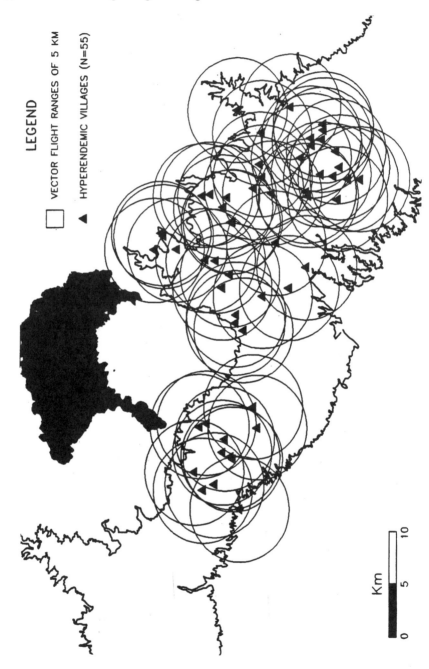

Source: Author's calculations.

Figure 8.6 Central Endemic Zone for Onchocerciasis
Hyperendemic target area

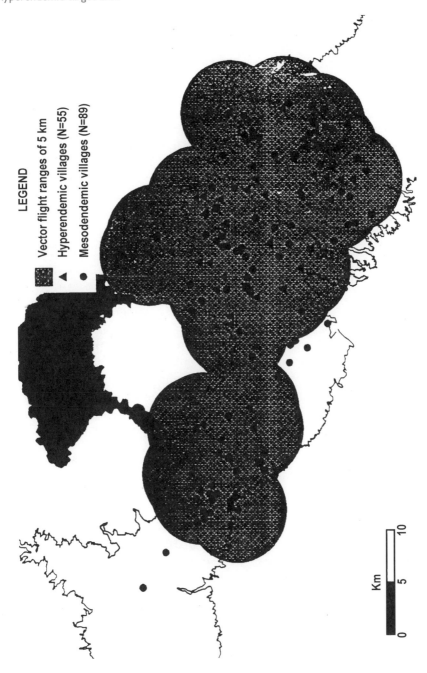

Source: Author's calculations.

capture all communities in need of treatment. Therefore, a second GIS-targeting strategy (figure 8.7) was run to buffer around both the 55 hyperendemic communities and the 89 mesoendemic villages. This second disease-endemic area had GIS-calculated plane dimensions of 162 kilometers perimeter, 1,109 square kilometers area, maximum east-west extent 58 kilometers, and maximum north-south extent 32 kilometers. Within the newly defined disease-endemic area, there was a total of 482 villages (67 percent of the CEZ community inventory—table 8.2), of which (1) 144 (29 percent) were the meso- or hyperendemic communities used for buffering, (2) 108 (22 percent) were communities for which there existed MOH data indicating less severe onchocerciasis, (3) 40 (8 percent) had already been determined to be nonendemic by MOH survey, and (4) 190 (39 percent) were communities for which no MOH data were available. Eighty percent of suspect villages in the Community Inventory (CI) were captured. This last exercise provided the final analysis of the target for either ivermectin distribution, or additional (fringe area) rapid assessment: 190 (47 percent) of the 408 communities without data should be evaluated or treated in the program.

Alternative Data Products

Figure 8.8 shows the comparison of community inventories in the onchocerciasis target area derived from the three different data sources. Despite having over 100,000 place name entries, only three human settlement points, all unnamed, were found inside the target area defined in figure 8.7. In contrast, the 1984 gazetteer data showed 204 communities inside the defined target area, and so was a much better source of information than the DCW. However, note that of the 256 disease-endemic communities found in the CEZ, only 125 (49 percent) could be matched in the gazetteer data set (versus 93 percent in the 1:50,000 community inventory before being supplemented with GPS readings). The success in matching MOH epidemiology data to that in the gazetteer is presented in table 8.3. Only 51 percent of meso- or hyperendemic communities in the MOH data set would have been matched if the gazetteer data had been used.

A comparison of distances was made between the 197 communities that were found in both the gazetteer and the 1:50,000 community inventory (figure 8.9). Three community pairs were excluded from the analysis since their relative positions were extreme outliers (separated by greater than 3 kilometers). The mean distance of separation among the 194 community pairs was 800 meters, suggesting that the error between the two data sets which was approximately ten times the difference of GPS and 1:50,000 map readings (85 meters).

Despite the considerable time required for their production, we found that the hard copy "tourist road maps" were received by the field workers

Figure 8.7 Central Endemic Zone for Onchocerciasis

Final targeted area for rapid assessment or Invermectin distribution

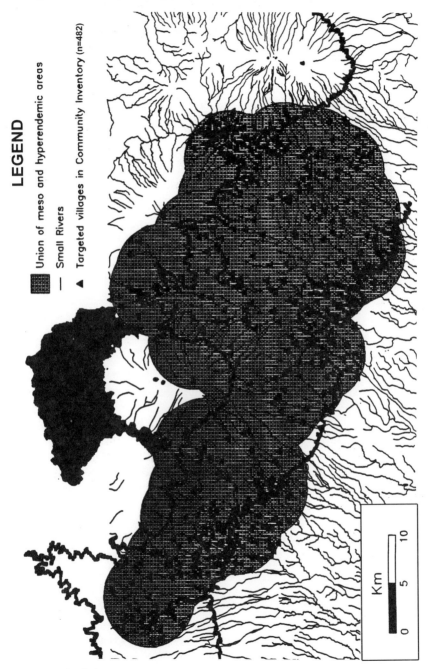

Source: Author's calculations.

Figure 8.8 Comparison of Three Data Sets for Community Positions in the Target Area: Digital Chart of the World (DCW), Gazetteer (GAZ), and Digitized 1:50,000 Data (DIG)

Number of communities in area in the data set

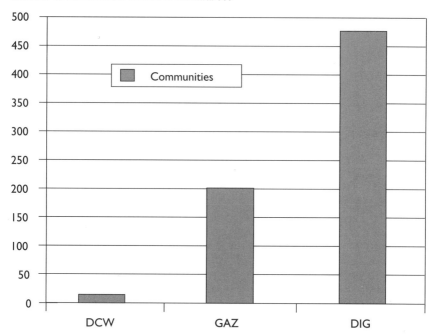

Source: Author's calculations.

with enthusiasm. They provided corrections (new communities, changes in position, and so on) by placing notes directly on the maps while in the field. The maps that were later returned to the GIS unit at the Universidad del Valle were tattered and torn—evidence of their usefulness; the notes on the maps were used to update the GIS so that new and improved maps could be generated. The feedback loop mechanism that characterizes an accurate

Table 8.3 Endemic Communities Identified in the Gazetteer Database

Endemic class	Total endemic communities	No in gazetteer (percent total)
Hyperendemic	55	28 (50%)
Mesoendemic	89	45 (51%)
Hypoendemic	112	52 (46%)
Total	256	125 (49%)

Source: Guatemalan Instituto Geographico, in collaboration with the U.S. Defense Mapping Agency.

Figure 8.9 Comparison of Two Sources for Community Inventory Data (Digitized 1:50,000 Data Base Versus Gazetteer): Distances between Positions Given for Identical Communities (n=194)

Number of pairs

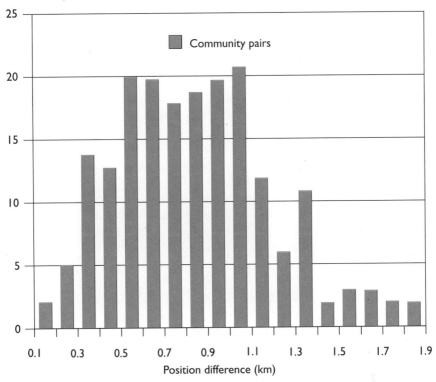

Source: Author's calculations.

surveillance system is based on the premise that those who produce data need it returned to them later as a useful analytic product.

Discussion

We describe the use of a GIS to target a public health intervention in a developing country. Georeferenced databases, not software, were the keys to this exercise. Three databases were created: (1) a digital map (that is, a spatial geographic database created by digitizing maps of different scales); (2) a georeferenced community inventory database (created by entering latitude and longitude data from maps and GPS units); and (3) an MOH epidemiologic database (relationally linked by unique ID numbers to the community inventory). The result of the analysis was a set of targeted communities generated through the use of a unique GIS function called buffering. Communities falling inside the buffer area were targeted for an intervention (treatment or further assessment); those outside were not. Accordingly, this spatial process generated new data to stratify communities that otherwise were without epidemiological information, and program management found new guidance in decisionmaking related to field activities of a control program.

Obtaining a relatively complete listing and position of the smallest and most marginal of rural villages inside and around the known disease-endemic areas was challenging (Estes 1994, Hastings and Clark 1991). Large-scale ($\geq$1:200,000) maps are usually not readily available in developing countries, and if found they are frequently out of date, incomplete (that is, missing adjoining sheets), or restricted by security forces. In 1987, paper maps at scales of 1:100,000 were available for only 59 percent of the earth's surface, with the developing world being that part of the globe least well mapped. Even in the United States, where coverage at 1:100,000 is 100 percent, only 14 percent of these maps were printed within the last 10 years, and 9 percent of what is available was produced 40 years ago (Estes 1994). However, finding maps of scale 1:500,000 to 1:1,000,000 is not difficult, and indeed may be obtained in a digital format (for example, from the gazetteer and DCW).

In contrast to rapid "address-matching" and "zip-coding" programs that are commonly included with GIS software for marketing and business applications, georeferencing of existing MOH field records was time-consuming and labor-intensive. Difficulties encountered included the repetition of community names, use of different scales, lack of maps with county and state boundaries, and data inconsistencies. Frequent plotting exercises, meetings with MOH field workers, and field reconnaissance opportunities were needed to review the results, ask questions, identify missing communities, and estimate positions. It is important to recognize that this tedious process was necessary despite the fact that we enjoyed the advantage of working at a relatively large (1:50,000) scale. Onchocerciasis-mapping efforts in Africa are usually not so fortunate (Ngoumou and Walsh 1993, Mace and others 1997, DeSole 1991).

Throughout the targeting exercise we had to keep in mind that we were not cartographers. The failure to produce a perfect map was not an excuse to slow the project; nor did we find that slight imperfections jeopardized the general usefulness of the final GIS for decisionmaking. Health officials, and their GIS consultants, must recognize that detail and scale may (and should) be sacrificed for the sake of time, money, and a higher purpose. Similarly, the paper maps we created would not have met a cartographer's standards, since they contained data from different scales, and were only specifically detailed to assist managers and field teams in accomplishing their programmatic objectives.

Although the community inventory could have been developed as an internal point layer from within Atlas*GIS (AGIS), we chose to make the community inventory database an independent point file that could stand alone, separate from the software itself. Rather than restricting ourselves to an internal position code generated within Atlas*GIS, we wanted our data in an industry-standard code (FoxPro®), and georeferenced with universal position coordinates (latitude and longitude). This strategy allowed easy transfer of the community inventory into other GIS formats (if a more sophisticated spatial analysis were required), and provided data safety in what was then a highly volatile software market (that is, rapid entry and exit of companies, formats, and data protocols). Using latitude and longitude coordinates also allowed easy addition of GPS data.

About 8 percent of the communities listed in the MOH database could not be found on the large-scale maps, so field readings on-site with a GPS became indispensable for completing the GIS. Horizontal position readings taken with the hand-held units could easily be introduced into a database of 1:50,000 scale. Elevation readings with a GPS, however, were not sufficiently accurate for our needs.

In contrast to GPS, readily available digital data (gazetteer and DCW) were not useful, as neither were sufficiently accurate to meet the demands of our MOH matching exercise. If we had used these readily available data sets we would have saved the time and costs of entering community data from large-scale formats (1:50,000 maps in this case) at the expense of completeness and accuracy when matching to MOH data files during the georeferencing phase of the project. The costs incurred building a digital map and community inventory from nondigital sources is decreasing now that maps can be converted to digital files using new scanning hardware. In any event, these costs should only be borne once, as other projects using a GIS should be able to benefit from the investment. Sharing of GIS data between units and institutions is important, but better yet is data trading of one data set or layer for another developed by other projects or sectors (such as agriculture or hydrology). GIS networking should be encouraged, since data trades can be a win-win situation for all involved (Hastings and Clark 1991).

GIS projects must make an effort to generate products helpful to the computer-illiterate field worker. Unless the GIS application is of use to the field workers actually involved in operations, the field workers will not provide observations to assist in the GIS development, and as a result the accuracy and validity of the GIS suffer. We found that production of GIS-generated paper field maps improved collaboration with the field teams, linked the office-based GIS unit to the actual field situation, and provided a route for the feedback needed to keep the GIS current. Printing large color maps is now becoming more feasible in developing countries as the prices of large-format plotters drop.

For the present, GIS applications in the developing world have to be built, not bought. Training programs that teach new geographic positioning technology must devote time to developing "building" skills such as map digitizing, the importation of data from diverse sources, data sharing, and the use of GPS. Course curricula should provide exercises based on these real-life experiences, appreciation of scale, and anticipation of the problems of retrospective data review and georeferencing described here. If GISs are to be used in decisionmaking, the users must become efficient at combining and manipulating information from different sources and scales to get a timely result.

In conclusion, geographical information systems and georeferenced databases will play an increasingly important role in disease targeting activities in the future. The work and cost of building a GIS should decrease with increasing availability and cataloging of detailed (large-scale) digital data sets. We cannot envision, however, a way to avoid the major task of georeferencing existing epidemiologic data, which was the key element in this targeting exercise.

Notes

Frank O. Richards, M.D., is at the Division of Parasitic Diseases; National Center for Infectious Disease; Centers for Disease Control and Prevention.

Testing the GPS Unit

1. Thirty-three GPS readings were taken at the same open site (the NE corner of the football field on the campus of the Universidad del Valle de Guatemala, or UVG). GPS readings were compared with a position read from the appropriate 1:50,000 map. Figure 8.1 shows a spatial analysis (each tick = 100 meters) of the horizontal plain of the UVG football field. The star in the figure indicates the position read from the map. The central position of the GPS readings was 85 meters SSW from the map position. Figure 8.2 shows a plot of horizontal and vertical distances from the map position. Similar to the findings on the horizontal plane, 79 percent (26) of elevation observations fell within 100 meters of the map position.

References

Brandling-Bennett, A. D., J. Anderson, H. Fuglsang, and R.C. Collins. 1981. "Onchocerciasis in Guatemala: Epidemiology in Fincas of Various Intensities of Infection." *Am J Trop Med Hyg* 30: 970–81.

Collins, R.C., J. O. Ochoa, E. W. Cupp, C. Gonzales-Peralta, and C. H. Porter. 1992. "Microepidemiology of Onchocerciasis in Guatemala: Dispersal and Survival of *Simulium Ochraceum*." *Am J Trop Med Hyg* 47: 147–55.

DeSole G., J. Fiese, F.M. Keita, and others. 1991. "Detailed Epidemiological Mapping of Three Onchocerciasis Foci in West Africa." *Acta Trop* (Basel) 48: 203–13.

Estes, M. 1994. "The Mythical Map." *Photometric Engineering* 60: 24–27.

Hastings, D.A., and D.M. Clark. 1991 "GIS in Africa: Problems, Challenges and Opportunities for Co-operation." *Int J Geographical Information Systems* 5: 29–39.

Hopkins, D., and F. Richards. 1997. "Visionary Campaign: Eliminating River Blindness." *Encyclopedia Britannica Medical and Health Annual* 1997: 9–23.

Mace, J.M, M. Boussinesq, P. Ngoumou, J. Enyegue Oye, A. Koeranga, and C. Godin. 1997. "Country-Wide Rapid Epidemiological Mapping of Onchocerciasis (REMO) in Cameroon." *Annals Trop. Med. Parasitol* 91: 379–91.

Mectizan® Expert Committee. 1990. "The Mectizan® Donation Program: Community-Based Mass Treatment of Onchocerciasis," Parts I & II. One Copenhill, Atlanta, GA 30307. November.

Ngoumou, P., and J.F. Walsh. 1993. "A Manual for Rapid Epidemiological Mapping of Onchocerciasis." World Health Organization, TDR/TDE/Oncho/93.4.

Ramirez, Perez J. 1986. "Human Onchocerciasis Foci and Vectors in the American Tropics and Subtropics." *Bull Pan Am Health Organ* 20: 381–402.

Richards, F. 1993. "Computer Mapping of Guatemalan Communities with Suspected Onchocerciasis." *PAHO Bull.* 27: 52–5.

Shelly, A.J. 1988. "Vector Aspects of the Epidemiology of Onchocerciasis in Latin America." *Ann Rev Entomol.* 30: 337–66.

Tada, I., Y. Aoki, E. Rimola, and others. 1979. "Onchocerciasis in San Vicente Pacaya, Guatemala." *Am J Trop Med Hyg.* 28: 67–71.

Taylor, H., B.O.L. Duke, and B. Munoz. 1992. "The Selection of Communities for Treatment of Onchocerciasis with Ivermectin." *Annals Trop. Med. Parasitol.* 43: 267–70.

Taylor, H.R., and B.M. Greene. 1989. "The Status of Ivermectin in the Treatment of Human Onchocerciasis." *Am J Trop Med Hyg.* 41: 460–66.

World Health Organization (WHO). 1987. WHO Expert Committee on Onchocerciasis, Third Report. Technical Report Series 752.

———. 1995. "Onchocerciasis and Its Control." Report of a WHO expert committee on onchocerciasis control. Technical Report Series 852.

———. 1996. "Onchocerciasis, Progress Towards Elimination in the Americas." *Weekly Epidemiological Record* 71: 277–80.

———. 1997. "Annual Onchocerciasis Report from the InterAmerican Conference on Onchocerciasis in Oaxaca, Mexico." *Weekly Epidemiological Record* 72: 215–8.

Yamagata, Y., T. Suzuki, and G.A. Garcia Manzo. 1986. "Geographical Distribution of the Prevalence of Nodules of *Onchocerca volvulus* in Guatemala over the Last Four Decades." *Trop Med Parasitol.* 37: 28–34.

9

A Geographical Information System Applied to a Malaria Field Study

Allen W. Hightower, Maurice Ombok, Richard Otieno, Richard Odhiambo, and William A. Hawley

HOW MANY PEOPLE LIVE WITHIN FIVE KILOMETERS of the proposed clinic location? Where are the houses in the village that were included in a survey of the use and acceptance of insecticide-impregnated bednets? What spatial features, such as proximity to seasonal streams, are associated with the prevalence of households that have elevated malaria transmission pressure, even during the dry season? During the dry season, are there focal areas of elevated mosquito abundance that can be targeted for an effective control program? These questions demonstrate just a few of the reasons that the analysis of spatial relationships has long been an integral part of public health planning, day-to-day operations, and research activities. Although affordable geographical information system software has simplified this effort, an accurate base map is required for any GIS analysis. Lack of such maps is a substantial obstacle for researchers wishing to perform geographic analysis in tropical disease research since studies are often conducted in areas where existing maps are inaccurate, insufficiently detailed, or outdated. Various methods, each applicable to particular circumstances, can be used for base map production. Performance of a geographic survey requires special skills beyond the reach of those not professionally trained in these methods. Sketch maps are normally created only for operational purposes. They are inaccurate and lack a coordinate system needed for spatial analysis. Satellite images and remotely sensed data are useful when finely detailed spatial analysis is not required (Beck and others 1994, Clarke and others 1991, Malone and others 1994, Malhotra and Srivastava 1996). Aerial photography is expensive if archived aerial photographs are not available to the researcher (Gunawardena and others 1996). Furthermore, security concerns can make access difficult. Use of the global positioning systems can provide an accurate, detailed map of any tropical site. As explained in more detail later, a GPS unit is a hand-held electronic tool that uses signals from satellites to compute the longitude, latitude, and altitude of a location. Without differential correction, GPSs provide adequate, but not extraordinarily accurate maps (Snow and others 1993, Richards 1993). A simple modification of a GPS, known as differential GPS (DGPS), can be used to produce a highly accurate base map in a tropical area. In this chapter we detail the use of differential GPS to map an area in western Kenya where two large-scale studies are being conducted, perform some simple spatial analyses by linking study data from these and other projects to these maps, and discuss the other applications of this system. The GPS and GIS mapping technology presented here will also be contrasted with that presented earlier to demonstrate how this technology has improved rapidly from the standpoint of user friendliness over the past few years (Hightower and others 1998).

Two collaborative studies between the Kenya Medical Research Institute (KEMRI) and the Centers for Disease Control (CDC) of the development of natural immunity to malaria and the use of insecticide-impregnated bednets in reducing childhood mortality in western Kenya provided the framework for this effort. The longitudinal study of the development of immunity to malaria in young children was carried out in a 70-square-kilometer area in Siaya district in western Kenya, approximately 50 kilometers southwest of Kisumu (Shi and others 1996). Clinical, hematologic, parasitologic, immunologic, entomologic, and demographic data were regularly collected for each participating family in 15 villages. The demographic data consisted primarily of census data collected at the beginning of each project and updated regularly. The entomologic data consisted of weekly trap collections for each study household. Clinical data were collected biweekly. Blood samples were obtained monthly or whenever any fever was reported. Blood samples were used to measure parasitemia, hemoglobin levels, and on certain subsamples, immunologic parameters. Since all of these data were collected with household identifiers, opportunities for examining spatial hypotheses exist in many disciplines if a map of study households, health care centers, mosquito larval habitat, bodies of water (such as rivers and lakes), roads, and other features of interest could be produced in a computer-readable format and linked to the various study databases through a GIS and other statistical software. Existing maps and aerial photography were either unavailable, inaccurate, or too outdated to be useful for mapping households and many of the other features of interest (Survey of Kenya 1970).

The second project, which includes the 15 villages in the natural immunity project and over 60 more in adjacent areas, evaluates the effect of insecticide-impregnated bednets on childhood mortality. This is a simple and inexpensive intervention. Bednets are soaked in an odorless insecticide and draped over beds to keep mosquitoes out. The insecticide prevents the mosquitoes from entering the net, even if there are small holes in the net. Because malaria-transmitting mosquitoes feed only at night, sleeping under the nets should effectively reduce illness and mortality due to this disease. All of the villages in this project have now received bednets. Since the Immunity study villages were also included in this chapter's study, we had detailed longitudinal data on a subset that allowed us to evaluate the effects of using impregnated bednets on the development of a child's immune system, as well as their impact on mosquito populations in the study area.

Methods

The Global Positioning System

Twenty-four satellites (21 for navigational purposes, 3 active reserves) orbiting at an altitude of approximately 10,900 miles (20,200 kilometers) form the global positioning satellite network (French 1996). GPS satellites continuously broadcast the time and their orbital path to provide the information used by a terrestrial GPS unit. Data received from four satellites allow the GPS unit to calculate latitude, longitude, and altitude, while data from three other satellites allow calculation of latitude and longitude only. The exact methodology for how position fixes are computed is described in detail elsewhere (French 1996, Herring 1996).

GPS Errors

The computations of a GPS position fix are subject to error from several uncontrolled factors—among others, atmospheric conditions (French 1996, Herring 1996, Magellan Systems Corporation 1995). The largest error component, selective availability (SA), is the intentional error component added for security purposes at each satellite. Because SA error varies with time and from one satellite to the next, when a GPS unit changes the group of satellites it is using to compute a position fix, the different SA error term results in a sudden change in the computed location. As long as the same set of satellites is in use by the GPS unit, errors are highly correlated with respect to time. This prevents short-term averaging of GPS readings to circumvent the deleterious effects of SA. A single reading on a standard GPS unit has an error of 100 meters horizontal, and 156 meters vertical (French 1996, Herring 1996). Approximately 55 meters of the horizontal error is due to SA (Magellan Systems Corporation 1995).

Differential GPS

Errors of 100 meters for horizontal measurements (latitude and longitude) and 150 meters for vertical accuracy are far too large to make simple GPS use practical for mapping the locations of objects that are relatively close together, such as households within villages. Such large errors will result in gross distortion of the true spatial relationships between the measured points, and make a map produced with simple GPS readings very confusing to use for operational purposes.

Differential GPS circumvents the effects of SA and environmental errors to produce a highly accurate position fix. Several different approaches to DGPS exist, but each employs the principle of having two GPS units simultaneously taking readings from the same set of satellites. One GPS unit is located at a fixed control site, preferably a known location, and the others become the roving field units. As a result, the position fixes for both GPS units are subject to the same SA and clock error terms. If the units are relatively near to each other (under 50 kilometers), the precisely timed GPS signals travel through similar ionospheric and tropospheric conditions (Magellan Systems Corporation 1995). For both units, each position fix is stored to a computer file, along with the exact time of the reading and the set of satellites used to compute the location. The matching files for the two GPS units are then downloaded to a computer. Software is used to pair or synchronize readings that were taken at exactly the same time. There are several techniques for doing this, but for each, the location of the remote GPS unit is computed by adding the distance between the two GPS units to the known location of the control GPS unit. In our application, this involved simultaneous creation of computer files on control and remote GPS units, followed by copying these files to a computer and running software to figure calibrated positions.

We established a GPS base station to serve as a control point near at the computer center in our field station near Kisumu, Kenya. A collapsible 8-meter antenna was constructed to lift the receiver above any obstacles that might block satellite signals. A cable connected the antenna to the GPS unit, which in turn, was connected to the computer. The exact location of the control GPS unit was unknown, so thousands of readings were taken over several days and averaged to provide an estimate of the true location. Because this position was used as a correction factor for all remote sessions, any error associated with estimating the control location was consistent across all remote points—having the effect of moving the entire map in one direction or another.

Equipment and Personnel

We used four Magellan Pro Mark Xcp GPS units (Magellan Systems Corporation 1995). (Use of trade names is for identification only and does not imply endorsement by the Public Health Service or by the U.S. Department of Health and Human Services.) These units use the latest "all-in-view" technology described below. The units record data from all available GPS satellites, unlike previous generations which required manual selection satellites based on a software analysis of satellite orbits (Hightower and others 1998). One unit is used for the permanent GPS base station, and the other three are field units. Tripod antenna extensions (2.5 meters) for each field GPS unit, battery powered hand held radios, replacement batteries for the GPS units, and a list of compounds to be mapped round out the equipment list for the field teams. Total equipment and software costs were approximately US$25,000 for the GPS equipment and GIS software. (Note that all dollar amounts in this paper are U.S.) One person is needed to operate each of the three field GPS units. A local village health worker who knows where to find the points (compounds, stores, and so forth) to be mapped meets each field GPS team member. A computer specialist, working part-time on this project, was responsible for GPS to PC data communications at the field station, using the Microsoft Windows® 95–based post-processing software to compute the calibrated positions, to enter data on a Pentium® computer.

About one hour of computer work was necessary to process six hours of GPS data—generally between 6 and 8 megabytes of data representing roughly 100 positions. Approximately six person-months of effort were required for the fieldwork, post processing, and data entry for this relatively large-scale mapping project. Total costs of labor and supplies to map the bednet project area have not exceeded $10,000. However, these costs are highly dependent upon where the work is being done, and will vary with different mapping projects.

GIS Analysis

Atlas GIS (Environmental Systems Research Institute, Inc. 1991), ArcView 3.0 (Environmental Systems Research Institute, Inc. 1996a), and SAS (SAS Institute 1989) were used for all spatial analyses. Location information was linked to parasitology and entomology databases through common identifiers. In the Immunity project, there was entomologic, immunologic, epidemiologic, meteorologic, demographic, and parasitologic information that could be linked to each household.

Automated or batch computing of distances between one group of points to another is a feature that is not available in the popular entry-level GIS programs unless supplemental programming tools or extension modules are purchased. A SAS program was developed that computes all possible distances from one group of points to another, chooses the smallest distance from each point in the first group to any point in the second group, and then creates an output database with household identifiers and the desired distances. The distance computations account for the curvature of the earth by computing arc length instead of linear distance (USGS paper 1395). This distance is then used as a basis for computing spatial statistics (that is, the parasitemia rate for households 0–200 meters, 201–400 meters, and so on from the nearest mosquito breeding site) or can be used in further statistical modeling. This process is called buffer creation and is available in virtually all entry-level GIS packages without supplementary programming.

GIS software is necessary for displaying data on maps and customized map production. GIS maps consist of layers. A map layer is defined by the user's convenience, but normally consists of a group of related features. For example, compounds, roads, streams, medicine stores, and schools are stored in separate map layers in this system. We can turn layers on or off as desired, highlight compounds to be visited for survey purposes, or restrict the map to a subset of villages to produce customized maps. Data can be associated with any map layer. Buffer zones can be created (for example, to highlight all households with 500 meters of the lakeshore). A map that displays data, such as the number of mosquitoes trapped in a household during a specific time period, is called a thematic map. Data of this type can be presented with a dot at the compound's location, with the size of the dot being proportional to the magnitude of the variable mapped. A map of the United States with the states having color or shading that is related to the incidence of a particular disease is another example of a thematic map. In our application, virtually all of the databases are related to households, or individuals within the households. For several years, Atlas GIS, an entry-level GIS product, met all of our customized mapping and thematic mapping needs.

However, modules that greatly expand the spatial analysis capabilities of entry-level GIS software can be purchased and used, if statistical programming expertise is not available. ArcView has many of the same features as Atlas GIS, but it is more expandable from the standpoint of offering several specialized analysis modules. While not inexpensive, these modules offer greatly enhanced analytic capabilities in specialized areas. The ArcView Spatial Analyst module (Environmental Systems Research Institute, Inc. 1996b) was used for the surface interpolations. Surface interpolation takes the concept of the thematic map a step further by expanding the analysis from the compound locations to the entire area containing the compounds. Given the map of compound-level mosquito abundance, it finds the best-fitting surface that smooths the observed data points. Such a surface shows the contours of mosquito abundance or malaria risk for the study area and could be used to identify areas of high, medium, and low mosquito abundance or malaria risk. High-risk abundance areas would then be logical targets for focal control efforts, if these areas could be demonstrated to be reasonably consistent across time. They would also allow the estimation of the vector abundance for any proposed building site in the study area. Spline functions, kriging, and inverse distance weighting are a few of the methodologies for estimating these surfaces (Cressie 1993). For this chapter, inverse distance weighting was used to interpolate surfaces. The map of the study area is divided into a grid, and the observed data for the dozen nearest compounds to the centroid of the grid cell are then averaged with weights inversely proportional to the distance from each compound. This process is repeated for each cell of the grid to obtain the smoothed surface for the variable of interest. The estimates can then be categorized to form contour lines, if desired. This is a general methodology that allows many of the fitting parameters to be varied as desired, such as the number of nearest neighbors used, the criteria for determining nearest neighbors, or the functional form of the inverse proportionality (linear, quadratic, or other polynomial).

Quality Assessment

Maps of each of the 15 villages were produced and distributed to village monitors, who assessed their accuracy and completeness. Special opportunities often arose for external validation. Many households were near roads, so they were checked to verify that the map showed them on the proper side of the road and at the correct approximate distance. Households or compounds that were clustered were also checked for proper distances and relative geometric relationships. Features of interest that had not been mapped were noted for later inclusion.

The performance of the GPS units and the post-processing software, as well as correct usage by the operators, was checked by placing the two units next to each other, designating one as the control unit, collecting positional information for 20 sessions of 5 minutes each, and computing the calibrated location of the remote unit. The mean and standard deviations of the calibrated longitudes, latitudes, and altitudes of the remote units were then computed.

Demonstration Data

Entomology and parasitemia data from the Immunity study for the months of June and September 1995 are presented to represent rainy and dry seasons, respectively. Parasitemic compounds were defined as having at least one child under five with any malaria parasitemia during the month in question. We had parasitologic and sufficient entomologic data (three or more visits during the month) for 394 households in June and 416 households in September. Potential larval habitats were defined as the lakeshore, streams and rivers, and pits dug to collect water for cattle. Multiple linear regression, correlation coefficients, and r-square statistics for each month were used to examine the relationship between distance from major mosquito breeding sites and average numbers of trapped mosquitoes by species for each month.

Results

The Bednet project (figure 9.1) covered an area of 192 square kilometers over a rectangular area roughly 12 kilometers long and 7 kilometers wide, encompassing 75 villages. Geographic features included 7,209 compounds, 65 schools, 1 nursery, 1 polytechnic school, 110 churches, 9 health care facilities, 1 rural AIDS counseling center, 70 major mosquito breeding sites, 10 borehole wells, 7 shopping areas, major roads, streams, and the shore of Lake Victoria. In terms of distances, 42.0 kilometers of roads, 54.3 kilometers of streams, and 15.0 kilometers of lakeshore were mapped. The Immunity project area (figure 9.2) contains 15 villages in the southeastern section of the Bednet project.

Of the twenty sessions taken with the two GPS units stationed next to each other, one (5 percent) had insufficient overlapping data to estimate a calibrated position. This is normally caused by the loss of a satellite signal during a session. Of the 19 remaining sessions, the longitudes had a standard deviation of 4.01 meters, the latitudes had a standard deviation of 5.34 meters, and the altitudes had a standard deviation of 4.78 meters. The two-dimensional standard deviation of these sessions was 3.11 meters and the standard error of the mean was 0.714 meters.

Table 9.1 relates parasitemia prevalence and entomologic measures to the distance from the household to the nearest major larval habitat. For the month of June 1995 (a rainy month), the average household prevalence of parasitemia in children less than 5 years old steadily decreased with

Figure 9.1 Map of the Bednet Study Area

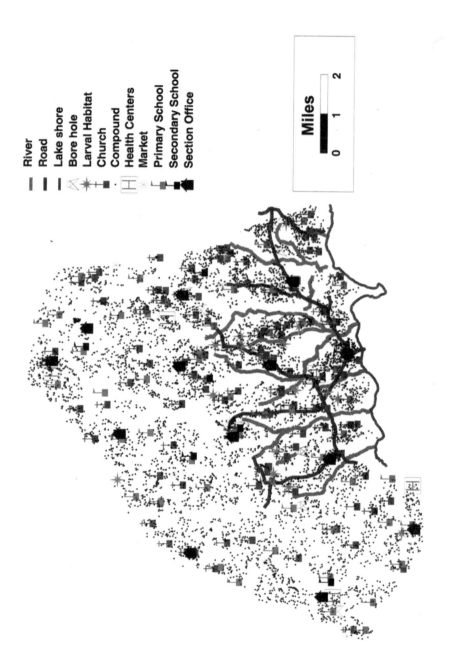

Source: Author's calculations.

Figure 9.2 Map of the Immunity Study Area

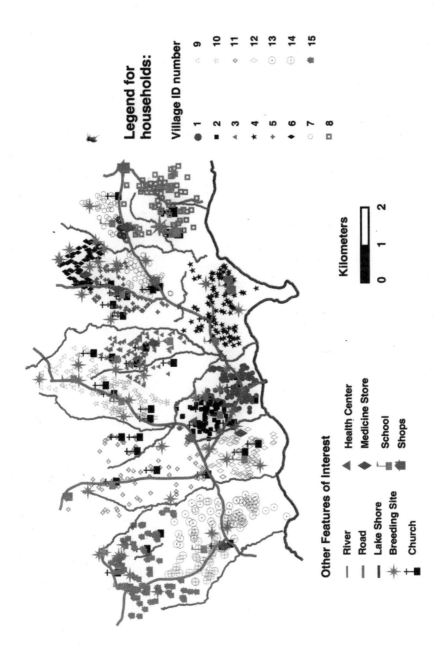

Table 9.1 Parasitemia Prevalence and Entomologic Measures by Household and Distance to the Nearest Mosquito Larval Habitat, June and September 1995

Distance to nearest larval habitat	Parasitemia rate (percent) in children < 5 years		Anopheles gambiae: average number trapped per colllection	
	Month		Month	
	June	September	June	September
0–200 meters	75.8+39.1	58.5+47.8	1.76+2.53	0.09+0.19
	n=75	n=71	n=69	n=57
201–400 meters	71.1+42.7	69.4+43.4	1.49+1.71	0.05+0.18
	n=214	n=206	n=176	n=164
401–600 meters	70.2+43.1	64.7+45.3	1.90+2.31	0.03+0.10
	n=117	n=109	n=113	n=108
>600 meters	67.1+46.3	57.8+47.7	2.09+2.05	0.02+0.06
	n=39	n=30	n=37	n=33
p-value*	0.3437	0.5594	0.1530	0.0039

Note:
* Linear regression, two-tailed test. Percent of children in household with parasitemia or average number of mosquitoes captured per weekly trapping session versus minimum distance (in meters) from household to nearest larval habitat.
n = number of mosquitoes captured.
Source: Hightower, Otieno, and others 1998.

increasing household distance (defined in 200-meter buffer categories) from larval habitat, but this difference was not statistically significant ($p = 0.3437$ linear regression). There was no relationship between distance to larval habitat and average parasitemia prevalence for the month of September, a dry month. Average numbers of trapped mosquitoes were related to the distance of the household to the nearest breeding site for *Anopheles gambiae* for the dry month, but not the wet month (September: $p = 0.0039$; June: $p = 0.1530$, linear regression).

Figure 9.3 shows the average number of trapped *Anopheles gambiae* weekly by household for the months of June and September 1995. The size of the dot for each household is proportional to the average number of mosquitoes collected during the weekly trappings for that month. Mosquito abundance drops off rapidly from June to September. Villages vary significantly in the numbers of mosquitoes trapped by household (all months, p < 0.01, one way analysis of variance). There is considerable variation in mosquito abundance both within and between villages.

Figure 9.4 shows the interpolated surfaces for the average number of *Anopheles gambiae* trapped weekly for the same two months of July and September 1995. Overlaid on the surfaces are the compound-specific abun-

Figure 9.3 Average Numbers of Anopheles Gambiae Trapped per Continent

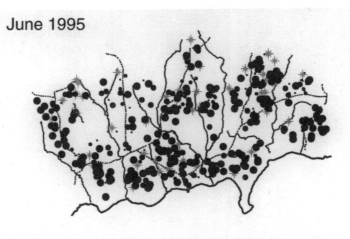

June 1995

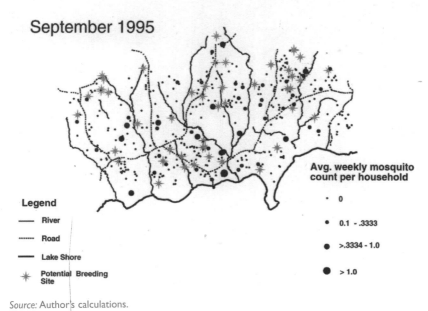

September 1995

Legend

— River

······ Road

— Lake Shore

∗ Potential Breeding Site

Avg. weekly mosquito count per household

· 0

• 0.1 - .3333

● >.3334 - 1.0

⬤ > 1.0

Source: Author's calculations.

dance measures shown in figure 9.3. Assessment of the overall trends is much easier in figure 9.4 than in figure 9.3. For example, in June, most of the study area is in the two highest categories. In September, most of the study area is in the two highest categories. Also, notice that it is much easier to see specific details in the transition in the areas of high and low transmission pressure from rainy to dry season in these maps when compared to the

Figure 9.4 Estimated Areas of High, Mid-High, Mid-Low, and Low Mosquito Abundance

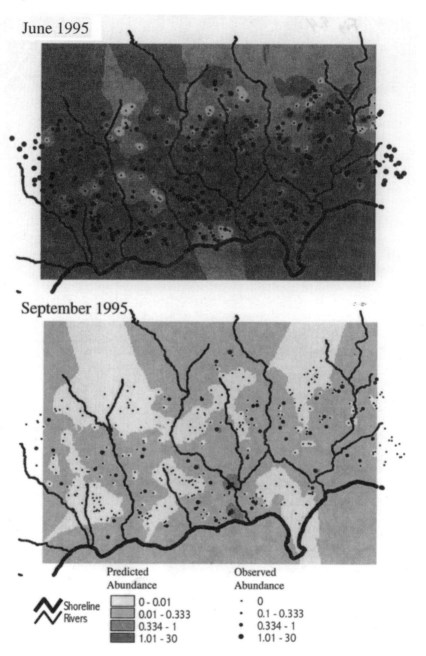

Source: Author's calculations.

maps just showing vector abundance by compound. Assessment of the potential mosquito abundance at proposed new construction sites is also much more easily done with figure 9.4 than figure 9.3.

Discussion

We have shown that it is feasible to use differential GPS to produce a highly accurate map of study households and other points of interest in a large-scale study of malaria in an area encompassing more than 75 villages over 190 square kilometers. Without differential GPS, positional errors are such that any mapping of objects within 200 meters or so of each other will yield inconsistent spatial relationships between map features, since the errors associated with use of nondifferential GPS can be on the scale of 100 meters. Use of simple GPS readings is appropriate when the objects to be mapped, such as villages, are relatively far apart (Richards 1993). In addition, we have shown that it is easy to map linear features such as roads, rivers, and lakeshores. The comprehensive maps have considerable use in the operational activities of the project and a GIS allows customized maps to be produced rapidly.

Even though DGPS was used to map our entire study area, other groups may find different existing digitized base maps a useful starting point, such as the Digital Chart of the World (Defense Mapping Agency of the United States); digitizing existing small-scale maps can also provide a basis for geographic mapping. Searching the Internet or querying GIS interest groups on the Internet is a worthwhile activity to find such maps. In our experience, these maps were quite old, and when checked, not accurate enough for our needs. It is relatively simple to combine GPS-produced maps with existing digitized maps, but one must be careful to convert both types of maps to the same map-projection system (like UTM) before combining them. This is easily done even in entry-level GIS software.

Our efforts at quality assessment raise several points. First, the results from the 20 sessions with the GPS units adjacent to each other demonstrate the greatly increased precision associated with differential GPS. A previous study not using DGPS reported a standard error of 47 meters associated with repeat measurements of 43 randomly selected households (Snow and others 1993), with an average discrepancy of 36 meters from the original measurement. In our example using DGPS, the standard error (variability of the mean of a group of 19 measurements) was 0.714 meters, or a standard deviation of 3.11 meters (reflecting the variability in the calibrated readings). Thus, DGPS greatly reduces the errors and variability in positional measurements associated with mapping. This allows mapping of features that are close together in a manner that will maintain spatial relationships with a high degree of integrity.

The expense and effort required to create this GIS was small relative to the other costs of the two field projects, with expenses being approximately $35,000. Of this amount, approximately $25,000 was for hardware and software. The GIS maps, databases, and GPS equipment and expertise continue to be used on other field activities. Those conducting smaller scale projects or one-time studies should consider renting DGPS equipment to reduce costs. DGPS equipment has made dramatic improvements in user friendliness and novices can become quite proficient in less than a week. DGPS units can be rented for approximately $150 per week, depending upon features. Rental of 4 high-end units for a month would then cost about $2,500— a substantial savings. Given the differential between purchase and rental costs, renting equipment and bringing in an expert consultant is a financially viable option in many cases.

Training field staff to perform the necessary duties for DGPS mapping presented no difficulties. Because existing staff were employed for the mapping operations on a part-time basis, the new duties were a novelty, and the opportunity to use recent aerospace technology to produce a map of the study area was exciting to all involved. Moreover, recent improvements in GPS technology have greatly simplified mapping operations. Improvements include faster GPS-to-PC communications, and the ability to obtain sub-meter accuracy with data collection sessions of less than 10 minutes. The net effect is to make the use of differential GPS a much simpler process than just two years ago. Our experience with even newer differential GPS units confirms that they continue to become even more user friendly.

A system such as DPGS has several applications outside of the mission of our operation. Since there is census and demographic information available for each compound, a GIS could be used for many types of public health planning for activities in the area. The system could be used, with the inclusion of buffers, to summarize the population characteristics within the catchment areas, or within walking distance of existing or proposed health care delivery systems such as clinics, medicine stores, nutrition programs, or vaccination campaigns. Indeed, many of the urban planning and marketing applications of GISs could have parallel uses in public health planning. Other surveys conducted in the study area could be linked to the GIS as long as they use the same compound identifiers.

The analyses presented here were intentionally simple and were intended to present only some of the potential uses of the GIS and GPS data. We have shown that GIS software need not be mastered to conduct many useful spatial analyses once locational information has been obtained. Indeed, the spatial capabilities of the most popular entry-level GIS programs are limited, and the automated computation of distances requires supplementary programming efforts or purchases (Kitron and others 1994). Fortunately, computation can be easily done in most statistical programs.

Our example used distance in 200-meter categories (or buffers) from the household to the nearest major potential larval habitat. However, many other distance variables, such as distance to the nearest health clinic or medicine store, could just as easily be computed and additionally incorporated into a statistical analysis.

However, GIS software is necessary for displaying data on maps, because it can produce customized maps, using observed data at many points (in our case, compounds), of a study area to estimate areas of high and low risk of disease or abundance of a vector. Most of these tasks can be handled by any entry-level GIS program, which will also handle most day-to-day operational mapping needs of the project. An entry-level GIS provides the tools needed for most, if not all, planning operational activities. Creation of buffer zones to see how many people live within 5 kilometers of a proposed clinic site is an example of such a task. Buffer zones can be used to assess risk factors, such as nearness to rivers during dry seasons. A GIS gives control programs the ability to monitor exactly what is happening down to the compound level. Entry-level products can be used to produce monthly maps of mosquito abundance by compound. More advanced GIS and spatial analysis topics include examining issues of time-space clustering and surface interpolation, which are more germane to the research and control aspects of a program. Surface interpolation allows the estimation of risk or prevalence contours, which allows targeting of control or treatment programs. These two tasks require the use of a mid-level GIS program with the purchase of supplemental modules or the availability of a person with statistical or GIS programming expertise.

Key to making a GIS work is the availability of personnel with expertise in GIS software to the operational and research staff of the project. This person should have a relatively well-equipped, but not necessarily expensive, Pentium-class computer with generous memory and hard drive capacity, at least a 17-inch monitor, and a reasonable color inkjet printer available with sufficient supplies for the needs of daily map production. All of this can be purchased for well under $3,000. GIS software can be purchased for as little as $800 to as much as $5,000, depending upon the sophistication of the product and the number of add-on modules. As entry-level GIS software can be easily mastered, this level of expertise should be easy to develop within an existing organization.

Our current activities include more in-depth analyses of the entomological and parasitological data (Hawley and others 1998, Hightower, Ombok, and others 1998, Hightower and others 1997, Gimnig and others 1998). Remote sensing data on vegetation zones and hydrology taken at several times during the study period will be added for analysis of the effects of ecological change on the study outcomes. Cross-sectional surveys on the prevalence of bloody diarrhea and childhood mortality have been linked to a GIS to investigate clustering for these issues. Researchers using data from this field site now have the option of investigating the spatial aspects of virtually any topic they are pursuing.

We have shown that survey-grade GPS mapping and GIS analysis are affordable, feasible, and useful in the planning, operational, and research activities of a tropical disease research site. These tools, once the province of highly trained professionals, have become sufficiently user-friendly that even novices can successfully employ them. As a result, applications are becoming more commonplace, and GISs and GPSs are becoming part of the everyday vocabulary. Public health professionals would be well advised to consider the benefits of GISs and GPSs while they are planning new tropical disease field activities.

Notes

The author would like to thank Joseph Omolo and Christopher Lwoba for their computer support and Daniel Colley for his support during the time it took to master, transfer, and apply this new technology.

Allen Hightower and William Hawley are at the Division of Parasitic Diseases, National Center for Infectious Diseases, National Centers for Disease Control and Prevention, Atlanta, Georgia. Maurice Ombok, Richard Otieno, and Richard Odhiambo are at the Kenya Medical Research Institute.

References

Beck, L.R., M.H. Rodrigues, S.W. Dister, A.D. Rodriguez, E. Rejmankova, A. Ulloa, R.A. Mesa, D.R. Roberts, J.F. Paris, M.A. Spanner, R.K. Washino, C. Hacker, and L. Legters. 1994. "Remote Sensing as a Landscape Epidemiologic Tool to Identify Villages at High Risk for Malaria Transmission. *Am J Tropical Medicine Hyg* 51: 271–280.

Clarke, K.C., J.R. Osleeb, J.M. Sherry, J.P. Meert, and R.W. Larsson. 1991. "The Use of Remote Sensing and Geographic Information Systems in UNICEF's *Dracunculiasis* (Guinea Worm) Eradication Effort." *Preventive Vetenary Medicine* 11: 229–35.

Cressie, N.A.C. 1993. *Statistics for Spatial Data.* New York: Wiley.

Defense Mapping Agency of the United States. "Digital Chart of the World Fact Sheet." http://www.dma.gov/information/facts/

Environmental Systems Research Institute, Inc. 1996a. ArcView GIS. The Geographic Information System for Everyone. Redlands, California: Environmental Systems Research Institute, Inc.

Environmental Systems Research Institute, Inc. 1996b. ArcView Spatial Analyst. Redlands, CA: Environmental Systems Research Institute, Inc.

Environmental Systems Research Institute, Inc. 1991. *Reference Manual.* Atlas GIS, Version 2.1 (DOS). Redlands, California: Environmental Systems Research Institute, Inc.

French, G. T. 1996. *Understanding the GPS, An Introduction to the Global Positioning System.* Bethesda, MD: GeoResearch, Inc.

Gimnig, J., A. Hightower, P. Phillips-Howard, G. Olang, J. Vulule, B. Nahlen, F. ter Kuile, and W.A. Hawley. 1998. "Divergence or Mass Effect: The Impact of Impregnated Bednets on Mosquito Abundance in Neighboring Houses." Abstract submitted for the American Society of Tropical Medicine and Hygiene Annual Meeting, October. San Juan, Puerto Rico.

Gunawardena, D.M., Lal Muthuwattac, S. Weerasingha, J. Rajakaruna, U.W. Kumara, T. Senanayaka, P.K. Kotta, A.R. Wickremasinghe, R. Carter, and K.N. Mendis. 1996. "Spatial Analysis of Malaria Risk in an Endemic Region of Sri Lanka." International Development Research Centre Website http://www/idrc.ca/books/focus/766/gunawar.html).

Hawley, W.A., G. Olang, M. Ombok, and A.W. Hightower. 1998. "Spatial and Temporal Analysis of Malaria Transmission Patterns in Asembo, Western Kenya." Abstract P-8.1, International Conference on Emerging Infectious Diseases, March, Atlanta, Georgia.

Herring, T.A. 1996. "The Global Positioning System." *Scientific American* February: 44–50.

Hightower, A.W., M. Ombok, R. Otieno, R. Odhiambo, A.J. Oloo, A.A. Lal, B.L. Nahlen, and W.A. Hawley. 1998. "A Geographic Information System Applied to a Malaria Field Study in Western Kenya." *Am J Trop Med Hyg* 58(3): 266–272.

Hightower, A.W., M. Ombok, G. Olang, and W.A. Hawley. 1998. "GPS and GIS Applied to a Malaria Field Study in Western Kenya." Abstract P-8.2, International Conference on Emerging Infectious Diseases, March, Atlanta, Georgia.

Hightower, A.W., G. Olang, A.A. Lal, B.L. Nahlen, A.J. Oloo, and W.A. Hawley. 1997. "Spatial and Longitudinal Analysis of Entomological Data from Western Kenya." Abstract. American Society of Tropical Medicine and Hygiene, Annual Meeting, December. Orlando, Florida USA.

Kitron, U., H. Pener, C. Costin, L. Orshan, Z. Greenberg, and U. Shalom. 1994. "Geographic Information System in Malaria Surveillance: Mosquito Breeding and Imported Cases in Israel, 1992." *Am J Trop Med Hyg* 50: 550–556.

Magellan Systems Corporation. 1995.*User Guide for the Magellan GPS ProMARK X-CP*, 1995. San Dimas, California: Magellan Systems Corporation.

Malone, J., O. Huh, D. Fehler, P. Wilson, D. Wilensky, R. Holmes, and A. Elmagdoug. 1994. "Temperature Data from Satellite Imagery and the Distribution of Schistosomiasis in Egypt." *Am J Trop Med* 50: 714–722.

Malhotra, M.S., and A. Srivastava. 1996. "Diagnostic Features of Malaria Transmission in Nadiad using Remote Sensing and GIS." International

Development Research Centre website (http://www/idrc.ca/books/focus/766/malhot.html).

Richards, F.O. 1993. "Use of Geographic Information Systems in Control Programs for Onchocerciasis in Guatemala." *Bull Pan Am Health Organ* 27: 52–5.

SAS Institute Inc. 1989. *SAS/STAT Users Guide, Version 6*. Fourth Edition, Volume 2. Cary NC: SAS Institute Inc.

Shi, Y.P., U. Sayed, S.H. Qari, J.R. Roberts, V. Udhayakumar, A.J. Oloo, W.A. Hawley, D.C. Kaslow, B.L. Nahlen, and A.A. Lal. 1996. *"Plasmodium falciparum* MSP-1: Variation in the C-Terminal Region from Field-Derived Isolates and Antigenic Cross Reactivity of the Variant Determinants." *Infect Immun* 64: 2716–2723.

Snow, R.W., R.M. Armstrong-Schellenberg, N. Peshu, D. Forster, C.R.J.C. Newton, P.A. Winstanley, I. Mwangi, C. Waruiru, P.A. Warn, C. Newbold, and K. Marsh. 1993. "Periodicity and Space-Time Clustering of Severe Childhood Malaria on the Coast of Kenya." *Trans Roy Soc Trop Med Hyg* 87: 386–390.

Survey of Kenya. 1970. Series Y731 (DOS 423). Sheet 115/2. Edition 5-DOS, 1970. Nairobi, Kenya.

Unites States Geological Survey (USGS). "Map Projections—A Working Manual." Professional Paper 1395, p. 30, formula 5-3a.

10

A Geographical Information System as a Component of the Animal Health Information System in Thailand

Pramod Sharma and Angus Cameron

IN MOST DEVELOPING COUNTRIES, AGRICULTURE is the major sector in the economy, and employs a large proportion of the population. For agriculturalists in these countries livestock are often one of their most important assets, second only to land. The Paris-based Office International des Épizooties (OIE) estimates that animal disease may result in losses of up to 20 percent of production (OIE 1993). Diseases of livestock have serious effects at many levels, especially as they are usually more severe, more widespread, and inflict more social and economic damage than in industrial countries. At the same time, the resources available to identify, assess, and control these diseases are often scarce. For this reason, it is important that any resources available are effectively targeted to achieve the most benefit.

Accurate information about the health status of a nation's animal population is critical in the fight against animal diseases. Without measures of the frequency and economic importance of a particular disease, a government's task of targeting disease control is almost impossible. Without comprehensive disease reporting systems and ongoing measures of recording disease incidence, the efficacy and endpoint of any control program is impossible to measure. Without an internationally acceptable system of epidemiological surveillance and animal health information management, the establishment of national freedom from disease or a disease-free zone is impossible to achieve.

Unfortunately, in many developing countries the systems in place for the collection, management, and reporting of animal health information are not able to gather the type of information required for informed priority setting, disease control program planning, implementation, and monitoring. Nor are these data-collection systems able to meet international requirements for the substantiation of claims of freedom from disease. This is despite some-times substantial investment in veterinary infrastructure and disease control activities, such as laboratory diagnostic facilities and vaccination programs.

This chapter reports on research that was carried out in Thailand and the Lao People's Democratic Republic (Lao PDR). The Thai study area consist-ed of the three northern provinces, Lampang, Lamphun, and Chiang Mai. The area covers about 40,000 square kilometers and approximately 3,000 vil-lages. The Lao PDR study area selected consisted of Vientiane Municipality, covering about 3,600 square kilometers and containing approximately 500 villages. In Lao PDR, there has previously been virtually no development of an animal health information system. While Thailand represents one of the most advanced of the developing nations in Southeast Asia, Lao PDR is one of the least developed, and the need for improved animal health informa-tion is obvious.

Farming systems in Thailand and Lao PDR are similar, despite differ-ences in their levels of development. The main livestock species are cattle, buffalo, pigs, and chickens. Foot-and-mouth disease (FMD) in village cattle and buffalo was chosen as the "model" disease for the development of the techniques. This disease was chosen because it has a significant impact on the livestock industries of countries in which it is endemic and it arouses a great deal of international interest and funding (mainly because of its importance to trade).

The purpose of the research project was to improve animal health by addressing the problems of a lack of reliable population-based information, poor data management, and reporting in both countries. We proposed that a strategic approach, involving the introduction of two core elements of an animal health information system, could effectively address the problems of the systems currently used in developing countries. These core elements are (a) the collection of key animal health information using active surveillance techniques, and (b) the introduction of appropriate information technology (including a GIS), to improve the collection, management, analysis, and reporting of animal health information.

Animal Health Information System in Thailand and Lao PDR

An animal health information system is a system for the collection, storage, analysis, and reporting of information related to the health of animals. As such, virtually every country has some form of animal health information system. There are, however, a wide range of systems that reflect the inter-action of the following factors and limitations: disease situations (generally endemic diseases with high morbidity or high mortality, or both); depend-ence on agriculture (when the agricultural sector is a major employer); vet-erinary infrastructure (generally poorly developed with staff having only basic skills), physical infrastructure (where poor communications and trans-port systems can make it difficult to provide services and gather relevant information); financial resources (where the collection of animal health information has lower priority); and integration of technology (where dom-inant paper-based systems can limit efficiency).

While published materials are scarce, we can evaluate the characteristics of existing animal health information systems in terms of their ability to achieve four broad objectives: (a) to collect basic animal health information; (b) to help assess priorities and develop policies; (c) to support the imple-mentation of disease control programs; and (d) to meet international dis-ease-reporting obligations. This discussion is limited to an examination of the animal health information systems of Thailand and Lao PDR.

Both the Thai and Lao PDR systems are only partly able to identify which diseases are present and their geographic distribution. Information from laboratory submissions may only be used to identify which diseases are being diagnosed more often or which diseases are resulting in laborato-ry submissions, but it does not indicate the significance of those diseases. Both Thai and Lao PDR systems are unable to make valid incidence or prevalence estimates. The disease information upon which these estimates must be based comes from the diagnostic laboratory submissions. The pro-portion of actual cases of diseases that results in submissions is unknown, and the source population is unknown.

Thailand's FMD serosurveillance system attempts to collect data from a representative sample of villages to estimate the proportion of animals with protective titres against FMD. Unlike passive data collection systems, it uses survey techniques to collect data from a sample of livestock and uses data from this sample to make inferences about the population. While the data from the serosurveillance is potentially much more representative of the population than passively acquired data, the sampling strategy employed (purposive sampling of villages, and convenience sampling of animals) results in biased data of unknown precision.

Neither system is able to collect the valid, quantitative epidemiological data that is necessary to determine the epidemiology, geographic, and tem-poral patterns of disease, and risk factors associated with the major prob-lems. There is virtually no capability to manage, analyze, or report information on the spatial distribution of disease, except in crude tabular form, or through the use of inaccurate, hand-drawn maps. Neither system routinely collects information on the impact of diseases or the losses associated with them.

Village livestock population figures are collected by both countries, and these figures may be used to estimate the population at risk for incidence or prevalence calculations. Similarly, livestock movement and vaccination data are collected. Although these data sources may be reported, there is no integration of this data with the rest of the system, and no analysis. For instance, vaccine usage data for a particular area cannot be easily linked to outbreak data from the submissions database, or to population data to help determine the likely number of susceptible animals in the area. Livestock movement data is not analyzed for movement patterns that could be linked to outbreak data to predict areas where disease is likely to spread. There is no capability for this type of spatial analysis or modeling.

The information currently collected by both systems may be used for setting priorities. However, the limitations of these reporting systems, such as the inability to make assessments of the relative economic impact of different diseases, mean that the basis on which decisions are made may not be valid. Reporting systems are based on the use of written or verbal descriptions, and tabulated data and the right information are often not available for decisionmakers.

No continuous disease monitoring is taking place in Lao PDR. Rabies and FMD monitoring is used in Thailand to support the control programs. Figures gathered might certainly assist in program evaluation, but problems with sampling mean that there is a danger that the results could be misleading. Analysis of this data is unable to properly describe variations in the geographic distribution of the diseases, which may be important to the understanding of the epidemiology and control of the disease. The laboratory submission system currently in place in both countries is appropriate for the detection of emerging diseases However, the systems used in Thailand and Lao PDR are unable to provide convincing measures of disease occurrence nor support claims of freedom from disease.

Data-handling systems are not adequate to provide consistent and reliable figures. For example, two Thai sources differ almost fifty-fold in reporting the total number of animals having contacted FMD in 1992. Such discrepancies in internationally published data undermine the credibility of disease status claims. For international trade purposes, trading partners are now in a position to demand epidemiologically sound substantiation of claims of disease freedom or of disease prevalence levels. The systems in Thailand and Lao PDR are not able to provide proofs that would withstand epidemiological scrutiny. It appears that most of the reasons why animal health information systems fail in developing countries are outside the control of veterinary authorities. However, it is clear that two key problems within the veterinary authorities' control severely limit the effectiveness of systems: the absence of valid measures of disease occurrence at the population level, and problems with data management.

Disease information in the systems described is collected primarily through the diagnostic laboratory submission system and represents a passive surveillance system. The livestock owner initiates submission of specimens in order to make a diagnosis and solve the disease problem. Passively acquired data has the advantage that it may be less expensive to collect than other data sources (Martin and others 1987, Willeberg 1985). All that is needed is a recording system, as the data is already being generated for diagnostic purposes. The disadvantages of passive surveillance systems are that the disease information is usually incomplete and biased, and reliable measures of disease occurrence cannot be calculated (Hueston 1993). The concerns regarding limitations of passive surveillance are well documented (see, for example, Oka and others 1992, Ogundipe and others 1989, McCallon and Beal 1982, and Hurd and others 1994).

Animal health information systems use data from a range of sources. Currently in Thailand and Laos PDR, each type of data is analyzed and reported in isolation—laboratory submission data, livestock population data, livestock movement data, surveillance data, and vaccination data. To provide value-added information to decisionmakers and disease control program administrators, these different data sources need to be integrated so that the relationships between them can be better understood. Centralized data storage systems that manage data at a fine level of detail are required.

In Thailand, although complex reporting systems exist, the presentation of data is often confusing and difficult to interpret. Information relating directly to animal health may be buried amongst administrative data, and long series of tables deter the reader from searching out the real meaning. For instance, the Livestock Development Regional Annual Reports from the Department of Livestock Development (DLD) in Bangkok are the main reporting instruments for animal disease in each of the nine regions. The 1994 report for Region 5 contains 173 pages, made up of one map, one graph, and the rest tables and text descriptions. Administrative information makes up 82 percent of the report, and disease information 18 percent. Only one percent contains any form of analysis and interpretation. A great deal of data is contained within the report, but it is in a form which makes it hard to interpret and difficult to access.

Improving the Animal Health Information System

A wide range of solutions would be needed to address the many problems that have been identified. Our research proposed that the main limitations of the information systems could be addressed using a strategic approach to implement the core elements necessary for an effective system. These core elements are improved information gathering, based on active surveillance, to quickly collect data for reliable, unbiased measurements of disease occurrence; and appropriate implementation of information technology in the form of a geographical information system (GIS) to improve animal health information management and reporting.

In order for these core elements to be effective in the developing country context, they must meet a set of four key criteria arising from the constraints faced by Thailand and Lao PDR: (a) any solution must be able to be implemented at a reasonable cost; (b) information must be able to be gathered and processed quickly, so that it is still relevant when it is used for decision-making; (c) information must be reliable; and (d) any solution must be able to be practically applied and be appropriate for the situation in which it will be used.

Active surveillance involves the active collection of accurate and representative field data on the health of the livestock population (Martin and others 1987). To maximize the value of active surveillance, it must be based on statistically sound survey techniques (Hueston 1993). In theory a survey can be a total count of the population—a prohibitively expensive exercise. Usually the survey is based on a small proportion of animals in the population (that is, a sample). The validity of sample estimates from a survey depends on how representative the sample is of the study population.

There are many ways to select a sample from a population for a survey (Cochran 1977, Levy and Lemeshow 1991, Kish 1995). Every sampling strategy is a compromise between many competing factors, such as data accuracy, cost, ease of field operations, and complexity of analytical procedures. These considerations mean that the use of more complex sampling designs are beyond the capacity of the veterinary services of most developing countries, without the assistance of external statistical expertise for survey design and analysis. They explain in part the failure of developing countries to adopt active surveillance techniques. Clearly, problems of resources and infrastructure must be addressed in the larger national context. However, the research undertaken in our study attempted to address some of the reasons for lack of adoption of sound active surveillance techniques. The question of how active surveillance techniques could be implemented in developing countries was also considered. The use of a GIS in this context was regarded as crucial.

A GIS is a specialized computer database that handles two types of information: geographic information (the location of features, be they countries, administrative boundaries, rivers, roads, villages, or farms); and attribute data (for example, the attributes of a village may include the name, the number of each species of animals present, diseases that have occurred, the average titre of the animals to a particular pathogen, feed available and so on). What makes a GIS different from a standard database is its ability to perform spatial analysis on the information stored. The spatial relationship between features and their associated attributes can be analyzed to reveal underlying patterns.

One of the objectives of an animal health information system is to provide a better understanding of the epidemiology of disease. An important component of the epidemiology of a disease is the distribution of that disease in relation to a number of factors (such as species, age, sex, and time). One of the most important of these factors is the disease's geographic distribution (Garner and Nunn 1991). The use of a GIS offers the ability to include the spatial distribution of disease in the analysis of all the other factors (Clarke and others 1996).

Examination of the spatial component of animal health data via a GIS also provides the ability to quickly identify data errors, since missing and out-of-range data are easily identified when the data is mapped. Disease maps are able to convey the relative levels of disease graphically, through the use of color or different symbols. They also convey the relationships between different geographic areas. The production of accurate, attractive, well-presented disease maps can be completely automated, and achieved in seconds, given a database of up-to-date information.

Many authors have recommended the specific inclusion of a GIS in an animal health information system (Morley 1988; Sharma 1994, Thrusfield 1995). A GIS has been successfully applied to a number of specific problems in veterinary epidemiology, such as estimating the risk of East Coast Fever to livestock in Africa (Lessard and others 1988); the analysis of chemical residue data from abattoirs (Van der Logt and others 1994); examination of the epidemiology of tuberculosis in possums (Pfeiffer and Morris, 1994); or of Aujeszky's disease in pigs (Marsh and others 1991; Belfrage and others 1994; McGinn and others 1994). One of the more common uses of the technology has been as an aid in the control of disease outbreaks, especially FMD (Sanson and others 1991a, 1991b, and 1994).

There are however relatively few examples of the inclusion of a GIS as an integral part of an animal health information system. These examples demonstrate the acknowledged need for an understanding of the spatial distribution of disease, but eschew the use of a fully functional GIS, probably because of the perceived expense and complexity of setting up such a system. The potential benefits for an animal health information system are clear, but the use of powerful GIS systems seems to be limited to specific research projects and a few information systems in industrial countries

Making a GIS Part of an Animal Health Information System

In Thailand, a pilot system was established covering three provinces in the north of the country. This system is now being extended to give complete national coverage. The base geographic data used consisted of provincial, district, and subdistrict boundaries, and village point locations. The village was used as the finest level of detail. Epidemiologically, all the livestock in a single village can be treated as a single herd, as they are in relatively close contact and share the same disease risks. The geographic data was digitized using 1:50 000 maps maintained by the Thai National Statistics Office. Other spatial data included in the system are roads, waterways, livestock market locations, and veterinary office locations. Climactic data maps (showing rain and temperature) were also incorporated into the system. In keeping with the objective of establishing an effective system, appropriate for use in developing countries at reasonable cost, all the data was maintained on two Pentium® desktop computers. These were capable of managing all the data required for a national system covering over 60,000 villages. The software used was ArcInfo and ArcView (from Environmental Systems Research Institute, Redlands, California).

Attribute data was maintained at the village level, and aggregated up to the subdistrict, district, or provincial level for various types of analysis. The various data sources were linked to the maps using standard village and subdivision codes maintained by the National Statistics Office. The main data sources were village livestock populations, collected by the Department of Livestock Development, and disease records from the regional diagnostic laboratory. Other data included (human demographics, agricultural data, and so forth) were derived from two village-level censuses, run by the National Statistics Office and Thammasat University. The Thai system was used for data management, livestock disease and population mapping, development and implementation of improved active surveillance sampling techniques, assisting with disease outbreak response management, and the tempero-spatial analysis of epidemiological data.

In Lao PDR, a GIS was specifically set up to improve the efficiency and validity of sampling strategies as part of active surveillance activities. The system included provincial and district boundaries, village locations (with, however, incomplete coverage), and it incorporated both raster-format aerial photographs and vector format–interpreted satellite images showing land-use data. Lao PDR lacks the sophisticated statistical infrastructure of Thailand, and the data used in our project was acquired from other projects in our area of interest.

Disease and Livestock Population Mapping

In Thailand a range of data sources can be used to produce disease maps. Passive disease reporting, usually in the form of reports of disease events, or through diagnostic laboratory submissions, remains a key source of disease incidence information. This is, therefore, the information that is most likely to be used for disease mapping. Disease reports or submissions are associated with their place of origin, be it a farm, village, suburb, or province. An alternative to the use of passively acquired data is active surveillance. Special purpose surveys can yield estimates (usually of disease prevalence) for defined geographic areas. Besides data on the occurrence of disease, it is necessary to have information on the livestock population at risk of disease in order to calculate meaningful incidence or prevalence estimates. This information is routinely collected by many government veterinary services or may be available through agricultural census information. It is a core component of any GIS for animal health.

Disease maps can take many forms. The simplest is a point map showing the location of disease events over a period ("pin maps"). While this displays the distribution of disease, it does not take into account the distribution of the underlying population. Similarly, choropleth maps of the number of disease events in subregions may be useful for planning the veterinary needs of an area, but they do not provide any information about risk. Converting counts of disease events into rates and mapping incidence or prevalence allows a more meaningful interpretation of the disease situation. The main purpose of these maps is to identify areas of greater or lesser risk of disease than the average. Choropleth maps of the relative risk for each geographic subdivision are quickly able to show the location of problem areas. The routine production of these maps has the potential to provide a more realistic, easy to interpret picture of the disease situation to decision-makers. The generation of these maps can be completely automated.

A GIS as a Survey Tool

Traditionally, random sampling depends on the presence of a reliable sampling frame, in which every member of the population is listed and has a known probability of selection (Levy and Lemeshow 1991). Work in Lao PDR on the development of active surveillance techniques for developing countries has shown that such a sampling frame does not always exist. Sometimes no frame exists at all, the frame may be incomplete, or a frame exists, but its reliability is not known. In any case, it may be necessary to draw a random sample independently of, or in the absence of, the sampling frame.

Random geographic coordinate sampling (RGCS) offers a technique for the selection of a random sample without the need for a sampling frame. In RGCS, pairs of random numbers are generated, which are interpreted as the x and y coordinates of a geographic point. All the villages within a certain radius of the random point are identified, and one is chosen at random. The technique used in Lao PDR and Thailand is a modification of previously used geographic sampling approaches.

This technique can be carried out successfully with a hand-held GPS unit and a four-wheel drive vehicle. It can be, however, very expensive. Human population tends to cluster along valleys or roads, and large areas of a district often have no villages at all. Access to these areas may be difficult, and random points falling in these areas will yield no villages. In cases where the spread of villages is uneven, much time and effort can be wasted in locating remote points with no villages nearby.

A serological survey using random geographic coordinate sampling was carried out in Lao PDR. A GIS was used to plan the survey, and to increase the efficiency of the fieldwork by incorporating data from remote sensing images into the system. First, a GIS was used to automate the task of selecting random points. Although no detailed digital maps of the survey area existed, a simple map of district boundaries was digitized. A program was written which generated a number of random points within the boundaries of the study area. These random points were printed out and entered into the GPS.

Random points need to be visited to determine if any villages lie within a certain radius of these points. No reliable maps for the study area showing villages existed, as they were either incomplete or out of date. The use of remote sensing data offered an opportunity to visually inspect the area around a randomly selected point to determine if a village is likely to be nearby. Two sources of data were available from projects working within the same government ministry: interpreted SPOT satellite images for the entire study area,[1] being used by a forest inventory project; and aerial photography for a smaller part of the study area, being used by a forestry training project. The data was loaded into ArcView and displayed as a backdrop to the map of the study area. The program used to generate the random points also drew circles of the required radius around these points. It was then a simple matter to examine each point to see if there was evidence of a village within that radius.

The aerial photography data was very detailed, with individual buildings being clearly distinguishable. In the satellite photos, villages were often less easy to identify, but agricultural land (mainly rice fields) was easily distinguished from forested areas. A conservative approach was used, in which any point in or near agricultural land was visited by the survey team to confirm if a village was present. Points lying in the middle of forest areas with no sign of human habitation were excluded. The sample size for the survey was 40 villages. Of the initial random points selected, 44 were excluded using the GIS with remotely sensed data, and a further 82 points were visited to obtain the sample of 40 villages.

A GIS for Targeting Disease Outbreak Response

Thailand is currently undertaking a very large control and eradication program for foot-and-mouth disease. One control option available is the use of ring vaccination around an outbreak. When ring vaccination is used, all animals within a defined radius of the outbreak are vaccinated, to help prevent the local spread of the disease. To be effective, ring vaccination must be carried out very quickly, to ensure that nearby animals develop protective antibodies before they are exposed to the virus. When managing the response to an outbreak, veterinary authorities require a great deal of information to be made quickly available: where is the outbreak, where are the neighboring villages, how many fall within a defined radius of the outbreak, how many animals need to be vaccinated, and so on. To collect this type of information manually can require days or weeks.

A GIS can access multiple data sources instantly, and interpret the spatial relationships between them. As part of the pilot GIS implementation in northern Thailand, a program was developed to quickly provide all the information required to manage the response to a disease outbreak. The program user first identifies in which village the outbreak has occurred, and specifies the radius of the ring vaccination buffer. The program, displaying a map of the area, including all villages, administrative boundaries and roads, then does a series of calculations and produces reports. First a circle is drawn on the display, representing the boundary of the ring vaccination buffer. Then all villages inside the buffer are identified, and their total susceptible livestock population calculated. Next, this data is broken down by district. District Veterinary Officers deliver field veterinary services in Thailand. In an outbreak, district officers are responsible for vaccinating those villages falling within their district. The number of villages and total livestock numbers for each district are calculated; and the name, telephone number, and distance from the outbreak of the relevant district officers are identified. An important part of the outbreak response is to control livestock movements in and out of the buffer by setting up roadblocks. The program calculates the number and location of roadblocks, giving their map coordinates and the type of road. In some parts of the country, access to villages is difficult, especially during the rainy season. The program identifies the villages that lie more than two kilometers from the nearest road.

The results of all these calculations are then reported. The on-screen map shows the location of the outbreak, all villages in the ring vaccination zone, the location of district veterinary offices, and the location of all roadblocks. This map can be zoomed, interactively interrogated to find the names or populations of particular villages, or printed. A report is produced listing the total number of livestock that need to be vaccinated, and the breakdown by district, roadblock location and types, and the number of remote villages. Finally, a listing of all villages requiring vaccination, with available figures on the population of all species, is displayed.

The key features of this system are as follows: It can provide almost all the relevant information needed by the veterinary authorities in charge of planning a ring vaccination response to an outbreak, quickly and simply; it is based on the integration of data from a range of preexisting sources; it was developed quickly and at almost zero cost (once the GIS was established); and it is easy to modify and enhance as more data becomes available (such as vaccination records that may show which villages require revaccination, and which are probably already protected).

GISs and Visualization

One of the roles of epidemiology is the identification of patterns in the distribution of disease. Such patterns may lead to a better understanding of the mechanisms of disease, and offer insights into potential control options. The distribution of diseases may be examined in many ways—distributions with respect to sex, age, diet, genetic makeup, space, time, and so forth. When a pattern is detected (for example, disease is more common in animals of a certain age), control options can be developed (such as targeted vaccination for that age group). Once the data is collected, the first step is to examine it for patterns. A GIS offers, through the production of disease maps, the ability to examine the spatial distribution of disease and find meaningful patterns. An armory of statistical techniques exists for the analysis of such patterns. Similarly, graphical and analytical techniques exist for analysis of the temporal distribution of disease (time-series techniques). However, the simultaneous examination of the spatial and temporal distribution of disease is more difficult. If we observe on a map that many cases appear to occur in the same area, are they occurring simultaneously? If we look at a graph of disease incidence over time and notice a peak, are these cases occurring in the same place? Statistical techniques exist to analyze the space-time "distance" between disease events, but little data is available for the identification of these patterns in the first place.

Using a GIS in Thailand, a tool for exploratory data analysis was developed that allowed simultaneous display of the temporal and spatial distribution of a disease. The data displayed came from the diagnostic laboratory submissions database, and contained a disease diagnosis, the origin of the submission, and a submission date. This provided the three necessary components for analysis: the *what, where,* and *when.*

A program was developed with the ArcView programming language (Avenue). The user creates a map of all disease events in a certain period. The program then "animates" the map by passing through the chosen period one day at a time, displaying new disease events (for an arbitrary period chosen by the user) and then erasing them. Using this simple technique, it is easy to see the wave of progression of an epidemic, or the random scatter of a sporadic disease. The program was used to examine several diseases in the study area, and revealed new patterns, suggesting new hypotheses. For example, while two serotypes of one disease were known to occur in all parts of the study area, and follow an annual cycle, it was not known that mixed outbreaks did not occur; only one serotype occurred in an area at a particular time. A natural divide down the center of the study area separated the two types, which tended to appear alternately on one side of the divide and then the other, from year to year. This observation led to new hypotheses as to the immunity of the population, and the source of the pathogen. The program can be used to examine any disease information that has a location and a date associated with it (and not only disease information). It is a simple yet powerful data visualization tool.

Conclusion

From our research reported here, we do not have much confidence that most developing countries are in a position to mount an across-the-board attack on their animal health problems. In addition, while incremental improvements in their passive surveillance based systems are possible, these improvements are unlikely to yield the type and quality of information that is urgently required for various purposes. Our research has demonstrated that active surveillance techniques coupled with the appropriate injection of modern computing technology can yield dramatic improvements in data availability.

To target control of livestock diseases, one must first understand the diseases and the way in which they are distributed through the population. One important aspect of this is the geographic distribution of disease. A GIS for livestock disease control retains all the data management and analytical power of a traditional database system, but it adds the ability to include the spatial distribution of livestock and their diseases in the analysis. It is another tool in the epidemiologist's armory.

A GIS thrives on high-powered computers and vast amounts of data and is often seen as the preserve of well-funded government departments, universities, or businesses. The research presented here shows that this is not necessarily the case. Affordable personal computers that are currently available provide enough power to run a full-fledged GIS package. A simple national system could conceivably be run on a single machine. Also, while the data requirements are quite demanding if one wants to utilize the powerful capabilities of the system, we have shown that even when data availability is limited, an effective GIS system can be implemented. It is true that as the available range of data increases, so do the capabilities of the system. However, when data availability is limited, as in many developing countries, establishing a very useful and cost-effective system is still possible.

Notes

The authors are at the University of Queensland, Brisbane, Australia.

1. Système Probatoire d'Observation de la Terre (SPOT) is a French satellite system similar in objectives to the U.S. LANDSAT system.

References

Belfrage, J.B., M.D. Salman, J. Freier, J. Nuckols, and D. Otto. 1994. "A Geographic Information System Analysis of Pseudorabies (Aujesky's Disease) in Four Counties in Iowa, USA." *Kenyan Veterinarian* 18: 500.

Clarke, K.C., S.L. McLafferty, and B.J. Tempalski. 1996. "On Epidemiology and Geographic Information Systems: A Review and Discussion of Future Directions." *Emerging Infectious Diseases* 2: 85–92.

Cochran, W.G. 1977. *Sampling Techniques*, 3rd ed. New York: John Wiley & Sons, Inc.

Garner, M.G. and M.J. Nunn. 1991. "Requirements for an Australian Animal Health Information System." In E.S.G. Sergeant, ed., *Epidemiology Chapter Proceedings*. AVA/NZVA Pan-Pacific Conference on Veterinarians and the Environment, Sydney, May. Sydney: Australian College of Veterinary Scientists.

Hueston, W.D. 1993. "Assessment of National Systems for the Surveillance and Monitoring of Animal Disease." *Revue Scientific Technique Office International Épizooties* 12: 1187–1196.

Hurd, H.S., D.D. Hancock, L.A. Thomas, and S.J. Wells. 1994. "Salmonella prevalence in US dairy calves and a comparison of active and passive surveillance systems." In *Proceedings of the VIIIth Congress of the International Society for Animal Hygiene*, St. Paul, Minnesota. St. Paul: International Society for Animal Hygiene.

Kish, L. 1995. *Survey Sampling*. New York: John Wiley and Sons.

Lessard, P., R. l'Eplattenier, R.A.I. Norval, B.D. Perry, T.T. Dolan, A. Burrill, H. Croze, M. Sorensen, J.G. Grootenhuis, and A.D. Irvin. 1988. "The Use of Geographical Information Systems in Estimating East Coast Fever Risk to African Livestock." *Acta Veterinaria Scandinavia*: 234–236.

Levy, P.S. and S. Lemeshow. 1991. *Sampling of Populations: Methods and Applications*, 2nd ed. New York: John Wiley & Sons, Inc.

Marsh, W.E., T. Damrongwatanapokin, K. Larntz, and R.B. Morrison. 1991. "The Use of a Geographic Information System in an Epidemiological Study of Pseudorabies (Aujeszky's Disease) in Minnesota Swine Herds." *Preventative Veterinary Medicine* 11: 249–254.

Martin, S.W., A.H. Meek, and P. Willeberg. 1987. *Veterinary Epidemiology—Principles and Methods*, 1st ed. Ames: Iowa State University Press.

McCallon, W.R., and V.C. Beal, Jr. 1982. "The Fallacy of Drawing Inferences from Biased Data: Some Case Examples." In *Proceedings of the 86th Annual Meeting of United States Animal Health Association*. Richmond: United States Animal Health Association.

McGinn, T.J., III, D.W. Wray, and P. Cowen. 1994. "Medical Geography of Aujesky's Disease in North Carolina, USA: The Effect of Density of Swine and Prevalence of Infection on a Neighbouring Aujesky's Disease Status." *Kenyan Veterinarian* 18: 499.

Morley, R.S. 1988. "National Animal Health Information System, Agriculture Canada. *Revue Scientific Technique Office International Épizooties* 7: 577–581.

Office International des Épizooties (OIE). 1993. *World Animal Health in 1993.* Paris: Office International des Épizooties.

Ogundipe, G.A.T., S.B. Oluokun, and G.O. Esuruoso. 1989. "The Development and Efficiency of the Animal Health Information System in Nigeria." *Preventative Veterinary Medicine* 7: 121–135.

Oka, M., N. Widowati, N. Lubis, and S. Holden. 1992. "The Role of Laboratory and Veterinary Diagnosis in Indonesia's National Disease Surveillance System." In P.W. Daniels, S. Holden, E. Lewin, and S. Dadi, eds., *Livestock Services for Smallholders: A Critical Evaluation of the Delivery of Animal Health and Production Services to the Small-Scale Farmer in the Developing World.* Proceedings of an International Seminar held at Yogyakarta, Indonesia, November 15–21. Yogyakarta, Indonesia: Directorate General of Livestock Services.

Pfeiffer, D.U., and R.S. Morris. 1994. "Spatial Analysis Techniques in Veterinary Epidemiology." *Kenyan Veterinarian* 18: 483–485.

Sanson, R.L., H. Liberona, and R.S. Morris. 1991a. "The Use of a Geographical Information System in the Management of a Foot-and-Mouth Disease Epidemic." *Preventative Veterinary Medicine* 11: 309–313.

———. 1991b. "The Development of an Epidemiological Management System for a Foot-and-Mouth Disease Emergency." In S.W. Martin, ed., *Proceedings of the 6th ISVEE Symposium,* Ottawa, Canada, August 12–16. Ontario: University of Guelph.

Sanson, R.L., D.U. Pfeiffer, and R.S. Morris. 1994. "Geographic Information Systems: Their Application in Animal Disease Control." *Revue Scientific Technique Office International Épizooties* 10: 179–195.

Sharma, P. 1994. "Use of Geographic Information Systems in Animal Health Information Programs." In J.W. Copland, L.J. Gleeson, and C. Chamnanpood, eds., ACIAR Proceedings No. 51: *Diagnosis and Epidemiology of Foot-and-Mouth Disease in Southeast Asia.* Proceedings of an international workshop held at Lampang, Thailand, September 6–9, 1993. Canberra: Australian Centre for International Agricultural Research.

Thrusfield, M. 1995. *Veterinary Epidemiology,* 2nd ed. Oxford: Blackwell Science.

Van der Logt, P.B., R.S. Morris, and S.C. Hathaway. 1994. "The Analysis of Chemical Residue Data Gathered at Abattoirs by Means of Geographical Information Systems." *Kenyan Veterinarian* 18: 496–498.

Willeberg, P. 1985. "Epidemiologic Use of Routinely Collected Veterinary Data: Risks and Benefits." In *Proceedings of the 4th International Symposium on Veterinary Epidemiology & Economics,* Singapore, November 18–22. Singapore: International Society for Veterinary Epidemiology and Economics (ISVEE).

11

Location Criteria of Nongovernmental Organizations Providing Credit to the Poor: The Experience in Bangladesh

Manohar Sharma and Manfred Zeller

IN RECENT YEARS, BANGLADESH HAS TAKEN MAJOR STRIDES in delivering financial services to the rural poor. The providers of these services have mainly been innovative group-based credit programs run by several nongovernmental organizations (NGOs). A number of studies are now available that describe how these new institutional arrangements dispensed with physical collateral and facilitated access of the poor to savings and credit services (Zeller, Sharma, and Ahmed 1996; Hossain 1988). However, scant attention has so far been given to the determinants of *placement* of NGO branch institutions and the client coverage of their operations across regions. Khandker, Khalily, and Khan (1995) find that commercial banks in Bangladesh favor economically better-off areas, and a study in India (Binswanger, Khandker, and Rosenzweig 1993) concluded that commercial banks were more likely to be located in places where the road infrastructure and marketing system are relatively developed. Is this also the case with the group-based credit systems of NGOs? In other words, do NGO programs target their services to the poor in relatively underdeveloped or disadvantaged regions, or do they locate their branches in the relatively better-endowed areas? What kinds of tensions arise among mission goals, performance standards, and operational restraints at the operations level? Once branches have been placed, what does client coverage look like across branches? For example, do the decisions on branch placement and client coverage follow similar patterns, or is there evidence of discontinuity? To what extent does the decision related to client coverage appear to be decentralized

(Ravallion and Wodon 1998)? Knowing whether certain types of areas are systematically favored or disfavored is of interest and importance to policy-makers as well as to program managers. This knowledge can also assist in disentangling program effects from location effects and hence it is useful for an assessment of the impact of group-based credit programs (Rosenzweig, Pitt, and Gibbons 1995).

For administrative purposes, Bangladesh is divided into four divisions and 64 districts. Each district is further divided into *thanas*. A thana is an administrative unit that corresponds with the jurisdiction of a police station. This chapter makes use of secondary level data from 391 thanas to examine the placement of branches and group coverage of three well-known NGO credit institutions in Bangladesh: Association of Social Advancement (ASA), Bangladesh Rural Advancement Committee (BRAC), and Proshika Manobik Unnayan Kendra (PROSHIKA). In the next section ("The Institutions"), major characteristics of these NGO institutions are described (see Zeller, Sharma, and Ahmed (1996) for more detail). The third section ("Factors Affecting the Placement of Branches") proposes a number of hypotheses on placement of branches that were tested econometrically, and the results are presented in the fourth section ("Econometric Specification"). Client coverage of NGOs branches is analyzed in the fifth section ("Client Coverage"). The last section summarizes conclusions and policy implications.

The Institutions

There are five common threads in the institutional structures of the ASA, BRAC, and PROSHIKA: First, services are strictly targeted to a well-defined set of clients: The most common criterion is the amount of land owned, and all three NGOs target landless or near-landless households. Second, credit is always provided to small groups of borrowers on the basis of joint liabil-ity and without the pledging of any physical collateral. Third, even though loans are made out to individual members, the entire group is denied fur-ther credit when outstanding arrears exist for any one of the members. Fourth, lending activities are supplemented by training activities in areas such as entrepreneurial skill development, management of microenterpris-es like shopkeeping and crafts production, education on social awareness, and family planning activities. Fifth, groups are required to contribute to an emergency fund that may be used when members experience household and other emergencies.

Loan recovery rates of all three institutions are impressive when com-pared with those of commercial banks: During the period 1992–1993, for example, they were 100 percent for ASA, 98 percent for BRAC, and 93 per-cent for PROSHIKA. Additional institution-specific details follow below.

Association for Social Advancement (ASA)

ASA, one of the largest indigenous NGOs in Bangladesh, was set up in 1978. It implements programs in the areas of income generation, integrated health, and education and empowerment of the poor, and its Income Generation through Credit Program (IGCP) was launched in 1989. The principal objective of the program is to increase income levels and purchasing power of poor households. ASA extends credit facilities to the female members of poor households for investment in various income-generating activities. The major income-generating activities receiving support under the IGCP program are paddy husking, cow and goat rearing, poultry farming, small trading, and handicrafts. Nearly 190,000 members received loans under the program in 1993.

Bangladesh Rural Advancement Committee (BRAC)

BRAC was set up in 1972, following the independence of the country in 1971. At its inception the primary goal of BRAC was to participate in the post-independence rehabilitation work of the war-ravaged country. It launched its campaign with a small rehabilitation project in Sylhet district in the northeast of Bangladesh. Gradually BRAC expanded its operation to other parts of the country. BRAC initiated its credit program in 1976 (BRAC 1991). The present form of the program, which was introduced in 1990, is known as the Rural Credit Project (RCP). RCP is an important component of BRAC's larger Rural Development Project (RDP). The objectives of RDP are four-fold: (1) to generate employment opportunity for both males and females; (2) to mobilize underutilized and unutilized resources; (3) to assist in diffusing appropriate technology in rural areas; and (4) to promote better health care. The cumulative amount of loans disbursed through RCP from 1990 through 1992 stood at 1,745 million taka (approximately US$ 45 billion), and during 1992, short-term loans accounted for 94 percent of total disbursement. Loans are generally extended for a specified line of projects. In 1992, for example, rural trading and food processing accounted for nearly 73 percent of the loans. Livestock, agriculture, rural industry, and irrigation accounted for another 23 percent. As of June 1993, 70 branches of RCP were in operation with a coverage of 379,000 members.

Proshika Manobik Unnayan Kendra (PROSHIKA)

PROSHIKA was founded in 1976 with the aim of empowering the poor by enabling them to participate in mainstream economic activities. Its objectives include achieving structural poverty alleviation, improving the status of women, and increasing people's participation in public institutions. PROSHIKA operates group savings and revolving loan fund activities under its Employment and Income Generating (EIG) program. The revolving loan fund program was launched in 1983 and in the 1992–1993 financial year funded 10,809 projects with total fund disbursements of nearly 224 million taka.

Factors Affecting the Placement of Branches

The placement rule followed by NGOs is specified in equation 11.1, where the decision to place a branch, B_i, by an NGO credit institution is specified as a function of

$$B_i = f\left(P_i, E(D_i), E(C_i), R_i\right) \tag{11.1}$$

where P_i is a vector that describes poverty conditions in thana i, $E(D_i)$ is the expected level of demand for credit services in that thana, $E(C_i)$ is the expected level of cost of providing services, and R_i is an index of the risk of conducting credit-related business in the thana. Each of these is discussed below.

Poverty Targeting

All three NGOs, which are among the largest in the microfinance NGO movement in Bangladesh (Credit and Development Forum 1996), claim to be guided, first and foremost, by a common mission to serve the poorest in the rural areas (ASA 1996a and 1996b, Lovell 1992, BRAC 1994). ASA, which provides credit exclusively to women, for example, aims at creating "a broader space for marginalized women of rural areas so they can participate in income generation activities to increase income" (ASA 1994). BRAC, on the other hand, aims to work "exclusively with disadvantaged sections of the community" (Chowdhury, Mahmood, and Abed 1991) and focuses on poor, landless groups, and PROSHIKA has an explicit mission to "empower the poor" (Jahangir and Zeller 1995). Given these kinds of mission statements, a reasonable hypothesis is that, conditional upon other factors, thanas with higher poverty levels will have a higher probability of a branch placement.

There are, however, two additional questions: (1) What criteria of poverty do these institutions apply with respect to *individuals* in targeting their operations, and (2) What criteria do these institutions apply in making the operational decisions on which *areas* to target their activities? The answer to the first question is relatively straightforward. All three programs have clear and strict poverty-based eligibility rules that are well enforced. BRAC lends only to those who own less than 0.5 acres of land and additionally work as laborers for at least 100 days in a year (Lovell 1992). ASA, on the other hand, lends to women owning less than 0.5 acres of land, whose income do not exceed 1,200 taka (approximately US$ 31) per month, and who also sell their labor for at least 200 days a year. However, the response of NGOs to differences of poverty levels across different locations when making decisions about branch placement is a more difficult question. A reasonable assumption is that the NGOs base their decisions on various types of indicators of poverty. One testable hypothesis is that NGOs locate their branches in thanas that have larger proportions of households owning less than 0.5 acres of land, as this criterion most closely defines their target households. This need not be the only criterion, however. Two additional criteria are proposed in this study: literacy rates per thana, and thana-based levels of the "distress" index developed by the Helen Keller Institute (HKI) in Dhaka, Bangladesh. Literacy rates generally highly correlate with poverty levels, and the HKI distress index combines information on susceptibility to flooding (a frequently occurring natural disaster in Bangladesh), general wage levels, and availability of irrigation facilities—all being major factors affecting the level of well-being in Bangladesh.

Expected Level of Demand for Credit Services

The expected level of demand for credit services in an area is likely to receive important consideration for two reasons. First, it would be important for the NGOs to avoid areas where credit demand is likely to be either non-existent or lower than some minimum threshold making credit delivery prohibitively costly to administer. Second, the marginal impact of NGO services on participating households, a major concern for the NGOs, is likely to be the highest in areas with the strongest credit demand. This is because credit demand is likely to be the strongest in areas that are affected relatively less by other constraints—for instance, on labor and product markets, transportation, and information. Hence, expected demand for credit is expressed as equation 11.2:

$$D(D_i) = g(W_i) \tag{11.2}$$

where the vector W_i consists of thana-level variables that affect the level of credit demand and may include the following variables:

- Level of physical infrastructural development such as access to markets, roads, electricity, irrigation, and other services
- Agroclimatic conditions, and general income levels
- The level of urbanization and commercialization of the local economy.

Cost of Supplying Services

In general, profit-seeking institutions select locations where expected revenues are at least as high as expected total cost (fixed costs plus variable costs). However, this may not necessarily be the case of NGOs as they do not have profit maximization as their explicit objective. Also, the NGOs receive subsidies of different types to operate in specific geographical areas and also implement various types of cross-subsidization schemes between branches. For these reasons they are not likely to base their placement decision solely on potential net revenues. How expected unit-costs of operation affect placement of branches, therefore, is essentially an empirical issue.

There are at least two other cost-related issues that are likely to be important in the placement calculation. These concern general security and the availability of banking services. Credit transactions necessarily involve the handling of cash, which raises security concerns. Proximity to police stations and other law and order establishments, therefore, is likely to be important. Moreover, when NGOs do not provide their own banking services but depend on the branch of a commercial or parastatal bank to make cash disbursements and deposits, convenient proximity to commercial banks becomes important. If commercial banks are generally located in areas that are more urbanized or benefit from better infrastructure, as Binswanger, Khandkar, and Rosenzweig (1993) have shown, then NGOs may also tend to place branches in or near these locations.

A third issue relates to staffing of branches. Since branch managers are recruited from a central pool, and since salaries and other compensations do not reward appointments in more remote locations, managers are likely to prefer locations that have fairly well-developed services (such as education, market, and health). If these considerations are significant in the decision to place branches, placement will be higher in thanas that have such services.

To account for all these consideration, we let the expected total cost function be specified as shown in equation 11.3:

$$E(C_i) = g(Z_i) \tag{11.3}$$

where the vector Z_i consists of thana-level variables that affect the level of unit service delivery costs. In practice, vectors W_i in equation 11.2 and Z_i in 11.3 are likely to be very similar if not identical.

Perceived Riskiness

An important goal of NGO-administered credit programs is to maintain high repayment rates. Indeed, as noted earlier, all NGO programs report repayment rates in excess of 90 percent. Maintaining near-perfect repayment rates is critical for NGOs. This is because most of the subsidies they receive from national and international donors appear to be conditional on maintaining such rates. This objective of maintaining high repayment rates may also affect the placement of branches. In particular, NGOs are likely to avoid areas where marginal returns from new microenterprises are low (poor, backward areas where complementary services either do not exist or are highly inadequate). They are also likely to avoid areas that are highly susceptible to natural disasters such as flooding and other covariant risks. We let the risk expectation function be specified as equation 11.4:

$$E(C_i) = g(V_i).\qquad(11.4)$$

Elements in V_i include poverty indicators such as literacy rate, level and distribution of landholding, and also the HKI distress level indicator described earlier.

Econometric Specification

A linear specification of the placement equation 11.1, upon substituting for 11.2 through 11.4, would be equation 11.5:

$$B_i = P_i\alpha + W_i\beta + Z_i\gamma + V_i\delta.\qquad(11.5)$$

However, as indicated in the previous section, it is, in principle, (and also because of data limitations) very difficult to identify P, W, Z, and V separately. For example, it is very difficult to find variables that affect poverty levels but not credit demand or riskiness of conducting business. A more practical formulation is therefore to regard the elements in P, W, Z, and V to be common and represented by the vector X_i, as in equation 11.6:

$$B_i = \Sigma\,\eta_i X_i + \mu_d + e_i\qquad(11.6)$$

and interpreting its coefficient $\eta_i = (\alpha_i + \beta_i + \gamma_i + \delta_i)$ as the combined effects of the four determinants of placement. After all, infrastructure, urbanization, and other community-level endowments are likely to jointly affect levels of poverty as well as demand for credit services, the cost of credit service delivery, and the riskiness of conducting business. Similarly, susceptibility to natural disasters simultaneously affects poverty, credit demand patterns, and the riskiness and costs of doing business. Note that a priori expectations on the sign of η_i are difficult to place unless α_i, β_i, γ_i, and δ_i are of the same expected signs. In some cases, however, it is still possible to make some inferences by computing the estimated sign of η_i with expected signs of α_i, β_i, γ_i, δ_i. This is done below in the fifth section of this chapter.

A different consideration is the effect of unobservables. If placement of government infrastructural programs and levels of poverty are functions of unobservable factors (such as agro-climactic potentials of lands, or historical or political considerations), then exclusion of such factors in equation 11.6 is likely to lead to biased estimates of ηs. In order to minimize bias arising out of location-specific unobservables, a district level of effect μ_d is included in equation 11.6. Since B_i in 11.6 is a binary-dependent variable taking the value (0,1), the equation is estimated using the fixed-effects logit estimation that sweeps out the effects of district-level unobservables.

The vector X in equation 11.6 contains the following variables (see table 11.1 for descriptive statistics):

Poverty-related variables:
- Landsize. The percentage of farms in the thana that are below 0.5 acres in size.

Table 11.1 Descriptive Statistics of Regression Variables—Thana Level (n = 391)

Variables	Mean	Standard deviation	Minimum	Maximum
Dependent variables:				
Presence of NGO				
(dummy variable)	0.40	0.49	0.00	1.00
Client density[1]	17.86	33.01	0.00	297.59
Independent variables:				
Electricity	6.96	8.47	0.00	54.90
Landsize	23.90	7.60	1.97	52.87
Literate	24.54	9.94	11.0	60.4
Market	26.22	13.37	1	75
Density	791.10	666.54	93.20	10,557.35
Urban	11.26	16.58	0.00	100.00
Road	0.17	0.21	0.00	2.61
Post office	16.18	9.69	1	82
Hospital	12,576.33	11,499.45	0	99,726
Doctor	42,905.03	44,555.82	0	329,739
Distress	1.1	0.15	1.0	1.5

1. Client density is defined as the number of NGO clients in the thana divided by the thana's total population.
Source: Statistical Yearbooks (various issues), Bureau of Statistics, Dhaka; BRAC Statistical Report, RDP and RCP, 1989–1993; ASA Annual Report, 1994; Grameen Bank Annual Report, 1994; Data for PROSHIKA obtained in interviews from Head Office; Helen Keller International, Dhaka (for distress index).

- Literacy. The percentage of population literate in the thana.

Infrastructure-related variables:

- Electricity. The percentage of villages electrified in the thana.
- Market. The number of number of market centers in the thana.
- Density. The population density of the thana.
- Urban. The percentage of urban population in the thana.
- Road. The kilometer of metaled road per 1,000 persons in the thana
- Hospital. The number of population per hospital bed in the thana.
- Doctor. The number of population per doctor in the thana.
- Post office. The number of post offices in the thana.

Risk/poverty-related variables:

- Distress. The thana-level distress index (HKI) computed by the Helen Keller Institute.

All data, except for the distress level which has been directly obtained from Helen Keller International in Dhaka, are published in various issues of the statistical yearbook of Bangladesh, published by the Bangladesh Bureau of Statistics (1994). Data on the dependent variables for the different programs have been obtained from annual reports from BRAC, ASA, and Grameen Bank for 1994 (BRAC 1994; ASA 1994; Grameen Bank 1994). The data for PROSHIKA also refer to 1994, and were obtained through interviews with staff from its headquarters in Dhaka.

Econometric Results: Placement of Branches

The estimated logit equation on branch placement is presented in table 11.2. A number of interesting results are discussed below. The coefficients of *Road* and *Post office* are positive and significant at the 5 percent level. These are both infrastructural variables measuring the extent of transportation and communication facilities in the thana. The percentage of urban population in the thana (*Urban*) and population density (*Density*) are not statistically significant. Neither are the two health service indicators, *Hospital* and *Doctor*, the number of market centers in the thana (*Market*), or the percentage of villages that are electrified in the thana (*Electricity*). It appears, therefore, that placement decisions are attentive to transportation and communication facilities, but that the **net** effect of other infrastructural facilities measured or proxied by population concentration, urbanization, and the availability of medical and health services appears to be insignificant.

The coefficient of *Literate* is negative and is strongly significant. Hence placement of branches appears to respond to literacy rates, with more branches being placed in thanas with lower literacy rates. Note that if considerations of demand, costs, and riskiness favor thana with higher literacy rates—that is, if $(\beta_{litertate} + \gamma_{litertate} + \delta_{litertate}) > 0$—then it may be concluded that

Table 11.2 Placement of NGOs: Estimated Fixed-Effects Logit Equation

Variables	Coefficients	t-Values
Landsize	0.0242372	0.987
Literate	−0.102779	−3.631**
Electricity	0.0156035	0.842
Market	0.0144544	1.162
Population	−0.0002954	0.593
Urban	0.0099031	0.893
Road	1.373573	2.156**
Hospital	4.11×10^{-6}	0.294
Doctor	-4.30×10^{-6}	−1.241
Post office	0.0344091	1.875*
Distress	−3.255817	−2.684**

Note: * Significant at 10 percent level. ** Significant at 5 percent level.

Log likelihood = −172.79; $c^2_{11,391}$ = 39.08

Source: Statistical Yearbooks (various issues), Bureau of Statistics, Dhaka; BRAC Statistical Report, RDP and RCP, 1989–1993; ASA Annual Report, 1994; Grameen Bank Annual Report, 1994; Data for PROSHIKA obtained in interviews from Head Office; Helen Keller International, Dhaka (for distress index).

the poverty consideration ($\alpha_{literate}$) is sufficiently large enough to overturn the combined positive effect so that the net effect is negative; that is, $| \alpha_{litert} | > | b_{litert} + g_{litert} + d_{litert} |$. The coefficient of the landholding variable *Landsize* has a similar interpretation—that the poverty effects of the smaller landsize more than outweighs the combined effects on credit demand and risk costs. *Landsize*, however, is not significant at the 10 percent level.

The coefficient of *Distress* is negative and significant at the five-percent level. NGOs thus are less likely to place branches in high distress locations. Unlike the case of *Literate* above, it appears that poverty considerations (that are attendant with high level distress) are not strong enough to compensate for the negative effects arising out of conducting business in risk-prone areas. Significantly, this result indicates the inability of even large NGO's, such as BRAC and ASA, to effectively deal with risks.

Overall, the estimated branch placement equation indicates while NGOs appear to respond to poverty, they are more likely to place branches in locations that have favorable infrastructure. They also are less likely to place branches in high distress location.

Client Coverage

Having examined branch placement outcomes of the three NGOs, we now go on to examine factors that influence the client outreach of thana-level branches. Apart from learning what types of poverty characteristics affect client density, it is also of interest to examine whether any type of decentralization process characterizes geographical distribution of service delivery. As Ravallion and Wodon (1998) point out, in many targeted programs, it may be the case that the headquarters (or the central government) makes a decision on where to place a branch, but subsequently leaves it up to local managers (or local governments) to determine the scale of operation of the established branch. Is this also the case of Bangladeshi NGOs? In this section, we use participation density (*Outreach*), measured as the number of participants in a specific program per 1,000 people in the thana, as an indicator of client outreach.

The econometric specification of the outreach regression equations is similar to the branch placement equation 11.6, except that the dependent variable *Outreach* is a continuous but truncated variable: client coverage is observed only in thanas that have branches. The procedure used to correct this sample selection bias is the two-stage Heckman procedure (1979) whereby a Mills ratio—*Lamda*—computed from the branch placement (logit) equation is used as an additional regressor in the participation density equation and appropriate adjustments are made in the computation of standard errors (Greene 1993). An additional variable *Years* is used in the outreach equation to control for the fact that client density is expected to increase with years of operation of the branch. *Years* is the number of years for which the branch has been in operation. However, because *Years* was not available for PROSHIKA, the outreach equation was estimated using data for BRAC and ASA only, with *Years* computed as the sum of years that branches of both ASA and BRAC (or both) in the thana had been in operation. The combined outreach equation estimated for ASA and BRAC is presented in table 11.3.

In the outreach equation in table 11.3, only the coefficients of three variables are significant: these are *Years*, *Landsize*, and *Distress*. These variables are discussed below.

- The coefficient of *Years* is positive and highly significant, indicating that NGO institutions have expanded their client base through time. Indeed if it was the case that *Years* was the only variable significant in the equation, this would have suggested that, once a branch was placed in a particular location, client coverage was mostly determined without significant reference to local specificities. However, this is not the case since at least two other area characteristics appear to influence outreach.

- Outreach is significantly higher in thanas that have a higher distress index. This result is completely opposite to that of the placement equation, which had indicated that placement rule disfavored high distress

Table 11.3 Outreach Equation: BRAC and ASA

Variables	Coefficients	t-Values
Years	3.6693	6.305**
Electricity	0.83156×10^{-1}	0.219
Landsize	−1.1799	−1.782*
Literate	0.22979	0.377
Market	−0.28682	−1.164
Population	$−0.77299 \times 10^{-2}$	−0.569
Percurbt	$−0.89751 \times 10^{-1}$	−0.283
Road	−0.62777	−0.023
Post Office	$−0.84270 \times 10^{-1}$	−0.213
Hospital	$−0.15839 \times 10^{-3}$	−0.595
Doctor	$−0.33360 \times 10^{-4}$	−0.462
Distress	53.777	4.175**
Lambda	−5.4164	−0.629

Notes: * Significant at 10 percent level. ** Significant at 5 percent level.
Log likelihood = −572.11; $F_{12,108}$ = 4.62 Selected sample contains 108 observations.
Source: Statistical Yearbooks (various issues), Bureau of Statistics, Dhaka; BRAC Statistical Report, RDP and RCP, 1989–1993; ASA Annual Report, 1994; Grameen Bank Annual Report, 1994; Data for PROSHIKA obtained in interviews from Head Office; Helen Keller International, Dhaka (for distress index).

areas. The result thus suggests that though branches are less likely to be placed in high distress areas, once established, they have higher client densities. This is a plausible scenario. First, it may be that demand for special financial services like those provided by the NGO institutions is especially large in these backward, high-risk thanas, especially since these areas are inadequately served by other market-based or government-sponsored organizations. Second, it may indeed be part of institution policy to have higher levels of outreach in relatively more depressed areas. Third, as suggested above, it may also be reflective of partial decentralization in service delivery whereby local branch managers, once the branch is set up, exercise more control in outreach-related decision functions that are more responsive to local conditions. Indeed it is possible that the high-outreach requirements of branches placed in distressed areas may in fact put pressure on NGOs to limit the number of branches operating in such areas.

- Outreach is significantly lower in thanas that have a higher proportion of marginal farmers, as shown by the negative coefficient of *Landsize*. But it remains unclear whether this result is driven by supply or demand factors. In the second section of this chapter it was noted that a significant proportion of the projects financed by NGOs were off-farm microenterprises engaging in rural trading, food processing, and handicraft production. If financing off-farm microenterprises (rather than agricultural production) is indeed one of the main objectives of the NGO institutions, then outreach would be responsive not just to the proportion of the population owning less than 0.5 acres of land, but also to the presence of landless wage laborers who are likely to be even poorer.

- Though it was clear from the placement equations that branches were more likely to be established in thanas with better communication and transportation infrastructure, there is no evidence that, once a branch is established, client outreach also responds to infrastructure-related characteristics. This once again suggests discontinuities between the placement and outreach decision functions.

Conclusions and Policy Recommendations

Our analysis indicates that even though the placement of branches of NGO institutions was attentive to poverty considerations, other considerations fared more prominently and branches were more likely to be established in locations that had better access to transport and communication infrastructure. Hence it appears that NGO services are geared more toward the poor who reside in relatively well-developed areas rather than toward the poor in more remote and less developed regions. Client density of the existing branches, however, did not exhibit such a feature and actually tended to be better in less favorable and more distressed locations.

Greater concentration of branches in the better areas may in part be the result of a search for locations where the marginal impact of credit services is the greatest. Typically, accompanying constraints on production or income—such as those imposed by the lack of markets, transportation, or communications—are likely to be less severe in areas that have good infrastructure. For example, loans for financing the production of highly market-dependent outputs, such as production of commercial crops, and other non-farm microenterprises, are less suitable for remote areas. Moreover, banking services become especially risky in remote areas where covariance in household incomes is likely to be very high. In such areas, the high repayment rates necessary to maintain an NGOs' access to subsidized funds from various agencies are harder to maintain. Furthermore, the unavailability of commercial banks limits financial operations in remote or poor locations. Hence, as suggested in the previous section, NGOs may follow a strategy of placing fewer branches in distressed areas, but with each of these branches serving a larger number of clients.

Simultaneous efforts to reach the poor, to maximize marginal impact of services, and to keep loan delinquency at the minimum introduces considerable tension in service placement decisions of NGOs. Solutions for reducing this tension lie in innovative lending technologies that reduce transactions costs for both lenders and borrowers and increase marginal returns of loans for the poor in disadvantaged locations. We suggest four strategies towards this end. These are: (1) area-specific innovations and differentiations in financial products; (2) performance and location incentives for branch staff; (3) reduction in dependence on branch offices of commercial banks; and (4) increased donor support for expansion of programs in the remote and vulnerable areas.

   1. Area-specific innovations and differentiations in financial products. A range of area-specific factors affects the demand for different types of loan and savings services. Reducing the cost of credit delivery and increasing the marginal impact of credit on borrowers depends on the extent to which credit and savings services are responsive to area-specific characteristics. However, it is presently the case that financial products of nongovernmental organizations are usually standardized for the entire country. While branch managers have sufficient decision flexibility in managing the headquarters-prescribed array of financial products, they do not have the flexibility to design new financial products or introduce modifications to existing ones. Presumably, headquarter offices do not possess enough information to evaluate the potentials and constraints of service branches. Hence, it is suggested that lower-tier institutions, such as divisional or district offices, be given some flexibility and incentives for modifying existing financial and other services or to introduce new services on a pilot level. Such area-specific modification and innovation may well cover the terms of the credit contract, including spatial differentiation of interest rates.

   2. Performance and location incentives for branch staff. To improve outreach and cost recovery in bank branches, managers and their staff could receive special incentives for above-average performance. Successful innovations by branch or district managers, as mentioned above, could be especially rewarded. Furthermore, if the presumed self-selection of good managers to urban areas is valid, some form of compensatory payments could be given to managing staff or branch offices that operate in remote areas where access to basic social services and economic infrastructure is lacking.

   3. Reduction in dependence on branch offices of commercial banks. NGO branches currently depend on a commercial bank office at which funds are deposited and withdrawn. This has the effect of limiting the outreach of the NGOs to those areas where such bank branches exist. Grameen Bank, one of the pioneers of microcredit, has chosen to maintain its own network of branch offices that perform all functions of money transfer between branches and regional offices and headquarters. When other NGO-supported financial systems reach a critical size, they may well follow this example; BRAC, for example, actually plans to develop a rural bank branch network of its own. However, for the smaller NGOs, this would not be economical. A solution here may lie in the establishment of subdistrict NGO units in remote areas that act as "NGO bank branches" by mediating between individual branch offices and commercial bank branches. The establishment of such units may well be supported by a consortium of NGOs targeting a particularly vulnerable area, so that the unit services a number of NGOs at the same time. Another possibility is that of mobile banking, where remote branch offices are served by regional or district NGOs or commercial bank offices on a prescribed time schedule. In so far as above-average-skill managers exhibit preference in locating themselves near towns, the system of mobile banking would allow remote branches to be continued to be served by a cadre of qualified managers instead of being "trainee branches." For the borrower or saver, it provides access where it was not available before.

4. *Increased government and donor support for expansion of programs in particularly remote and vulnerable areas.* The placement of a branch office, the recruitment and training of its personnel, and the formation and training of groups requires considerable up-front investments, especially in remoter areas. However, it is also likely that many remote thanas in Bangladesh that are currently not served have sufficient long-term demand to support total cost of operation. Hence, donor and government support to target selected remote areas, and accelerate expansion of the branch network in these areas, can be in many cases justified, both from the efficiency and equity perspectives.

Note

Manohar Sharma and Manfred Zeller are at the International Food Policy Research Institute.

References

Association for Social Advancement (ASA). 1994. *Annual Report.* Dhaka, Bangladesh.
———. 1996a. *Impact of Income Generation Through Credit Programs (IGP) on Family Income and Expenditure.* Dhaka, Bangladesh.
———. 1996b. *ASA in Micro-Finance 1996.* Annual Report 1996. Dhaka, Bangladesh.
Lovell, Catherine H. 1992. *Breaking the Cycle of Poverty: The BRAC Strategy.* Westport, CT: Kumarian Press, Inc.
Bangladesh Bureau of Statistics. 1991–1994. *Statistical Yearbook.* Dhaka: Ministry of Planning.
Bangladesh Rural Advancement Committee (BRAC). 1989–1994. *Statistical Report, RDP and RCP.* Dhaka, Bangladesh.
Binswanger, H., S.R. Khandakar, and M. Rosenzweig. 1993. "How Infrastructure and Financial Institutions Affect Agricultural Output and Investment in India." *Journal of Development Economics* 41: 337–366.

Chowdhury, A.M.R., M. Mahmood, and F.H. Abed. 1991. "Credit for the Rural Poor in Bangladesh." *Small Enterprise Development* 2(3): 4–11.

Credit and Development Forum (CDF). 1996. *Savings and Credit Information of NGOs.* Vol. 2, No.1. Data of March and June, 1996. Dhaka, Bangladesh.

Grameen Bank. 1994. *Annual Report.* Dhaka, Bangladesh.

Green. W. 1993. *Econometric Analysis.* Englewoods Cliffs, N.J.: Prentice Hall.

Heckman, J. 1979. "Sample Bias as a Specification Error." *Econometrica* 47(1): 153–161.

Hossain, M. 1988. "Credit for Alleviation of Rural Poverty: The Grameen Bank in Bangladesh." Research Report 65. Washington, D.C.: International Food Policy Research Institute.

Jahangir, A.S.M., and M. Zeller. 1995. "Rural Finance Programs for the Poor in Bangladesh—A Review of Five Major Programs." Washington, D.C.: International Food Policy Research Institute. Processed.

Khandker, S., B. Khalily, and Z. Khan. 1995 "Grameen Bank: Performance and Sustainability." Discussion Paper 306. Washington, D.C.: The World Bank.

Pill, M., Rosenzweig, M., and D. Gibbons. 1995. "The Determinants and Consequences of the Placement of Government Programs in Indonesia." In D. Van de Walle and K. Nead, eds., *Public Spending and the Poor.* Baltimore: Johns Hopkins Press.

Ravallion, M., and Q. Wodon. 1999. "Evaluating a Targeted Social Program When Placement is Decentralized." Washington, D.C.: The World Bank. Processed.

Sharma, M., and M. Zeller. 1997. "Repayment Performance in Group-Based Credit Programs in Bangladesh: An Empirical Analysis." *World Development* 25(10): 1731–42.

Zeller, M., M. Sharma, and A. Ahmed. 1996. "Credit for the Rural Poor: Country Case Bangladesh." Final report submitted to German Agency for Technical Cooperation (GTZ). Washington, D.C.: International Food Policy Research Institute.